Historic Figures of the Arthurian Era

ALSO BY FRANK D. RENO

The Historic King Arthur: Authenticating the Celtic Hero of Post-Roman Britain
(McFarland, 1996; paperback 2007)

Historic Figures of the Arthurian Era

Authenticating the Enemies and Allies of Britain's Post-Roman King

FRANK D. RENO

McFarland & Company, Inc., Publishers
Jefferson, North Carolina, and London

The present work is a reprint of the library bound edition of Historic Figures of the Arthurian Era: Authenticating the Enemies and Allies of Britain's Post-Roman King, *first published in 2000 by McFarland.*

LIBRARY OF CONGRESS CATALOGUING-IN-PUBLICATION DATA

Reno, Frank D., 1937–
Historic figures of the Arthurian era : authenticating the enemies and allies of Britain's post–Roman king / by Frank D. Reno.
p. cm.
Includes bibliographical references (p.) and index.

ISBN 978-0-7864-4509-7
softcover : 50# alkaline paper ♾

1. Great Britain—History—To 1066—Biography. 2. Arthur, King—Contemporaries—Biography. 3. Anglo-Saxons—Biography. 4. Britons—Biography. I. Title.
DA152.R45 2010
942.01—dc21 99-55343

British Library Cataloguing-in-Publication data are available

Manufactured in the United States of America

McFarland & Company, Inc., Publishers
Box 611, Jefferson, North Carolina 28640
www.mcfarlandpub.com

In memory of my mother,
Helen Genevieve,
and my father, Frank Anthony

Table of Contents

List of Illustrations

List of Abbreviations of Works Cited in the Text

AA	*The Age of Arthur*
AB	*Arthur's Britain*
AC	*Annales Cambriae*
AE	*The Arthurian Encyclopedia*
AMC	*The Arthurian Material in the Chronicles*
ASC	*The Anglo-Saxon Chronicle*
AW	*Arthur of the Welsh*
BH	*British History*
CODEP	*The Concise English Dictionary of English Place-names*
DA	*De Antiquitate Glastonie Ecclesie*
DE	*De Excidio*
DKA	*The Discovery of King Arthur*
DR	"Dream of Rhonabwy"
GP	Genealogical Preface
GRA	*Gestis Regum Anglorum*
HB	*Historia Brittonum*
HCWO	"How Culhwch Won Olwen"
HECP	*History of the English Church and People*
HKA	*The Historic King Arthur*
HKB	*The History of the Kings of Britain*
KAA	*King Arthur's Avalon*
QAB	*Quest for Arthur's Britain*
RBEE	*Roman Britain and Early England*
WG	Welsh genealogies
WTC	*Was This Camelot?*

Prologue

Researching the early and central medieval periods can aptly be likened to crossing a desert. Only very, very rarely is there an oasis—the symbol of life itself—in the scorched, barren wasteland, a watering hole of original ancient manuscripts with its pools of replicas, copies, and fragments. The myriads of dunes, some which hinder progress to an oasis and some which offer a more panoramic view to spot one, are the mounds of manuscripts produced by critics, analysts, interpolaters, and translators of the ancient manuscripts. The small sandy knolls are discouraging because they do not provide an extensive vista; they are tediously monotonous, seemingly the same ground which has been covered hundreds of times. The larger promontories, megatons of sand deposited throughout the centuries, symbolize the aggregation of multitudinous commentators. Although much more difficult to scale because of sheer volume, they link the laborious ascent with the anticipation of what will be discovered from the summit. Sometimes, too, even if the dune is lofty enough to reveal a haven, there are those who, distrustful of their senses, will turn away, believing that what they see is a mirage, something too fortuitous to be real.

Yet for the individual with hope and persistence who pursues his vision, the rewards are satisfyingly rejuvenating. Like some before him, because the surroundings are Utopian, he might choose to spend his lifetime at one fountain of specialty rather than venture back into the wastelands. Like others, he could risk the dangers to explore new oases, comparing the coolness or clarity of water, the depth and configuration of the pools, the palm trees and grass nurtured by the water of life. Or like the resourceful few who know the lay of the land, he might navigate caravans from one haven to the next, allowing others to luxuriate in a guided expedition.

As the analogy suggests, there are only a finite number of original manuscripts which can unlock the secrets of the past. A prolific outpouring of interpretations, contentions, and postulations far outnumber the originals. The best researchers are those who have not only dipped into the pools of ancient manuscripts but have also expended energy to sift through the towering dunes for the proverbial needle. Individuals of that caliber have a right to become tour guides because they themselves might propose alternate routes which lead to the true wellspring of the watering hole.

Only the guides themselves, the ones who sift through the accumulations of a thousand-year period, are aware of the difficult complexity of trying to decipher truth and accuracy as opposed to fiction and interpolation. These creators who have devoted a lifetime of research in one narrow confinement of endeavor sometimes face only bleak prospects of innovative discoveries, while other times their careful, deliberate judgments are unappreciated. The chasm between the creator and the censor can be bridged by both passive tolerance and active open-mindedness. Because delving so deeply into an idea requires dedication and resolve, the resultant innovation or theory should be given due consideration rather than offhandedly being discarded.

Of the early and central medieval period, more than one researcher has stated that more than likely, no further ancient original manuscripts will ever be discovered, but if it does happen, it will be nothing short of a miracle exposing a missing link to the exciting past. Until then, however, it is necessary to heed the admonition of those same scholars to scrutinize the existing manuscripts for substantial clues which cut new windows into the unknown past. Hence, works from invaluable contributors such as Acton Griscom, R. H. Fletcher, J. G. Evans, William Skene, and Charles Plummer must be viewed as timeless rather than dated; these writers have been the creators of building blocks for future progressions. The more recent researchers—Leslie Alcock, Geoffrey Ashe, John Morris, Thomas O'Sullivan, and A. W. Wade-Evans, plus a host of others—have styled and added their building blocks to earlier foundations, helping to create new and different ever-evolving structures.

Since the beginning of the twentieth century, the invaluable works of several distinguished scholars have unfortunately been buried by the succeeding avalanche of the written word. Because of new theories embracing new ideas, some of these earlier works have been characterized as irrelevant, of no further value, or only of mild, modern-day curiosity, and hence have nearly been forgotten. One such contributor is Acton Griscom, whose work on Geoffrey of Monmouth first appeared about 1929. In a random and very unscientific survey, of twenty books on Arthuriana published in 1959 or thereafter, I discovered that only four include Griscom's name in the bibliography or index: A. W. Wade-Evans's *The Emergence of England & Wales; The Quest for Arthur's Britain* edited by Geoffrey Ashe; Richard Barber's *The Figure of Arthur;* and Michael Curley's *Geoffrey of Monmouth.* This is not necessarily an indictment against those who pass over earlier works such as Griscom's; a more probable reason than any listed above is oversight, as exemplified by Griscom's absence from the bibliography of *The Historic King Arthur.*

In *Arthuriana,* Volume 5, Number 3, fall 1995, an article titled "The

Origins of the Arthurian Legend" appeared in which Geoffrey Ashe reiterates material about the historic King Arthur from several of his previous books. On the opening page he writes,

> [Historians in search of Arthur have dismissed] the medieval literature (Geoffrey of Monmouth and everything later), ... [reducing] the data to two Latin documents.

In fairness, this isn't quite true, for the authors in quest of the historic Arthur do in fact scour literary material, but in its rightful place as a secondary source. There are also more than just two Latin documents; true, there are only two which *name* a figure called Arthur, but there are many other bona fide histories which verify his milieu. Although Ashe must be credited with the majority of postulations about the historic King Arthur, each reflecting thoughtful support (unlike the unsubstantiated generalities by some critics who refute his work), there are some common misconceptions that have led him down the wrong paths.

One occurs on the second page of the article, where Ashe writes that Arthur of the fifth or sixth century was "embroiled chiefly with encroaching Saxons." As I proposed in my first book, *The Historic King Arthur,* this is one of the misconceptions which has for so long misplaced the Arthurian milieu in southern Britain. Arthur was *not* fighting German Saxons who were infiltrating the island from the mainland. Instead, he was engaged in *internal* wars with the *English* Saxons, part of the generic group labeled as *Saxones* by the Romans. These Saxons, about whom Gildas Badonicus wrote in the *De Excidio,* had been settled on the island for two or three generations.

A couple of paragraphs later Ashe writes of Dumville's attacks on various books and articles which defend the existence of the historic Arthur. Dumville categorizes "historical Arthur" books as being "contradictory, wildly unscholarly, and sometimes worse," which is why I structured my first book with such heavy documentation, including over five hundred endnotes, more than seventy illustrations, a glossary, and a cross-referenced index. The historic Arthur lies under six centuries of layer upon layer of fabulous tales, legends, and myths between his lifespan and Monmouth's "pseudohistory," followed by three more centuries of folkloric and Britannic additions.

Yet despite Ashe's having specifically written that "Far-fetched elements in a story do not discredit [Arthur's history], nor do far-fetched elements in a career disprove its protagonist's reality," it is precisely this which his critics attack. One example will suffice. Ashe is absolutely accurate in relating that by far the majority of terms identifying characters in Arthur's milieu (including Arthur himself) are *epithets,* and beyond a doubt *not* proper names: *Arthus; superbus tyrannus;* Vortigern; Vortimer; Vortiporix; all the words with *cunos-* as an affix (including Maglocunus, Cunedda, Cunorix, Cuneglases, and Cunobelinus); Caesar; Augustus; Utherpendragon; Aurelius Caninus; and

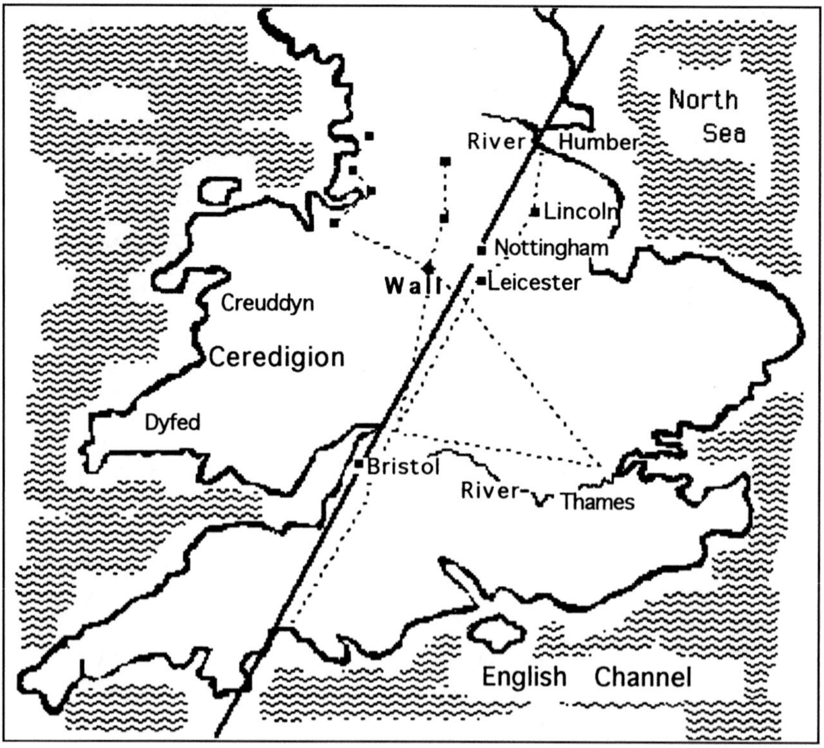

Map 1. Roman civil and military boundaries.

Riothamus. In spite of this massive evidence, critics still insist on pointing to one singular Roman named Lucius Artorius Castus of the second century as the incipience for the popularity of the name Arthur. It is no longer possible to hide behind a theory that Arthur's namesake was a Roman legionnaire who lived three centuries before the king's era.

Other misconceptions forwarded by Ashe are the three locales he selected for Arthur's story—Tintagel, Glastonbury, and South Cadbury—all of which are based upon the erroneous assumption that Arthur was warring with an influx of *German* Saxons. Since there are only a finite number of ancient manuscripts and variations upon which to focus, we must rely upon those for different perspectives other than the interpretations which have been accepted for centuries. The first is in regard to Tintagel. During the Roman occupation, and into the Arthurian age after the Empire's withdrawal, the southwestern peninsula of Britain was known as Dumnonii, not Cornwall. It did not acquire the name of Cornwall until several hundred years after the post-Roman period, when migrants from the *Cornovii* territories in the midlands began to populate the domains of Dunmonii. Hence, when Monmouth

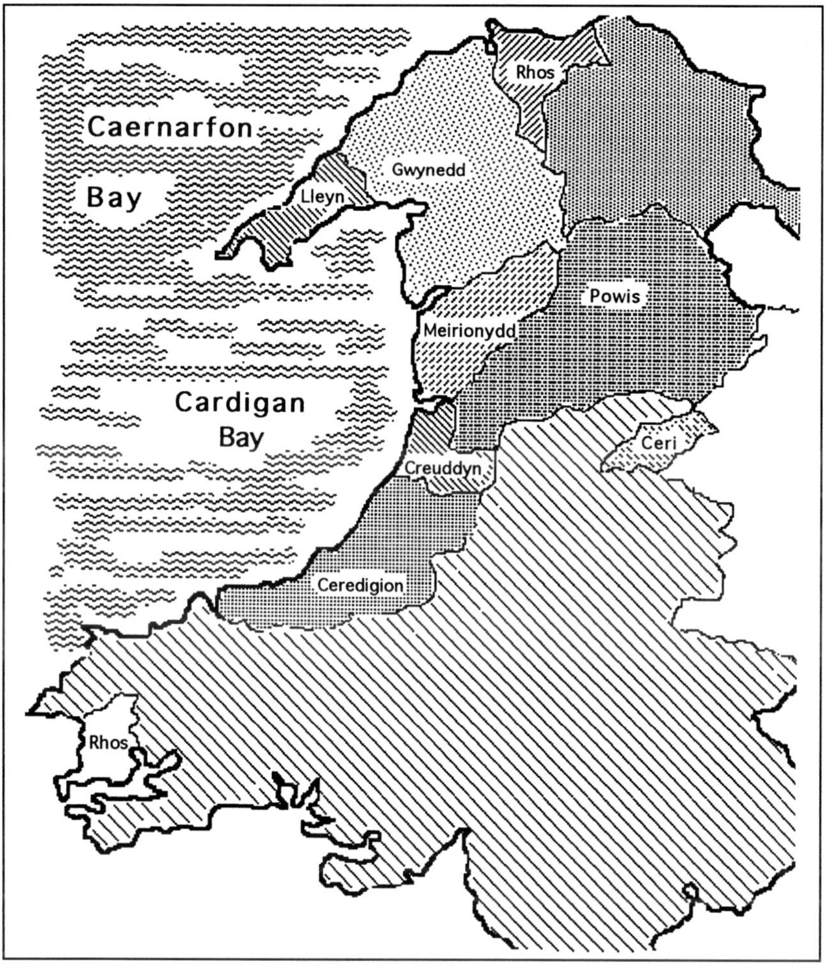

Map 2. Early Welsh provinces.

settled upon a likely site for the conception of Arthur, he was mistakenly thinking of the Cornwall peninsula instead of the Cornovii heartland.

The second location—Arthur's burial site—is not listed as Glastonbury by Monmouth. Monmouth writes that Arthur was transported to Avalon, where his wounds were tended. The equation of Avalon with Glastonbury did not transpire until several decades subsequent to the Monmouth manuscript, and after that, from Giraldus Cambrensis through John of Glastonbury, Adam of Domerham, and John Leland, a gradual connection—mystical, enigmatic, and overlaid with spuriousness—was made between Glastonbury and the otherworldly Avalon. Other works, too, have considered a connection with a different Avallon on the continent, but no theory is definitive about Arthur's burial site.

The last site, South Cadbury, attained fame as Arthur's Camelot for a variety of reasons. One is its southern locale, another is its proximity to Glastonbury, and a third is its easy access to Southampton Water and the southern coast. But the main impetus came from Leslie Alcock's excavations there during the late 1960s and early 1970, when he found evidence of Arthurian-age fortifications. Even though Alcock himself stressed that Camelot—a fictitious name for Arthur's court—was a term coined by Chretien de Troyes, it was John Leland's sixteenth-century label which entrenched South Cadbury as Camelot Fort. Geoffrey Ashe refers to this on page 5 of the article cited above, writing that "advocates of a northern Arthur have produced no comparable sites," which is true, but he neglects the vital Cornovii territory in central Britain. Wroxeter (Viroconium) and its neighboring hillfort of the Wrekin have been methodically detailed by Graham Webster, Philip Barker, and Barry Cunliffe, showing that the area was occupied continuously after the Roman evacuation into the sixth century and beyond. This site, too, had easy access to the Thames Valley and London via Watling Street, to the northeast and southwest via Foss Way, to the north via Ryknild Street, and to the northwest via several different Roman roads, all of which would have been in excellent condition during the Arthurian era. Additionally, the navigable River Severn skirted the city walls and flowed due south for an easy access to Gloucester and eventually to Bridgwater Bay. This suggests that Arthur's court very well could have been located somewhere in the Midlands.

All of these conditions shift attention to Arthur's true arena of operations—Wales and the Midlands. A close analysis, as provided by *The Historic King Arthur,* reveals that the *Historia Brittonum* is not a Kentish Chronicle, but a Welsh one, supported by the meticulous extraction of information from the *Annales Cambriae, The Anglo-Saxon Chronicle,* and surprisingly, the *De Excidio.* As stated in the preface of *The Historic King Arthur* and demonstrated by the first eight of the twelve chapters, the search for a historic King Arthur is accurately more of a search for the history of the Dark Ages; no doorknockers identifying Ambrosius's or Arthur's residences will be unearthed, no leather gerkins stamped "property of Arthurex" will ever be discovered, and it is even highly unlikely that inscribed stones bearing epitaphs will ever come to light, although, astoundingly, two such stones for Maglocunus ap Clutor and Vitalinus exist.

Nevertheless, there are some who, for various reasons ranging from academic pedantry to legitimate skepticism, walk away with upturned noses from the mere mention of Monmouth; he has been fiercely maligned by critics, especially in relation to what they claim are his false assertions about the notorious *liber vetustissimus.* As demonstrated by Griscom, and more recently, Geoffrey Ashe, though, Monmouth's bona fide reflection of history (the proverbial baby) cannot be thrown out with his creativity and invention (the bath-water). A person must refrain from rolling his eyes, shaking his head, and shunning the single most influential piece of Arthurian material ever written, in spite of its nerve-wracking inconsistencies and literary license. For literally centuries, the concept has been accepted that the Welsh chronicles, including the *Tysilio* and the *Brut y Brenhined,* were Welsh (or Breton) translations of Monmouth's *History of the Kings of Britain,* averring, therefore, that they were written *after* Monmouth's manuscript. But one seemingly trivial contention, proposed by Griscom over sixty years ago, gives an amazing new perspective and leads to astounding accuracy if accepted as credible. Griscom's stance, almost laughably simplistic, is this: The Welsh *Bruts,* including the *Tysilio* and the *Brut y Brenhined, precede* Monmouth's manuscript. Stated differently, if Monmouth is taken at his word, the compilation of these manuscripts could have been the very ancient book to which he refers. Though the *original* compilation has been lost, there are still, according to Griscom, fifty-eight (yes, fifty-eight!) *versions* or *fragments* extant, only three of which (during Griscom's time) had been translated by expert Welsh or Breton scholars. Contemporary work, reflected by texts such as *The Arthur of the Welsh,* indicate that some advance has been made on the Welsh chronicles and early Welsh Arthurian poetry, and that there seems to be tentative agreement that none of the early Welsh poems "seem to owe much to Geoffrey of Monmouth's realism; indeed, many of them may have been composed before the *Historia Regum Britanniae* appeared," a statement made on page 61 by Sims-Williams in the above text, which agrees with Griscom's belief.

That minute shift—the Welsh manuscripts *preceding* Monmouth instead of *following* him—becomes an astonishing eye-opener of what Monmouth presented as a copyist distinct from what he contributed as his own. Special entitlements must go to Acton Griscom for his in-depth exploration relating to the importance of the Welsh chronicles and background on Monmouth. The revelations of bona fide history—along with the confirmations substantiated in my first book, *The Historic King Arthur,* and further substantiations provided in Chapter 3 of this text—fulfill at least the nascence of Griscom's dream that British history, after centuries of neglect, can now claim its rightful niche.

Undying gratitude must therefore be the beacon for the predecessors of the romances of the thirteenth and fourteenth centuries. Beginning with Gildas Badonicus, there would have been no Celtic hero of post-Roman Britain upon which to build one of the greatest figures of all times. In spite of negligence heaped upon Gildas as a historian because he seldom records proper names, he provided the first peg—Ambrosius Aurelianus—on which to hang the legends. And upon reflective scrutiny, he provides other names and epithets which allow quite a comprehensive history, including those of Constantine (a historical reference to Constantine III), Aurelius Conanus,

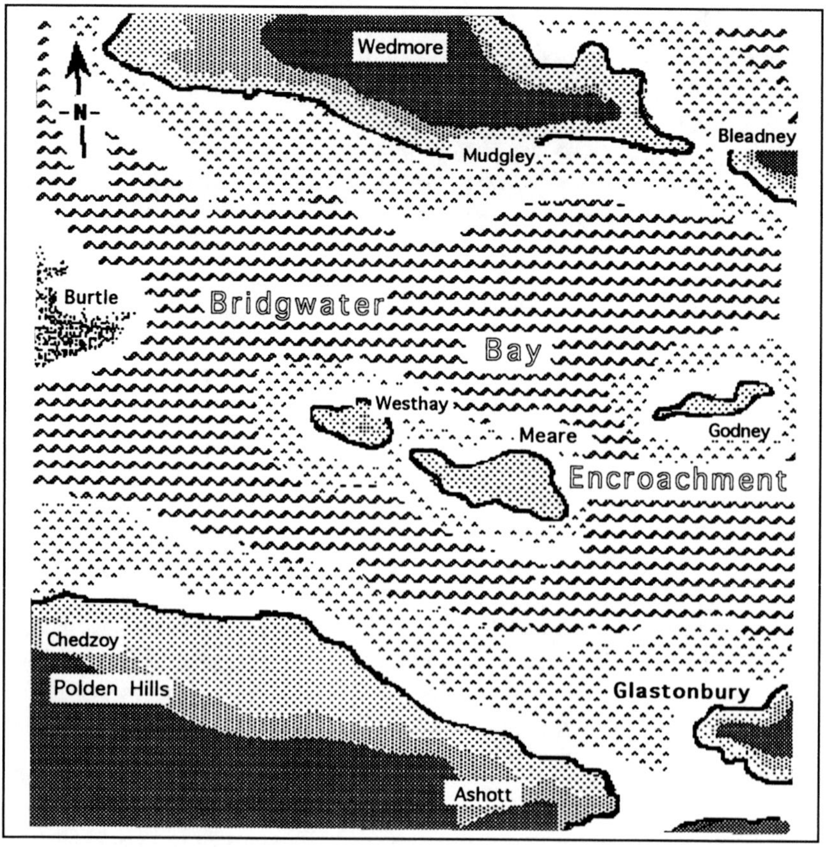

Map 3. The encroachment of Bridgwater Bay on the Glastonbury area.

Vortiporus, Maglocunus, and the *superbus tyrannus.* Likewise, the copyist of the *Historia Brittonum*—and to a lesser degree Bede and the Welsh genealogies—added details about Ambrosius, about Cunedda and his eight sons (particularly Cerdic and Enniaun Girt), and about their offspring Creyuddin, Eugein Dantguin, and Maglocunus. The *Historia* must also be credited for Vitalinus, for the creation of Merlinus, for more detail on the distinction between the English and German Saxons, and for the three Saxon *Adventi,* especially the last two, which deal with Hengist, Horsa, and Octha.

The *Annales Cambriae* and *The Anglo-Saxon Chronicle* also play indispensable roles, the former for providing not only the epithet of Arthur but some type of time-frame (albeit inaccurate), and the latter for inspiring its offshoot, the *Æthelweard Chronicle,* and its perspective of Arthur's enemies, the five most important being Hengist, Octha, Cerdic, Creoda, and Cynric. From these sources sprang the important Welsh *Bruts*, some indistinctively attached to the parent Irish annals, which then set the stage for the much-maligned work by Monmouth, by Malmsbury (including his heavily interpolated *De Antiquitate)*, and by John of Glastonbury.

There should also be the same indebtedness to pathfinders such as Leslie Alcock, John Morris, and Geoffrey Ashe. Without the contributions of Alcock, Arthurian studies would figuratively still be in the Dark Ages. Rather than critics focusing upon insignificant shortcomings and finding fault with this scholar, Alcock must instead be judged upon the more comprehensive broad picture which he portrays. A case in point is written by Alcock himself in the "Supplementary Bibliography" to the most recent edition of *Arthur's Britain.* In his earlier edition, he labeled the text of the *Historia Brittonum*, the Welsh Annals, and other historical or quasi-historical material as "*The British Historical Miscellany,*" and was in essence apologizing for attempting to treat these various manuscripts as a unified source, based upon their mergence in the Harleian 3859. The criticism of this affixation should not overshadow Alcock's monumental accretions to the Arthurian matter in areas such as chronological calibrations, the Saxon *Adventi,* Ogham stones, his diligent approach to Arthurian-age discoveries, and the history of Roman and sub-Roman Britain, written in concise, straightforward, easily understandable prose. The merits and value of *Arthur's Britain* far outweigh any shortcomings it might have, and it certainly isn't dated or obsolete.

John Morris, another important contributor, is out of favor, since *The Age of Arthur* has been labeled as a mixture of fact and fantasy, which is misleading. If a book's "mixture of fact and fancy" is the sole judgment of its worth, then the preponderance of texts would be disfavored. In spite of accusations that Morris lacked critical judgment concerning the value of some of his sources, his work, like Alcock's, is monumental, sometimes including obscure sources which are absolutely essential for an understanding of the history of the Arthurian age. Without his work as one of the building blocks, once again the reconstruction of this particular era would not have progressed as far as it has. Similar to the criticisms directed also at Geoffrey of Monmouth, if the main criterion in judging a book is indeed its mixture of fact and fancy, what would be left to read about King Arthur?

One of the greatest debts should be accorded to Geoffrey Ashe, particularly because of his book *The Discovery of King Arthur.* He endorses a process of analysis which he terms "lateral thinking," a procedure which *all* researchers should embrace. The term "patterned thinking" which I use in *The Historic King Arthur,* is basically the same principle stated conversely. Concisely, it is this: In studying the ancient manuscripts (and their translations), interpretations given by previous analysts become embedded in the brain as "fact," and this malaise of "mind-set" paralyzes the brain to shield the pattern of thinking set forth by these earlier writers. This patterned thinking—unlike Ashe's fresh concepts for old topics—must first be dismantled before new perspectives can be constructed. Both *The Discovery of King Arthur* and *The Historic King Arthur* are products of lateral thinking. The Welsh/Breton matter is of supreme importance in Arthuriana, but because the distinction between the two is so hazy, Ashe tends to discount the Welsh influence and stress the Breton, whereby I attempted to balance the two. The point, however, is that both perspectives value the Welsh/Breton *Bruts* rather than deriding them as "worthless history."

Further, Ashe's theory—that Riothamus, an epithet for Arthur, recounted Arthur's Gallic exploits on the continent—allowed my "lateral thinking" to move one step further: Ambrosius Aurelianus, the one proper name depicting a Romano-Briton historical figure, had to be the actual name for two homologs which also occur in the histories. The first, "Riothamus," meaning "supreme king," who was known to the continental historians as the "King of the Britons," *had* to be a reference to Ambrosius Aurelianus. Likewise, "Arthur," derived from the Welsh/Roman "Arthus" or "Arthurex," meaning "high king," also *had* to refer to Ambrosius. As more and more discoveries revealed (and continue to reveal), Ambrosius's history encompasses from 422 to around 460, when he drops from the histories; Riothamus's appearance is from approximately 460 to 470; Arthur's coronation is traditionally set in about 475 and his death in the second decade of the sixth century. The combination of these three floruits coincides with what the legends tell us, that Arthur was almost a centenarian when he died. And even though accepting the "reasonable age" concept as important, insular Roman monuments verify that life-spans of ninety years are not uncommon. The point to be reiterated, though, is that patterned thinking can be destructive and restrictive while lateral thinking can be constructive and expansive.

Alcock opens Chapter One of *Arthur's Britain* by writing that "The major task of research consists in looking at the existing texts in new ways"; on the second page he states a need to re-examine "old finds, and the dogmas based on them, in the light of each new discovery." By assuming this stance, Alcock is much too hard on himself when he writes in the revised preface of 1987 that *Arthur's Britain* is "no longer a reliable guide to the present state of knowledge, hypothesis and opinion." In fact, the opposite is true; the book is a prodigious tribute to Arthurian data, and it will continue to influence future generations in the exploration of the Dark Ages. On pages xiv and xv in the Introduction to *The Age of Arthur,* John Morris writes that the historian must not only collect and assess information, but also interpret the evidence. He encourages the pupils of history to make judgments, even though at times they will not be able to proclaim certainty. Ashe basically states the same thing; in fact, *The Discovery of King Arthur* epitomizes Ashe's concept of "lateral thinking," fresh perspectives on old manuscripts. Throughout the entire book, Ashe uses terms such as "new discoveries" manifested from the ancient manuscripts, "fresh concepts," new ways, new vistas, and new lives.

Based, then, upon the advice of these giants of Arthurian contributions, the old manuscripts can yield new insights heretofore not considered, either because of a dogmatic attachment to traditional interpretations or an unthinking acceptance of terms and conditions as reported centuries earlier. Examples of these age-old misconceptions—by no means exhaustively listed—are:

1. the traditional stance that the Arthurian milieu is set in southeastern Britain, rather than Wales and the midlands, thus not making the crucial distinction between "Welsh" and "Britons";
2. the references to the "English" or the "Saxons" in the early manuscripts were to those barbarians from across the Channel, rather than distinguishing between the "English (insular) Saxons" who had been settled on the island several generations, dating back to times when the Romans still occupied Britain, as opposed to the "German (continental) Saxons" who encroached upon the insular territories from across the Channel;
3. the inherent inference that there was only one Anglo-Saxon influx instead of three distinctive ones, which in turn suggests that Hengist and Horsa were Saxon (rather than Angle) leaders of the first *Adventus* instead of the second and third *Adventi;*
4. the belief that battles of Arthur's era—specifically the conflicts at Derguentid, Tanet, the Inscribed Stone, and Ægælesthrep—were fought near or along the southern shores of Britain;
5. the same distorted belief that the battles attributed to Arthur would also be in this milieu in southern Britain.

Examples of the latter—that terms were misinterpreted or simply passed over or not specifically defined—also present a long list, part of which is

1. the term "homeland" can mean a variety of things, depending upon whether its contextual reference is to English Saxons, to German Saxons, to Hengist or Octha's point of origin, to Cunedda's native base *before* his migration, to Cunedda's headquarters *after* migration, or to Vortigern's original kingdoms;
2. identification of sites near the "inscribed stone," particularly because stones bearing inscriptions exist within specifically defined regions, *none* of which are along the southern or southwestern coasts of Britain;
3. original Latin references which could be either to proper-name places or common descriptive markers for a site—Bath versus bath, Wall versus wall, or North versus north;
4. one proper name, whether used for an individual or a geographic locale, used interchangeably with another such as Gildas Badonicus/

Gildas Albanius, Wessex/West Saxon, Manau Gododdin/Gododdin, Cerdicesora/Cerdicesford, Cornwall/Cornovii, Briton/Welsh, Scotti/Scottish, City of Legion/Caerleon, or Oghgul/Angeln;

5. general terms which can be defined in radically different ways, such as a) "north" referring to Pictish regions beyond the Antonine Wall or to the kingdoms between the Antonine Wall and Hadrian's Wall, or the area north of the midlands but south of Hadrian's Wall; b) "obtaining" or "ruling" a kingdom as being synonymous with "conquering" a kingdom; c) "discord" being interpreted as "conflict" or "battle."

Curious as to why Arthur's ubiquitous fame has endured for so many centuries, people commonly ask, "Why Arthur?" The inquiry is ironic—seemingly simple but deceptively and profoundly complex. Indeed, why, among all of the ancient leaders of the early medieval period, did Arthur, above all others, achieve such stature and lasting fame, particularly since his authenticity has remained so concealed over the last 1,500 years? A seemingly simple answer can match the question: "Because Arthur is Celtic," a response equally as laden with complexities. Arthur is not a figment of the imagination; that is, he is not simply the outgrowth of a mythological explanation. He is every bit as real as Julius Caesar, Alexander, and Hannibal from an earlier era, or Euric the Visigoth, Attila the Hun, and Theodoric from his own era. Although his exploits are clothed in legends and romances, it is his heretofore unveiled real and historic accomplishments which have elevated him to unequaled fame and popularity.

By definition, a hero is a selfless man of exceptional values and qualities, thus distinguishing himself through deeds and accomplishments in spite of insuperable odds. Like Abraham Lincoln, King Arthur fits that definition because of his compassion, fortitude, and sense of honor; in spite of insuperable odds he saved his country from internal annihilation for seven decades after the Romans literally abandoned the island and left the *Britanni* to fend for themselves.

Unfortunately, Arthur's identity was lost because of the silence of the Dark Ages. He has been buried under layers of epithets, homologs, and titles for literally thousands of years, but Arthur's appeal has persisted during those centuries. Little by little, truths about his authenticity are being discovered. As pieces of the puzzle are put together and misinformation is disregarded, his image becomes more distinctive, making it more and more evident that the figure behind the facade of legends is the impelling force which makes the tales so great.

At this time, archaeological discoveries have contributed as much to the understanding of a historic Arthur as the redefinition of the ancient manuscripts. Sir Mortimer Wheeler, C.A.R. Ralegh Radford, and Phillip Rahtz, in addition to Leslie Alcock, must also be recognized. Special appreciation is likewise extended to translators such as Patrick Ford, Michael Winterbottom, Charles Plummer, G. N. Garmonsway, Lewis Thorpe, Josephus Stevenson, and Jeffrey Gantz for their commitment to accuracy.

Furthermore, it is refreshing to read new nonfiction theories as proposed by Graham Phillips and Martin Keatman. Neither their work, nor *The Historic King Arthur,* nor this book, however, should mark a definitive end of the quest for the historic Arthur. As new interpretations to the ancient manuscripts—or perhaps, even more fortuitously, as public or private collections are studied—an even clearer picture will show the reality of a true Celtic hero and make, if possible, the legendary romances even more alluring.

And last, writers with an accurate grasp of the period's history coupled with an ability to breathe life into figures previously believed to be illusions will indelibly imprint Arthur's image in man's collective mind. One such individual, Parke Godwin, on page 2 of the opening chapter of *Firelord* (Avon Books, New York, May 1994), views Arthur "as historical as Lincoln or Julius Caesar, merely less documented." Viewed in these terms, Godwin then has Arthur, as he lay dying at Avalon, ponder the unimportance of what monks write and bards sing. Arthur wants people to remember the way he and his comrades were

> before some pedant petrifies us in an epic and substitutes his current ideal for ours. As for poets and bards, let one of *them* redecorate your life and you'll never be able to find any of it again.

Godwin's philosophy is that the images of authentic figures become frozen and distorted when immersed in legend; in reality, they are constantly moving between the end of one thing and the beginning of another, affirming that

> Guenevere wouldn't sit still while Time painted her in serenity, and God *knows*—Morgana? Catch the lightning, friend. Chain the wind.
>
> No legend then. I give them their world as it was and let them stride.

Arthur and all those associated with him should not, therefore, be locked in legend. They should be remembered in their historic milieu, and *then* we should let them stride.

1

New Perspectives of Ancient Insular History

Any scrutiny of the historic King Arthur must unequivocally depend upon the manuscripts closest to his era, meaning that one must reach back in time over six hundred years from the timeless chapter titled "Arthur of Britain" in Geoffrey of Monmouth's *History of the Kings of Britain.* Stated differently, one must reach back over nine hundred years from the romances of Chretien de Troyes and the tales of Malory. To place even more emphasis upon the passage of time, writers such as T. H. White and Marion Zimmer Bradley based their work on a figure dating back 1,500 years. Bridging that span is a monumental task, considering the fall and plunder of empires and the appalling desecration of the written word.

That anything at all has survived is miraculous and should be treated with thankful humility. There are researchers who sigh and roll their eyes at the mere mention of these surviving manuscripts, especially those who have already offered their own opinions, probably because their belief is that these relics couldn't possibly have anything more to contribute after fifteen centuries of analysis. Or worse yet, there are those pessimistically resigned researchers who deprecate the obstinate radicals who never give up searching old ground for new material. Thankfully, though, there are those die-hard free-thinkers who satisfy themselves with what is available and continually strive to add building blocks for new perspectives rather than rehashing standardized, tired theories. It is to these latter innovators that we must turn.

Leslie Alcock is aware of the limited resources and doesn't harbor false hopes that different manuscripts or variants remain to be discovered. Although he views the so-called Arthurian histories as a static body of information, his field, archaeology, still in a stage of infancy but constantly growing, continues to uncover new information related to the Arthurian age and to re-examine old tenets in a new light. Nevertheless, he has not abandoned the written word. In relation to the manuscripts of the Dark Ages and the early medieval period, which have become tainted over the last millennium and a half, he effectively verbalized the problem experienced by so many researchers. Sometimes when a scribe copied a document which contained a reference to King Arthur, that scribe might be tempted to add his own comments. Even though that interpolated material might have been derived from a reliable source, future scribes wouldn't know whether the addition was factual or fictitious. Hence, it becomes obvious that

> the difficulties of distinguishing between authentic and interpolated material [is] one of the major cruxes of Arthurian scholarship.[1]

This leads Alcock to his admonishment that "Consequently the major task of research [for the students of Arthurian Britain] consists in looking at the existing texts in new ways."[2]

A prime series of examples demonstrating deceptive interpolation are the phases of manipulation which William of Malmsbury's manuscript underwent. Neither fiction nor literature, *De Antiquitate Glastonie Ecclesie* was written for Glastonbury Abbey as pure history; Malmsbury was extremely careful to avoid references which he knew were not based in fact. Yet his manuscript, which was left at the Abbey and thus subjected to rampant modifications—sometimes for self-serving purposes—is laden with interpolations, misleading statements, and downright lies added over a period of centuries. Fortunately for the students of Glastonbury history, Malmsbury himself had included the first part of the *De Antiquitate* in a subsequent edition of another of his works titled *Gestis Regum Anglorum,* which appeared in 1140. The number of interpolations in the *De Antiquitate* left at the Abbey is astounding. If the students of history had not been left with copies of *Gestis Regum,* then there most certainly would have been a manipulated view of the period. This distortion of history is a perfect illustration of the problem, and by no means an isolated incident.

In addition, other deceptions—inadvertent or deliberate—must be guarded against. Most are detailed in the preface of my first book, *The Historic King Arthur.* In order to follow Alcock's exhortation to look at the old manuscripts in new ways, those old manuscripts which have been scrutinized for centuries must be emended; that is, the manuscript in its purest form (the oldest variant of it in its original language) must relinquish its sacrosanctity itself for a fresh new perspective. As in my first book, the textual corrections will be gingerly handled here in an attempt to weed out altered or corrupt text, which is most commonly referred to as interpolations. Besides interpolations, misinformation pervading the ancient manuscripts must be identified because of translocation (geographic displacement because of faulty translations), transpicuousness (clearly seeing and understanding the milieu of Arthur's time), and transvaluation (the re-evaluation spanning not only Arthurian history but also later satellite modifications which repudiate accepted standards not satisfactorily reconciled over the last fifteen centuries).

Thanks to Leslie Alcock's work, his clarification of the three methods of calibration allow a much more precise time frame for the historical era in question. Exposing the faulty nature of spurious insertions, particularly in the *Historia Brittonum,* leads to a much more enlightened view of the chronological framework, which in turn drastically affects the geography of the period. Erroneous headings—which have been inserted between the original, existing parts of any ancient manuscript by a later hand—absolutely must be disregarded, and any liberty of this sort propagated by future translators should be considered a heinous desecration of history, punishable by law. Whenever *any* heading is encountered, it behooves the reader to check the earliest variant of the original manuscript to determine if, in fact, that heading or subheading is included there. If not, expunge it from memory. Only then can accurate interpretations be hoped for. This is one of the processes which gives new insights into old manuscripts.

Associated with this, changes in geographic names present other major stumbling blocks in explicating the history of the period. In the old manuscripts, natural topography was most commonly used for identifying sites, so that an original description of "the river crossing by the steep white cliff" was adequate. The passage of centuries led to other word symbols, but these, most commonly, failed. The word *Derventio* illustrates the problem: It was a common root based upon *derva* and *entio,* meaning "oak near a river" or "river where oaks were common." Variations of the word are Derwent, Darwent, Darwen, Darent, Darenth (in Kent), and Dart, with variant spellings throughout the centuries compounding the problem: Deruuent, Deowentan, Derewent, Derventione, Derventione, Diorente, Dærentan, Daerintan, Dærætan, Tarent.[3] Even further, new descriptors were added: Lower Darwen, Over Darwen, Netherderwent.[4] There's a Darwen and a Lower Darwen near the mouth of the River Ribble in Lancashire; there's a Derwen in the central part of northern Wales, six miles southwest of Ruthin; there's a Darenth in the southeast suburbs of London in Kent; there's a Derwen in northern Wales about eighteen miles from the coast. Furthermore, a River Derwent flows north-south between the city of York and the North Sea; another River Derwent originates about twenty miles east of Manchester and flows into the River Trent; and still a third River Darwent originates in the Cumbrian Mountains and flows into the Solway Firth on the western coast of Wales at Workington. It becomes absurd, therefore, to blindly accept the belief of earlier scribes or researchers who insist that a battle fought at Darenth was located in Kent, particularly when the information comes from a *Welsh* chronicle. Instances like this, as it turns out, are the rule rather than the exception, including all the battles attributed to Vortimer in the *Historia Brittonum.*

Still another difficulty derives from the style (or lack thereof) used for reporting events. In any series of events, it's a safe assumption (but not an uncontested fact) that they occurred in that sequence, yet neither the time lapse between events nor the importance of one event compared to another can be judged. Small skirmishes might be allowed the same amount of space as huge battles. Although John Morris writes about battles and chaotic politics in Gaul during the mid-fifth century, what he proffers is equally pertinent in Britain during the century following Roman abandonment when he relates that "The events are confusing, because four or five different armies changed alliances rapidly; and the account is unclear, because it is no more than a local report of what the armies did in one district."[5] As this applies to King Arthur's battles listed in the *Historia Brittonum,* complex difficulties arise in establishing any chronological framework or geographic limitations; there is no way to determine if two battles were two months or twenty years apart, or if they occurred two miles or two hundred miles apart. Britain was in chaos, and there were civil wars, as Gildas Badonicus indicates, plus continental alliances, as Jordanes, Gregory, and Sidonius relate.

Identification of characters also poses a major hurdle. For instance, even though it can be asserted that Hengist's son is a historically verifiable figure, he appears in various reports as Octha, Octa, Osla, Oesc, and Æsc, the "Ochta" variations appearing in the *Britanni* works, and the "Æsc" used in the Saxon versions. Thus, once a proposal is made that Octha in a Briton tale is the same individual as Oesc or Æsc in a Saxon manuscript, establishing and analyzing floruits and life spans must verify or nullify the postulation. A name like "Owein" and its host of variations presents even more of a problem. "Owein" has the same etymological root as "Eugein" and its variants, and if a scribe incorrectly interpolated that Owein son of Urien from the late 500s (or worse yet, Owein son of Maredudd from the early 800s) was a companion and comrade to Arthur in the early 500s, then a genealogical search is the only way to resolve the perplexity. The problem is even more complex concerning the name Owein because there are several figures by that name who lived during Arthur's era. Because there was an Owein Finduu and an Owein (Eugein Dantguin ap Enniaun Girt), even more investigation is needed to determine who fought against Arthur.

The historic King Arthur, then, is buried beneath the debris of fifteen centuries. Since then there have been layers upon layers of folktales, legends, romances, and novels which have contributed to the obscurity of his genuine existence. Reaching as far back as possible for any written record about Arthur leaves the history enthusiast with no more than a handful of documents. Gildas writes of a post-Roman hero by the name of Ambrosius Aurelianus who snatches Britain from the edge of defeat, but does not name Arthur as the leader of the famous Battle of Mount Badon—listed in three of the four major historical manuscripts of the era—between the *Britanni* and the *Saxones.* Several centuries later, Nennius also records events of the historic Ambrosius mentioned in Gildas, but adds details about Ambrosius as the son of a Roman consul and as a wizard with supernatural powers. Just as important, Nennius (probably as a copyist) also devotes Book 56 to the "Campaigns of Arthur," and lists Arthur as the leader at the Battle of Mount Badon, preceded by eleven other conflicts with the Saxons.

Only one other manuscript in the first millennium records the name of Arthur. In a typically abbreviated chronicle format, the *Annales Cambriae* lists Arthur's name twice. In Year 72 of the calibration used, Arthur, under the banner of Jesus Christ, fights his enemies at Mount Badon for three days and three nights and is victorious. Year 93 of the cycle once again records the name of Arthur, coupled with the name of Medraut; both fall in the Battle of Camlann. Similar to Nennius in the *Historia Brittonum,* Arthur's name is thus linked to the Battle of Mount Badon. Missing are the details that Arthur was the leader of the battle, and that the enemies were the Saxons. But the one important addition is the Battle of Camlann, in which Arthur is killed. Medraut, along with the Saxons typically listed as the enemies, fade into historical oblivion.

My first book, *The Historic King Arthur*, was dedicated to the research and documentation of the numerous facets of Arthur's historicity. The four main scriptural texts used—three of them already mentioned above—were the *De Excidio* by Gildas, the *Historia Brittonum* attributed to Nennius, the *Annales Cambriae,* plus *The Anglo-Saxon Chronicle.* Independent of verifying Arthur's authentication, each manuscript has developed inaccuracies over the centuries, mainly by the addition of incorrect subtitles or misleading interpolations. A summary of the modifications for each of those manuscripts were given in the Preface of that text and substantiated in detail throughout.

The *De Excidio* of Gildas Badonicus

Although Gildas doesn't even record the name of Arthur, he is the best single source of information about the Arthurian age because he is from that era, and any source used to validate the authentic Arthur should be as close as possible to the period of the great king. This is a different approach from that of Norma Goodrich, who indicates that in order to verify King Arthur

> A good knowledge of medieval French is essential to the understanding of the manuscripts from the twelfth and thirteenth centuries, when Old French was also the official language of Britain. It will prove to be the key that opens the doors to discovery [of Arthur's authenticity], that allows us to pierce not only the upper level of the texts but their hidden, secret language.[6]

While there is no disagreement that the original language of a manuscript (or any literary work, for that matter) must be the primary reference, looking for a fifth-century figure by beginning with the twelfth- and thirteenth-century romances seems to be the reverse of how the search for the historical Arthur should be conducted. The analysis of the romances begins seven to eight hundred years *after* the death of Arthur and therefore the attempts to verify him with this subsequent material seem misplaced. Inherent in the acceptance of a premise which states that the nearer to the original source the better, then that premise applies to working with the meager sources very close to Arthur's time, and *afterwards* trying to verify the later, divorced, literary references to him. Hence, the knowledge of languages should be Irish, Welsh, and Latin rather than Medieval French. The passage of several centuries can profoundly alter any manuscript through interpolation, errors in transcription, misinterpretations, and manipulation of facts to better suit artistic considerations or ecclesiastic expediencies.

Ms. Goodrich is an excellent example of why paying very close attention to the ancient manuscripts and properly documenting the material is essential. She writes that "an intellectual 'clerc' is our best source [of information], even though he was a tired 105 years old,"[7] without ever revealing to whom she is referring. She also proposes a thesis statement: "It has become clear that the earliest versions of the Arthurian story are not fiction."[8] Yet she does not confirm this determination with specific supportive evidence. She makes one other puzzling statement:

> He [the tired, old intellectual clerc Gildas? Nennius?] also gave King Arthur's career and military rank and mentioned his twelve victories, especially that of Mount Badon, which this witness knew because it was his own birthplace.[9]

Details about Nennius's life are scarce, and although the work attributed to him does give Arthur's rank and his twelve battles, Mount Badon definitely cannot be Nennius's birthplace, especially because the location of Badon has been so controversial over the centuries. If this is a reference to Gildas Badonicus, as it most certainly must be because Gildas is the only scribe who equates his *birth-year* with the Battle of Badon, then it is very misleading on several accounts. First, Gildas does not give the name of Arthur, nor does he give Arthur's career or his military rank. Second, it is *Nennius* during a later era who records Arthur's twelve victories, not Gildas. Third, Gildas was not born *at* Mount Badon but instead he was born in the same year that the Battle of Badon was fought. Because of passages such as these—assertions with no substantiations and misleading information—Goodrich's belief that Arthur's milieu was in the far north is discredited.

Goodrich compounds these shortcomings by her claim that Geoffrey of Monmouth is an unimpeachable source. Further, she offers far too many apologies for Monmouth's inaccuracies.[10] In her work, no evidence manifests itself, except in Chapter 3, which is itself superficial in nature. In this chapter, Goodrich calls the written evidence her "particular province," and then indicates that this evidence comes from the "High Middle Ages from persons known and unknown, who lived six and seven hundred years after the death of King Arthur."[11]

The *written* records, whether reliable or not, are scarce indeed in the interim between Arthur and Geoffrey of Monmouth, and the written *historical* records, which are considered the most reliable, are even more scarce. Astute scholars have shown that during a passage of six to seven centuries scribal errors, interpolations, deliberate deceits, and selfish motivations reshaped what was truthful. From the tenth century onward, many of the Arthurian stories which were passed down from generation to generation were of *oral* tradition, meaning that, unquestionably, over the span of six hundred to a thousand years, the information likely was garbled beyond recognition. For this reason, the contentions of this text and its predecessor, *The Historic King Arthur,* have been to stay as near to the historical sources as possible (Gildas Badonicus, Nennius, Bede, the *Annales Cambriae, The Anglo-Saxon Chronicle),* use documented archaeological evidence, geomorphic changes, and past reliable scholarship as much as possible, and then finalize the depiction through literary resources (Monmouth, Taliessin, Aneirin, *The Mabinogion)* for the most comprehensive picture. Of the three possibly different Arthurs mentioned by Richard Barber, *The Historic King Arthur* amasses a great deal of evidence to show that the great king is of Welsh origin. Analysis of the *De Excidio* is one of the sources which supports this contention.

According to W. F. Skene, there were three surviving manuscripts of the *De Excidio,* but the oldest of these, the Cottonian Library (Vit A, vi) was destroyed by fire. Of the two remaining, however, one of those—Josseline's edition in 1568—accurately represents the destroyed version.[12] Commonly, the work is divided into five sections, but of major interest to the Arthurian researcher are Chapters 1 through 13, which give a brief background on the land of Britain and Britain under the rule of the Romans. This sketch is followed by the abandonment of the Romans and the struggle of the *Britanni* to salvage their nation. The information Gildas gives, though weak in detail, is reliable and verified by other sources. There are no sources which deny the circumstances surrounding Rome's abandonment of Britain. Gildas expresses an opinion about Maximus's role in British history, but although his opinion might be questioned, Maximus's role cannot be denied. The western Empire was beginning to crumble because of the continued attacks by the barbarians on the mainland, and Honorius, wanting to consolidate his defenses, left Britain to fend for itself. Britain was caught in the dilemma of continued survival under Roman rule or destruction by the barbarians, and therefore beseeched Rome several times to return to the island and protect it from the invaders—all attested to by the Aëtius letter, another undeniable historical fact.

However, of utmost importance are chapters 22 through 26, describing the coming of the Saxons and the victory at Mount Badonis, because Gildas gives objective, although sometimes impassioned, reports. He candidly and forthrightly expresses his hatred of the Saxons, but the basic details are accurate. He writes of:

1. the *Scotti* (Irish) and the Picts renewing their attacks, especially since no help was forthcoming from Aëtius;
2. a plague shortly before the second Saxon *Adventus,* identified by later scholars as the "pestifera lues" and labeled as the Plague of 442 by C. E. Stevens;[13]
3. the three *adventi* of the Saxons (similar to Leslie Alcock's report,[14] although in a "compacted sequence"), unlike the *Historia Brittonum* and the later Monmouth work, which name specific Saxon leaders for the first *Adventus*;
4. praises for Ambrosius Aurelianus, one of the few Romano-Britons referred to by a proper name rather than an epithet;
5. (by inference) the Briton leader of the Battle of Monte Badonis being Ambrosius, thus eliminating the need for an explanation of why Gildas does not specifically name Arthur;
6. *civil* wars which are tearing the country apart with the *English* Saxons, and not *external* wars with the *German* Saxons;

Following this, chapters 27 through 36 on the castigation of the five kings are crucial because of the historical details they supply. Because the coming of the Saxons and the Battle of Badon were historical facts, Gildas, in his own day, would have been exposed as a prevaricator, thus destroying his credibility as an honest monk, if he had tried to fictionalize either these episodes or the existence of the kings whom he rebukes. Of these five kings, O'Sullivan writes

> It is clear that these pedigrees [of the five kings] were not manufactured to authenticate the *De Excidio.* In the first place, nobody in the middle ages doubted its authenticity. Secondly, the later linguistic forms which the names take in the Harleian document indicate a long preservation, presumably as oral genealogy, rather than direct derivation from the ancient *De Excidio* text. It might finally be pointed out that, although we have for obvious reasons emphasized the names and their contemporaneity in the table above, they are given no particular prominence in the original text.[15]

Two of the five kings are solidly entrenched not only in history but in the genealogies of the period. The last and most important is Maglocunus, whose name appears in the *De Excidio,* in the *Historia Brittonum,* and in the *Annales Cambriae.* My book, *The Historic King Arthur,* methodically established a cardinal year which verified the recording of his death in the year 547 according to the *Annales Cambriae.* However, because the purpose of the book was only to verify a chronological framework, Maglocunus's role in British history wasn't pursued any further. However, his name not only crops up again here, but serves as the promulgation of another theory in a later chapter.

MAGLOCUNUS

Gildas supplies more information about Maglocunus than about any other historical person. Information from a host of ancient sources coupled with new theories in *The Historic King Arthur* corroborate Maglocunus as a powerful and influential king. For simplicity, the following genealogies differentiate between the traditional modes of thought and the new proposals established in *The Historic King Arthur,* the former listed in normal type and the latter in italics.

Cunedda *435–465* *(420–480)*		
| Cerdic [Fifth Son] *465–495* *(450–510)*	Enniaun Girt [Seventh Son] *469–499* *(454–514)*	
| *Creoda* *495–525* *(480–540)*	| Eugein Dantguin *499–529* *(484–544)*	Catgolaun Lauhir *495–525* *(480–540)*
| *Cynric* *525–555* *(510–570)*	| Cinglas *529–559* *(514–574)*	| Maglocunus *525–555* *(510–570)*

Because of their very nature, the floruits and the parenthetical life spans should, of course, be viewed as broad generalizations; for example, the floruits and life spans between Cerdic and Enniaun Girt are separated by an arbitrary time of four years, logistically taking into account an intermediate son and a passage of two years between each sibling. Each floruit or life span, therefore, could vary by ± three years.

A great deal of uncertainty surrounds Cunedda, the root of this particular genealogy. That Cunedda is the great-grandfather of Maelgwn, however, is accepted "indeed by practically everyone."[16] Likewise, Cunedda does not appears in the ancient manuscripts as a young man when he migrates from Manau Gododdin to Wales,[17] which means his floruit/life span could easily be off by several years. In contrast, though, the date of his migration and the motive behind it are controversial and are still being hotly debated. An analysis of the above genealogies offers some interesting answers, even though some might not be iron-clad facts.

In relation to Cunedda's date of migration, the *Historia Brittonum* relates that Cunedda came down from Manau Guotodin 146 years *(centum quadraginta sex annis)* before Maelgwn's reign. The book *The Historic King Arthur,* as all other scholarly works, rejects that particular length of time because it places Cunedda's migration too early for the events of the period. Most scholars agree, too, that scribal error isn't likely because the length of time is written out in the original manuscripts rather than being recorded numerically. Since that number of years is irreconcilable with other data of the period, it is passed over in favor of the term *atavus* and the more general forms of reckoning, floruits and life spans, placing Cunedda's movement somewhere near the fourth decade of the fifth century.

Several researchers, however, have attempted to resolve the one hundred and forty-six years with other accepted facts. Wade-Evans, for example, sought a solution by looking at the number of years in the context of the *Historia.* He avers that the history just prior to this passage concentrates on the northern provinces of Din Guaire and Bernicia, and hence specifically to the reign of Ida. He deduces, therefore, that the 146-year time span should be figured between Ida's reign and Cunedda's migration. Bede provides the date of DXLVII (547) for the beginning of Ida's reign, and 146 years prior would set Cunedda's migration in A.D. 401. This is the date which Wade-Evans feels confident is the beginning of Cunedda's movement, resolving the issue of 146 years by explaining that *Maelgwn's* reign inadvertently replaced *Ida's* reign. By strange coincidence, the beginning of Ida's reign is identical to the date of Maelgwn's death in the *Annales Cambriae,* 547. This has given rise to some theories that Cunedda's migration must be figured from the end of Maelgwn's reign, not the beginning.

Either way, A.D. 401 is still too early a date for Cunedda's migration, particularly when his migration is viewed as stemming from an invitation by Vortigern during the middle of Vortigern's reign. But Wade-Evans's pattern of thinking is excellent: one way to attempt a resolution of the 146 years is to look at it in its historical, contextual framework. Wade-Evans used the right process, but he backed up too far. In the segment immediately preceding the section on Maelgwn and Cunedda, the name Dutigern (Outigern) appears in one line, conveying that he "fought bravely against the English nation." That is the total amount of information provided on this mysterious king. Three shaky conjectures are possible from this one sentence about this singular king who has been historically bypassed. One is that he reigned after Ida's death; the second is that the bard Talhearne Tad Awen sung of Outigern's praises, but unfortunately, only fragments of Aneirin's and Taliesin's songs remain; and third is that Outigern is aligned against several English kings, not just one.

In order to re-configure the 146 years in a different format, three separate steps are needed, a type of reversal from Wade-Evans's method. Step one is to use dates typically assigned to Cunedda's migration tied to the simultaneous uprisings of the Irish and the Saxons, which are set either in the opening years of the fourth decade in the fifth century, around the common date of the Saxon Revolt, 442, or around the third Saxon *Adventus,* around A.D. 449. Next is the addition of the 146-year span to those dates in order to try to determine a probable span of Outigern's reign, since there is no clue of it in any recorded history. That supplies the dates from 588 to 595. The last step is to check that time-span in an independent source, *The Anglo-Saxon Chronicle,* to determine if possibly a Briton king was warring against several Saxon kings. The entry of major interest which manifests itself is entry A.D. 593. In that year Ceawlin, Cwichelm, and Crida perish. Æthefrith then succeeds to the kingdom. The obvious impact is that three English kings are killed in some major war, judging from the previous entry about "great slaughter."

Of hidden significance is evidence of the shift in English power. Ceawlin, Cwichelm, and evidently Crida (although he is not listed in the genealogic tracts) are a part of the West-Saxon royal house, and upon their deaths the power of the West Saxons seems to dwindle and emphasis shifts a bit farther to the north: Northumbria, Deira, and Bernicia. Entry 597 confirms a divisiveness in its report that Ceolwulf (of the west-Saxon house) is continually fighting against not only the Britons, the Picts, and the Scots, but also the English. Getting back to the main point, then, if the name Outigern rather than Maglocunus should have been used in its reference to Cunedda's migration, then the date for that would be 593. A subtraction of 146 years from the period of Outigern's reign brings us to 447, giving an almost ideal date for the movement. This is about the only way that the 146-year span would be workable.

Accepting Cunedda's date of migration and Maglocunus's floruit and life span after this seeming diversion, it is now necessary to examine Cerdic's line in conjunction with the Maglocunus material. Based upon the premise in *The Historic King Arthur* that Cerdic, son of Cunedda, was also the same individual who became the West-Saxon king during the holocaust of civil wars after Roman abandonment, then the brothers Eugein Dantguin and Catgolaun Lauhir would be Creoda's first cousins. Eugein Dantguin is a variation of the name Owein, and in the *HKA* was identified as the Owein who played four games of gwyddbwyll with Arthur at the Battle of Badon in the "Dream of Rhonobwy," thus correctly identifying the king's enemies as offspring of Cunedda, those Welshmen who in the civil wars ended up allying themselves with the English Saxons. Cerdic, who became known as the West-Saxon king, was also at that battle, as was Octha, son of Hengist, another Saxon (or more accurately, Angle) king.

Of Maglocunus, Gildas writes

> Did you not, [Maglocunus], in the first years of your youth, use sword and spear and flame in the cruel despatch of the king your uncle and nearly his bravest soldiers, whose faces in battle were not very different from those of lions' whelps?[18]

From what can be pieced together—which is appallingly little since Maglocunus would have had probably eight uncles springing from Cunedda—some interesting speculations emerge. Creoda is the lost generation from Cerdic's genealogy, and if this information is combined with the quotation above, it could explain why. After reconciling Plummer's discrepancy between the Genealogical Preface and the *ASC,* Creoda's reign ended in 534. Using the life span for Maglocunus, his age would have been between 21 and 27, not really in the "first years of his youth," but still within the realm of reason if he assassinated his uncle Creoda.

Two other factors are also intriguing. The first is the geographic location where this would have happened. Maelgwn's province as Gwynedd in northwestern Wales is basically unchallenged. Because the name Rhos appears not only in the *Annales Cambriae* but also Welsh vernacular texts[19], an exhaustive search focused upon this ancient cantref. As typical in this period, there are two widely separated cantrefi by that name, in addition to two different

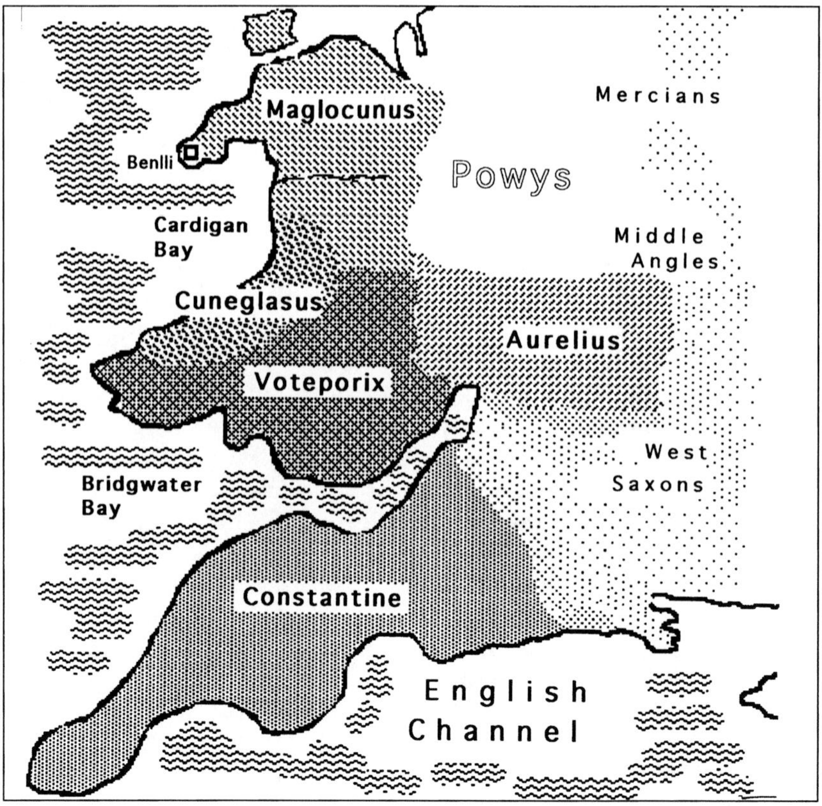

Map 4. Domains of the five kings listed by Gildas Badonicus.

villages called Rhos. Malmsbury's *Deeds of the Kings of Britain* also refers to Rhos[20], but this is unquestionably in southwest Wales in the province of Dyfed, where Gawain's grave is located. The reference to Rhos in the *Annales Cambriae* entry of 547 is the cantref along the *northern* coast of Wales, encompassing Llandudno and Abergele. Maglocunus died from the Great Death (mortalitas magna) reported by an interpolation in the *Annales Cambriae,* but Welsh tradition goes into more elaborate detail involving Taliesin's curse upon Maglocunus, whereupon Maglocunus sees Vad Velen (Yellow Pestilence) through the church keyhole in Rhos and perishes as a consequence.

Knowing the location of Rhos is important in determining what might be Maglocunus's motive for killing Creoda. Virtually no accurate representations showing definitive boundaries of provinces, cantrefi, cymydau, and gwlads exist for the fifth and sixth centuries. There is, however, sketchy information which can be pieced together about two cantrefi, plus two villages named Rhos. In reference to the two villages (not the cantrefi), one is in Glamorganshire, but of more interest is the one in Dyfed, Vortigern's home base. This particular Rhos is approximately a mile from the River Teifi, the *southern* boundary marker for the vast territory between the River Dee and the River Teifi promised to Cunedda if he migrated south to help crush the Irish and Saxon incursions. This southern boundary near the River Teifi is of additional interest because this Rhos borders the territory of Ceredigion, named after Cunedda's son, Cerdic. In turn, Creoda (Cerdic's son) establishes the province of Creuddyn just to the north and even closer to Gwynedd. And most noteworthy, this village of Rhos is within fifteen miles of Nevern, near Fishguard on the coast of Wales, which is the site of an Ogham[21] stone bearing an inscription for an ancestral Maglocunus. This obscure memorial—evidently not the object of any research projects—is embedded as part of a window sill at the church of Saint Brynach in Nevern. Appropriately called the Maglocunus Stone, the irregular slab is 62½ inches long. Its bilingual inscription is as follows:

> Latin. MAGLOCVNI (miscut MAGLOCVVI) FILI CLVTOR
>
> Ogham. MAGLICUNAS MAQI CLUTAR [I] (read right to left).
>
> The meaning of both is "(THE MONUMENT) OF MAGLOCUNUS (MAELGWN) SON OF CLUTORIUS."[22]

The slashes of Ogham, dating to the fifth century A.D. indicate the Goidelic language. "Maqi" is a variation of "Map," "Mab," or "ap," meaning "son of." This is not Maglocunus son of Catgolaun Lauhir from the middle of the sixth century, but an ancestor of the same name from a century or so earlier. Maglocunus of Gwynedd had ties to this area, granting land to the church here, a circumstance made even more interesting because of its regional connections to Cerdic and Creoda the "West-Saxon" kings. Based upon the scathing invectives which Gildas heaps upon the profligate Maglocunus, it would be easy to appraise him as an avaricious and unscrupulous tyrant capable of murder.

Vortipor

Whereas Gildas writes several pages castigating Maglocunus, he grants Vortipor only two short paragraphs. Even so, Gildas provides some important information which can be tracked: Vortipor is in his late years (his hair is whitening and the end of his life is drawing near); he is the bad son of a good king; he is the tyrant of Demetae; and he raped his shameless daughter.[23] Neither the name Vortipor nor any variants appear in the *HB*, the *AC*, or the *ASC*. According to Thomas O'Sullivan, his name is listed, however, as Guortepir in the *Harleian Pedigrees*.

Tracing the details of Vortipor's lineage is outside the scope of this investigation, though, because there is no thread which would connect him to Arthur or Arthur's enemies; his name is incidentally important only in that it corroborates his reign during Gildas's lifetime and solidifies documentation even further. Nevertheless, there is some satellite information which is of relevance and interest. One is that through "The Expulsion of the Dési," Vortipor is linked to Irish origins through an ancestor named Gartbuir, who migrated to Demed, and left sons and grandsons there before his death. There are undeniable ties, then, to Vortigern and Vortimer (if the latter is a factual figure), to the migration, and to the territories of Dyfed. During this period, it is commonly acknowledged that there were Irish raids to the western and southern coasts of Wales during the latter part of the Roman period, and that in the waning decades before Roman abandonment, there were Irish settlements in areas such as Dyfed, Ceredigion, and Gwynedd. As time passed, these settled Irish families became allied to Rome and then helped to protect the frontiers, a very common Roman strategy.

Several modern researchers have contributed details connected to this basic information. Both Alcock and O'Sullivan describe Vortipor's gravestone at Gastell Dwyran in Carmarthenshire,[24] and explain some of the ramifications of its inscription. Neither researcher supplies a name for the grave marker, but Sir Ifor Williams labels it the Llanfallteg stone.[25] O'Sullivan and Morris calibrate a floruit for Vortipor, but arrive at different conclusions. At one point, O'Sullivan assigned Guortepir a death-year of around 508,[26] but then through later calculations offers a floruit of around 503.[27] Morris, on the other hand, lists in his "Table of Dates" Vortipor's reign as around 515 to 540,[28] evidently arriving at that conjecture by an earlier observation that "Agricola (Longhand) is well dated to about 500, for he was the father of Vortipor, who was old and grey when Gildas wrote about 540."[29] Morris and Alcock also list Agricola Longhand (a variant of Aircol) as Vortipor's father,[30] but only

Morris uses the name Agricola Longhand, to distinguish this individual from Julius Agricola of the late first century.[31] Incidentally, Morris's date for the penning of the *De Excidio* circa 540 varies by only one year, 541, from the date established in the *HKA;* O'Sullivan's two dates of 503 and 508, therefore, are difficult to accept, since it is obvious that this particular king was alive simultaneously with Gildas, and Gildas's manuscript can quite accurately be dated to the beginning of the fourth decade of the sixth century.

The Annales Cambriae

In the *AC* there are four major emendations which have to be made, two entries which actually name Arthur. In the *HKA* these emendations, referred

Anno Domini	Pre-Christian	Event
•428	Nulla	The first Saxon landing
438	Nulla	The compilation, purification, and writing of the *Annals of Ireland*
•440	Nulla	The second Saxon landing
•		Cunedda migration
•453	ix	Easter altered by Pope Leo I
•		The year of the (third) Saxon landing
467	xxiii	The death of Bishop Benignus
•455-516	Nulla	Cerdic son of Cunedda
•455-516	v/xiv	Cerdic the interpreter
•497	liii	The Battle of Badon, in which Arthur and the Britons were victorious
••		Cerdic and Cynric came in five ships to Britain and fought against the Britons
•		The Birth of Gildas Badonicus
•518	lxxxiv	The Battle of Camlann, death of Arthur
••		Cerdic and Cynric succeed to the kingdom of the West Saxons
••521	lxxvii	The Birth of Saint Columba
••541	iiic	The Penning of the *De excidio,* Gildas age 44
•547	ciii	The Great Death
•		The death of Maelgwn, King of Gwynedd
••563	cxix	Saint Columba's voyage to Britain
••569	cxxv	The Synod of Victory at Caerleon
••570	cxxvi	The death of Gildas, age 73
••597	cliii	The death of Saint Columba

Table 1. Cardinal/Ordinal Years for Arthurian Chronology: • = Cardinal; •• = Ordinal.

to as Cardinal Years, are important because they relate directly to Arthur's milieu, and without them it would be impossible to establish an accurate chronology for the era. The first of these is the year in which Easter was altered by Pope Leo I, the foundation used by all chronographers. In simplistic terms it means that Year Nulla (0) is equated to the Christian reckoning of A.D. 444, ± two years. The second is the entry for Year 72, which converts to 516, when Arthur fought against the Saxons at the Battle of Badon and was victorious. Coincidentally, this is Gildas's birth-year, so that his penning the *DE* 44 years later also becomes a satellite Ordinal Year. The third is Year 93, converted to A.D. 537, the Battle of Camlann, in which both Arthur and Medraut fell. The last is the death of Maelgwn, King of Gwynedd in Year CIII (103), A.D. 547, important because of Maelgwn's relationship to Cunedda and Cerdic, Arthur's Welsh enemies who sided with the English Saxons.

Credit for the calculations of an emended accurate chronology goes to Leslie Alcock's work on Easter Tables, the Victorius of Aquitaine method, the Dionysius Exiguus method, and then his later adaptation according to the nineteen-year lunar cycles. The adjusted years which have been devised for significant events are summarized in Table 1 on page 29.[32] Although this might seem like an insufficient summary for such a valuable source, it has a far-reaching significance which would have been impossible without it.

The *Historia Brittonum*

The *HB*, too, is an indispensable work. It is part of a collection which Leslie Alcock called the British Historical Miscellany, a fitting name because it is an assorted collection of miscellaneous documents from a variety of sources, aimed at relaying early British history. Dating the origin of this work as the first half of the ninth century, Alcock writes that

> Since no facsimile of [the British Historical Miscellany] has ever been published, the student must refer to the original manuscript if he wishes to know where the scribe thought breaks were necessary.[33]

However, in 1980 John Morris translated this miscellany, which was titled *Nennius: British History and the Welsh Annals,* published by Phillimore & Company. It is a small volume of large impact, with only one significant drawback voiced above by Alcock. Morris's translation uses interpolated headings and subheadings not in the original earlier manuscripts. The superficial headings cause severe problems with correct geographic determinations, a difficulty to be addressed in detail later.

Alcock likewise shows an awareness of the problem created by inaccurate headings in the early manuscripts. Referring to Harley 3859, he writes that Arthur's battle list is separated from a *Kentish* reference by a colored drop-letter, which suggests that it introduces a new section altogether. He concludes that

> The termination of the Arthurian section ... is less easy to define, for it runs indistinguishably into a statement about Ida of Northumbria, which in turn leads on into the "Northern British History." The question has been asked, therefore, whether the battle list itself is part of the "Northern British History."[34]

The misfortune is that Alcock doesn't emphasize that the Kentish references are inappropriate and Arthur's battle list is indeed connected to the midlands further north.

This is probably the singular most important ramification affecting the search for the historic Arthur: emendations for the headings and subheadings of the *HB* must be made. A study of the earlier original manuscripts shows that no major headings were given. However, as time passed, scribes, antiquarians, and even modern scholars added headings, which for centuries have created puzzling contradictions because those headings have been accepted as fact. The segments of the chronicles in the *HB* should not be labeled as the Kentish Chronicles, Parts I, II, and II. Josephus Stevenson, one of the leading authorities on the *HB*, shows no titles between Books 30 and 57, yet the translations insert all of the following: "The Fifth Century," "The Kentish Chronicle Part 1," "The Kentish Chronicle Part 2," "The Life of Saint Germanus Part 2," "The Tale of Emrys," "The Kentish Chronicle Part 3," "The Life of Saint Germanus Part 3," "The Life of Saint Patrick," and "The Campaigns of Arthur."

Between Books 57 and 58 Stevenson records the titles of "The Genealogies of the Kings of Kent," and "The Genealogies," but adds in a footnote that "These titles are added in A(.) by a later hand, and are not found in any other MSS."[35] That one title adds "of Kent" and the other omits it is in itself an indication that the locale of Kent for the genealogies is spurious. The heading of "The Kentish Chronicle Part I" is based solely upon one word, Tanet. Evidently, from a very early date, that word had been translated as the geographic site of Thanet, which is located in Kent. No one has bothered since then to question why a Welsh-based king, recorded in a Welsh manuscript, would be granting territories to the Saxons two hundred miles away in Kent. The word Tanet would much more realistically refer to the River Tanat in northern Wales, which formed an island as it flowed southeasterly for about thirty miles and joined the River Severn.

Other information under the incorrect heading of "The Kentish Chronicle Part 2" also shows that the heading is geographically very misleading. Book 37 relates that Hengist took counsel with the elders of Oghgul. This has been incorrectly interpreted either as Angeln, the territory to the east later called Anglia in the old Roman Britannia Flavia segment of the island, or as the dominions of the Schleswig-Jutland peninsula on the continent. In fact, however, Manuscript A of the *HB* uses the term "insula Oghgul," the *island* of Oghgul, and Manuscript *a* uses the word Oehgul, both which are ancient terms for Ireland. The dynasty of the Dési (Vortigern's tribe) migrated from Ireland specifically to Dementia (the later province of Dyfed), one of Vortigern's kingdoms and strongholds. This, then, places Hengist and Vortigern in the proper locale of southern Wales, and as a very important aside, Hengist is negotiating with *Vortigern's council of elders,* not with his own counselors.

Leslie Alcock indirectly verifies this locale of Wales in his discussion on Ogham stones. Ogham, of course, is a cognate of the word Oghgul meaning "Irish" and in relation to its history, Alcock writes that the roots are traceable as imports from Ireland to Britain

> along with the Irish language, the Ogham script, and the pagan idea of setting up rough stone memorials. The immigrant tribe or dynasty of the *Dési* [Vortigern's tribe] would have had the chief responsibility for the introduction of these *Irish* customs. [Italics mine][36]

Continuing about these stones in Group I, Alcock writes that there are nearly two hundred of them dating from the fifth, sixth, and seventh centuries, and of that number, "Wales has the overwhelming bulk, some 140 concentrated in Gwynedd, Dyfed, and Brycheiniog...."[37] This alone shows unquestionably that the geographic locale for Vortigern's and Hengist's operations would be in Wales, and not in Kent.

Yet there is even more evidence. In that same paragraph of the *HB* is a passage in Manuscript *a* stating that Hengist was granted the country (our equivalent of province or kingdom) "quæ vocatur [which is called] Anglice Centland, Britannice autem Cæint."[38] The word "Anglice," corroborated by John Morris, is "a general term for the Germanic settlers in Britain who were not Frisian."[39] And from Book 31 of the *HB* itself, Hengist is labeled as "an exile from Germany" who had already settled on the island. More important, however, is the Briton word for the country which was granted to Hengist, *Cæint,* which (to the modern researcher's dismay) was translated as *Chent,* for Kent, probably because of the interpolated titles associated with it. However, Eilert Ekwall points out that "Cant is an Old Britain river-name, which may be related to Caint R (Wales) and KENN D., So."[40] The River Cain is also in northern Wales, only about two miles south of the River Tanat, and also flows into the Severn. It would be too far-fetched to be mere coincidence that Vortigern first grants land to Hengist at "insula Tanet", and then Hengist later acquires more land in Cæint in the same vicinity; without a doubt, the territories are in northern Wales—which Vortigern has a right to grant—and *not* in the distant province of Kent, where he has no jurisdiction.

Book 38 of the *HB* continues to stress the locale as Wales and not Kent.

In pressing Vortigern for even more land, Hengist promises more reinforcements, including his son Octha, to fight against the *Scottos,* which is the ancient name for the Irish. The Irish were settled in Wales, and because of incursions from Ireland and the havoc which the invaders were creating in Vortigern's provinces in Wales, Hengist was promising protection against them. For this historical period, it is ludicrous to imagine that Irish invaders were threatening Kent. Book 38 then ends with the word *Cantorum,* once again unfortunately translated as *Chent* (Kent).

"The Tale of Emrys," Books 40 through 42, also gives additional support to the contention that all of this activity is taking place in Wales and not Kent. When Vortigern's wizards search for a boy without a father, they explore provinces and many countries, including Maes Elledi in Gleguissing, which is in southern Wales. Once they find him, they take him to the site of Vortigern's future fortress, at Dinas Emrys, which is near Beddgelert in the Snowdonias of northern Wales. After Vortigern becomes fearful of the boy's magical powers, he grants the kingdoms of the western part of Britain (i.e., Wales) to the boy and flees farther north to the Gwynessi territory, also a province in Wales.

Books 43 and 44 also give clues that Wales is the key to interpreting events of the period, but several are more conjectural, though still logical. Book 43 once again records the locale of Tanet, followed by Vortimer's (not Vortigern's) battle on the Derguentid (Derwent). The etymology of the word Derguentid was given earlier, and rather than reiterating information, the approach for locating the 'correct' Derwent should follow a reverse logic; that is, assuming that the Derwent in Kent is *not* the correct location, where would the location be in Wales that logistically fits Vortimer's battle with the treasonous Saxons? Two probabilities emerge. One is the River Derwent, whose origin is about fifteen miles to the east of Manchester. This is an area slightly to the northeast of Wales, but still conceivably within the vague boundaries provided by the Romans for the Cornovii territory, which was a no-man's-land after the abandonment. The second probability is the River Derwent, about fifteen miles southeast of Manchester, likewise on the boundaries of the old Cornovii territory. Although a location cannot be pinpointed with certainty, the commonality does become obvious that the word "Derwent" focuses much more on the Welsh rather than the Kentish kingdom: Two River Darwents, a Darwen and Lower Darwen, and Derwen.[41]

The site for another of Vortimer's battles would add even more confusion to the already thorny problem of trying to decipher geographic location, but a fortuitous clue diverts the search once more toward Wales, rather than once again allowing a quick jump to the wrong conclusion that Kent is the proper site. The fortuitous clue is that the entry adds that Horsa was killed in this particular battle, and hence, it is listed not only in the *HB,* but also in the *ASC* at A.D. 455. We can turn, therefore, to the *ASC* entry to determine (from a source more likely to be accurate since it deals with one of its heroes) that Horsa was killed at a place called Ægælesthrep. The balloon of hopeful identification is a bit deflated because the identification of a Welsh site is not immediately forthcoming, but it does point to the unreliability of some of the early copyists: The site is listed in the *HB* as Episford, undoubtedly spawned by the misconception that the titles identifying Kent were correct. The difficulty is compounded because the *HB* adds that the Briton name for that site is Rit Hergabail, an obvious Welsh name, but there is continued deflation because there is no modern site by that name. The only straw left to grasp is that if three of Vortimer's battles took place in Wales, then it follows that the fourth probably did too.

There is one last and undeniable clincher that these conflicts between the Britons and the English Saxons took place in Wales. Vortimer's last battle is "in the open country near the Lapidem Tituli (Inscribed Stone) near the shores of the Gallici Sea."[42] As earlier cited, Leslie Alcock related that of the two hundred inscribed stones, 140 of them are in Wales. *None of those ogham stones have ever been discovered in Kent.* That means, then, the stone in question is on the shores of the *Gaelic* Sea and *not* the Gallic Sea. With this kind of massive proof, there should be no doubt that the *HB* has given an excellent account of geographic reliability, but for centuries, scribes and researchers have been trying to squeeze round pegs into square holes because of interpolated headings and subheadings.

There are several other minor emendations which must be made in the *HB*, not as obvious when examining each by itself. The first is the implication that Hengist and Horsa were the leaders of the first Saxon *Adventus.* Without going into elaborate detail here and instead referring the reader to the three Saxon *Adventi* in the *HKA*, it is sufficient to relate that Hengist and Horsa were the leaders of the second and third *Adventi;* the first took place around the year A.D. 428,[43] twenty-one years *before* Hengist and Horsa make their first appearance in the *ASC.* The *HKA* establishes the involvement of those two leaders in British affairs during the year 440, the *second* Saxon incursion. Their reign carries over to the year 453 which is the date normally given as *the* Saxon *Adventus,* but which is actually the third. Gildas in the *DE* writes about Vortigern and the invitation to the Saxons, but because of "compacting" which was so common in the early documents, the *Historia Brittonum* makes the Vortigern/first Adventus/Hengist connection in Book 31, tying these three aspects together and then recording the donation of land to the Saxon allies.

The second minor adjustment focuses upon Octha's involvement. The *HB* reports that Octha was sent to the "north about the wall which is called Guaul."[44] The assumption which has been made to date is that the "wall" is a reference to either Hadrian's Wall or, from J. A. Giles, the Antonine Wall, and hence Octha was sent quite far north, which could have been anywhere

Photograph 1. Octha's location in the north when he was sent to Guaul (Wall). This text identifies this site, Wall-by-Lichfield, known also as the Roman name Letocetum, as Octha's headquarters.

along two different frontiers. And nowhere along this barrier is there a site named Guaul. There is, however, a Roman way-station in the midlands which was called Guaul or Wall, more formally known by the Romans as Letocetum. The *HKA* postulates that this was the site where Octha was sent, particularly in light of the fact that Octha was involved in the Battle of Mount Badon, which would have occurred only about thirty miles away and would have been the epicenter of the Briton/Saxon wars.[45]

The third incorrect assumption is Cerdic's identity in Book 37. In 1899, Charles Plummer, an authority on the manuscripts of the *ASC*, comments in a reference to the *HB*, "It is worth noting in Nennius, § 37, Ceretic is the name of Hengest's *interpreter.*"[46] The language of the passage is garbled and therefore can cause difficulty for copyists and translators interpreting it. J. A. Giles relates, "And now the Saxon chief prepared an entertainment, to which he invited the king, his officers, and Cerdic, his interpreter, having previously enjoined his daughter to serve them so profusely with wine and ale, that they might soon become intoxicated."[47] John Morris in his translation writes, "When the keels had arrived, Hengest held a banquet for Vortigern, and his men and his interpreter, whose name was Ceretic, and he told the girl to serve their wine and spirits."[48] The many repetitions of "his" makes it difficult to determine if Ceretic is Hengist's interpreter, or Vortigern's.

There are extensive ramifications, however, so that it is important to stress that Ceretic is *Vortigern's* interpreter. One of the major postulations in the *HKA* is that Cerdic the Interpreter, and Cerdic son of Cunedda, *and* Cerdic the West-Saxon King are all the same individual. Although the first mention appears in the *HB*, the second in Welsh genealogies, and the third in the *ASC*, one floruit fits all three roles, resolving a great deal of the puzzling historical aspects of the period. Cunedda's young son, Cerdic, fraternized with the English Saxons, who were initially allies with Vortigern fighting the Irish and the Picts. He had a penchant for the Saxon language (and might even be Gwrhyr Interpreter of Languages in the "Culhwch," "Rhonabwy," and "Gereint" tales of *The Mabinogion*, although this thread is never traced). Once the split developed between the Britons and the Saxons, Cerdic became a Saxon sympathizer, rose as a leader in the power struggle, and finally became known as a Saxon rather than a Briton king because of his treasonous or selfish inclinations. This would coincide with Gildas's description of civil war, raging from coast to coast and tearing the island asunder. It would likewise explain the lack of a Saxon genealogy for one of the most powerful kings of the era, as well as Arthur's tolerance for the continual disturbances caused by Cerdic. Because Cerdic is a figure pervading the histories, there will be further discussion of him later.

The fourth and last adjustment is the introductory passage prior to Arthur's battle list. The *HB* relates that "On Hengist's death, Octha came down from the north."[49] But after a great deal of mathematical calculation, and the calibration of floruits and life spans for the Saxon leaders, the *HKA* emends that to read "Octha came down from the north upon *Horsa's* death."[50] This shifts attention to several puzzling entries in the *ASC*.

The *Anglo-Saxon Chronicle*

One other major supplement must be considered in the attempt to verify the historic Arthur, even though neither his name nor any ancestors appear in the variant versions. That work is the *ASC*, the counterpart to the Briton histories. The major focus is on two separate segments, The Genealogical Preface and the *Chronicle* itself, narrowed to the period between A.D. 420 and 535. The overlapping reigns of Hengist, Horsa, Octha, Cerdic, and Ælle are crucial in establishing Arthur as their adversary in Britain following Vortigern's rise to power after the Romans abandoned the island. This, then, is not independent of Arthur's origins, but instead an integral part of his roots, even though modifications and changes in the *Chronicle* can stand on their own merits without any link to King Arthur. When used in conjunction with the *DE* of Gildas, the *HB*, and the *AC*, the *Anglo-Saxon Chronicle* contributes to an accurate chronological calibration of Arthur's lifetime.

For the most part, the dates in the *Chronicle* are fairly accurate, in that there is not a great deal of confusion among the Dionysiac, the Victorian, and the lunar cycle of calibrations. Chapter 3 of the *HKA* deals with the methods of reckonings and reconciles those dates which are important in establishing the historicity of Arthur; they are accurate and have been verified, and any questions are validated through the book's documentation.

Leslie Alcock expressed concern that a significant portion of the *Chronicle* reflected only leap years and thus were artificial. However, the dates within Arthur's time span would be 496, 500, 504, 508, 512, 516, 520, and 524, and the actual dates in the *Chronicle* are 495, 501, 508, 514, 519, and 527. Only one date, A.D. 508, falls on a leap year, showing that these dates do not reflect that portion of the annals which follows a four-year cycle. Alcock's hypothesis might apply to other segments which reflect only leap years in the Easter Tables, but his concern is not applicable when looking at the crucial dates between 495 and 520.

Two other general misconceptions should be addressed before moving on to specific entries. The first is that distinctions in the *Chronicle* entries should be made between references to the Welsh and to the Britons. Unfortunately, the two terms are used synonymously in the various versions, but the difference is crucial to the understanding of the history of the period. The Welsh are an outgrowth of the Britons, and as such, when they are mentioned, it means that the conflicts with the English Saxons are taking place in the western midlands and in Wales, as opposed to the Thames Valley or the southern coast. The *Chronicle* entries of 465, 473, 477, 485, 495, and 508 record that the Saxons (and the Saxon sympathizers)—Hengist, Horsa, Octha, Ælle, and Cerdic—are battling the *Welsh;* battles elsewhere involve the Saxons and the *Britons.*

The second general misconception is the subtle distinction between the geographic locations of Cerdicesora and Cerdicesford, both which are, of course, epynomic for the West-Saxon king, a common practice for many place-names. Lamentably, these two locales have been used interchangeably. There is no solidly based proof that the two sites are different, but nevertheless the entries which mention these spots imply they are different. For example, Year A.D. 495 relates that Cerdic was fighting the *Welsh* at Cerdicesora, but in entry A.D. 519 Cerdic is fighting the *Britons* at Cerdicesford. In that interim there seems to have been a switch from specific in-fighting and civil war, to a more general malaise which was devastating the island.

Other than these *general* deficiencies, the problem is not that an incorrect method of calibration was used, but instead one of replicating some entries and misplacing others. Chapter 3, "Cerdic as Vortigern's Interpreter: Cardinal Year #10," in *The Historic King Arthur* gives all of the relevant research and verification for establishing a composite chronology for Hengist and Octha. The generalities are relatively simple: The English Saxons are no longer allies with the Welsh, meaning that Hengist and Vortigern are now mortal enemies and camps have been divided; Horsa is killed in one of the battles, and Octha succeeds to the kingdom and reigns jointly with his father until his father dies.

The specifics are not quite as easy. Vortigern is mentioned in two entries: Year A.D. 449, where there is a hint that even though the English Saxons have been invited in as mercenaries, dissatisfaction and treason are brewing: and Year A.D. 455, relating that Hengist and Horsa fought against Vortigern and Horsa is killed. Vortigern drops from the scene without any explanation of his fate. Hengist's last appearance is in Year A.D. 473 but his death is not recorded, and Octha's succession to the kingdom is listed in Year A.D. 488, after which he reigns for twenty-four years.

The last entry, Year A.D. 488, is the one which is most jarringly out of place. Technically, Octha succeeds to the kingdom twice: once in 455 when Horsa is killed and he reunites with Hengist in joint reign, and then again after his father's death, when he becomes the sole ruler. If we accept 488 as Octha's succession to the kingdom with a twenty-four-year reign, then his death-year would be 522. If he jointly reigned with his father in 455, that would have been sixty-seven years prior to his death. Assuming that he was approximately twenty years old when he began his joint rule with his father, he would have been born in 435 and hence eighty-seven years old when he died. Although there are records of people living to that age and even older (as in Arthur's case), it is the exception rather than the rule during this era, and lies beyond the "reasonable age" concept.

What is common in the *Chronicle* is that at the last entry where an individual is mentioned, there is an inference of a death-year plus a succession to the kingdom. If we apply this common practice of simultaneously listing a succession and inferring the predecessor's death, then Octha's life span falls into alignment while at the same time putting Hengist's span within the "reasonable age" concept. If Hengist's death occurred in A.D. 473, his floruit would be 428–458, and his life span would be 413–473. He would have been twenty-nine years old when he led the second *Adventus,* overlapping Vortigern's and Octha's life spans. If Octha's sole rule began in the year 473 and he reigned for twenty-four years, he would have died in 497. His floruit would have been 452–482 and his life span 437 to 497, suggesting that he was five years old during the Saxon Revolt, eighteen years old when he began his joint reign with his father, and thirty-six years old when his father died. One surprising bonus is that the *Chronicle* attests to the *Historia* report that Octha fought against Arthur in his campaigns, and even more surprising, infers that he was killed at the Battle of Mount Badon in 497. "The Dream of Rhonabwy" in *The Mabinogion* is a third source which corroborates that Arthur and Osla Big Knife fought at the Battle of Badon. And then, in a circular fashion, Octha's death in 497 leads to Cerdic's rise as the West Saxon King as recorded in the *Chronicle* for the year 495.

Preface		**Chronicle**		
Cerdic	500 + 16 = 516			
Creoda	517 + 17 = **534**	34 years:	500–**534**	
Cynric	534 + 26 = **560**	26 years:	534–**560**	
Ceawlin	560 + 25 = 585			
Ceol	585 + 6 = **591**	31 years:	560–**591**	
Ceolwulf	591 + 17 = **608**	14 years:	597–**611**	
Cynegils	608 + 31 = **639**	31 years:	611–**642**	
Cenwalh	639 + 31 = **670**	29 years:	643–672	Parker Chronicle Ā
			641–**670**	Mss A, B, C,E
Sexburg	670 + 1 = **671**	1 year:	672–673	
			670–**671**	
Aescwine	671 + 2 = **673**	2 years:	673–**675**	

Table 2. The reconciliation of discrepancies between the *ASC* and its GP. The bold-faced dates show the striking similarities of dates. Compare to Plummer's chart.

Undoubtedly, the most important reconciliation of dates is between the *Anglo-Saxon Chronicle* and its Genealogical Preface, a discrepancy first noted by Charles Plummer in 1899 and later deemed that it was "impossible to harmonize the two series of dates."[51] Propitiously, however, after almost a century, one of the ancillary outcomes in the *HKA* was a reconciliation of those dates, perhaps the breakthrough with the most far-reaching implications because the reconciliation directly relates to chronological calibrations for the fifth and sixth centuries—unexpected but fortuitous. The details can be checked in Chapter 2, "Deciphering Differences between the Preface and *The Anglo-Saxon Chronicle*"; a summary of the findings is reflected in Table 2.

The first column of Table 2 shows the information as it appears in the Genealogical Preface; the Preface records, for instance, that Cerdic succeeded to the kingship in A.D. 500 and ruled for sixteen years, then Creoda succeeded to the throne and he ruled for seventeen years. The second column indicates what was recorded in the *Chronicle;* that is, the Creoda generation is omitted from the *ASC* (even though he appears in the genealogical table in the appendix), and instead Cerdic is listed as ruling for thirty-four years. The explanation of one more example should suffice. In the Preface, Ceawlin assumed the throne in 560 and ruled for twenty-five years, and when he died Ceol assumed leadership and ruled for six years before he died. Their combined reign, therefore would be a total of thirty-one years. However, there was a discrepancy in the *Chronicle* because it listed Ceawlin's reign as thirty-one years, then tacked on another six years for Ceol's reign, which gave instead a total reign of thirty-seven years. This means that the *Chronicle* therefore erroneously listed Ceol's succession in 591 and his death in 597, which of course threw off all the succeeding reigns of the kings.

Some of the dates have a two- or three-year discrepancy, but as Plummer states, it is a small matter if there is a one-to three-year difference when dealing with history dating back fifteen centuries.

Table 3 shows the emendations which have to made to the *Chronicle* entries. In entry 495, for example, the name Creoda has to be substituted for Cynric, since Cynric was Cerdic's grandson and not his son. The rest of the table should be self-explanatory.

One last peculiarity about *The Anglo-Saxon Chronicle* which has a direct bearing on the era of Arthur is the term *Bretwalda* or *Breotenwalda,*[52] which very few historians have dealt with. Leslie Alcock and Geoffrey Ashe (technically they could be categorized as Arthurian historians) touch upon the term. Ashe tersely mentions the first three Saxon kings who held the title of Bretwalda and gives the impression that it was only an honorary title because the kings could not have coordinated regional sovereignties.[53] Alcock gives more detail, first defining the term as "ruler of Britain," and then indicating that the term is based on Bede's account. He then names the first four who reigned south of the Humber and adds three others who were of the north.[54]

Of the individuals who would be more appropriately called a historian, John Morris touches but lightly upon the term. He, like Alcock, lists Bede who identified these kings "holding empire," *imperium,* which in the English language was termed Bretwalda. Morris then adds slightly more by drawing a similarity with the imperial title *Brytwalda,* which means "wide ruler" and was occasionally used for the Roman emperors.[55] In a footnote he names Æthelbert as the Bretwalda south of the Humber who was the third to hold the title, which came by the seventh century to mean an over-king.[56] John Davies is the most laconic and the most confusing. He identifies Edwin as "the first English king to be called Bretwalda" and then writes that "Catguollaun

PREFACE	CHRONICLE
494—Cerdic and *Creoda* his son landed at Cerdicesora with five ships	**495**—In this year two princes, Cerdic and *Creoda* his son, came to Britain in five ships at a place which is called Cerdicesora.
500—Six years after they landed they conquered the kingdom of Wessex. These were the first kings who conquered the land of Wessex from the Welsh. Cerdic holds the kingdom for sixteen years.	**500**—[Æthelweardian chronicle] In the sixth year after their arrival they conquered the western part of Britain which is now called Wessex: Whitelock, footnote 5, page. 11.
516—*Cerdic* held the kingdom sixteen years, and when he died his son *Creoda* succeeded to the kingdom.	**519**—In this year *Creoda* obtained the kingdom of the West Saxons; the same year they fought against the Britons at Cerdicesford.[1]

PREFACE	CHRONICLE
534—*In this year Creoda died.* Cynric inherited the kingdom of the West Saxons and ruled for twenty-six years.	**534**—In this year *Creoda* died and his son Cynric ruled for twenty-seven years.[2]
560—*When Cynric passed away, his son Ceawlin succeeded to the kingdom and held it twenty-five years.*	**560**—In this year Ceawlin succeeded to the kingdom in Wessex; Ælle to the kingdom of the Northumbrians.
585—When *Ceawlin* died, Ceol succeeded to the kingdom and held it for six years.	
591—When Ceol died his brother Ceolwulf succeeded and ruled seventeen years, and their ancestry goes back to Cerdic.	**591**—In this year Ceol reigned for *six* years. [MSS E and A give six years instead of five.]
	593—In this year Ceawlin, Cwichelm, and Crida perished.
608—Then Cynegils, Ceolwulf's brother's son, succeeded to the kingdom and ruled thirty-one years, and he was the first of the West Saxon kings to receive baptism.	**611**—In this year Cynegils succeeded to the kingdom in Wessex, and held it for thirty-one years. Cynegils was the son of Ceola, the son of Cutha, the son of Cynric.[3]
639—Then Cenwalh succeeded and held it thirty-one years; and that Cenwalh was the son of Cynegils.	**641**—And Cenwalh succeeded to the kingdom of the West Saxons and held it for thirty-one years.[5]
671—Then Cenwalh's queen Seaxburh held the kingdom one year after him.	**672**—In this year Cenwalh died, and his queen Seaxburh reigned one year after him.

1. Based upon the clue from the Preface, Cerdic dies or is killed at this point, and the name Creoda should replace the name Cerdic in all entries until entry 534.
2. The name Cerdic should be replaced with the name Creoda to account for the lost generation. This would mean that Creoda ruled for eighteen years.
3. *611 + 31 = 642, but Cynegils's death is given as 641. This one-year discrepancy gives credence to the date of 609 in the Preface for Cynegils' succession.
4. See information in Preface, year 609.
5. **At this point MSS A, B, C, E are two years behind Ā.

Table 3. Comparison/contrast of dates from the *ASC* and GP, resolved in *HKA*.

was Cadwallon of the line of Maelgwn Fawr, a man who was himself not without claims to the status of *Bretwalda*."[57] Davies then abandons the subject without explaining whether or not he was being figurative.

Peter Hunter Blair is the most lucid on the subject of Bretwalda. In an appendix he lists the eight kings who were identified as Bretwalda and clarifies the origin of the term by explaining that it was first used in a ninth-century annal of *The Anglo-Saxon Chronicle* for eight kings, seven of whom were also mentioned by Bede.[58] The first of these is Ælle, commonly identified as a South Saxon, whose kingdom was small and seemed of no earth-shaking political consequence. If indeed the term Bretwalda was an honorary title as suggested by both Ashe and Blair, then the circumstances which allowed Ælle to reach such a status is hidden, a common misfortune when seeking answers about Arthur's era. Ælle, whose reign is contemporary with that of Arthur, is the only Saxon to acquire such a prominent title during this period. Forty-two years after Arthur's death, Ceawlin, Cerdic's great-grandson,[59] is the second king and the first from the West-Saxon house to acquire the title. The third Bretwalda is Æthelbert, the king of Kent whose rule began in 560.

It is not surprising that the haunting question about Bretwaldas hasn't been directly assaulted by the *ASC* historians, since there are so many intertwined strands of events which must be explained before the core question can be asked. The best approach is to set aside any questions about the Bretwalda and first clarify (or explicate) events of the period. One crucial clarification is a determination of Ælle's territory. Throughout history he has been labeled as a South Saxon and hence his territory has been identified (or translated) as the Owers to the south of Selsey Bill which is now under the sea, plus the Sussex Weald and Anderida in Pevensey. But this impression must be exposed as a falsehood because of all the evidence to the contrary. *The Historic King Arthur* skirted the issue of Bretwalda, but it does point out the inconsistencies as they appear in the *ASC*.[60] Of the three entries about Ælle, the first two assert that he fought against the Welsh; in one entry he slew many Welsh and the remainder fled into the woods, and in the other he fought against the Welsh near the banks of a stream. The inconsistency of entry 477 is that the Welsh would be fighting a battle on the far southern coast near Selsey Bill and the Weald; the inconsistency of entry 485 is that the Welsh would still be hanging about the southern coast eight years later. The entry of 491, on the other hand is not contradictory. It reports that Ælle slew all of the Britons at Andredescester. If Andredescester is interpreted as Anderida on the southern coast, then it is correct to assume that Ælle is slaying Britons and not Welsh.

A further inconsistency is the name of one of Ælle's sons (Cymen) and the eponymic geographic location named after him (Cymenesora). The entry of 477 opens with "In this year Ælle came to Britain with his three sons Cymen, Wlencing, and Cissa in three ships at the place which is called Cymenesora."[61] In a different context, Rachel Bromwich provides a consequential clue about Cymen and his place-name in a chapter which is ironically significant in the search for the definition of Bretwalda. She introduces the material about the *Cymry* by explaining that the inhabitants of the British districts called themselves Britons, and the inhabitants of Little Britain (or Brittany) in France called themselves Bretons. She then relates that the people of

> Wales and Strathclyde ... began to call themselves also *Cymry*, the plural of *Cymro*, a compound of *com-* a prefix meaning "together," and *bro* "border, coast, district." ... [S]o *Cymro* means ... a fellow

> countryman. Cornishmen were never known as *cymry*, but the people of *Cumberland* were; ... Cumberland means "the land of the Cymry." ...
>
> In older Welsh usage *Cymry* denoted both the country and the people; later *Cymru* came to be the name for Wales, and *cymro*, pl. *Cymry*, the name for the people of the country.[62]

"Cymen" and "Cymenesora" are cognates of "Cymry," "Cymro," and "Cymru," signifying *northern* territories just east of what is now called Wales, *not* anything associated with the southern coast or Sussex; according to the *ASC* entry, Ælle is fighting against the Welsh in Welsh territory.

An entry from Eilert Ekwall's dictionary of place-names further verifies a different *ASC* entry, which relates that in 485 "Ælle fought against the Welsh near the bank of Mearcrædesburna."[63] Mearcrædesburna has not been specifically identified by any modern scholar, but the prefix is quite revealing. Of it *(Mearc-)* Ekwall writes

> O[ld] E[nglish] **mearc** "mark, boundary mark, boundary, border, border district." The last sense is found in OE *mierce* "Mercians," lit[erally] "borderers." In pl[ural] n[oun]s the usual meaning is no doubt "boundary mark, boundary."[64]

Ælle, therefore, is fighting the Welsh on the borderlands between Cymru (Wales) and Mercia, *in the north*. Mercia is the name for the earlier Roman territory known as Cornovii, which is the heart of all the Saxon/Briton and Saxon/Welsh conflicts which were taking place. The two entries in the *ASC* are surprisingly accurate in pinpointing the arenas of war: Wales, Cumbria, Northumbria, and Mercia. The final entry about this particular Ælle in 491 suggests a different set of circumstances because of the word "Briton" and the geographic location of Andredescester.

One other minor clue also leads to the proper identification of Ælle's kingdom. The Ælle of our inquiry is the Ælle of the late 470s, the 480s, and the beginning of the 490s. There is one other king by the name of Ælle recorded in the *ASC* who reigned during the 560s, 570s, and 580s. From entries 560 and 588, this particular Ælle is described as the king of the Northumbrians who succeeded to the kingdom after Ida had died, and who in turn was succeeded in 588 by Æthelric. It is a safe assumption that Ælle of the mid–400s was an ancestor of the Ælle of the latter-half of the 500s and that the last-recorded Ælle inherited the kingdom of Northumbria through his namesake. The kingdom inherited was not along the southern shores of the island, but to the north and east of Cymry territories. After the passing of the second Ælle, Edwin reigned.

It is necessary to now turn to two circumstances which seem not only unrelated to each other but also unrelated to the term Bretwalda. The first of these is the distinction which must be made between the *English* Saxons and the *German* Saxons. *The Historic King Arthur* points out that the

> ethnic group "Saxons" is not limited to the continentals who persistently tried to invade Britain. "Saxons" can also refer to the prior two generations who settled in Britain, sanctioned not only by the Romans but later by the Britons themselves. The present text later distinguishes between the *English* Saxons (who were settlers on the island) and the *German* Saxons (continentals who are newcomers.)[65]

Wade-Evans makes the same distinction by defining the word *Britanni* as a generic term used by the Romans to identify all of the inhabitants of Britain, including immigrants, who would by no means be termed "Britons." He then makes a distinction between "Saxons" and "Britons" (in modern terms the English and the Welsh), confirming that the English Saxons lived "toward the east" and the Britons "toward the west."[66]

These observations also clarify several references in Gildas's *De Excidio.* At one point in Chapter 24 Gildas writes of the *orientali sacrilegorum,* which is a reference to the Saxons from the eastern part of the island, in Britannia Secunda. He accuses these "easterners" of trying to capture territory from sea to sea and leaving devastation in their wake. This relates to his comment in Chapter 26: "External wars may have stopped, but not civil ones."[67] The implication is that the Britons, during this time of upheaval after the Roman abandonment, are fighting two distinctive factions, one group generically labeled as the German Saxons (from the continent) who are responsible for the external wars, and the other group labeled as the English Saxons (settled for generations on the island) who are creating the civil, internal conflicts by attempting to overrun the Britons (settled to the far west) once the buffer zone (the Cornovii territory previously occupied by the Romans) is left vacant.

The second seemingly unrelated circumstance is a condition reported in Chapter 26 of the *Historia Brittonum.* After Arthur's twelve successful battles against the Saxons, the *HB* records that when the Saxons were defeated in these campaigns, the English Saxons sought help from their counterparts, the German Saxons, from the continent. The Saxons on the island increased in number, and the German kings came to Britain to rule over the Britons until the reign of Ida, "who was the son of Eobba." Using different terminology, the English Saxons, who had been defeated by Arthurex Ambrosius, appealed to their ancestors, the German Saxons on the continent, to ally themselves with their insular kinsmen so that as a coalition they could conquer the island. The English and German Saxons joined forces, and after the death of Arthurex, the German Saxons held domain until Ida's reign.

All of the information about Ælle, about the distinction between English and German Saxons, and about the concluding segment of Chapter 56 in the *Historia Brittonum* must now be bound together in order to give the long-awaited answer to the question about the term Bretwalda. In an attempt to decipher the term, P. H. Blair suggests that perhaps "the title itself was an invention of the ninth century in which it is first found recorded."[68] But that seems extremely unlikely. Why would a scribe retrospectively apply the term to the mid-fifth century (five centuries prior to his time)? Even more puzzling, why would a copyist ascribe the term Bretwalda to Ælle in particular, since he could have selected a *Saxone* who would have been much more prominent, such as Hengist, Horsa, Æsc, or Cerdic?

Bretwalda embodies a position of eminence, an equivalence of *Vortigern* or *Vortimer*, meaning an overlord or a chieftain above other chieftains. It was not inherited or passed down from one generation to the next in a royal family, nor was it a title of inherent authority; it was bestowed or won, perhaps by either administrative civil importance or military competence or both. Blair writes that there is nothing known of Ælle's circumstances to warrant this distinction for him, but then adds

> We can only conjecture that at some time in the second half of the sixth century he was recognized as the leader of the Anglo-Saxon assault against the British in the south-eastern part of the country as a whole.[69]

This is not a bad surmise, but it's even better if "sixth century" is emended to the fifth, and "the south-eastern part of the country" is emended to "the Mercian and Cumbrian territories of the Midlands," as the bulk of evidence dictates.

The answer to the question "Why Ælle?" begins to unfold. The *ASC* itself shows that Ælle's kingdom is not etched out along the southeastern coast (an idea which has been accepted as fact for so long), but instead is at the very core of conflict during his era. The *HB* then contributes the essential information that after the English Saxons were defeated in all their battles against Arthurex, they sent for German Saxons to rule over them in Britain. By implication this means that Ælle was a German Saxon king who joined his English Saxon allies to fight against the Welsh. By this time, the English Saxon leaders Hengist and Horsa were dead, and Octha and Cerdic had been defeated. Ælle, therefore, would have been the impelling force behind the successful reclamation of some insular territories.

If the definition of *Bretwalda* is initially accepted as a German-Saxon King (or ally) ruling in Britain, then the analysis of another Bretwalda should either deny or confirm the definition. If it does the former, then the definition must be scrapped and the search must be continued in a different direction; if it does the latter, then the word Bretwalda is finally defined as an expressive epithet.

According to emended calibrations, Hengist was one of the Angle leaders during the second and third *Adventi*. In the year 455 his brother and co-chieftain was killed in a battle against Vortimer, perpetrating Octha's move from the north to join his father as co-chieftain. Father and son ruled jointly until Hengist's death in 473, at which point Octha became the sole ruler. Octha ruled for twenty-four years, from 473 until 497, meaning that the entry for 488 which split Ælle's reign should be stricken. Sometime during this interim period, tradition portrays Octha as Arthurex's comrade, but between this and a later tradition he became an enemy. The transition suggests that at first the Welsh and English Saxons were fighting side-by-side against the Irish and the Picts, but when the alliance crumbled, Octha of course chose the Saxon side. In 497, based upon the interweaving of several historical and literary sources, Octha is killed at the Battle of Badon, thus ending Hengist's line of Angle rulers.

Along similar lines, Cerdic emerges from nowhere as the powerful king of the West-Saxon house. The genealogy provided for him in the *ASC* is bogus for a Saxon, but as the son of a British chieftain, he is revealed as a Briton with Saxon allegiance. Whereby his father is true to the Briton cause, Cerdic traitorously sides with the Saxons to try to carve out a kingdom of his own. He and his son Creoda jointly rule for an indeterminate length of time. John of Glastonbury records that there was continuous feuding between Arthurex and Cerdic until a pact was made granting Cerdic the kingdom of Wessex in return for his fealty to the high king. Cerdic reneges on the pact, and in at least one instance, he takes a stand at Mount Badon, in league with Octha against Arthurex. A truce is reached after Octha's death, but the struggle between Cerdic and Arthurex continues until both are killed at the Battle of Camlann in 518. Creoda reigns as the sole king until 534, at which time Cynric becomes the sole ruler until he is joined by his son in 556. Four years later Cynric dies, and Ceawlin becomes the sole successor.

The important name in this winding trail to the definition of Bretwalda is that of Ceawlin in the West-Saxon house, the second individual to be granted the title of Bretwalda. What, if any, is the link between Ceawlin and Ælle? Distressingly, there is a breach in the West-Saxon genealogical line in addition to a host of other complexities. Creoda's generation is missing and there are only four applicable entries between the death of Cerdic in 518 (519 in the *ASC)* and the appearance of Ceawlin's name in entry 556. The first is the entry of 527, in which the West-Saxon leaders (presumably Creoda and Cynric) fight against the Britons at a place called Cerdicesleag. The only key word in this entry is "Britons"; the West Saxons are *not* fighting the Welsh, but the locale is an enigma. Contextually, Cerdicesora can be identified as a place in Wales and Cerdicesford can be identified as a place in south-central Britain near the coast. Cerdicesleag, though, is mystifying.

The second entry is for the year 534, which records the death of Cerdic and Cynric's rise as sole successor. There is, of course, a need to emend "Cerdic" to "Creoda" for the missing generation; not only does this properly insert Creoda into the line of West Saxons, but it also satisfies the "reasonable age" concept for Cerdic and his progeny.

The 547 entry is more complex. It states, "In this year Ida, from whom sprang the royal race of the Northumbrians, succeeded to the kingdom."[70] The important connection is to the name "Ida" in the last segment of Chapter 56 in the *HB,* which explains that the German-Saxon kings ruled over the English Saxons until the time when Ida reigned. In order to understand the full impact, it becomes necessary to jump to entry 560 because several events happened in rapid succession. This later entry states that in this year (560) Ceawlin succeeded to the kingdom in Wessex, and then Ceawlin's name is linked to the second Ælle, who simultaneously succeeded to the kingdom of the Northumbrians. The Parker version of the *Chronicle* adds a lengthy interpolation for the year 565 about Æthelbert succeeding to the kingdom of Kent, an odd coincidence (if it is such) because Æthelbert is the third Bretwalda.

The remainder of entry 552 shows that Cynric, named alone and evidently the sole ruler, fought against the Britons at a place called *Searoburh* and put the Britons to flight. This is a much more informative entry. For one, Ceawlin hasn't made an appearance yet; either he is too young, or he is not on the island. Second, the word "Briton" is used twice, indicating that the locale is *not* Wales. And most important, *Searoburh* is easily identifiable as Old Sarum, just north of Salisbury. The accepted histories relate that the southern heartland of Britain had not been pierced as deeply prior to this time. The Britons do flee, but there is nothing in the entry to indicate that Cynric succeeded to the kingdom, or even that he won a victory. Instead, this suggests that the territory is still in Briton hands. The narrative of Cerdic "obtaining the kingdom" from Arthur can then be extended. Once Cerdic broke his oath, he was driven out by Arthurex, who reclaimed the land. Even after Arthur's death there was strong Briton resistance to the German Saxons, and the heartland of Wessex was still a Briton stronghold.

The very next entry (556) names both Cynric and Ceawlin, who are still fighting against the Britons at Beranburh (Wiltshire) in the southcentral part of the island. It is reasonable to assume that Cynric and Ceawlin are German Saxons, crossing the Channel and sailing up Southampton Water in order to conquer more Briton domains. Cynric's death occurs sometime between the entry of 556 and 560, since he is not listed as a co-chieftain with Ceawlin. If indeed he had survived, he, too, would undoubtedly been accorded the title of Bretwalda, because in 560 Ceawlin, a German-Saxon king, succeeded to the kingdom of Wessex. Perhaps the phrase "regained the kingdom" would be more accurate and expressive, since Ceawlin finally conquers what his great-grandfather had been given four decades earlier.

The dates for Æthelbert and particularly Rædwald are tangled and uncertain. For good reason, P. H. Blair glosses over Æthelbert's reign in Kent, indicating that throughout the period, the Kentish kings were dependent upon Wessex. The Parker and the Laud Chronicles are widely divergent at this point, giving a great deal of different information. Rædwald and his slaying of Æthelfrith of Northumbria are chronicled briefly in the same entry with Edwin, Ælle, Eanfrith, Oswald, Oswy, Oslac, Oswudu, Oslaf, and Offa. Although it is impossible to trace the Bretwaldas any further, the definition as set forth from the existent evidence should be sufficient. What makes the outcome so interesting is that no one, single source can be used to arrive at an answer; the only way to piece together the puzzle is to objectively analyze Gildas, Bede, Nennius, and the compilers of *The Anglo-Saxon Chronicle.*

2

Other Early Manuscripts

Other minor manuscripts also offer important information to clarify the picture of Arthur's historical period. One source, John of Glastonbury, narrates a history of the Abbey. In one segment of his manuscript he provides a backdrop for events of the tenth century which contributed to the Arthurian matter; in addition, he records information about Cerdic and Arthur as opponents, including some details not provided by any of the other early manuscripts. Another, Giraldus Cambrensis, writes of Glastonbury as Arthur's burial place, detailing an intriguing account of Arthur's alleged exhumation. And as objective unrelated sources, Gregory of Tours, Sidonius, and Jordanes from the continent supply a different perspective through very abbreviated passages and letters, offering circumstances which meld Riothamus's activities with those of Arthur's.

Like a Celtic weave, the separate strands all these sources intertwine to create a tapestry of pattern and detail, of unity and sensibility, of deduction and logic. My first book, *The Historic King Arthur*, accomplishes that purpose; at times the separate threads of the intricate interlace seemed too convoluted to trace, but in spite of reckoning disparities, identical or similar geographic sites, and *persona* confusions, scattered remnants of information can be collected and glued together, much like an archaeologist who tirelessly extracts shards of pottery from a ruined site and literally pieces together a drinking vessel which symbolically reflects an era of history. Thanks to Leslie Alcock, the calibrations have already been analyzed and resolved.[1]

John of Glastonbury, even though he was at times deluded by William of Malmsbury's manuscript which had been heavily interpolated over the centuries, contributes a good deal to the clarification of Arthur's historicity. One item of great consequence is his account of Saint Gildas's relationship with the historic Arthur, which he incidentally but fortuitously resolves. If Arthur's life span was from the second decade of the fifth century to the first decade of the sixth, and if Gildas (who wrote the *De Excidio)* lived from 497 until 570, what explanation is there that their lives overlapped, according to all the oral tradition and accounts in the Saints' Lives?

What seems to be an irreconcilable problem is easily untangled by John's innocent candor: John is writing about a different Saint Gildas. All of Glastonbury's records, including the manuscript of Caradoc of Llancarvan's *Life of Gildas* and the succeeding associations between Arthur and Gildas in the *Mabinogion* tales, are about Gildas, son of Caw, who becomes known as Gildas Albanius, distinct from the Gildas (Gildas Badonicus) who wrote the *De Excidio.* Since he was "the son of a king of Scotland named Kau (Caw) who had twenty-three other sons who were warlike soldiers,"[2] the surname "Albanius" was logistically attached: This particular Gildas was born at Arglud, later known as Albania, Scotland.[3] Unfortunately, Lacy's encyclopedia glosses over two possible Gildases by averring that hagiography "treats [the two Gildases] as the same person, and that assumption may be allowed to stand."[4] Conversely, however, Josephus Stevenson is much more thorough[5] and relates that Gildas Albanius was born about 425 and died around 512, a near-contemporary of Gildas Badonicus. Once the existence of Saint Gildas Albanius is accepted, all literature of that period falls into a proper perspective. As one of the sons who was a warlike soldier, Gildas Albanius would have been in his prime during many of Arthur's conflicts. The saint's brother Hueil, who never submitted to another's hand, was killed by Arthur, but in spite of that, Gildas Albanius is portrayed as Arthur's close comrade. For one, the saint forges a truce between Melwas and Arthur when Melwas kidnaps Guinevere. Likewise, in the "Culhwch" tale of *The Mabinogion,* Gildas is among Arthur's warriors invoked by Culhwch. In "Gereint and Enid" Gildas is asked to escort Guinevere back to the court during one of Arthur's hunts, and in the "Rhonabwy" tale, the saint is listed as one of Arthur's advisors. More important, in this last tale Gildas is one of the warriors at Badon in 497, an impossibility for Gildas Badonicus because this latter Gildas was *born* in the same year that the Battle of Badon was fought.

John of Glastonbury also supplies some interesting details about Cerdic, the West-Saxon king. In Chapter 33 he writes

> King Arthur fought mightily against the Saxons and wore them down; he waged twelve battles against them, conquering and routing them in all twelve instances. Often he struggled with Cerdic, who, if one month Arthur vanquished him, rose up the next fiercer for the fight. Finally, when Arthur tired of the conflict, he accepted Cerdic's fealty and gave him Hampshire and Somerset, which Cerdic called Wessex.[6]

The first sentence offers nothing new; that information appears to have been extracted from the *Historia Brittonum.* The second sentence, however, is interesting because neither the *Historia Brittonum* nor any other early work—including the *De Excidio,* the *Annales Cambriae,* or *The Anglo-Saxon Chronicle*—link Cerdic and Arthur. Carley writes that "Henry of Huntingdon is the first author I can locate who places Cerdic and Arthur in the same period,"[7] then suggests that John of Glastonbury takes the next step of making

Cerdic and Arthur enemies. At first this rings a discordant bell, but after a close reading of Geoffrey of Monmouth, Carley's statement holds true. Monmouth only vaguely mentions a Cherdic who travels to Britain with Octa, but he records that the battle at Badon is fought between Arthur and Cheldric. It could easily be that the historical material went from Henry of Huntingdon, through Ranulph Higden, and to John of Glastonbury. The connection nevertheless makes sense.

What also seems to hold true, as proposed in *The Historic King Arthur*, is John's last sentence from the above quotation. Æthelweard's chronicle, among others, bears out that Cerdic did not *conquer* Wessex; the key word used by Æthelweard is *circumierunt*, translated as Cerdic "encircling the western area of Britain now known as Wessex."[8] But probably more descriptively, the interpretation should be "encompassing" or "incorporating" or "adjoining," to convey that Wessex had now become part of the West-Saxon territories. Instead of Cerdic conquering the new provinces by force, therefore, he was granted it, or given jurisdiction over it, implying what John writes: Through a treaty or a pact, Arthur gave the territories to Cerdic, hoping that the incessant conflicts which were tearing the island asunder would terminate. This further suggests, as attested to by the Genealogical Preface of the *ASC*, that Cerdic survived the Battle of Badon in which his ally, Octha, was killed. As West-Saxon king, he lived until A.D. 516 and most probably was killed in the Battle of Camlann along with Arthur and Mordred.

Attention must then focus upon two sets of terms which are not synonymous, even though most researchers make no distinction; the first is "West Saxon" as opposed to "Wessex" and the second is "Cerdicesora" versus "Cerdicesford." To more easily understand the term "West Saxon," my earlier book *The Historic King Arthur* pointed out that entries 495 and 514 in the *ASC* were doublets, created by a confusion of a nineteen-year lunar cycle, and because of that, Entry 514 should be stricken. Entry 495 would then correctly read, "In this year two West Saxon princes, Cerdic and his son Creoda, came with five ships to Britain at a place called Cerdicesora, and they fought against the Welsh on the same day."

This one entry is laden with information. First, the word "princes," a translation of *ealdormen*, which signifies royalty, indicates that Cerdic and Creoda are offspring of a king. Even more significant, however, this entry connects the terms West Saxon, Cerdicesora, and Wales. West-Saxon territories are in *Wales*, not the south-central coast of England, verified by the later territory named Ceredigion (after Cerdic) and an adjoining province named Creuddyn (after Creoda) along the west-central coast of Wales. Furthermore, as the *HKA* averred, Cerdicesora is therefore in *West-Saxon* territory in Wales. In contrast, *Wessex* refers to Hampshire and Somerset in the south-central part of the island, and *Cerdicesford* is a part of that territory, where Cerdic and Creoda would be fighting the Britons and *not* the Welsh.

The discrepancy between the back-to-back entries of 514 and 519 in the *Chronicle* can also be resolved with the information as reported in the Genealogical Preface. If indeed entry 514 is stricken because it is a doublet of 495, then the Genealogical Preface is conveying that six years after Cerdic and Creoda landed at Cerdicesora, they were granted the kingdom of Wessex by Arthur, which would be in the year 501. Æthelweard's chronicle confirms this sequence. He writes that in 494 (a one-year differentiation from the *ASC)* Cerdic and Cynric (an error which must be corrected to Creoda) landed at Cerdicesora, and six years later Wessex was annexed to the West-Saxon kingdom. Both Æthelweard and the *ASC* then complete the sequence at Year 519: Cerdic and Creoda now inherit the *kingship* of West Saxon, which includes Wessex, and they fight a battle at Cerdicesford in Wessex, chronologically matching Arthur's fateful battle at Camlann in 518. Upon the defeat of the great King Arthur, the West Saxons ruled in Britain from that day onward.

Although Alcock cautions that the history of the *ASC* has not be completely verified on the basis of archaeological evidence, what he writes about his findings suggests the sequence as outlined above. He conveys that archaeology contributes to early English history, something which verbal evidence alone cannot do. He writes

> Whereas the story in the *Chronicle* is of a band of adventurers landing in Southampton Water and battling their way inland over some three generations, archaeology demonstrates that the nucleus of Wessex was a peasant settlement in the mid- and upper Thames valley, going back a generation *before* [italics added] the *Chronicle* date for Cerdic's landing.[9]

When the West-Saxon intrusion into Britain is viewed as a patterned Saxon continuity from the River Thames to Selsey Bill to Southampton Water, then the Saxon settlements dating a generation *earlier* are perplexing. However, when the distinction is made between the original West Saxon kingdom and Wessex, then the movement from Wales in a southeasterly direction to Southampton Water fits Alcock's archaeological pattern. As a recapitulation, then, the locales West Saxon and Cerdicesora are in Welsh territory, but Wessex and Cerdicesford are in the area generalized as Briton.

Giraldus Cambrensis also contributes an interesting morsel of Arthurian information. The manuscript's main attraction is, of course, its age; Arthur's grave was allegedly discovered in Glastonbury Abbey's cemetery in 1191, and Giraldus first wrote of the exhumation in his manuscript entitled *De Instructione Principis* during 1192 or 1193, incorporating the story in his *Speculum Ecclesiae* about twenty-five years later. Although the narrative is very brief—only about two printed pages—it now occupies an important niche in the lore of Arthur's burial. The so-called discovery is highly controversial, but Giraldus's account is simple and straightforward. The hollowed-oak entombment was discovered between two stone pyramids, buried to a depth of sixteen feet. Along with the hollowed oak was a stone, and affixed to the underside of the stone was a leaden cross bearing the inscription

> Hic jacet inclitus rex Arturius cum Wenneveria uxore sua secunda in insula Avallonis sepultus.

This translates to "Here lies the famous King Arthur with Guinevere his second wife in the Isle of Avalon buried." Giraldus claims to have seen the cross, describing the letters as being engraved (turned inward) and not embossed (projecting or standing out). There is a discrepancy in the inscription between his two versions, and also variances between his reports and those by Ralph of Coggeshall and John Leland. But these particular differences should not be magnified to a point of scorning the narrative or rejecting the authenticity of the exhumation; as Alcock so adequately conveys, Richard Robinson's translation of Leland's text varied at four points even though Robinson had the original in front of him. Hence, despite this, "we can [still] readily accept minor discrepancies in the transcription of the text without doubting the authenticity of the original."[10]

Although Giraldus states outright that he personally saw the cross, there is only an implication that he viewed the bones. He indicates that Arthur's bones were huge; the shank bone was at least three inches longer than any man's there, and the skull, showing ten or more wounds with one hole larger than the rest, had eye-sockets a palm's width in size. Because of other more serious extenuating circumstances—not the minor transcriptional errors—the account of the exhumation has encountered heavy resistance as to it reliability and authenticity, mainly from the possibility of a hoax initiated by the monks and abbot themselves. For a more definitive resolution, additional evidence must be uncovered.

Accepting the condition that Arthur is a triadic homolog, other intriguing glimpses of this great king filter across the Channel from the continent in the form of Riothamus. After Ambrosius Aurelianus fades from the histories on the island at the advent of the second migration to Brittany during the waning years of the fifth decade in the fifth century, he regenerates as the Briton king in Gaul, his sojourn there evidently sparking the later romances of Arthur's continental episodes. Jordanes[11] records only one small piece of information about Riotimus, and although Sidonius doesn't format his material as history, he also refers to a Briton king named Riothamo. The only other pre-Monmouth antiquarian who provides suggestive overtones of Riothamus as a homolog for Arthur is the author of the *Legend of St. Goeznovius* who writes that

> ... this same Arthur, after many victories which he won gloriously in Britain and in Gaul, was summoned at last from human activity.[12]

Stripped of all the uncertainties and doubts which have tainted Monmouth's manuscript, these three writers link Arthur to Gaul; since there is no earlier manuscript which ties King Arthur to the continent—and specifically to Gaul—then a logical assumption is that Arthur was known by the epithet Riothamus, the Briton king from beyond Ocean.

Geoffrey of Monmouth: Pseudohistory and the Welsh Chronicles

The next stepping stone chronologically which contributes to the Arthurian matter is Geoffrey of Monmouth's pseudohistory, *The History of the Kings of Britain.* It provides a repository of information about Arthur in astonishing complexity; what the outline of extant histories cannot provide is patternistically laid out by this pre-romance document. Unquestionably, it is not solidly based as an objective and irrefutable historical work, yet neither can it be derisively labeled as pure fiction. No uncontaminated nuggets have survived in other sources; what is available is only the raw ore, and it is the responsibility of the modern researcher to extract the valuable metals from the mountainous tons of slag as meticulously as possible .

One of the scholars from the early 1900s who must rightfully be recognized for his expertise on Monmouth is Acton Griscom. All the versions of the *HB* are a lot to scrutinize, but they pale next to the "one hundred and ninety-eight manuscripts of Geoffrey of Monmouth's *Historia Regum Britanniae* ... forty-eight [which] are unquestionably of the twelfth century ... and a dozen more of the early thirteenth."[13] A re-examination of the twelfth-century manuscripts shows that there were minor progressive alterations done by Monmouth, and as he was critically attacked, he admonished other historians not to write of things about which they were ignorant. The progression of the versions can accurately be judged by his change of patrons, and what makes his earlier manuscripts so important is that internal historical evidence suggests that Monmouth's work is derived from a Welsh/Breton original.[14] Admittedly, in Griscom's time and even now the evidence proving this last statement is scanty. Griscom emphatically claims that up until 1929—the publication of his book—of fifty-eight surviving Welsh/Breton manuscript chronicles, only three had been published, "two of them uncritically,"[15] and only one of the two had been translated into English.

Griscom builds a strong case which is too complex to be detailed here,[16] but one illustration which he gives builds a strong case for his belief that the Welsh/Breton chronicles *preceded* Monmouth's manuscript rather than *followed* it. He writes

> The spelling and pronunciation of Welsh names are notoriously almost impossible in Anglo-Saxon or Latin. Latin scribes could

> make nothing of these strange Welsh spellings of the names of early British characters or places, and it is obvious that they were modified to accommodate Latin modes of speech.[17]

This observation is not contentious, and as *The Historic King Arthur* points out, Sir Ifor Williams in several lectures discussed the various blends and assimilations undergone between Welsh and Latin. To make his point, Griscom focuses upon the name of a pre-Roman British king which cannot be reproduced by our present alphabet, but it looks similar to *g6rgant 6aryft6rch,* which has been translated to Gurgiunt Brabtruc, gurguitus brabtrucus, and Gurguintus Brabtrucus. The last two (brabtrucus, Brabtrucus) display the Latin *-us* suffixes which Sir Ifor states were added onto Welsh words to give them prestige, again, something observed in the *HKA* as it applied to *Arthus.*

Of this, Griscom continues that this name meant "'Gurgant of the cut (or shorn) beard,' or Gurgant Cutbeard: *barf* meaning beard, and *trwch* meaning cut or mutilated."[18] There is corruption among manuscripts turning *barbtruc* into *brabtruc, batruc,* or *Bartruhc,* and because the natural and thoroughly Welsh original is thus distorted, this indicates that Monmouth would not have invented it. Griscom concludes

> Internal evidence of this nature will go far towards re-establishing the fact of Geoffrey's dependence upon native, written records. When his romantic embellishments are sufficiently discounted, there will remain a body of material upon which the historian, the anthropologist, the archaeologist, and the student of linguistics, in collaboration, may yet reconstruct for us the all but forgotten ancient history of the British Isles.[19]

In his recent book on Geoffrey of Monmouth, Michael Curley seems, if I am interpreting him correctly, to directly contradict Griscom by writing that "The Welsh Bruts are all later than Geoffrey and many of them are clearly influenced by him."[20] In the next paragraph he indicates that Monmouth was deliberate in scattering evidence of his knowledge of the Welsh language throughout the *History of the Kings of Britain,* but "most of these passages have to do with the meaning of place and personal names and do not imply more than a superficial knowledge of the language on his part."[21]

Yet he immediately follows these two observations by writing that Monmouth might have had a deeper knowledge of Welsh than at first anticipated. Based upon a witty comment about the Welsh word *Cymraeg,* Monmouth demonstrates not only an understanding of "academic folk etymology," but more importantly, "a knowledge of Welsh initial consonantal mutation (lenition) ... attached to form the word *camroeg, ... Cymraeg.*"[22] Based upon this and the dispute about Monmouth's very ancient book, Curley asserts that "There is nothing improbable about Geoffrey's claim that Walter brought this book from Brittany *(ex Britannia)*, although this statement occurs only in some of the manuscripts of the *HRB*,"[23] and that "It seems unlikely that a *single* [italics added] source will ever be identified as Geoffrey's 'very ancient book in the British Language.'"[24]

Because of the complexity of the matter, it is difficult to reiterate Curley's intent, but he seems to be indirectly expressing the same basic affirmations as Griscom. That is, they both seem to agree that 1) the Welsh *Bruts* are linked to Monmouth, 2) it is not improbable that Walter brought this book from Brittany, and 3) Monmouth's very ancient book is not a *single* source. The contention seems to lie with a proper definition of the "very ancient book." Curley writes that "... no such continuous historic narrative in the British language has come down to us from Geoffrey's day or before," and stresses later that Monmouth's ancient book cannot be identified as a *single* source. Griscom does not take a stand on either of these issues; he makes no claims of Monmouth's source being one continuous historic narrative.

Instead, Griscom focuses his attention particularly upon the *Tysilio* to show that Monmouth's conglomerate of sources under one cover referred to as the *liber vetustissimus* points to the Welsh/Breton chronicles which Monmouth used as the inception for his book. Otherwise, it would indeed be baffling why Monmouth would have included Welsh etymology in his text if it would have been nonsense to all except a few of his readers. In that context it would be more realistic to believe that in the *HKB* he was at times translating ancient Welsh material into Latin, and that his understanding of the Welsh language was bona fide, especially in light of the fact that he himself was native Welsh.

Neither does Griscom claim that the existing Welsh/Breton chronicles are Monmouth's very ancient book. As a matter of fact, he emphatically writes

> However, for fear of misunderstanding, let it be clearly stated at the start that no one of the existing Welsh manuscripts known to me represents exactly, or perhaps even closely, the *vetustissimus liber* itself.[25]

Griscom was advocating that the issue of Monmouth's *liber vetustissimus* not be forgotten or brushed aside, but instead *all* of the surviving Welsh manuscripts should be critically examined by competent specialists of medieval Welsh and a careful comparison made with Monmouth's *HKB* to show exactly where Monmouth expanded his narrative by distinguishing it from the original chronicle records. This would allow us to "conclude, therefore, that certain important contributions in the *Historia* are not imaginative, and that Geoffrey did not always 'invent.'"[26] It does border on impossibility that Geoffrey could have written such a narrative based solely upon the sparse material offered by the *De Excidio,* the *Historia Brittonum,* the *Annales Cambriae,* Bede, and perhaps *The Anglo-Saxon Chronicle.* Similarly, it is insultingly presumptuous that Walter, an archdeacon, or Geoffrey himself should be labeled as historical liars or daring fabulists.

Griscom's purpose is twofold. One is to create a rightful and appropriate niche in British history for the Welsh *Bruts*. In the introduction to Chapter VII, he writes

> Many, if not most, of the best modern scholars have considered this question [of Monmouth's sources] to have been so definitely answered by preceding generations, that they have not themselves troubled to examine it at first hand, but have repeated the opinions of earlier writers.[27]

This is a common pitfall, an inhibitive trap which intimidates the modern researcher who develops the attitude that ancient manuscripts, scribes, and antiquarians are infallible or sacrosanct. It is like treading on hallowed ground, and a trespasser would not dare commit sacrilege by asking questions. Yet as shown in the *HKA* the ancient manuscripts are laden with misleading interpolations and assertions which over the centuries have glazed into fact: the *Annales Cambriae* incorrectly calibrates some chronologies, notably the years in which the Battle of Badon and the Battle of Camlann were fought; the *Historia Brittonum* erroneously lists Hengist and Horsa as the Saxon leaders of the first Saxon *Adventus* and incorrectly infers that they are Kentish Saxons, very frequently confusing geographic locales such as Cæint, Tanet, Darenth, Guaul, and Anglia, and also erroneously relating that Octha came down from the north after Hengist's death instead of Horsa's; the *Anglo-Saxon Chronicle* has at least nine entries which must be emended for a sensible chronology; and lastly, for centuries the discrepancies between the Genealogical Preface and *The Anglo-Saxon Chronicle* had never been reconciled.

Griscom is simply pointing out that if an individual works from faulty text and translations, then the results themselves are faulty. Thus, to avoid that, he suggests that it is imperative to examine closely any manuscript, plus any parent or offspring versions when possible. In this specific instance, he is hoping to force attention to a whole body of Welsh chronicle material which has been (and for the most part seemingly still is) ignored. He mentions in particular the *Tysilio* and points out that

> Even Dr. Hodgkin, when discussing both Geoffrey who copied from Tysilio, and also the Breton *Brut* from which Tysilio originates, ignores Tysilio, as also do the recent studies by Baldwin Brown, Munro Chadwick, T. W. Shore, J. W. Jeudwine, E. McClure, and Henry Sharpe.[28]

Six decades later, the same still seems to be true. Very few researchers mention the *Tysilio* even in passing, and to my knowledge no contemporary researcher of Arthurian history refers to or makes use of this manuscript or its translation. This, combined with fifty other manuscripts which have been largely ignored, is an astonishing failure.

The blame, however, does not fall on the normal researcher. In his day, Griscom claimed that of the fifty-eight Welsh manuscripts, only three had been printed, and only one had been translated from the Welsh.[29] The manuscripts are difficult to come by for a variety of reasons. For one, there are probably very few scholars who are competent in the medieval Welsh language, and undoubtedly those experts who are qualified are also inundated with myriad other pursuits. Second, as Griscom points out, many of the manuscripts are now in private collections and hence not accessible. And third, in Griscom's day, the work of translation fell to one man, J. G. Evans, who was responsible for describing 894 manuscripts.[30]

The scraps of information about the *Tysilio* which *are* available are astonishing eye-openers, and when these Welsh manuscripts are translated, all of British history and therefore Arthuriana will take a quantum leap. R. H. Fletcher, one of the few who did write about the *Tysilio,* passes on this information: Eigr appears in Monmouth's work as Ygerna, but although she is identified as the daughter of Amlawdd the Great in the *Tysilio,* Amlawdd is not named in Geoffrey's work; Gwenhwyfar is translated in Monmouth as Guanhamara and her father's name does appear; Cador, father of the Constantine (Constantine III) to whom Arthur leaves the kingdom, is the son of Gorlois; Arthur himself killed Medrod. Fletcher then admits that "All these statements may possibly be details of the old British tradition from which Geoffrey drew...."[31] even though he still suspects that they are fanciful elaborations. Assuming that these pieces of information are, in fact, originally from the *Tysilio*, a side-by-side comparison of these details with those in the *HKB* provides some revelations.

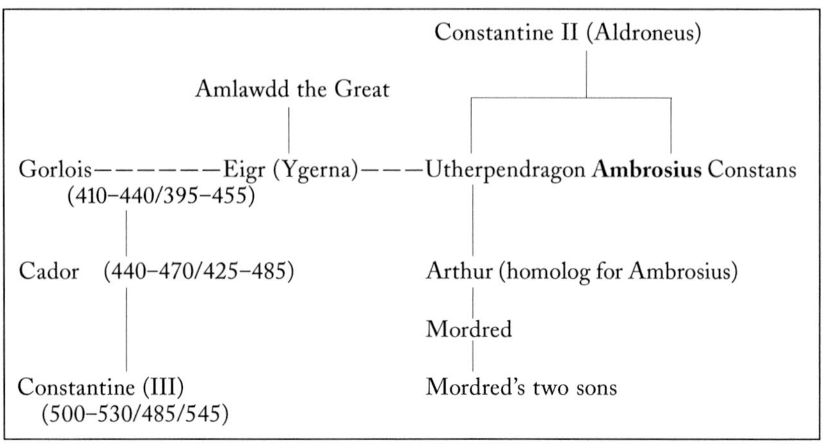

Table 4—The combination of two genealogical trees, the one on the left from the Tysilio and the one on the right reflecting narratives from *The History of the Kings of Britain* about the House of Constantine.

It must be kept uppermost in mind that Utherpendragon is considered by scholars of the historical Arthur as a fictional character based upon three things: First, the word is actually an epithet meaning "Head of the Dragon"; second, the clipped version "Uther" seems to be an anagram of the word Arthur; and third, the epithet doesn't seem to link with a bona fide historical figure of the era. Additionally, *The Historic King Arthur* postulates that Arthur is an epithet for Ambrosius Aurelianus, something which was established at least five years prior to my discovery of the *Tysilio* information. The interesting thing, then, is to see how contents of the *Tysilio* meld not only with the Arthur/Ambrosius Aurelianus theory presented in *The Historic King Arthur* but how it relates to *The History of the Kings of Britain.*

The Historic King Arthur established that Ambrosius Aurelianus's life span was from *c.* A.D. 422 to 518, and that the epithet "Arthus" (Arthur) was ascribed to him *c.* 475 after his return from the continent, where he had been known as Riothamus. The book also calibrated the date of A.D. 541 as the penning of the *DE.* Because Gildas writes that Constantine was still alive, Constantine's floruit/life span, albeit general, must overlap the period when Gildas was writing. In fact, Gildas specifically writes that in the very same year when he was writing the *DE,* Constantine (III?) bound himself by oath to refrain from evil only to break his vow by killing two close relatives and their guardians. This dispute of parricide will be focused upon later, but for the present the emphasis must remain solely upon the time-frame. The *Tysilio* lists Cador as Constantine III's father, and as Gorlois' son, locking their respective floruits/life spans into place according to Table 4.

The proposal that Aurelius Ambrosius seduced Ygraine on the basis that neither Utherpendragon nor Arthur exist as separate entities in the histories seems extremely tenuous, a very weak link in comparing the parallels, especially because Ambrosius Aurelianus is portrayed with such integrity by Gildas Badonicus and Sidonius. In any event, according to what exists in the *Tysilio* and *The History of the Kings of Britain,*

1. Aurelius Ambrosius's son (not Utherpendragon's) would have been a bastard, since Ygerna's seduction would not have yet been sanctioned by marriage.
2. Aurelius Ambrosius and Gorlois would have been contemporaries, whose floruits and life spans overlap.
3. In a laconic passage, Gildas lists Ambrosius Aurelianus as honorable Roman nobility, and the *Tysilio* seems to confirm this by adding more historical detail, even though neither it nor the *HKB* mentions the name Aurelian or Lucius Domitius Aurelianus. Monmouth's use of the name Aurelius, however, is interesting, suggesting that perhaps he was indeed copying part of his narrative; his use of the name Aurelius Ambrosius, which makes an etymological and genealogical connection of Aurelius/Aurelian, could have

come from some other mysterious source rather than it being an adaptation of Gildas's Ambrosius Aurelianus. *The Historic King Arthur* genealogically linked Ambrosius Aurelianus and Lucius Domitius Aurelianus initially because of their *cognomen.* Beyond that, Lucius Aurelianus was the first in a series of Illyrian emperors who can be directly traced to Constantius I and his three sons, also of Illyrian stock. The *HKB* picks up the Constantinian chronology in the third generation, but it is beyond credibility that Monmouth selected the Constantinian dynasty because of the Illyrian connection, particularly since there is an irreconcilable gap between Constantine II and Ambrosius Aurelianus. Constantine II was murdered by Constans I in A.D. 340, almost a hundred years prior to Ambrosius Aurelianus's birth, averring, of course, that Constantine II could not possibly have been Aurelius Ambrosius's father. As part of the triumvirate, Constantine II was responsible for the security of Britain and Gaul, but because he was killed at age 23, there is no direct link with Ambrosius Aurelianus in Britain or in Gaul. Monmouth also writes of Constantine III as Arthur's successor, but there was no one with that designation in the Constantinian dynasty. Gildas castigates a king of Dumnonii by the name of Constantine, but there are no numerals attached to the name, suggesting that it was a name carried on by the Welsh kings after the Roman withdrawal. This particular Constantine would have been known as Constantine the Briton. The impact of all this on British history will be picked up in Chapter 4. The genealogical line from the Constantinian dynasty to Ambrosius Aurelianus—if it exists—must be resolved either by a different source or more information.

According to Fletcher, based on John Hardyng's Chronicle, "The first part of [the Welsh chronicles] consists in a condensed and interpolated version of Geoffrey's story. Most of Geoffrey's incidents, with the exception of several of the least credible ones, are reproduced or mentioned; but the divergences in details, in some of which Hardyng agrees with the *Brut,* show that the source is not primarily Geoffrey's narrative. As points of difference from Geoffrey, the following may be especially mentioned."[32] These are some of the items then listed:

1. The assassination of Constantine II is ascribed to Vortiger's [sic] instigation.
2. Cador is called Arthur's brother "of his mother's side," implying half-brothers.
3. Constantine [III] is definitely represented as Arthur's nephew.
4. Arthur in person kills Modred and receives his death wound from him.
5. Arthur is said to have given Westsex to Cordryk after the battle of Bath. (Not all the items are listed, nor are they numbered or ordered this way in Fletcher.)

These additional scraps of information also allow in-depth explanations to the above genealogical connections. To continue what has already been given, the assassination of Constantine II by Vortigern provides the motive of why Vitalinus, as Ambrosius's guardian, would send Aurelius Ambrosius to Britanny, as proposed in *The Historic King Arthur.* The *Tysilio* shows, then, that in the ensuing struggle for power after the Roman abandonment, the Welsh king known as Vortigern, after killing Constantine II, would have to eliminate only one more heir—Ambrosius—to ascend to the throne. To prevent that, Vitalinus places Ambrosius under the protection of Budicius of Britanny. These circumstances agree with what is recounted in two of the earliest sources. The *DE* narrates that in the civil wars among those *Britanni* who were pro-Roman and those who sided with the Saxons, Ambrosius Aurelianus's parents were killed. The *HB* elaborates on the account, first with the preface that Vortigern feared the Picts and the Irish, he was frightened by a Roman return to the island, but most of all, he had a "dread of Ambrosius."[33] The *Tysilio* provides an answer to the question of why, above all other things, Vortigern was in dread of Ambrosius: Vortigern, who was a war-chief of Dementia, killed Ambrosius's father, who was the Roman consul of Dumnonia. As the rightful successor according to Roman law, Ambrosius posed a more ominous threat than either the Picts or the Irish, particularly because he had the support of those Romans who had remained on the island.

In the above comparison, it also becomes obvious why the *Tysilio* labels Cador as Arthur's half-brother. Once again, there are matching floruits/life spans: the rise of the person known as "Arthur" is typically set by researchers in the year 475, and based upon floruits for Constantine III and Gorlois, Cador's floruit/life span would be 440–470/425–485. The *Tysilio* made the common mistake that Utherpendragon was a separate, bona fide figure, and based upon this assumption, listed Arthur and Cador as half-brothers, Gorlois being Cador's father and Utherpendragon being Arthur's father, but Ygerna being their mother. Because of that bond, they would naturally emerge in the romances as strong allies in their wars against the English and German Saxons. Cador, as Duke of Cornwall, is Arthur's right-hand man and one of the major war-leaders.

The next progression also becomes logical. As Cador's son, Constantine III would also have an indirect claim to the throne. Constantine III would be Arthur's nephew through Ygerna's bloodline. When Arthur kills his most immediate heir Mordred at the Battle of Camlann, the only direct heirs would be Arthur's grandsons, that is, Mordred's two sons. But because of Mordred's treachery in aligning with the Saxons and trying to grab Britain as his own, his two sons would likewise be considered as traitors to the cause. The logical individual to consider for succession to Arthur would be Constantine III.

This in turn casts illuminating explanation on Gildas Badonicus's castigation of Constantine, obviously a reference to Constantine III based upon the overlapping floruits/life spans of Constantine and Gildas and on other internal evidence in the *De Excidio.* Immediately after the praise of Ambrosius Aurelianus, Gildas wrote that Ambrosius's "descendants in our day have become greatly inferior to their grandfather's excellence,"[34] which accurately describes Ambrosius Aurelianus as Constantine III's grandfather through bloodlines to Ygerna. Gildas also labels Constantine as a tyrant whelp of Dumnonia, the earlier name for Cornwall, the kingdom also associated with Cador and Gorlois. In his tirade against this "whelp of Dumnonia," Gildas then writes of Constantine's parricide, the killing of two close relatives at the altar of a church.

Monmouth also records this episode, naming the two close relatives as Mordred's sons and adding the details that Constantine kills the two because they were in league with the Saxons and revolted against him, his narrative deviating a bit from Gildas's account by relating that one of Mordred's sons was killed in a church at Winchester, and the other at a monastery in London, whereas Gildas seems to infer that Mordred's sons were killed simultaneously in the same church. The two accounts differ, too, in their covert suggestions of motive; Gildas imputes that the brutal murders were assassinations of two innocent men of God, while Monmouth states outright that as traitors similar to their father they were threatening the rightful empire of Britain. Most scholars have branded Monmouth's account as creative imagination, claiming that Monmouth, of course aware of Gildas's material, simply embellished the story. But if one were to accept Monmouth's and Walter's claim that there was a *liber vetustissimus* based upon an early version of the *Tysilio,* then this information would have to be viewed in an entirely different light, because Monmouth would be functioning as a copyist, not as a prevaricator of fiction.

This possible link between Mordred's two sons as recorded in Monmouth and Gildas's account about the assassination of "two royal youths" by Constantine have an enigmatic link. Michael Winterbottom translates part of this passage from Gildas's *De Excidio* in this manner:

> [Constantine] tore [the youths], I say, at the holy altar, using as teeth his wicked sword and spear, so that the place of divine sacrifice was touched by the purple cloaks (as it were) of their drying blood.[35]

Winterbottom is an excellent translator, as evidenced by his meticulous and critically precise selection of synonymous words. In settling upon specific words, he also weighs the impact of connotative versus denotative influences on various passages. The above passage, especially the last clause, is particularly difficult to interpret in Gildas's original Latin. For years I have read and re-read the passage and bypassed trying to understand it, but I've always been allured by its mystique, principally because of the word "purple," which an Arthurian enthusiast notices immediately.

Gildas uses the word "purple" as a mark of Roman royalty in Chapter 25, where he relates that the Roman, Ambrosius Aurelianus, survived the fierce wars which had claimed his parents, who had worn the purple. It was only in the context of aligning Mordred's sons in Monmouth's account with Constantine in the *De Excidio* that the meaning of the passage finally became apparent. After close scrutiny, my translation relays that

> At the holy altar, (the attacking Roman), armed with his abominable sword and spear, mauled and slashed (the youths) as with teeth, so that the heavenly altar was purple from clotted gore.

This translation doesn't reinforce Winterbottom's "purple cloak" which symbolically suggests the attire of Roman royalty, but it does suggest internal conflicts between the *Romanophils* and other *Britanni.* In the original Latin manuscript, *pallia* means "clad as a Roman,"[36] positively identifying Constantine as a Roman. The word *attingere* can connote "touch," as Winterbottom used it, or it can signify, surprisingly, "attack." D. P. Simpson explains that the former ("touch") is a "transferred" definition—that is, used in an altered or metaphorical sense—but the latter ("attack") is a "literal" definition.[37]

Similar to Gildas's passage about Mount Badon, this segment about Constantine is somewhat garbled; sometimes when Gildas becomes entangled in his vilifications, his graphic descriptions hinder his grammatical precision. Nevertheless, from a variant but supportable syntactic approach, I've also transvaluated the passage—based upon the Latin words *ac si*—to mean

> (Constantine), with his abominable sword and spear, mauled and slashed (the youths) as with teeth, so that clotted gore tinged the heavenly altar purple, matching the cloak of the attacking Roman.

The Latin word *ac,* which is used before words beginning with consonants as opposed to *atque* which is used before words beginning with *h* or vowels, means "and moreover" or "and even" when adding a new point which is to follow. The Latin word which follows *ac* in Gildas's passage is *si,* a conjunction, and when this conjunction is preceded by *ac,* its specific use is for *comparisons,* in this instance comparing the purple gore on the altar with the purple of Constantine's cloak. Gildas is sometimes criticized for his ineptitude with Latin, but this passage indicates the opposite; Gildas refers to Latin as "our language," and is proficient in its use.

This perspective also unravels much of the confusion in Monmouth's book. As a preface, the *Annales Cambriae* tersely lists the "deaths" of Arthur and Medraut, but does nothing further in identifying either of them. The *Tysilio* clarifies that shortcoming by explaining that Mordred is a bastard son of Arthur/Ambrosius, and while Arthur aligns himself with the struggling Welsh, Mordred sides with the English Saxons. Monmouth's manuscript, like the *Tysilio,* would reflect the confusion because both would be unaware of the expression "Utherpendragon" as an *epithet* for Arthur's father rather than a proper name, and of course, neither would realize that the word "Arthur" is an epithet for Ambrosius Aurelianus. This would be the reason for all the confusion by Monmouth; as a copyist, Monmouth would sometimes be labeling Anna as Arthur's sister and sometimes as Ambrosius's sister; he would also sometimes identify Mordred as Arthur's nephew, and at other times Mordred as Arthur's bastard son. However, once a person realizes that "Arthur" and "Ambrosius Aurelianus" are references to a single individual, then the confusion disappears and the kinships become lucidly simple: Anna is Arthur/Ambrosius's sister, and hence Mordred is Arthur/Ambrosius's bastard son by Anna.

The last item from the *Tysilio* which must be clarified is the statement that Arthur gave Westsex to Cordryk after the battle of Bath. "Westsex" is *part* of the West-Saxon territory which appears as "Wessex" in the later manuscripts of the Genealogical Preface, *The Anglo-Saxon Chronicle,* the *Æthelweard Chronicle,* and John of Glastonbury's *Cronica.* "Cordryk" is the Welsh name which appears as "Cerdic," the interpreter for Vortigern in the *Historia Brittonum,* as "Ceredig," Cunedda's son in the Welsh genealogies, as "Cherdic," "Chelric," and "Cheldric" in Monmouth's *HRB,* and as "Cerdic," the West-Saxon king in *The Anglo-Saxon Chronicle.* The theory in *The Historic King Arthur* shows that all these name variations point to only one individual: a Briton born into an influential family, an interpreter as a young boy, a war-leader aligning himself with the English Saxons, and finally, the first, most powerful king of the West-Saxon house. And lastly, the battle of "Bath" is a reference to Badon as recorded in the *DE,* the *HB,* and the *AC*—Arthur/Ambrosius's renowned victory against the Saxons. Hopefully this at least partially fulfills Griscom's dream of reconstructing the all-but-forgotten ancient history of the British Isles.

All of these additions probably make Monmouth's work an even more discomforting mixture of bona fide history, confused renditions (either deliberate or inadvertent), and vivacious imagination. Because the *HB* is one of our only historical sources, we must accept its statement that Arthur was in conflict with the *Saxones,* and the Angle leaders (part of the generic term *Saxones)* during that era were Horsa, Hengist, and Octha. Yet after the deposal of Vortigern, Monmouth relates that Hengist and Horsa warred with Ambrosius and were killed before Utherpendragon's ascent to the throne. Octha becomes a Saxon leader at the end of Ambrosius's reign and into Utherpendragon's kingship, when he is killed while Arthur is still a boy. Hence, in Monmouth's account Hengist, Horsa, and Octha do not encounter Arthur.

Similarly, Monmouth grossly confuses Cerdic as a Saxon chieftain. At one point he relates that a Saxon named Cherdic sails with Octha to join Hengist in Britain, but thereafter Cherdic drops from the narrative. In his place, Monmouth inserts Cheldric the Saxon, who fights against Arthur and perishes at the Battle of Badon. Chelric succeeds to the kingdom after Cheldric's death, and Chelric, in league with Mordred, wars with Arthur at the Battle of Camlann, where all three perish. The Cherdic/Cheldric/Chelric episodes seem to replace the Cerdic reign from *The Anglo-Saxon Chronicle.* Monmouth also lists a Colgrin and a Baldulf as brothers and chieftains of the Saxons, but those two names don't appear in any of the variant manuscripts.

After the Battle of Badon, Monmouth depicts Arthur as going on a widespread rampage into Ireland, Gotland, the Orkneys, Norway, and Iceland. According to Monmouth, Arthur wants to conquer all of Europe, but the most discordant notes are conflicts with the Tribune Frollo in Gaul under Emperor Leo, and a later battle with Lucius Hiberius, a Procurator of Rome. The contradiction is that Arthur and his forebears were allies, not enemies, of Rome. When the Roman forces abandoned the island, there were several communiqués addressed to Aëtius requesting a Roman return; Monmouth has imbued Aurelius Ambrosius with Roman royalty through Constantine, and the wars in Gaul were an attempt to stem the barbaric tide and maintain the Roman dominance there.

From still another angle, Monmouth echoes material from *The Mabinogion.* He portrays Mordred as Arthur's foe at the Battle of Camlann, although, as mentioned, he hopelessly botches the kinship between the two. Not only several times, but consistently he confuses "Arthur" and "Ambrosius." Sometimes Mordred's mother (Anna) is listed as *Ambrosius's* sister, and at other times as *Arthur's* sister; she is at times *Lot's* wife, but at other times, she is married to *Budicius* of Brittany. This of course befuddles Mordred's kinship: He is either Arthur's nephew, or his son; he is either Gawain's brother, or Hoel's brother; he is either heir to the throne of Lodonesia, or to the throne of Brittany; he is either Ambrosius's son or his grandson.

In a similar vein Monmouth describes three conflicts from the battle list in the *Historia Brittonum,* but bypasses the other nine. With no supportive evidence, he places Kaerluideoit "between two rivers, in the province of Lindsey,"[38] a reference to Lincoln. However, in 66a of the *Historia Brittonum,* Caer Luit Coyt is listed as Wall-by-Lichfield,[39] a once-important Roman way-station, and one of the twenty-eight most important cities of Britain. Monmouth describes the second battle at Caledon Wood,[40] but does not identify it as Caledonia, instead leaving it vaguely untraceable. The third battle (numbered as the twelfth in the *HB)* was the Battle of Badon, which he places at Bath, on a neighboring hill,[41] keeping Arthur's troops as the attackers and the *Saxones* as the defenders, as narrated in "The Dream of Rhonabwy." Monmouth does not incorporate into his narrative the battle at the River Glein, the four battles at the River Douglas, the battle at the River Bassas, the battle at Guinnion Fort, the battle at the city of legions, the battle at the River Tryfrwyd, or the battle on the hill called Agned. Hence, the chapter on Arthur by Monmouth does not closely parallel the battle list from the *HB.*

3
Riardd Ambrosius

Only one other summary has to be given from *The Historic King Arthur* to complete the necessary base for constructing new frameworks. The major thesis of the book is that the figure we know as King Arthur is in reality an epithet for an authentic person named in the histories of the period.

Research to date, with some exceptions such as the book by Graham Phillips and Martin Keatman, consider Arthur as a proper name for the great king. Most, however, such as Kenneth Jackson, believe that it is derived from the Latin "Artorius," based upon a Roman officer named Lucius Artorius Castus.[1] This derivation is, in fact, questionable, and although Jackson writes that it was not rare in the histories, he cites only one Roman officer with the name of Artorius during the nearly four centuries of Roman rule in Britain. This particular individual is chronicled as an officer of the VIth Legion in the middle of the second century, three hundred years before Arthur's time, and hence it is highly unlikely that a Roman commander with the *nomen* Artorius recorded in the year A.D. 184 would be a carryover to the fifth-century King Arthur as a proper name; Arthur's parents probably weren't even aware of Castus, particularly since he did not emerge as a prominent leader.

Nevertheless, Rachel Bromwich also writes about the name of Arthur as having a Roman derivative from a proper name. She asserts that the name "Arturus" first appears in the *Historia Brittonum*, and then appeared in several Welsh poems dating back to approximately the same time.[2] The name does appear in the *Historia Brittonum*, but the reference is to *the* King Arthur, yet simply because it was used in Latin does not prove that it was a Latin derivative; that is, simply because an expression such as *hors d'oeuvre* exists in the American language, it does not indicate that it derived from English or American English. Likewise, names that appear in Welsh tradition might, in fact, be a reference to *the* King Arthur.

Bromwich further suggests that "Arthur" derives from a proper name by suggesting that names derived from Latin were common in early Welsh genealogies between A.D. 300 and 450.[3] There is no question that Latin had a great influence upon the Welsh language, or that Latin names entered the newly forming language, but if the above comment is being interpreted correctly, Bromwich is writing of Latin names *generically,* not as a specific reference to Arthur. Also, the name King Arthur is normally calibrated for A.D. 470 to 475, when such happenings would be less common.

This leads back to the original flaw: Only one name, Lucius Artorius Castus, appears in the histories, and that was three hundred years before the great king's time, showing that "Arthur" was an uncommon—not common—name. Richard Barber postulates several different Arthurs during the mid-500s, but instead of ascribing them to Artorius Castus, he convincingly refutes the association by writing that a link between Lucuis Artorius Castus and the Welsh Arthur would be extremely tenuous. He continues by writing that a bridge of tradition from a second-century Roman officer to the Welsh Arthur would be a "daring feat of imagination, but not admissible evidence."[4]

Several other researchers have abandoned claims such as those by Jackson and Bromwich, and instead follow the avenue of explaining Arthur's "name" as an epithet. R. H. Fletcher lists possible variations such as Arthure, Arthurus and Artus, but he doesn't develop any theory of his own. Jack Lindsey makes a possible connection between "Arthur" and the Celtic *artos,* meaning "bear," a suggestion which Graham Phillips and Martin Keatman elaborate upon. These two authors aver that Arthur has the tribal title of "Bear," based upon a combination of the Brythonic affix *Arth* and the Latin word *Ursus* to form the word *Arthurus,* which was later shortened to Arthur.[5] Unlike John Rhys's reference to a mythological god, this innovative concept—that the name Arthur is an epithet—is excellent, and the authors provide interesting support for what they conjecture.

Even so, there is a simpler explanation, as I believe I proposed in *The Historic King Arthur.* Eilert Ekwall opened the door for a different explanation because of his dictionary definition of *arth-*. In citing the etymology for Arthuret in Cumberland, he writes that the first element is identical with the Welsh *Ardd,* which translates to the early Welsh 'Arð' which means height or high.[6] This beginning is right on target because it is dealing with the Welsh and Early Welsh language plus Arthur's Welsh roots, from which all the Arthurian material—including that in the *Historia Brittonum,* the *Annales Cambriae,* and *The Mabinogion*—evolved. The doubled "d" and the diphthong ð are both pronounced like our unvoiced "th-" sound.

Anderson and Anderson further explain *ardd-* as an affix. In their book about Saint Columba they explain Adomnan's mixture of Old Irish stems, compounds, and spellings used in conjunction with Latin affixes. This was evidently a common linguistic practice during that era and applicable to the Arthurian material. Adomnan's technique was to add a Latin case-ending (such as *-us)* to an Irish noun and thus form a mutated word which eventually shifted from the nominative to the genitive case.[7] Hence, the Welsh affix *Ardd* (which would have been derived from its Irish parent) was commonly combined with the Latin suffix *-us* to form words such as Arddus or Arðus, pronounced as Arthus, a natural occurrence as the Welsh language developed.

Sir Ifor Williams also clarifies this process. He is referring to the name of Mailcunus as it appears in the *Historia Brittonum,* but it is equally applicable to the name of Arthur. He writes that in the name Mailcunus, the *-us* tacked onto the end shouldn't be taken too seriously because that Latin add-on was put there only to give dignity to the resulting Welsh name.[8] Providing even more clarification, in addition to the *-us* suffix giving the Welsh language more prestige, Sir Ifor also addresses the process of Welsh genitives becoming Welsh epithets, or more explicitly, how Welsh genitives became nominative Welsh names. He points out that the significance of this technique has not been fully realized by philologists, but what this blending of language has done is create a British grammar using a king's name in the genitive case.[9]

Hence, as a Welsh nominative epithet, Arthus (Arddus, Arðus) would have replaced the king's name, and in conjunction with his attained new title, he would have become Arthus Rex or Rex Arthus, the High King of Britain. Arthurex is a variation, so that, more realistically, Arthur's name evolved independent of Artorius. Had Phillips and Keatman translated "Arth" as the Brythonic word meaning "High," used with the Latin root "Urses" meaning "bear" as the great king's animal symbol, they would have ended up with "Arthursus," meaning High Bear, something parallel to Pendragon. In fact, this is the same technique which was used to invent the "fictitious" Utherpendragon.

Sir Ifor goes one step further to conclude his case. He explains that in any pedigree, whether it's Latin, Celtic, Old Irish, or Old Welsh, the first name is in the nominative case and every other name is in the genitive case. Over the course of time, the genitives become common fixtures, people forget that the forms are genitives, and the nominative forms become obsolete.

In Tatlock's scrutiny of sources, he cites the authority Sir J. E. Lloyd as writing, "Among the Early Welsh, Arthur is a very unusual person name."[10] After some seeming intensive investigation, Tatlock then observes that "The extreme paucity of Arthurs in early Wales, where one might look for evidence of a pre-Geoffrey Arthur tradition, encourages skepticism as to its vogue elsewhere."[11] A further survey of Breton sources also shows that although the name Arthur is very slightly more common, there is no name of Arthur recorded prior to 860.[12] Continuing his search, Tatlock concludes, "Needless to say the name is scarce in England and Scotland before Geoffrey's time."[13]

After this particular search for the commonality of the name Arthur, Tatlock turns to a slightly different perspective. He writes,

> As to why the king's name changed from Artur to Artus we cannot say. While a change from *s* to *r* is frequent in various languages

> and phonetically natural, the converse is not. In French (Paris and central France) there was at one time such a tendency, now surviving only in *chaise* for *chaire* (from *cathedra),* but there is no reason to believe this the cause here.[14]

He then provides a reason based upon the assumption that "Artur" or "Artus" is a proper name. But as *The Historic King Arthur* explained, and should be reiterated again here because of its importance, "Artus" is derived from the Welsh *arddus,* with the doubled "d" pronounced as an unvoiced th- "Arddus," meaning "high" was a genitive descriptor for Ambrosius Aurelianus, which became an epithet. The Latin *-us* suffix was commonly added to Briton (including Welsh) words to give them prestige, and what evolved was the term "Arddurex" (pronounced "Arthurex"), the High King Ambrosius.

E. K. Chambers, in his book *Arthur of Britain,* also was cognizant of the customary convention whereby an epithet took the place of a proper name. He admits not knowing the relationship between Arthur and Ambrosius Aurelianus, but he sensed that perhaps the names were doublets, that is, two different names for the same individual. He also sensed that these two figures in history had similar personalities, but their different names appeared in the *Historia Brittonum* under two separate name-forms which had undergone a scribal corruption from Aurelianus to Arthur.[15] His concept is faultless; however, seeking the answer as a scribal corruption from Aurelianus to Arthur unfortunately caused Chambers to back away from a precise and impressive postulation, or otherwise he would have solved part of the riddle about King Arthur in 1964.

No one—not even Geoffrey Ashe, who came very close—followed up on Chambers's speculation. In *The Discovery of King Arthur,* Ashe writes of a Riothamus on the continent, the Briton High King who sailed from the island "by way of Ocean" and fought in continental wars during the fifth century, and theorizes that this "Riothamus could have been the title of another royal or prominent Briton."[16] Through a process of elimination he considers and rejects the Briton heroes of the day, including Vortigern, Vortimer, and Ceredig. Then just as tersely he rejects Ambrosius Aurelianus based upon the premise that "Gildas does not call him a King."[17] That Ambrosius is not called a king in the *De Excidio* should not be considered a major obstacle which Ashe rejects so offhandedly; in truth, nowhere in any of the ancient manuscripts is *Arthur* ever called a king. Gildas Badonicus doesn't even record the name "Arthur," Nennius refers to him three times and simply calls him Arthur, and likewise in the two entries of the *Annales Cambriae* he is designated only as Arthur.

Similarly, Ashe elides too quickly over Ambrosius's title in the *Historia Brittonum* where Ambrosius is proclaimed "a great king among all the kings of the British nation."[18] This title leaves no doubt that Ambrosius is High

King, and yet Ashe dismisses that statement as "legend."[19] Why Ashe does this is a mystery, unless he jumped too quickly in an attempt to equate the epithet "Riothamus" with the word "Arthur," which he believed to be a proper name. If any surviving manuscript is to be labeled as a legend, it would be Monmouth's, which Ashe was using as his unimpeachable source.

Not only did Leon Fleuriot understand the important distinction between an epithet and a proper name, but he also realized the impact of interpreting history based upon that difference. He, too, sensed that Arthur's name was somehow enigmatically connected to an epithet. In his 1980 book, *Les Origins de la Bretagne,* he speculated that the great Briton leader of the fifth century, Ambrosius Aurelianius, named in Gildas Badonicus's *De Excidio,* carried the title of Riothamus, but that his achievements were later credited to another person named Arthur.[20] Fleuriot thus forms the equation that Ambrosius is Riothamus and both these names are connected to Arthur. He points to proof by citing a *HB* manuscript dated 1072, which records that Ambrosius was in Brittany during the same part of the Arthurian period when Riothamus was fighting wars there. This would additionally confirm an *Ambrosian* connection in Brittany rather than an Arthurian one.

Scholars basically concur that the word Riothamus is in itself an epithet. Norris Lacy in *The Arthurian Encyclopedia* explains that the word means "most kingly" or "supremely royal" and appears as "Riatham in Breton and Rhiadaf in Welsh."[21] Two apparent questions ensue; the first is "What part did this 'supreme king' play in the history of this era?," followed immediately by "What was the proper name for Riothamus?" There is very little history about Riothamus, but essentially there is enough information to ascertain his role in the Arthurian saga. His niche in continental history spans only about ten years, from A.D. 460 to 470. Interestingly, this interval is between the period traditionally set for Ambrosius Aurelianus from 420 to 460 and the one set for Arthur between 475 and 500.

Jordanes, in his *Gothic History* of 551, provides the motive for Ambrosius and his army sailing from the island to Gaul. As High King (or Riothamus), Ambrosius crossed the channel to help the Roman emperor Anthemius protect Gaul from Euric the Visigoth.[22] Contrary to the narrative that Monmouth weaves, this report shows that the Roman Empire and Britain were allies and not enemies. Although the motives for the British High King agreeing to this request are speculative, if Riothamus and Anthemius were bound by treaties of alliance, then Ambrosius might have expected help from Anthemius on the island later. Other histories show that this possible reciprocal agreement didn't happen; Rome was being attacked on so many fronts that it could not contain its borders, and no help was ever sent back to the island.

A fierce battle followed between Riothamus and Euric, with disastrous results to the Roman contingency. In 470, following the Battle of Angers,

Jordanes writes that Euric's innumerable army clashed with Riothamus's force of twelve thousand and after a long fight he routed Riothamus, king of the Brittones, before Anthemius and the Roman auxiliaries could join him. Without the Roman aid which was so badly needed, Riothamus lost a great part of his army and was forced to retreat with the remnants of his tattered troops into Burgundy, another tribe which was still allied with Rome. This devastating defeat followed the earlier Briton victory over the Saxons at Angers. History indicates that the Roman reinforcements never arrived because the Saxon army led by Childeric and the Franks, who had agreed to a treaty with the Romans, rebelled and engaged them in a separate fierce conflict.

Riothamus's army was decimated. Gregory of Tours in the *History of the Franks* gives a specific detail which is passed over by Jordanes. He, like Jordanes, writes that the Britons were driven from Bourges by Euric and the Visigoths, but then adds that many of the Britons had been slain at the village of Déols. This battle occurred around A.D. 470, and after Riothamus and the remnants of his army retreated into Burgundy, his name drops from the continental histories. Sidonius does not write of the devastating conflict between the Visigoths and the Britons, but he does validate one date of the confusing history of the period; the year was late 469.[23] The fourth of the antiquarians—William of 1019—leads to the next inquiry.

Asking for the proper name of the historical figure behind the two epithets leads to an answer that is simplistically obvious. The antiquarian William was the first to connect Arthur and Gaul, evoking a link between Arthur and Riothamus. Leon Fleuriot believed that Riothamus was Ambrosius Aurelianus; an obscure monk named Uriscampum of the 1170s and Geoffrey Ashe contend that Riothamus was Arthur; E. K. Chambers felt that Arthur was Ambrosius. There is no other possible conclusion because there is no other choice: It must be that Riothamus is a different epithet for Arthur, and by extension Arthur is an epithet for Ambrosius Aurelianus because Ambrosius is the only Briton designated by a proper name after Vortigern's rule.

Gildas Badonicus praises only one Briton leader, the one named Ambrosius Aurelianus, who succeeded Vortigern. He identified him as Roman, and relates that Ambrosius's parents, "who had worn the purple were slain in [the war with the treasonous Saxons],"[24] and goes on to say that under his leadership the Britons regained their strength and challenged the victors to battle. After back-and-forth successes, the Britons scored a major victory.

Although Ashe writes that Ambrosius was never referred to as a king, the implication of royalty through his parents is undeniable. John Morris explains that the word "king" was a colloquial expression for emperor, and that "wearing the purple" meant Ambrosius's "father was emperor, for no subject 'wore the purple.'"[25] The meticulous records of Roman emperors, which can be found in any general encyclopedia, verify Ambrosius's claim to royalty.

Independent of any historic sources attempting to verify the authenticity of King Arthur, Ambrosius's ancestry can be traced to Aurelian, a Roman emperor who ruled from A.D. 270 to 275, whose *praenomen, nomen,* and *cognomen* was Lucius Domitius Aurelianus, called by an epithet of Restitutor Orbis (Restorer of the City) because of credit given him for building the Aurelian Wall around Rome. Many of Aurelian's campaigns were in Gaul, and from there he rescued Britain from pretenders during A.D. 271, 272, and 273. He was murdered by conspirators in 275.

As a consequence, the early manuscripts, including the *De Excidio*, provide a great deal of information linking not only continental and insular history, but also Arthur and Riothamus to Ambrosisus. Enumerated for the sake of brevity, they are listed below.

1. The color purple was the Roman Ceasars' standard, a purple dragon insignia, accounting for Ambrosius's tie to Rome and his rise to the two *HB* titles of "the great king of all kings" and "the son of a Roman consul."
2. Ambrosius was a young boy during Vortigern's reign, as depicted in the *HB* under the title "The Tale of Emrys," the same individual who in the 460s at the age of approximately forty was Britain's savior.
3. The historical importance of Ambrosius as the great king among all the kings manifests itself in geographic locations in the midlands between the Severn and East Anglia—Ambrosden, Amberley, Amesbury, Ombersley, Emberton, Ambleston, Emborough—which would have been the Cornovian war zone between the Welsh to the west and the powerful Anglian kingdoms to the east.
4. It also explains his fictitious brother's heraldic shield, thirteen gold crowns on *purple* background, plus the use of a dragon.
5. Under Ambrosius's brilliant leadership, by the end of the 450s the appalling civil conflicts in Britain had diminished and almost ceased.
6. During this lull in warfare in the sixth decade of the fifth century, Riothamus, the supreme king of the Britons, crossed by way of Ocean to join forces with the Romans to fight against the Saxons and the Visigoths on the continent.
7. Riothamus fought a successful battle against the Saxons at Angers.
8. After a devastating defeat dealt by the Visigoths at the end of that decade, Riothamus escaped into the country of Burgundy, a sympathetic ally, and dropped from history.
9. At the same time—the early years of the seventh decade of the fifth century—the name of Arthur first appeared on the island.
10. The *HB* records Arthur's twelve battles against the Saxons, specifically Octha.
11. The name of Arthur appears in two entries of the *Annales Cambriae.*

12. Arthur's colloquial title was High King and his more formal title was Emperor throughout the tales of *The Mabinogion.*
13. Arthur and relatives such as Culhwch own purple banners and mantles adorned with red-gold apples.
14. The Ambrosian era was from approximately A.D. 422 to 460, the Riothamus one from the 460s to the 470s, and the Arthurian age from the early 470s to approximately 518.

4

Who's Who: Ambrosius's Father, the *Superbus Tyrannus* Vortigern

The House of Constantine

If the House of Constantine truly marks Ambrosius's ancestry, the search for Ambrosius's father can lead to only one real possibility. Monmouth lists Ambrosius's father as Constantine II, brother of Aldroneus King of Brittany. But historically the life span for Constantine II, the oldest son of Constantine I, was from 317 to 340, and he reigned from 337 to 340. Although he was the ruler of Gaul, Britain, and Spain, which would fit Monmouth's history, he was killed by Constans I in 340, almost a century before Ambrosius's time.

The only other real possibility recorded in Roman history is Constantius, proclaimed Constantius III by Honorius. He died in A.D. 421, which would properly place him one generation prior to Ambrosius, and hence he realistically could be Ambrosius's father. Because there is no direct link with Constantius II or the House of Constantine, there is not as much information attached to him as there normally is for bona fide Roman emperors. Nevertheless, in the Roman histories he is labeled as a member of a noble Roman family, which coincides with Gildas's entry that Ambrosius's parents wore the purple, and with the statement in the *Historia Brittonum* that Ambrosius's father was a Roman consul. He became master of the soldiers—the equivalency of a general—under Honorius, and in 411 he distinguished himself by overcoming various usurpers in Gaul, including Flavius Claudius Constantinus, who was a common soldier acclaiming regency in Britain near the end of the first decade of the fifth century. Initially, Flavius Constantinus overran Gaul and repelled attacks by Honorius, but he was eventually captured and executed in Ravenna in 411. This last detail incidentally shows that this usurper (who had the presumption to name his son Constans) could not be

Ambrosius's father because his death occurred over a decade before Ambrosius's birth.

The *Historia Brittonum* has two important and interesting references to Constantius which are easy to inadvertently overlook. The first is in Chapter 27, which relates that there were seven Roman imperators (emperors), extended to nine in the Latin manuscripts.

> The ninth was Constantius. He reigned sixteen years in Brittannia, and in the sixteenth year of his reign he died in Brittannia.[1]

The first reference clearly indicates that Welsh tradition does not name two additional emperors; it is only the Roman genealogies which claim their reigns in Britain. An initial check of the Roman genealogical charts indicate, however, that the order of these last two imperators should be reversed. Constantius III, who was in power from 411 until 421, even though he was not officially labeled as a co-emperor, was the eighth in line, and Severus, who ruled from 461 to 465, was the ninth. This "other" Severus (Septimius Severus and Flavius Valerius Severus were two predecessors) was Livius Severus, one of five emperors who was elevated to the throne and then later deposed by Ricimer, a Suevian barbarian who had been raised in the court of Valentinian III. It is hoped that future researchers will uncover Livius Severus's impact on British history, but the focus of this book is on Constantius III and his significance in insular history during this period.

Two transgressions in translations and two variances among the *Historia Brittonum* manuscripts are important. The first misinterpretation in translation is in John Morris's index for *British History,* where he lists Constantius as Constantine III, based, perhaps, upon Geoffrey of Monmouth's history. Morris then lists Constantius as the *ninth* emperor, either lured into the error by the order in the *HB* without checking the Roman genealogies, or assuming that the reference was to Constantine and not to Constantius. He then goes one step further and adds the gloss, "Constantius was the last emperor to rule the British in Britain,"[2] which doesn't appear anywhere in any of the manuscript variants. Much more significant, however, are early versions of the *HB*, which record that Constantius III was killed in Eboracum (York), and that, "according to reports" he was "treacherously murdered."[3]

This Constantius seemingly points to Constantius III, since there is no closer match. Both the *DE* and the *HB* strongly verify this. In narrating the rise of Ambrosius Aurelianus, Gildas Badonicus supplies a one-sentence reference of Ambrosius and his lineage:

> Their leader was Ambrosius Aurelianus, a gentleman who, perhaps alone of the Romans, had survived the shock of this notable storm: certainly his parents, who had worn the purple, were slain in it.[4]

Whereas this source asserts Roman nobility by the expression "wearing the purple," the Nennius manuscript relays the same precept in a different way. Atop Dinas Emrys, when Vortigern asks Ambrosius what family he comes from, Ambrosius replies

> My father is a Consulibus of the Roman people.[5]

The closest translation for a *consulibus* during the imperial period would be "a provincial governor of senatorial rank." Winterbottom translates the term *purpuram sumere* as a late Empire term meaning "to become emperor" and *purpuram induere* as carrying the slight suggestion of "assuming the throne without adequate qualification,"[6] but the definition most commonly used for *purpuratum* is "a man of high rank."[7] Whichever way it is interpreted, this would be a close match to Constantius III being described in the Roman genealogies as a member of a noble Roman family; he becomes a co-emperor not through direct descendancy but through appointment.

Six centuries later, whether it is with or without the *liber vetustissimus,* Geoffrey of Monmouth makes a connection between Ambrosius Aurelianus and the Constantinian dynasty. However, as mentioned in the introduction to this chapter, he names Constantine II, brother of Aldroneus King of Brittany, as Ambrosius's father. If this is a reference to the Constantine II of the Roman genealogies, then Monmouth displaces this king's reign by about eighty years. Additionally, instead of Constantine II being murdered by his brother Constans I in 340, as in the Roman genealogies, Monmouth relates that Constantine II was stabbed to death by a treacherous Pict. Similarly, Monmouth identifies Constantine III as son of Cador Duke of Cornwall, and as the successor to King Arthur. If Monmouth extracted this Constantine from Gildas Badonicus, then the appellation should simply be Constantine, not followed by any numerals. In Roman history, Constantine III was emperor for only three months in 641; there is no record of a Constantine III in Britain, who would have had a floruit of 500 to 530 or a life span from 485 to 545, contemporary with Vortipor or Maglocunus.

Monmouth gives one other misleading detail about the House of Constantine. He identifies Constans—no numerals affixed to the name—as the eldest son of Constantine II and a brother of Aurelius Ambrosius and Utherpendragon. This particular Constans is manipulated by Vortigern, and once Vortigern acquires the crown, he has Constans murdered by Pictish agents. When Monmouth labels Constans as the son of Constantine II, he once again must be referring to Aldroneus's brother and not to the Constantine II of the Roman genealogies. Monmouth's Constans cannot be Constans I, who killed his own brother Constantine II and then ruled as emperor of Gaul, Spain, Britain, Italy, and Africa until he was overthrown by Magnentius in 350. Neither can Monmouth's Constans be the son of Flavius Claudius Constantinus (sometimes called simply Constantine the Usurper). Constantine the

Usurper was executed in Ravenna in 411, and his son faded into oblivion.

This conundrum of genealogies evades an indisputable solution. Of all the figures associated with the House of Constantine, only two included in Monmouth's work resemble those listed in the bona fide Roman genealogies. When Monmouth names Constantius, the Senator and a legate sent to Britain who becomes King of Britain, he is correctly identifying Constantius I, who does, in fact, reconquer Britain, and who bore a son named Constantine I, who died at York. For the remainder, there are three possibilities.

The first is that Monmouth incorrectly identified Constantius III as Constantine II. If this is the case, then Ambrosius indeed would be the son of a Roman *consulibus* in agreement with the records left in the *DE* and the *HB*. The controversy over the Welsh genealogies touched upon in Chapter 1 of this book and exemplified by Griscom—whether they were recorded *before* or *after* Monmouth's manuscript—has a significant impact here. That Geoffrey was simply creating a historical fantasy would account for his sloppy apprisal; however, if he was copying material from some other source, as he claimed he was doing with the Mordred material, then he wouldn't have questioned the veracity of the information. It is this latter condition which seems to have caused at least some of the "lapses" in his narrative: the confusion between Arthur and Ambrosius, the contradictions about Anna's husbands, the ambiguity of where Mount Ambris was located, the association between Guithelinus and Aurelius Ambrosius as that of a guardian rather than an enemy, the blood ties between Cador and Constantine of Cornwall and Arthur, and the recurrent problem of the relationship between Arthur and Mordred. If in truth Geoffrey had been copying from the *liber vetustissimus,* then he at times would have been befuddled by the history of it in contrast to what he believed it to be. This would have given rise, as it did with Mordred, to Monmouth's avowal that he found the information "in the British treatise already referred to."[8]

The second plausible explanation of a connection between Arthur and the House of Constantine could be that, independent of the Constantinians in the Roman genealogies, there might have been a Constantine II in Breton history and a Constantine III in Cornish or Welsh history. There are no existent ancestral records for a Breton Constantine II, but Constantine III can be explained, as will be shown later, not only by the Welsh genealogies but by the writings of Gildas in the *DE*. From both of these sources, Monmouth might then have written what he believed was bona fide insular history, events which were the truth because they were verified by a reliable historical source and ingrained in ancient Welsh tradition.

The third possibility, which seems the most unlikely, is that Ambrosius (i.e., Arthur) had absolutely no connections to Roman royalty, and hence the ancient manuscripts such as the *DE*, the *HB*, the Welsh genealogies, and Monmouth's *The History of the Kings of Britain* are all bogus. This, probably, would be the easiest way to close the chapter on Arthur's historicity, but to do so means that this incredible spirit of Arthur must be relegated to the world of make-believe, a fantasy with no substance. Although the romances and fiction could probably now survive at this distance from the Arthurian age, a depressive pall of gloom would still obscure this majestic figure, consigning him to a position of fanciful imagination. That he was human is what now makes him larger than life. Even myth—natural circumstances explained by supernatural causes—has a base in reality; Arthur himself was not manufactured from nothingness. The reason he became such an imposing, memorable figure throughout the ages is that out of the annihilation of centuries-old civilization, he arose as the savior of a new nation. Nevertheless, for those non-believers, this option is the easy way out: Arthur is a mythical invention; the remaining scraps and pieces of information which have survived are the remnants of a massive superstructure erected only to make him appear human.

The first option—that Arthur is attached to the House of Constantine via Constantius III—was determined by a process of elimination. The information above, reiterated in a narrative style, shows that through verifiable Roman genealogies, the Constantinian dynasty (as it affects the later Arthurian era) was at its strongest peak when three brothers—Constantine II, Constantius II, and Constans I—ruled simultaneously. The triumvirate was violent; Constans I killed his brother Constantine II, but was overthrown ten years later by Magnentius. However, Constantius II then defeated Magnentius for Constans's share of the empire and became sole Emperor of the West. At that point, Constantinian successors become blurred. One Constantine (labeled as Constantine III by P. H. Blair), was executed by Honorius in A.D. 411; this particular Constantine was known as Constantine the Usurper, but his full name was Flavius Claudius Constantinus, a common soldier acclaimed Briton Emperor in 411 and executed in that same year.

This marks the termination of the Constantinian dynasty, with one exception: Constantius III. This individual is not validated as a blood relative of the Constantinian dynasty, but instead he is described simply as a member of a noble royal Roman family. Through distinguished service and marriage to Honorius's sister, he became the virtual ruler of the Western Roman Empire in A.D. 421, but died in that same year. Constantius III is the only figure left after this process of elimination, yet it is precisely this option which is the most plausible, built upon the amalgamation of the existing sources.

Some of the postulations from *Historic King Arthur* tie in remarkably well here. Using oral tradition, the writings of Layamon, and material in the *Historia Brittonum,* the *HKA* calculated Ambrosius Aurelianus's birth year as 422. This date was determined by subtracting Arthur's age at coronation (fifteen) from the date of discord between Vitalinus and Ambrosius (437).

The rationale behind this was actually expressed by Monmouth's narrative. Upon the death of Aurelius's and Utherpendragon's father, dissension broke out among the leaders as to who should be elevated to the kingship. Even though the two brothers (Aurelius and Utherpendragon) are the rightful heirs to the throne, they are too young to assume the responsibility, especially during those periods of unrest. Through deception and murder, Vortigern, the King of the Gewissae, seizes the crown, and Vitalinus, fearing that his two wards will be assassinated, flees to Brittany for their safekeeping.

At this point a review of material in Chapter 1 on Griscom and his contemporary, Professor Petrie, is in order. Griscom takes the stance that the Welsh/Breton chronicles *preceded* Geoffrey of Monmouth. In spite of some scholars who denigrated Griscom and Petrie, the Welsh/Breton chronicles cannot be dismissed that easily, and no one to date has seriously taken up their challenge. Of the very scanty information which *has* emerged from the *Tysilio Brut,* however, the genealogies blend well with other sources. In spite of the risk that disputants will express disdain at its simplicity, the following emended genealogy from Chapter 2 gives one representation of a very complex subject.

The most radical change is the name of Constantius III from Constantine II, brother of Aldroneus. The histories do not show that Constantius III

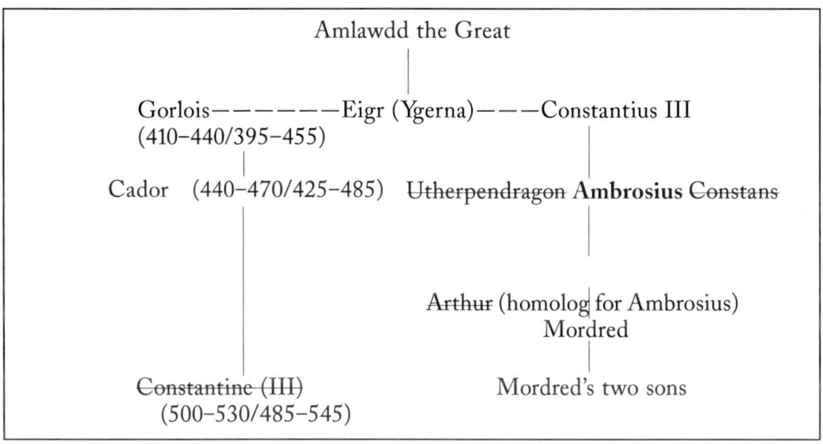

Table 5—The emendation of the House of Constantine based upon the *Brut Tysilio*, Monmouth's *The History of the Kings of Britain*, and the theories from *The Historic King Arthur*. (See also Chapter 2 of this text.)

had a brother who became the King of Brittany, but only that he cleared Gaul of usurpers.

Fletcher has written that

> [T]he *Brut Tysilio* follows Geoffrey rather closely, but with considerable condensation, with the addition of two or three distinct incidents in the non-Arthurian portion, and with some minor divergences. The following points deserve notice: Eiger (Geoffrey's Igerna) is called the daughter of Amlawdd the Great; Gwenhwyfar (Geoffrey's Guanhamara) is called the daughter of Gogyrfan the hero; and Cador, father of the Constantine to whom Arthur leaves the kingdom, is said to be the son of Gorlois. *All these statements may possibly be details of the old British tradition from which Geoffrey drew,* but it is quite as likely that they are elaborations on his text [italics added].[9]

Even though the italicized statement points to the Welsh/Breton chronicles as predecessors to Monmouth's manuscript, Fletcher for some reason still resists accepting that as fact. He further overlooks it when he claims that Wace, writing of the same genealogies, also added elaborations of his own. Fletcher was still in a state of denial when he wrote

> On closer consideration, however, most of the [details added by Wace not given in Monmouth] prove to be merely elaborations due to Wace himself. Such [elaborations] are several statements that one person was cousin to another....[10]

One of Fletcher's references is Guinevere's relationship to Cador. Wace writes that the beautiful Guinevere came from a noble Roman House, and Cador had raised her in his earldom of Cornwall, ending the description by adding "The maiden was the earl's near cousin, for by his mother, he too was of Roman blood."[11] In the sixteenth century John Leland also writes that Guinevere was cousin to Cador of Cornwall and daughter to the King of Briscay, probably borrowed from the Welsh/Breton chronicles, but Fletcher views this as "a monstrous romance or ballad idea."[12] It is puzzling why Fletcher refused to recognize that the Welsh chronicles were recorded about three decades prior to the Monmouth manuscripts, especially since he offers nothing more defensible than the belief that Monmouth, Wace, and Leland were just adding fanciful details.

Discrepancies exist, however, between the historical accounts in the Roman genealogies and those in the *Historia Brittonum.* For one, several versions of the *HB* claim that the eighth emperor of Britain (Constantius, with no numeral suffix) died at York; for another, there are versions which claim that this eighth emperor was treacherously murdered. Some scribe of a later version, evidently ignorant of empiric Roman emperors, assumed that the Constantius recorded in the *HB* must have been the same Constantius recorded in Monmouth's account, which relates that Constantius died at York. A further transgression was the confusion with the death of Monmouth's Constantine II, who was killed by a nameless Pict. The several versions of the *HB* which record Constantius's treacherous murder at York begin with

Manuscript D (the Cottonian MS. Caligula A viii), which was copied around 1153, almost two decades *after* Monmouth's book had been distributed. Prior to Manuscript D, the *HB* versions do not give explicit information either about Constantius's murder nor his locale in York.[13]

This serves as substantial proof that a scribe misidentified Constantius as the eighth emperor of Britain. The Constantius who died at York was more commonly known as Constantius I, whose reign was from 337 to 361. In actuality, the Constantius mentioned in the *Historia Brittonum* is Constantius III, who reigned from 417 to 421 and who was the immediate predecessor of Valentinian III. Constantius III, then, as initially proposed at the beginning of this chapter, is the only possibility as Ambrosius Aurelianus's father. Shifting the point of view to Aurelianus's father, however, means reversing the proposition: Can Ambrosius's father be Constantius III? Several specifics affirm this. First, Ambrosius Aurelianus and Constantius III fall into an ideal chronological framework; one floruit and life span overlaps the other and supports the details of Ambrosius's encounter as a young boy with Vortigern. Second, the occurrence of this event immediately follows the Roman withdrawal from Britain and the two decades or so afterwards. Third, because Ambrosius's father was a Roman *consulibus,* Ambrosius would automatically be viewed as a natural leader to assume kingship.

The fourth similarity, the close bond to Gaul, requires a bit more elaboration. Because Roman histories show beyond a doubt that Constantius III fought the majority of his campaigns in Gaul, what events likewise show that Ambrosius's father also had binding ties to Gaul? Honorius had inherited the Western Empire from his father Theodosius I in 395, but because Honorius was only seven years old at the time, the real power until 408 lay with Stilicho, who had been appointed his regent. When Honorius was twenty-four, public pressure led to the deposition of Stilicho. After Alaric and his Visigoths sacked Rome in 410, it was Constantius III who offset Honorius's ineffectiveness by eliminating the usurpers and re-securing Gaul.

On the issue of Gallic connections, Monmouth provides two important pieces of information. One is that after the death of Ambrosius's father, Ambrosius is spirited away to Brittany (a part of Gaul) in order to prevent a possible assassination. The other is that approximately sixty-five percent of the material on Arthur in the Monmouth manuscript centers on Gaul.

But because Monmouth's work is considered at best a pseudohistory, what other, more reliable information confirms a link between Ambrosius's father and Gaul? To better answer this question, it must be pointed out that the major thesis of *The Historic King Arthur* is that the figures of Ambrosius, Riothamus, and Arthur are embodied in one homolog, leading to the coined name Riardd Ambrosius. Chapter 2 of this text gives the basic premises of that thesis. The applicable segment centers upon Riothamus, the Briton King from across Ocean. Riothamus spends almost a decade in Gaul, allied with

Ægidius and Syagrius in an attempt to keep Gaul from falling to the barbarians. The emperor Anthemius and the Romans are a part of their coalition in the struggle against the Saxons, the Visigoths, the Franks, and the Huns. The histories of these wars are provided by independent, neutral sources, Gregory of Tours and Jordanes. The accord among the Romans, the Gauls, and the Britons suggest that their union was not transient. Even after the Roman withdrawal from Britain, there was continuous contact and reciprocal support and protection. It follows that the relationship was generational; Riothamus had an affinity for Gaul because it was in a sense his father's homeland. Just these four reasons, then, establish a persuasive possibility that Ambrosius's father is Constantius III.

Nevertheless, some jarring discrepancies must be assessed, most notably Constantius's marriage to Galla Placidia, Honorius's sister, who is detailed in Roman history in an even more significant role than that of Constantius. She was taken hostage by Alaric during the sack of Rome and held until 414. At that time she married Alaric's successor, Ataulphus, who died a year later. Soon after, she was returned and married Constantius in 417. Constantius subsequently became emperor of the West, even though Honorius didn't appoint him as co-emperor until February of 421. Most important, Placidia had a son (Valentinian III) by Constantius who was officially seated on the throne in 425 by Theodosius II. Because Valentinian was only six years old at his ascension, his mother was regent until her death toward the middle of the fifth century.

None of the histories nor traditions even remotely suggest that Galla Placidia reigned from Britain. That in itself casts doubt on the possibility of Constantius III being Ambrosius's father. Gildas writes that Ambrosius's parents (plural) were killed in the internal wars against the *Saxones*. Contextually, in addition to writing explicitly that both parents had been slain, Gildas leaves no room that these wars were the continental ones, and therefore the conflicts cannot be interpreted as being fought in Gaul. Without any doubt, Gildas is writing about internal (or civil) wars between the English Saxons and the Welsh. The conditions seem absolute and undeniable: Although Constantius III could have been fighting wars in Britain where he was killed, there is no possibility that Galla Placidia met the same fate under the same circumstances.

Yet there is one tiny loophole which creates a nagging plausibility. The *Historia Brittonum* gives a detailed story of Ambrosius. When Vortigern tries to build a fortified stronghold to defend himself, his attempts are supernaturally foiled several times. He consults his wizards, who tell the king that the stronghold must be sprinkled with the blood of a child without a father. Envoys search all of Britain and finally find a fatherless boy in the country called Glywysing. Upon questioning the mother, she denies that the boy has a father, claiming that she did not know how she conceived because she had never lain with a man. It is only later, when Ambrosius (also called Merlinus) has demonstrated his own powers, that Vortigern asks what family Ambrosius had come from, and Ambrosius replies that his father is a Roman *consulibus.*

This claim—that Abrosius's father is an incubus—makes its way into Welsh tradition as Constantius III's having a Briton woman as a concubine. The implications of this genealogically is shown in both Table 4 of Chapter 2 and in Table 5 of this chapter. By alleviating the epithetical character who is Constantius III's seemingly fictional son Utherpendragon and then adding those historical figures who are anachronistic (Constantine II, Constantine III, and Constans) and also adding the correct references to Constantius III and Constantine the Briton, the parallel genealogies add a new, interesting twist to an old story. After the Romans withdrew from Britain to fight the continuous conflicts flaring up on the continent, and after his mother and his father perished under unknown circumstances, Ambrosius Aurelianus was one of the few Romans of royalty left behind on the island.

Once of age, he gained control of the *Britanni* tribes and emerged as their unifying leader, stemming the *Saxone* tide and administering justice as none of his predecessors had been able to do. After Ambrosisu had pacified the northern section of the Midlands, he gathered together his tribal sub-kings to plan strategies for the unification of all of Britain. Among those whom he rallied together was Cador of Dumnonia, the peninsula later known as Cornwall. The two join forces not only as kinsmen with a common mother, (Ygerna), but as strong allies trying to stem Britain's demise. As a Pendragon, and because of his military success, Ambrosius becomes Arthurex, high king of the sub-kings, commonly referred to as "a king among all the kings of Britain."

When Mordred is born, he and his uncle Cador are almost a generation apart. As the years pass, deep rivalry develops between Cador, who claims connections to the throne of High King through his mother Ygerna, and Mordred, whose right to the throne is through his father Ambrosius. Cador's son, Constantine the Briton, also lays claim to the high throne from his mother's side, and a feud develops between him, Mordred, and Mordred's sons. When Mordred treasonously sells out to the Saxons, the door is open for Constantine's claim as high king upon Arthurex Ambrosius's death. As the monk Gildas Badonicus implies in his writing, once Constantine succeeds to the throne after the Battle of Camlann, in which both Arthurex and Mordred perish, he kills Mordred's two sons to protect his own inheritance.

The sequence of events is supported by a chronology for each of the individuals involved. Galla Placidia is governing the empire from Gaul on the continent, attempting to stem the onslaught from Attila the Hun through her capable commander Aëtius. Constantius III, part of the Roman contingency left on the island, is killed along with his Briton concubine by the tide of the Saxon advance. As rightful heir, Ambrosius Aurelianus is spirited off to Brittany while a young boy under possible threat of assassination, but returns later to ascend to the throne. Through the tumultuous decades of the mid-400s he is able to unite the *Britanni* against the triple perils posed by Picts, *Saxones,* and Irish. Though he stems the dangers from foreign invasions, he is plagued by internal conflicts, finally succumbing to civil wars which destroy what external powers could not overthrow. By the time Constantine and the other four regional kings gain control, the glory of a unified island has passed its zenith, while avarice and power replace the virtues of the previous era.

The *Superbus Tyrannus*

Although the above scenario is plausible, there are an enormous number of ramifications when coupling Arthurian history with these brief Roman capsules, particularly the account of Galla Placidia's bona fide son, Valentinian III, who, when paralleled with Welsh tradition, would be Ambrosius's half-brother. Valentinian was a weak, indecisive figurehead who never really ruled during the thirty years listed as the period of his reign. His savior, like Constantius was to Honorius before him, was Flavius Aëtius. Ironically, after Honorius's death, Aëtius had supported the usurper Joannes against the Empress Galla Placidia, but he was later reconciled with her and became Count of Italy, commander of the army, and chief advisor. Also like Constantius III, Aëtius was the embodiment of power in the Western empire. In 450, after Attila invaded Gaul, he was instrumental in tracking the Hun and defeating him in 453, thus destroying the Hun dominion. Because of Galla Placidia's death, the throne had finally passed to Valentinian, a vengeful recreant. With the threat of Hun power destroyed, Valentinian turned on Aëtius in a fit of envious rage and stabbed him to death in 454. His own death occurred a year later, but the records are unclear about the nature of his demise; some accounts indicate he was stabbed by Aëtius's former guards, and others relate that he was killed by Petronius Maximus, whose wife Valentinian had ravished.

One conspicuous detail which surged to the surface from this compelling reservoir of Roman history was Valentinian's reign from A.D. 425 to 455. As so often happens, at first no significance was attached to this seemingly prosaic piece of information. It, like hundreds of others, merely gave a time span in the most common and simplest format. Even when recognition struck, it was not earth-shaking: The reign attributed to Vortigern was likewise from 425 to 455. Alcock was aware of this similarity at least as far back as 1971, when *Arthur's Britain* was first published. In order to accurately establish Vortigern's reign, Alcock confirms that the best source of information about Vortigern is the set of chronological computations which preface the Easter Annals in what Alcock calls the *British Historical Miscellany.*[14] He writes of Vortigern holding rule during the consulship of Theodosius and Valentinian, and cites an error in the calculations because of the differentiation between the Dionysiac and Victorian modes of reckoning, relating that

> The first consulship of Theodosius and Valentinian was in 425 and an earlier, partly bungled calculation had alread equated the story of Vortigern's reign with that of Valentinian, again, 425.[15]

Because both dates are so ingrained in history, there was a mild reaction to the coincidence, but nothing of momentous consequence.

However, two other details, which have been accepted as fact for nearly a millennium and hence have become locked in what I termed "patterned thinking" in *The Historic King Arthur,* struck a disturbing and discordant note. First, Gildas Badonicus does not identify Vortigern as the *superbus tyrannus,* a piece of information commonly known to any researcher who studies the Dark Ages. Also commonly known is that Vortigern is not a proper name but an epithet. Yet ever since Bede in his *History of the English Church and People* identified the *superbus tyranus* as Urtigernus,[16] or Vortigern, the *superbus tyrannus* has become a Briton king who invited the hated German Saxons into Britain to fight the *Scotti* and the Picts. In that sentence Bede falls into the common copyist's trap of interpolating an original manuscript. He faithfully copied Gildas's inference to German instead of English Saxons, but by the one seemingly harmless change from *superbus tyrannus* to Vortigern, he distorted the understanding of insular history for all time. In order to rectify that blunder, historians, scholars, medievalists, etymologists, and logicians must take a step back and ask the simple question, "Who in heaven's name is the *superbus tyrannus,* the actual man behind the title?

Alcock attacks the question with an initial reminder that

> we have still to explain the emergence of the *superbus tyrannus* of Gildas out of the framework of Roman civil administration. Our only clue to the constitutional processes involved is the word *(superbus) tyrannus* itself.[17]

A quick survey shows that *superbus tyrannus* has variously been defined as high king,[18] supreme ruler,[19] great king,[20] over-lord,[21] haughty tyrant,[22] and most commonly, proud tyrant.[23] As a parallel, the epithet "Vortigern" is most commonly defined as over-chief or over-king.[24] Additionally, both Alcock and Ashe refer to Vortigern as a usurper.[25] As an interesting parallel, Ashe writes of Vortigern as having "power without legitimacy,"[26] and Lacy writes that Gildas's *superbus tyrannus* implies "not so much tyranny as doubtful legitimacy."[27]

All of these translations have merit; the word *tyrannus* generically means "an absolute ruler," although sometimes it was used by Ovid and Cicero to mean someone who overthrows the constitution of his state, or in other words, a usurper. Although it seems unlikely that Gildas would have been using the term in its narrower sense, it is impossible to state as a fact, especially since the preceding adjective is of no help. The neutral definition for *superbus* is "exalted," but it, too carries both positive and negative connotations. In a negative sense, it means "arrogant or overbearing," terms which could be equally applicable to Valentinian (judging from his attitude and treatment of Aëtius) or to Vortigern, if the latter were a Welsh usurper. In the positive sense, it implies "brilliant," magnificent," or "splendid," attributes that would apply to neither. Valentinian was an incompetent profligate whose majority of reign was handled by his mother until she died, and Vortigern earned the hatred of all the succeeding *Britanni* generations. As a concluding comment, it appears that if Gildas had indeed meant to label the *superbus tyrannus* as a usurper, he would have used a much more explicit expression such as *regnum occupare,* "to seize the throne," or "to seize authority," rather than using the obscure connotation "usurper" attached to the word *tyrannus.*

After deliberation, the answer to the question seems ludicrously simple, but because the response seems so obvious, the mind erects other barriers, those of trepidation and suspicion—trepidation for fear that the response might be viewed as foolish, and suspicion based on why no one else has yet voiced that possibility. Nevertheless, the risk must be taken and an answer voiced: The *superbus tyrannus* mentioned by Gildas Badonicus in the *De Excidio* is a reference to Valentinian III, and by extension, Vortigern is a different epithet for a chieftain appointed as an "over-king" of the mercenary tribes on the island, which would have followed typical Roman policy.

The difficulty, of course, is not really the leap, but the landing. Echoes of "Prove it!" will doubtlessly reverberate in the canyons of time. The epithet of Vortigern appears in the ancient historical manuscripts normally in brief one-or two-line notices, so that a substitution of one name for another is facile, and a quick check can be made to determine if historically, with the substitution, the sentence makes logistic sense. Much more complex are the two manuscripts which give the in-depth stories and genealogies of Vortigern, *The Historia Brittonum* and Monmouth's *History of the Kings of Britain;* they will require more explanation, which will, one hopes, be viewed open-mindedly rather than being rejected out-of-hand as mere rationalizations.

The best approach is to deal with the easy things first. Gildas writes,

> Then all the members of the council, together with the *superbus tyrannus,* were struck blind; ... they devised that the Saxons ... should be let into the island ... to beat back the peoples of the north.[28]

The sentence still makes sense if Valentinian III is substituted, but clarification is needed for the word "council," and some historical background must be given. In addition to addressing the term "council," Alcock also clarifies the adjective for *tyrannus:*

> The qualifying *superbus* implies that he [i.e., Valentinian] held sovereignty over several minor *tyranni.* He was not in modern terms, an unconstitutional despot, for he ruled with a group of *consiliarii* like a Roman governor ...[underline added].[29]

Valentinian was *the* Emperor of the West, not just an underling appointed by Roman authority; the "minor tyranni" or the "consiliarii" would have been tribal chieftains such as Vortigern or Romans of lower rank. Valentinian acted "like a Roman governor" because he *was* of royal birth.

In that same vein Alcock continues:

> Vortigern continued the line of British *tyranni* in the 420s and 430s, and continued likewise the Roman policy of settling Germans as *laeti* or *foederati* for the defence of Britain.[30]

If "Valentinian" is substituted for "Vortigern," the passage makes even more sense; he would, of course continue Roman policy, just as his immediate predecessor Honorius had done, and all the other emperors before him. The only other common misconception is that Alcock assumes that the Saxons were imported from the continent—that is, German Saxons, rather than the English Saxons already settled on the island. Earlier in his text, however, Alcock shows his cognizance that artifacts on the island indicate English Saxon settlement rather than just sporadic raiding that had begun "significantly before Bede's date for the *Adventus.*"[31]

The proper date for the *Adventus* raises the issue of chronology, specifically the year 410 as the date so commonly ascribed to the Roman abandonment of Britain. Vociferous objections might be made that Valentinian could not possibly have been the person behind Gildas's title of *superbus tyrannus* at such an early date. But fortuitously recorded history supports a much later date. The year 410 seems to have been arbitrarily selected because it coincides with Alaric's sacking of Rome, and evidently the assumption is thus made that the Western Roman Empire crumbled at that time. It is true, of course, that the West was in decline, but it was a gradual process which spanned approximately three decades. Even after withdrawal, Rome continued strong ties with Britain, as evidenced by the writing of Gildas and later historians. In the section on independent Britain, chapters 14 through 17, Gildas writes of two episodes of Roman aid. Then, after the second, he writes that the Romans (specifically, it would have been Honorius) notified the country that the legions could no longer make expeditions or be responsible for the island. Alcock exemplifies this by writing,

> But the effective outcome was made clear when Honorius wrote, not to the military commanders—the *dux* or *comes Britanniarum*—nor to the chief civilian administrator, the *vicarius*, but to the local councils, the *civitates*, telling them to undertake their own defence.[32]

The next plea, the letter to Aëtius, did not result in help. But this cannot be interpreted that the Romans had forfeited all claims to the island, or that Britain's decline was rapid or complete.

Writing about the events during the Roman withdrawal from Britain to protect its holdings in Gaul, Collingwood relates that

> ... the significance of [the deserted ruins in some of the major cities] must not be misunderstood. They do not imply a breakdown or abandonment of the system of local administration. Shrunken and impoverished though they were, these towns were still the capitals of self-governing tribes.[33]

As the period after the Romans have filtered from the island extends more and more, Collingwood writes of the historical progression, indicating that in the mid-fifth century, as had been the case at the turn of the century, "[c]auses being identical, it is hardly to be doubted that effects were identical too."[34] A sequence shows that prosperity declined and spiritual initiative decayed, but there was no *catastrophic* decline in lifestyle. Instead, Britain survives for about a quarter of a century with only intermittent aid and very little direct control from the weakening Roman regime. But the Western Empire held on from the beginning of the fifth century to the last quarter, the end probably being best marked by Anthemius's reign from 467 to 472. As attested to by Collingwood,

> But let us keep our hold on the archaeological facts. All four of the deserted major towns [Verulam, Silchester, Wroxeter, and Caistor-next-Norwich], and several minor ones, have been excavated; and the excavators have in every case looked for evidence that the towns finally perished in some such way [as Gildas's report of ruin and massacre]. The results are decisive. These towns came to an end, not by fire and sword, but by decay and evacuation. They were abandoned and left to fall down.[35]

With the Roman withdrawal, then, seen as a gradual process of general abandonment and eventual decay, Valentinian would have still been a figure of authority even though he might have been operating from Gaul. Britain remained under the general protectorate, and as such would have continued to be a subject of Roman policy. To continue, then, with the possibility of the word Vortigern mistakenly being an epithet for Valentinian, there are several other single references which should be checked. Independent of Gildas but close to his time chronologically, there are two other documents. The first, called the *Cronica Gallica a. CCCCLII* (the *Chronica Gallica of 452*) supports the contention that decay and ruin in Britain was an extended phenomenon, but even more important it acts as an introduction for the Valentinian/Vortigern issue. It reads

> XVIIII Britanniae usque ad hoc tempus variis cladibus eventibusque latae in dicionem Saxonum rediguntur.[36]

The Roman numeral (XVIIII) is a reference to the nineteenth year of Theodosius II, who was for a time the Emperor of the East simultaneously while Valentinian III was Emperor of the West. Their joint rule began in 423 after the death of Honorius, and hence the nineteenth year of his combined reign would have been in 442. In translation, the above reads as

> A.D. 442: Britain, which up to this time had suffered misfortunes of war and eventual retreats, was subjected to the power [authority] of the Saxons.

Although there is no mention here of Valentinian III, there are several important implications. The first is that the Roman policy of hiring mercenaries—in this instance the *Saxones*—had been invoked, and when the treacherous Saxons rebelled, the result was the Saxon Revolt of 442. Second, it is unclear if Galla Placidia as regent, or Valentinian himself was part of the plan, but nevertheless, Valentinian would have been involved as part of the policy, which was transferred to someone named Vortigern when Bede assumed that the *superbus tyrannus* was the Briton king.

The second source runs a close parallel to the first. It is the *Cronica Gallica a. DXI,* which reports that

> XVI Britanniae a Romanis amissae in dicionem Saxonum cedunt.[37]

Similarly, the Roman numeral (XVI) is a reference to the sixteenth year of the joint rule of Theodosius II and Valentinian III. Valentinian acceded to the throne in 425 (the same date ascribed to Vortigern), and sixteen years beyond that time would be 441. Likewise, the translation for the above would be

> A.D. 441: Britain, relinquished by the Romans, fell to the power [authority] of the Saxons.

Without a doubt, this entry spells out that the *Romans,* not the *Britanni,* relinquished the country, which exonerates the Briton king Vortigern. Although the Romans began a withdrawal as early as 410, they still held power over Britain, so that when their policy of hiring mercenaries backfired, they were helpless to prevent the Saxon rebellion. This entry, then, states outright that Valentinian, as the direct ruler of the Western Empire, was the impelling force behind the Saxon take-over of the budding *Britanni* government. The Roman Empire had committed itself to the use of mercenaries to fight the Picts and the Scotti, and because Aëtius was engaged with the Huns on the continent and the salvaging of Gaul, his army could not be detached to intervene in the civil war which was erupting in Britain. This is what makes Alcock's observation a moot point when he writes, "Despite the impression left by Gildas, Vortigern was not the first to recruit Germans to ward off the Picts."[38] Gildas did not even vaguely suggest that Vortigern was the instigator behind the use of the Saxons as mercenaries, and this particular Welsh king did not invite Germans in; the Saxons were settlers to the east of the Roman Cornovii territory, and hence these English had a vested interest in the island. It was Bede, two centuries later, who misplaced the blame.

Vortigern

If this is the case, then, who is the Welsh king, Vortigern, and how can he be explained? The *Historia Brittonum* gives a great deal of information, including a genealogy, which cannot be paralleled to Valentinian's life. Alcock is correct in asserting that the *HB* gives historically plausible information, but it is information which cannot be confirmed or denied because there are no other primary sources which deal with this history. Independent of Gildas Badonicus and his echo Bede, the *HB*, exclusive of the questionable material on Germanus and Patrick, provides historical detail which easily and accurately fits into the milieu of the period. At one point Alcock writes that

> ... these tales [in the *HB*] about Vortigern are of very uneven historicity. There is little doubt that some of the stories with a Welsh setting, like the tales about Garmon or Germanus, were invented in order to explain place names which had "Vortigern" as one element in them.[39]

Several other sources concur that some segments of the *HB* are fictional. As cited in *The Historic King Arthur*, Wade-Evans is instrumental in specifying that several episodes in the *HB* are *cyfarwyddiadau*, bardic tales, told by professional bards, which really stem from Nennius

> ... trying to make history to harmonize with Bede's disastrous misunderstanding of a "Saxon advent" as told in the *de excidio* and with all the guess-work he expended on it.[40]

He elaborates on this specifically with Octha and the episodes recorded in Chapter 38 dealing with Octha and Ebissa wasting the Orkney Islands. He writes,

> The *cyfarwydd* (professional bard) naturally made his audience to understand that Octa and Ebissa started from the North Sea in their forty keels, circumnavigating the Picts from east to west, wasting the Orkneys on their course and terrifying all Pictland.... [41]

Sir Ifor Williams expresses some of the same beliefs about various episodes in the *HB*. He asserts that Nennius wrote in 796, and the bardic songs reached Nennius possibly through records compiled in a Welsh monastery. If this were the case, the records would have been in Latin, and would *not* have supplied Welsh epithets. In that case, Sir Ifor conjectures,

> ... it [is] much more likely that Nennius' source was the oral tradition of the Welsh bards, handed down by these professional guardians of past history, in the form of sagas or long tales which they used to tell in the halls of their chieftains .... [42]

A footnote is added in which Sir Ifor deduces from the style and idioms of Nennius's Latin that an Old Welsh source underlies much of the *HB*. In particular, he argues that Nennius was reproducing a native tale or *cyfarwyddyd* concerning Gwrtheyrn (Vortigern).

However, his comment about Vortigern should not be interpreted to mean that Vortigern is not an authentic figure of history. Alcock counterbalances this possibility by citing information from a non-fiction source:

> Since the computations (folios 189B–190A) deal largely with Vortigern and the coming of the English to Britain, they have frequently been regarded as a summary or recapitulation of the "Life of Vortigern" which formed Sections 31–49 of the *Historia Brittonum*. But this is most unlikely. They are absent from most of the manuscripts of the *Historia Brittonum,* and occur only in Harleian 3895 and another manuscript derived from it. .... In that case they [the folios mentioned above] stand closer to Vortigern's own day than any other document that we possess, except possibly for brief entries in the Gallic Chronicles.[43]

The computations to which he is referring are the *calculi* at the head of the British Easter Table compiled in 455[44] which he believes are historically sound.

In trying to determine Vortigern's historical authenticity, the *HB* automatically comes under scrutiny, particularly since the entire story of Vortigern occurs in no other early source, including Gildas, except in two entries of *The Anglo-Saxon Chronicle.* J. N. L. Myres writes,

> How this straightforward tradition [the story of Vortigern and the Saxons] was developed in the Celtic lands before the eighth century was over, and how the story of Vortigern was interwoven with a mass of legend dealing with the miracles of St. Germanus, is amply illustrated in the pages of Nennius [the *Historia Brittonum]* and for the most part may be safely ignored by the historian.[45]

What Myres writes is slanted a bit by O'Sullivan, who gives the impression that the Vortigern segment in the *HB* should be ignored as history, but does not suggest the important contributions made by Welsh *tradition,* a word which should be preferred to "legend" as used in the above citation. Tradition can contain nuggets of historical accuracy, and therefore, even though all of the Vortigern material might not be accepted at face value historically, it is still wise to at least explore what other sources have to offer.

A few pages later Myres continues that,

> Vortigern's authority was thought of as extensive; after the first settlement of the invaders in Thanet, he proceeded in return for Hengist's daughter to hand over the rest of Kent without consulting its local king, and finally, after the murder of the British chieftains and his own capture, he recovered his freedom by the more interesting surrender of Essex, Sussex, and Middlesex.[46]

Although Myres labels the details of this story as worthless, perhaps the story needs only minor emendations to make it valuable. The information might not be applicable to Vortigern the Welsh King of the *HB,* but it fits well for the *superbus tyrannus*—that is, Valentinian III, the Emperor of the West. Valentinian's authority would indeed be extensive and as emperor he would have the right to hand over territory ruled by a minor king, a power which Vortigern as a Welsh king of a province two hundred miles away would not have. Eliminating the particulars of a reference to Thanet, Hengist's daughter, and Vortigern's "surrender," this passage could very well be relating that Valentinian instituted the Roman policy of using mercenary tribal chieftains, and when the Saxon kings rebelled in an all-out revolt and killed other mercenary chieftains, they were able to seize valuable territories in the south and southeast.

The Vortigern references which seem to be epithets to Valentinian in the *HB* must be compared as similarities to the entries naming Vortigern in *The Anglo-Saxon Chronicle.* Once again turning to Myres, he writes,

> The laconic entries of *The Anglo-Saxon Chronicle,* put together in their present form at the end of the ninth century, are derived in part from Bede, but they add topographical details of battles between the invaders and the Britons....[47]

That the name of Vortigern appears in the *ASC* and was derived from Bede immediately arouses suspicion, since Bede was the first antiquarian to equate the *superbus tyrannus* with Vortigern. Plummer, the expert on the variant manuscripts of the *ASC,* verifies the derivations from Bede; specifically for the entry of 449 he notes that this particular entry and its reference to Vortigern are taken from Bede, and variants A, B, and C further add the title of "Briton King."[48] There are several versions of the *ASC,* and each version varies, but in essence Vortigern, king of the Welsh invites in the English Saxons, specifically naming Hengist and Horsa as the leaders (similar to the *HB* but different from the *DE),* who came to Ypwinesfleot. Most of the versions are prefaced by a statement that 449 is the year when Maximianus (Mauritius, Mauricius, Marcian) and Valentinian (Valentinus) obtained the kingdom and reigned for seven years. The landing-place, Ypwinesfleot, is not listed in any *Britanni* manuscript, but instead of this giving an advantageous edge like names provided elsewhere in the *ASC,* it has provided a guessing-game, most commonly settling upon Ebbsfleet in Thanet. Unlike most entries which Myres described as "laconic," Manuscript A contains a long Canterbury addition and Manuscript E contains an equally long accretion suggesting its Northumbrian origin for the date of 449.

Based upon these observations, but particularly upon the strength of its derivation from Bede, King Vortigern is a reference not to a Briton submonarch, but to the *superbus tyrannus,* which again seems a more suitable conjecture. Valentinian, in joint rule, has just acceded to the throne, and he invites the Saxons to come to the aid of the Britons. The identification of the Saxon leaders as Hengist and Horsa seems spurious, another borrowing from Bede, which has led to the erroneous connection of these two Saxon leaders with only the third *Adventus.* More accurately, Hengist and Horsa were the leaders of the second *Adventus;* then as the *HB* narrates, Hengist asks for more warriors and fighting men from his country, and another envoy is sent for and arrives, it being the third *Adventus.* As detailed in *The Historic King Arthur,* Hengist and Horsa, therefore, are the leaders of the last two *Adventi.*

All of this information about Vortigern's *persona* seems to be evasive, since the question of who Vortigern was still has not been answered; we know who he was *not,* but now the inquiry has to shift the focus slightly. The name of Vortigern appears in only one other entry of the *ASC,* that for the year of 455. But the Vortigern of this entry has a different flavoring; whereas in the entry of 449 Vortigern has an empirical quality about him, in this entry he is definitely directly associated with the Briton/Saxon conflict on the island. Because there is no record of Valentinian personally ever having been in Britain, this, then, must be a reference to the Welsh (Briton) king. The first reaction might be that this entry, like that of 449, is again a direct derivative from Bede, which is exactly what Plummer indicates.

However, Plummer devotes his entire explanation of the entry to the geographic location of Ægælesthrep, and hence overlooks one jarring discrepancy. The *HB* emphasizes that after the death of Vortimer (Vortigern's son), Vortigern was still friends with the Saxons because of his concubine Rowena, and the Briton king did not want to drive the Saxons from Britain.[49] Nowhere in the *HB* is there ever war between *Vortigern* and the Saxons, which means, then, that the *ASC* does not draw upon Bede as its source for entry 455, but instead is almost a verbatim paraphrase of material from the *HB.* It is *Vortimer,* not Vortigern, who wars against the Saxons; the second battle between the two was at a place called Episford in the Saxon language and Rhyd yr afael in Welsh, where "fell Horsa and also Vortigern's son Cateyrn."[50]

As a comparison, the *ASC* entry has some interesting variations. It reports that

> In this year [455] Hengest and Horsa fought against king Vortigern at a place which is called Agælesthrep and his brother Horsa was slain. And after that Hengest succeeded to the kingdom and Æsc, his son.[51]

The geographic location changes from Episford to Agælesthrep, but most significant is the shift from the name Vortimer to Vortigern.

Typical in the quest for Arthur's historicity, one question is answered by the formulation of another question. In this instance, the initial question is, "Who is Vortigern?" and in attempting to clarify that issue, another question arises, "Who is Vortimer?" The enigma of Vortimer is addressed in the next chapter, but several comments about him merit attention here. The first reaction is to claim that the epithet "Vortimer" is a simple variant of "Vortigern," but this can be rejected almost immediately. Vortimer represents the opposite end of the continuum from Vortigern. Whereas Vortimer detests the Saxons and tries to drive them permanently from the island, Vortigern is in league with the Saxons and has an affinity with them as allies, even after some severe conflicts have almost driven them apart. Realizing a distinction between Vortimer and Vortigern, a process of elimination must apply to the most-likely historical figure for Vortigern. That task is very difficult because of the four major ancient manuscripts, Vortimer appears only in the *HB*, which lists Vortigern's line as follows:

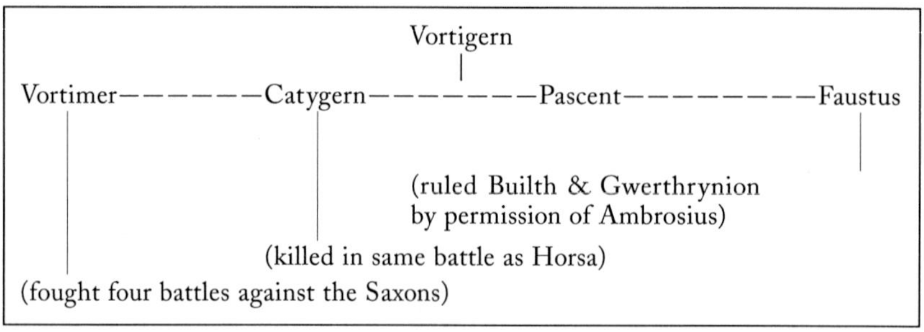

Catygern, Vortigern's second son by his first wife, is recorded not only in the *HB*, but also in the *ASC*, and on Eliseg's Pillar. He likewise appears in Monmouth's manuscript as Katigern, and, as in the *HB* and the *ASC*, he and Horsa are both killed, although Monmouth adds the detail that they kill each other in hand-to-hand combat. Vortigern's third son, Pascent, also appears in the *HB*, on the Pillar, and in Monmouth's manuscript as Paschent.

Yet Vortimer, who has a major role in the *HB*, does not appear on Eliseg's Pillar, at least not by that designation. Monmouth echoes the information from the *HB* that Vortimer fought four successful battles against the Saxons and that he asks to be buried according to specific instructions, which are disobeyed. The *HB* simply records that Vortimer died, but Monmouth elaborates that Vortimer's stepmother Renwein (Hengist's daughter) plots his death because of envy; she learns about noxious poisons, and then, by the hands of one of her servants through a bribe, she has him poisoned.

The contradictions which cloak the personage of Vortimer veil a mystifying story. Because Vortigern shunned the *Britanni's* advice, he was deposed and Vortimer was elevated to the kingship. Vortimer was loved by the Britons, and in four battles against the Saxons he proved himself to be an excellent military leader. He drove the Saxons from the land in spite of King Vortigern siding with the enemy. After the Saxons had departed for Germany, Vortimer began to return to the Britons possessions which had been torn from them. Affection and honor bound the leader and his people.

There are three variants of the *HB* which contain detailed additions of Vortimer's virtue and excellence, manuscripts I, K, and L.[52] The essence of the extended passages tells of the honorable Vortimer, proclaimed for his goodness by the multitude, accepting the kingship and stemming the tide of the Saxon onslaught. In savage combat he overthrew and destroyed his adversaries, and for a period of five years after the last battle, no enemy dared enter the island until after the downfall and destruction of Vortimer. This high praise of Vortimer sounds very much like Gildas's praise of Ambrosius Aurelianus in the *DE,* leading of course to the common conjecture that the *HB* is simply echoing the Gildas manuscript. Based upon this, R. H. Fletcher observes that the "Vortimer of Nennius practically replaces the Ambrosius of Gildas."[53]

As attractive as it is to forge a connection between the *persona* of Vortimer and that of Ambrosius, there are several items which prevent an easy link, the most notable being Vortimer's death. For those who ascribe to the belief that Arthur was a separate entity who inherited the Briton throne from Ambrosius, this presents no problem; Vortimer could conceivably have died at the end of the fourth or beginning of the fifth decade of the 400s. But even that theory presents a new problem: The *HB* relates that after Vortimer's death, Vortigern re-ascended to the throne, which is contrary to the histories claiming that if, in fact, Arthur and Ambrosius are two separate figures, then there was *not* an intermediate ruler between their two reigns.

If the premise is accepted that the term "Arthur" is an epithet for Ambrosius, as proposed in the *HKA,* then there are several ambiguities in the original Latin which could lead to different interpretations, touched upon in the next chapter. One other ambiguity, however, is the section describing the demise of Vortimer which is phrased as "...*usque ad obitum Guorthemir.*"[54] The Latin term *obitum* is normally associated with death, but two other common meanings are "downfall" or "destruction," as opposed to a later passage describing Vortimer's death as "...*Factum est autem post mortem Guorthemir...*"[55] meaning "now after the death of Vortimer...," the second passage leaving no doubt that the translation must be "death."

One of the peculiarities of Vortimer's death is the contradictory reports between the *HB* and the Welsh Triads. Both manuscripts relate that Vortimer was beloved by the Briton people. Before Vortimer died, he told his followers to construct his tomb in the port from where his enemies, the Saxons, had fled. If his followers were to do that, he guaranteed them that "[w]herever else [the Saxons] may hold a British port or may have settled, they will never again live in this land."[56] But then there is the very curious addition: "But [the Britons who loved him] ignored his command and did not bury him where he had told them"; the question of why the Britons would do that is left unanswered.

Unlike so many questions which arise about the Dark Ages and remain maddening enigmas, however, two of the Welsh Triads supply an answer. The first series is this:

> Three Fortunate Concealments of the Island of Britain:
> 1. The head of Brân the Blessed son of Llyr, which was concealed in the White Hill in London, with its face towards France. And while it was in the position in which it had been put there, no Saxon oppression ever came to this Island.
> 2. The second Fortunate Concealment: the Dragons which Lludd son of Beli concealed in Dinas Emreis.
> 3. And the third, the Bones of Gwerthefyr the Blessed (Vortimer) in the chief ports of this Island; and while they were in that concealment, no Saxon oppression ever came to this Island.

Bypassing any attempt to interpret the symbolism, the third item of this triad shows that the Britons did, in fact, respect the wishes of their beloved leader. Again bypassing any attempt of interpretation, a different set of Triads furnishes the reason that the Saxons were able to return:

> The Three Unfortunate Disclosures:
> 1. Gwrtheyrn the Thin (Vortigern) disclosed the bones of Gwerthefyr the Blessed [Vortimer] for the love of a woman; this was she, Ronnwen [Renwein, Rowena—Hengist's daughter] the pagan.
> 2. And [Vortigern] also disclosed the dragons.
> 3. And Arthur disclosed the head of Brân the Blessed from the White Hill, since he did not desire that this Island should be guarded by anyone's strength but his own.[57]

Vortigern, then, breaks the power of this oracular prediction and once again allows the Saxons into the island. The *HB* then conflates with the Triads by recording that "[T]he barbarians returned in force, for Vortigern was their friend, because of his wife, and none was resolute to drive them out."[58] When Monmouth's narrative appears, some new details have been added: out of envy and hatred Renwein poisoned Vortimer, and when Vortimer knew his end was near, he exhorted the Britons to construct a bronze pyramid as his tomb to frighten off any Saxon invaders, but the Britons did not honor the request. These new twists seemingly indicate that Monmouth drew upon the

Triads for the information about Renwein's role, but fell back upon the *Historia Brittonum's* version that the Britons did not honor Vortimer's request.

Even after amassing all these details, it is exceedingly difficult to draw any firm conclusions. One point, however, emerges as implausible: It is unlikely that "Vortimer" is an epithet for Ambrosius, not only because historical death-years do not match, but also because Ambrosius's reign was not an intervention with Vortigern's rule. Likewise, a later passage in the *HB* further supports the infeasibility that Vortimer can be equated with Ambrosius. As indicated in Table 7 of Vortigern's line, Pascent was Vortigern's third son. The important sentence in Chapter 48 on this particular issue states that Pascent ruled two countries in Britain, Buelt and Guorthigirniaun, after his father's death, by permission of Ambrosius, who was the great king among all the kings of the British nation.[59] The name Vortimer cannot be substituted for Ambrosius in this passage; Vortimer *preceded* his father in death, Vortigern *preceded* Ambrosius in death, and Ambrosius then became the great king of all kings in Britain.

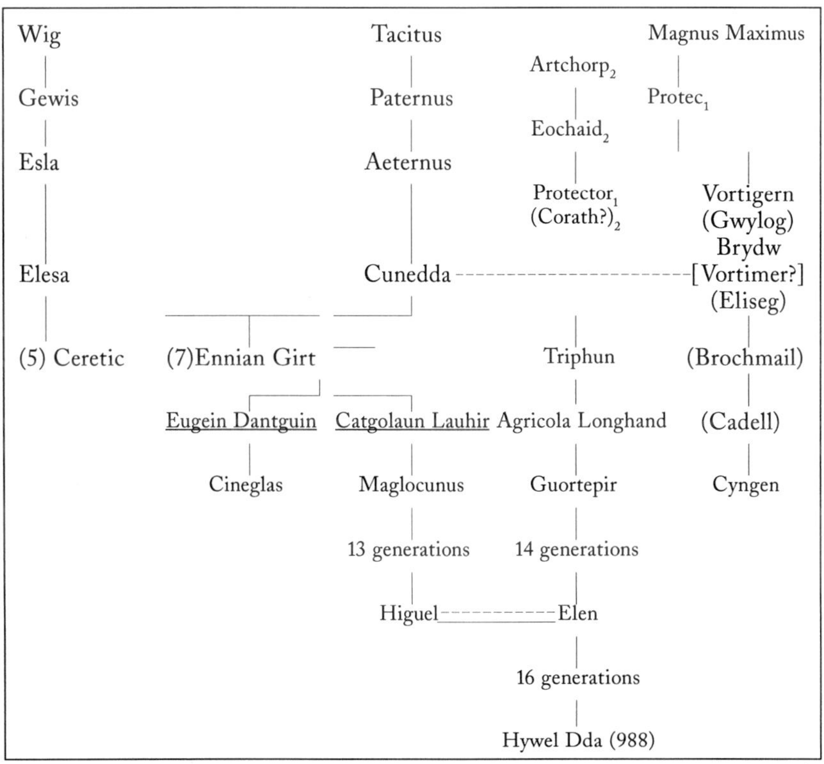

Table 6—Genealogical table combining information from *The Anglo-Saxon Chronicle*, the Welsh Chronicles and Genealogies, and Eliseg's Pillar.

As stated earlier, the name of Vortimer appears in only one of the four major historical documents of the period, the *HB*. The difficulty of tracing names and ancestry is monumentally compounded during this particular segment of history and at this particular crossroad in Britain. The *HKA* touches upon the convoluted blending of languages during this era: Latin, Breton, Brittisc, Wilsc, and *Saxones*, which in itself combined Saxons, Angles, and Frisians, all part of the complexity in piecing together the events of the period, as analyzed by Charles Plummer.[60] One individual could be referred to by his proper name, a nickname, a title, an epithet, an alias, or an appository descriptor, each with spelling variants. Combined with five or six language divergences, this could conceivably (and unknowingly to future researchers) lead to as many as thirty possible appellations for *one* person.

Photograph 2—Eliseg's Pillar, near Llangollen and Valle Crucis.

One such appositive for Vortimer given in the *HB* and carried over to the Welsh Triads and Monmouth's *History of the Kings of Britain* is "Vortimer, *Blessed by Saint Germanus.*" Using this appositive to identify Vortimer, an interesting conjecture arises about a specific inscription on Eliseg's Pillar. The appellation Gwrthemir (Vortimer) does not appear, but Line 8 on the Pillar, which was gratuitously still legible when Edward Lhuyd translated the inscription in 1696, reads

> But Brydw was the son of Gwrtheyrn [Vortigern], whom Germanus blessed and who was born to him by Severa, the daughter of Maximus the king, who slew the King of the Romans [Gratian].[61]

There is accord in all sources, therefore, that Brydw is unquestionably equated with the epithet Vortimer, confirmed by the expression "blessed by Germanus." Brydw would not yet have acquired the title of Vortimer (Overking) because *Vortigern* was still Overlord and Brydw was a prince next in line as heir to the throne.

For this period, then, there are only a finite number of bona fide historical figures who can be identified by the epithet "Vortimer." By blending several separate genealogies for Table 6, some very interesting observations emerge. The first column shows Cerdic's genealogy as a West-Saxon king in conjunction with that of his Briton/Welsh father, Cunedda. The third column is Cunedda's Welsh genealogy, and the last two columns are the variants of Magnus Maximus's offspring. Jacob Hammer provides the explicit details,[62] but upon close examination of two disparate documents linked, one principal postulation emerges, with logical satellite strings attached to it. Based upon the chronology of *Tysilio* devised by Hammer, Vortimer rises to the kingship in 434, ± two years, suggesting a birth year of 400, ± two years. Independent of Hammer's calculations, the *HKA* separately established Cunedda's floruit as 435–465 and his life span as 420–480. Even by using these general guidelines, the match in the rise to kingship is almost ideal. Cunedda's initial primary directive is to rid the island of the *Scotti,* but after that victory, instead of the island healing itself, it is then torn apart by savage conflict with their allies, the Saxons. Hence, both Cunedda and Vortimer would turn against the Saxons and drive them from the land.

The parallels then pervade the entire blended chronology. Brydw would be known more commonly as Vortimer, and Vortimer would most commonly be known as Cunedda. Because Cunedda's son Cerdic allied himself with the Saxons and became a powerful king, Cunedda is listed as Elesa in the Saxon genealogies, a very close parallel to the inscription of Eliseg on the Pillar. Cunedda's Latin father Æternus would bear the Welsh epithet Vortigern, the Over-King, known to the Saxons as Esla. The heretofore unidentified title of Protector would logistically apply to Æternus who would be under the direct command of the *superbus tyrannus,* Valentinian III. This in turn would explain the epithet for Paternus Red-Robe as Protec, who had Roman authority just below the rank of the Caesarean purple. Paternus, too, would be the authority or king of the entire Gewissae tribe, which ranged in the lower midlands just south of the Cornovii territory, thus giving rise to the name Gewis which the Saxons bestowed upon him.

The offspring from Cunedda forward also fit the pattern. Cerdic, Enniaun Girt and their other brothers are of the same generation as Triphun and

Brochmail; similarly, Eugein Dantguin, Catgolaun Lauhir, Agricola Longhand, and Cadell are of a close generation. The next generation, tying together Cineglas, Maglocunus, and Guortepir, are verified by the castigations in Gildas's *DE.* As it stands, Brochmail and Cadell listed in this comparison cannot be the same individuals recorded in the *Annales Cambriae,* since Brochmail and Cadell are listed as father/son, but in the *Annales Cambriae,* Brochmail's death is listed in 662 and the earliest Cador's death-year is given as 808, a separation of 146 years.

Based, then, upon several skimpy scraps of information, at this point Vortimer appears to be an epithet for the great Cunedda, who migrated from the north to rid the island of the *Scotti,* who in the process became embroiled in the battles against the Saxons. When he was eventually killed, by a method related only in the *Historia Brittonum,* there was just a short period of peace before the Saxons returned upon the direction of the Protector, also known as Vortigern and Æternus. After the deposal of Vortigern, the great king Ambrosius ascends to the throne following several years in exile, and the internal strife erupts again with fury. Britons such as Cerdic and his offspring align themselves with Octha and the English Saxons in back-and-forth conflicts for supremacy through twelve extensive battles. Simultaneously, wars rage on the continent as the disintegrating Western Roman Empire tries to hold the barbarians at bay. After literally decades of bloodshed, Arthurex Ambrosius is mortally wounded and Briton dominance cracks and begins to crumble. Both the old and the post-Roman system gives way to the rise of a new order.

Until firmer and broader-based clues manifest themselves, this seems to be the most comprehensive scenario which can be constructed at this time. Alcock sums it up well when he comments that these genealogical charts can contribute no more about Vortigern until "the essential work of source analysis has ... been carried out."[63] Comments by Acton Griscom, Flinders Petrie, and Jacob Hammer further admonish that much work has to be done in precise translations of the *Tysilio,* the Welsh Triads, and all of the versions of *The History of the Kings of Britain* before the neglected history of Britain can be rectified.

Conclusions

Table 7 will aid in following the events as proposed throughout this chapter. The most important consideration in determining if the sequence is feasible is to study the overlapping chronologies of those historical figures involved.

Table 7—Summary of historical figures and the sources for them.

Name or Epithet	*Floruit/ Life span*	*Name Variants/ Miscellaneous Info*	*Sources by abbreviations*
Æternus/ s. Paternus	405–435 390–450	Æternus, Etern	Welsh Genealogies, *Book of Taliessin*
Aëtius	b.396– d.454	Flavius Aëtius/ Chief advisor to Galla Placidia	Roman Genealogies, *DE*
Agricola Longhand/ s. Triphun	527–557 512–572	Vortiporus's father	*WG*, Expulsion of the Dessi, *DE*, Vortiporius Stone
Ambrosius Aurelianus	455–485 422–518	Aurelius Ambrosius, Arthur, Riardd Ambrosius	*DE*, *HB*, *HKB*, *HKA*
Brydw	435–465 420–480	son of Vortigern, unlisted in other sources	Eliseg's Pillar
Catgolaun Lauhir/ s. Enniaun Girt	497–527 482–542	brother of Eugein Dantguin (Owein)	WG
Catygern	435–465 420–480	second son of Vortigern, killed in 455	Eliseg's Pillar, *HB*, *ASC*, *HKB*
Cerdic/ s. Cunedda	465–495 450–510	Ceretic, Ceredig, Cherdic, Cheldric, Chelric, Cordyck/ king of the West Saxons, interpreter for Vortigern	*WG*, *HB*, *ASC*, Genealogical Preface *HKB*, John of Glastonbury
Cineglas/ s. Eugein Dantguin	527–557 512–572	first cousin of Maglocunus	WG, *DE*
Constans I	b.320– d.350	Emperor from 337-350, killed his brother Constantine II in 340, overthrown by Magnentius	RG
Constantine II	b.317– d.361	Emperor from 337-361—Asia, Egypt, defeats Magnentius for Constans I's share, become sole emperor.	RG
Constantine III/ s. Cador Duke of Cornwall		Succeeds Arthur as High King, kills Mordred's two sons, equated with one of the tyrants in the *De excidio*.	*HKB*, *DE*
Constantinus	d.411	usurper; full name = Flavius Claudius Constantinus, called Constantine. Common soldier, emperor 406-407. Executed by Honorius in 411.	RG
Constantius (III)	d.421	Identified only as a member of a noble Roman family, he became master of the soldiers under Honorius. In 411 distinguished himself by defeating usurpers. Married Galla Placidia, Honorius's sister, in 417, appointed co-emperor in 421, died September of that same year	RG, *HB* Sects. 27 & 66. Erroneously indexed by J. Morris in *BH* as Constantine III.

Table 7—*continued.*

Name or Epithet	*Floruit/ Life span*	*Name Variants/ Miscellaneous Info*	*Sources by abbreviations*
Corath			
Creoda/ s. Cerdic	495–525 480–540	Creuddyn, one of the generations omitted from *The Anglo-Saxon Chronicle*	GP, *ASC*
Cunedda/ s. Aeternus	435–465 420–480	Father of Cerdic and Enniaun Girt, from Manau Gododdin, settles in Wales.	WG, *HB*
Cynric/ s. Creoda	525–555 510–570	later King of the West Saxons	*ASC*, GP
Elesa/ s. Esla	435–465 420–480	Grandfather of Cerdic in the Anglo-Saxon genealogies	*ASC*, GP
Enniaun Girt/ s. Cunedda	467–497 452–512	Brother of Cerdic, father of Eugein Dantguin, grandfather of Cuneglases	WG, *HB*
Esla/ s. Gewis	405–435 390–450		*ASC*, GP
Eugein Dantguin/ s. Enniaun Girt	497–527 482–542	Eugein, Owein/ one of Arthur's adversaries at the Battle of Badon	*DE*, WG, *M*, *HKA*
Galla Placidia	405–435 390–450 b.388–d.450	sister of Honorius Flavius, wife of Constantius III, mother of Valentinian III	RG
Gewis	375–405 360–420	great-grandfather of Cerdic	*ASC*, GP
Hengist	428–458 413–473	co-chieftain w/ br. Horsa *Adventi 1 & 2* co-chieftain w/ s. Octha, d. 473	*ASC*, GP, *HB*, *HKB*, *HKA*
Honorius Flavius	b.384–d.423	Brother of Galla Placidia, brother-in-law of Constantius III, uncle of Valentinian III	RG
Horsa	d.455	co-chieftain with Hengist, *Adventi 1 & 2*, killed in 455	*ASC*, GP, *HB*, *HKB*, *HKA*
Maglocunus	527–557 512–572	Maelgwn, Maglo, Maglocunus, Maglocunu, Mailcun, Mailcon, Mailcunus/ king of Gwynedd	*DE*, *AC*, *HB*, *HKB*
Magnus Maximus	365–395 350–410	Magnus Clemens Maximus, usurper, d. 383	RG, Eliseg's Pillar, WG, M
Octha/ s. Hengist	452–482 437–497	co-chieftain 455-473; sole chieftain 473-497, d. 497 Battle of Badon	*ASC*, GP, *HKA*, *M*, *HKB*, *HB*
Pascent/ s. Vortigern	435–465 420–480	granted kingdoms of Builth and Gwerthrynion by Ambrosius, who was the great king among all the kings of Britain.	*HB*, Eliseg's Pillar, *HKB*
Paternus/ s. Tacitus	375–405 360–420	Patern Pesrut, Paternus of the Red Robe, grandfather of Cunedda	WG
Probus, Marcus Aurelius	b.232–d.282	succeeded Marcus Tacitus to throne; fought in Gaul, Britain in 280	RG
Tacitus	345–375 330–390	great-grandfather of Cunedda	WG

Table 7—*continued.*

Name or Epithet	*Floruit/ Life span*	*Name Variants/ Miscellaneous Info*	*Sources by abbreviations*
Tacitus, Marcus Claudius	b.200–d.276	ruled after Aurelian, Gothicus Maximus	RG
Valentinian III	b.419–d.455	*superbus tyrannus*, ruled 425-455, Galla Placidia = regent, killed his general Aëtius in 454.	*DE*, RG
Vortigern	405–435 390–450	First Briton King after Roman abandonment	*HB*, Eliseg's Pillar, Easter Tables, *ASC*
Vortimer/ s. Vortigern	435–465 420–480	Alleged son of Vortigern, fought four great battles against the Saxons	*HB*
Vortiporus/ s. Agricola Longhand	527–557 512–572	One of five tyrants castigated by Gildas	Vortiporius Stone, *DE*

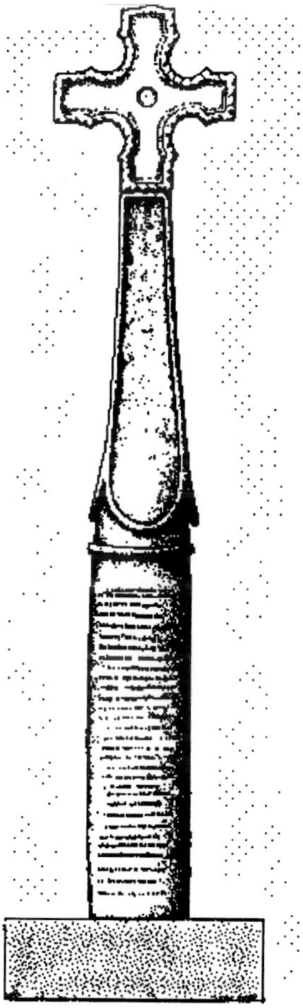

Drawing—The original structural design of Eliseg's Pillar. According to Jeremy K Knight, the cross was toppled during the Civil War and broken into two pieces. The upper shaft of the cross was re-erected and stood at an approximate height of twenty feet, but it was once again destroyed and never reconstructed.

Edward Llwyd translated the cross inscription, which by 1696 was badly weathered. It tells of Cyngen son of Cadell son of Brochwel son of Eliseg son of Gwylog. Also recorded are the names of Cattegirn, Pasgen, Brydw, Gwrtheyrn, Germanus, Severa, Maximus, and Cynfarch.

This information is printed at the back of the "Valle Crucis Abbey" booklet published by Cadw Welsh Historic Monuments.

5

Vortimer and Vitalinus: Arthurian Enigmas

Vortimer

Vortimer, or the synonymous name Guorthemir with variable spellings for both, is one of the most enigmatic characters in the *Historia Brittonum*. Curiously, his name is recorded in this historic manuscript only; Gildas in the *De Excidio* does not name Vortimer, nor does Bede, who for the most part echoes Gildas. Likewise, neither *The Anglo-Saxon Chronicle* nor the *Annales Cambriae* record such a historical figure. Normally there is a strong connection between the *De Excidio* and the *Historia Brittonum*, the former functioning as the outline and the latter providing the details, but in this instance it seems that either the *HB* was using some other unknown independent source, or that later interpolaters added (or changed) the material about Vortimer.

However, what is missing from the histories is detailed in Monmouth's narrative. As a lead-in to the role of Vortimer, Monmouth borrowed the introductory material from Chapter 36 of the *HB*. It gives only a passing mention of Hengist's daughter, but Monmouth elaborates upon the banquet. Hengist's beautiful daughter is identified by name, Renwein, who solicits advances from the king. Whereas the *HB* just briefly explains that Satan entered Vortigern's heart and made him covet the girl, the Monmouth account stresses that this was a major travesty because the king was a Christian and she was a pagan. This causes the deep rift between the Britons and their king and irreversible enmity between the king and his three sons, particularly Vortimer and Katigern.

To intensify the great chasm which has split the *Britanni* from the *Saxones*, Monmouth points not only to the corruption brought on by the king's association with a pagan concubine, but he cites also the Pelagian heresy poisoning the country, recorded in Bede's manuscript of several centuries earlier. The Britons are incensed that even more Germans are invited over and, because they are terrified by the prospect of a treasonable revolt, they pressure Vortigern to force the intruders to return to the continent. But because of his concubine, Vortigern "loved the Saxons above all other folk."[1] The Britons therefore immediately desert Vortigern and elevate Vortimer to the kingship. Unlike the *HB*, which makes no attempt whatsoever to explain Vortigern's deposal and Vortimer's rise, Monmouth's account thus provides the rationale of why Vortimer's rule intersperses that of Vortigern's.

Monmouth then turns once again to the *HB* and borrows the narrative of Vortimer's four battles against the *Saxones*. After Vortimer's successes, Monmouth adds details of his own. Vortimer is blessed by the Britons and Saint Germanus for restoring lands to the Britons, but Renwein plots the new king's death. She studies noxious poisons, and then through bribery convinces one of Vortimer's servants to administer a fatal dose to the king. Vortimer dies, and similar to the story related in the *HB* about the king's burial wishes, Monmouth writes basically the same thing, but adds more detail and changes the burial site from Lincoln to Trinovantum, a reference to London.

Vortigern is restored to the kingship and invites Hengist back into Britain. Through an elaborate account, Monmouth narrates that Hengist returns with 300,000 warriors, then treacherously betrays the Briton king, slaughters the Council at the Cloister of Ambris, and ransoms the king for territories, cities, and fortresses. Vortigern seeks advice from his magicians, then flees to northern Wales near Beddgelert, where the story about Emrys unfolds.

R. H. Fletcher approaches the issue of Vortimer by using the Chartres manuscript, a fragment pre-dating the Nennius manuscript and lacking the details of the *HB*, which stops where a deal is being struck between Vortigern and Hengist for Rowena (Renwein), the Saxon's daughter. In making comparisons between the *HB* and the *DE*, he formulates several interesting postulations, beginning with a comment on the noticeable variance already cited that "Guorthemir [Vortimer] practically replaces the Ambrosius of Gildas."[2] After pointing out the incongruities in the *HB* and granting that the Nennius story includes Ambrosian material but only in subordinate and inconsistent notices, he writes, "From these facts is seems not unreasonable to surmise that Nennius's story is that of the British faction in the island, as opposed to the Roman faction of Gildas...."[3]

Inevitably, this engenders an analysis of the word "Vortimer," which, not surprisingly, reveals the word as another epithet, something quite common in the quest for Arthur's origins. Ashe notes that

> In the form Vortigern the syllable *vor* means "over," the rest is "king" or "chieftain." Vortigern was the overking. While historians accept him as real, his son Vortimer, who Geoffrey [of Monmouth] portrays as briefly taking [Vortigern's] place, is viewed with more skepticism. ... The British original of Vortimer would have

> been Vortamorix. The *vor* is the same syllable as before, meaning "over"; *tamo* is the superlative suffix like the English "-est"; and *rix,* akin to the Latin *rex,* is another word for "king." So Vortimer means "over-most" or "highest" king. It is a different expression of the same paramountcy.[4]

Ashe is not implying that Vortigern and Vortimer refer to the same individual, but instead is saying that they have similar titles. The important realization is that it is *not* a proper name; the word "Vortimer," like "Vortigern," is an epithet.

Even without a great deal of psychic ability, it is simple to determine the next step in the procedure: Identify Vortimer. Although the step is simple, the identification isn't. Like an apparition, Vortimer mysteriously appears from nowhere; with no introduction or explanation, he simply materializes as a distinctively separate figure. The *HB* asserts that Vortimer's reign interrupted Vortigern's, but when Vortimer died, Vortigern once again became the ruler. This in itself is an assurance that there is not a confusion of the same titles, but there are two distinctive individuals. More consequential is that Vortimer is a bitter enemy of the Saxons, and Vortigern is unswervingly allied with them. The *Historia Brittonum* narrates in Chapter 43 that Vortimer, Vortigern's son, hated the Saxons and fought against their leaders, Hengist and Horsa. When he had expelled the enemies from the land, the English Saxons sent to Germany for warriors to fight against the Welsh, "sometimes victoriously advancing their frontiers, sometimes being defeated and expelled."[5]

Most versions of the *HB* are abrupt and unavailing about Vortimer's inception, but fortuitously there are three versions of Chapter 44 which offer some clarification. Version K has the explanation added in the margin, but versions I and L contain the information in the body of the text.[6] These versions provide the reason why Vortigern is deposed: The king incestuously defiles his own daughter and when they are confronted by Saint Germanus, they flee. Vortimer, an honorable and trustworthy man, accepts the kingship with the support of the multitude, and vows to drive the villainous Saxons from the shores of Britain. He breaks the spirit of the powerful, hostile forces and they take flight. They are expelled from Britain and for a period of five years afterwards, they dared not return, until the death of Vortimer. The three versions then merge with the other variants and relate the four battles of Vortimer against the Saxons.

In the *HB* there are no details about Vortimer's passing, but Saint Germanus blessed him in his prayers, another indication that Vortimer is not Vortigern since Saint Germanus and Vortigern were mortal enemies. It is Geoffrey of Monmouth several centuries later who supplies some of the details of Vortimer's death, specifics which must have come from the mysterious *liber vetustissimus,* since there aren't any other sources which record this narrative.

The *HB* continues that after Vortimer's death "The barbarians returned in force, for Vortigern was their friend..." and "it came to pass ... [that the Saxons] sent envoys to ask for peace and make a permanent treaty."[7] Vortigern agreed, Hengist treacherously killed all the Council of Elders, took Vortigern as hostage, and bartered for great tracts of land, including Essex, Middlesex, and Sussex. Thus was the destruction of Britain woven.

The *HB* refers to Vortimer twice as Vortigern's son, once in Chapter 43, where it is unceremoniously divulged that Vortigern's son Vortimer drives out the Saxons, and then again in Chapter 48, where a genealogical statement notes that Vortigern had three sons, one who was Vortimer. Nevertheless, most scholars do not view Vortimer as a historic figure. R. H. Fletcher is an exception. After writing about Vortimer's role in the *HB,* plus parallels in the *ASC* even though Vortimer is not named, Fletcher concludes that "...it does not seem very unreasonable that Vortigern, Vortimer, Ambrosius, and Arthur were real men who fought against the invaders."[8]

John Morris, too, views Vortimer as a real and separate entity, but goes into much more detail than Fletcher. Early in *The Age of Arthur* he directly quotes that Vortimer fought against Hengist and Horsa and expelled them (from where?) for five years. He uses as his source Chapter 43 of the *HB,* which he himself had edited and translated in 1980, but there is no mention that the Saxons were expelled from Kent, nor that it was for a period of five years. Putting this aside, though, he devotes a segment equating three battles from the *HB* with three battles listed in the *ASC,* reversing the order and modifying the dates. This would approximately set Vortimer's brief span during the fifth decade of the fifth century. Morris's speculations are interesting, but if accepted, negate the time frame given by Gildas, who relates that there was no intervening king or intervening time between Vortigern's reign and Ambrosius's rise to power.

Leslie Alcock, on the other hand writes

> [Ambrosius's, Vortigern's and Arthur's] claim to historicity is based on contemporary or near-contemporary notices: of Ambrosius by Gildas, of Vortigern in the *calculi* at the head of the British Easter Table compiled in 455, and of Arthur in the British Easter Annals.[9]

Alcock asserts several lines later that "In this sense, Ambrosius is the touchstone to prove the genuineness of Arthur."[10] Explicitly absent is the name of Vortimer, in diametric opposition to what R. H. Fletcher supposed. Alcock's viewpoint carries conviction, though, because Vortigern's name was recorded in the *calculi* and Vortimer's name was not. In addition to Alcock, who was quite familiar with the *HB* but still did not acknowledge Vortimer, Richard Barber bypasses that name in *Arthur of Albion* and refers to him only through Nennius in *The Figure of Arthur.* Also, E. K. Chambers in *Arthur of Britain* gives the name of Vortigern but writes nothing of a Vortimer or a Guothimer.

In response to the simple question of "Who, then, is the real person behind Vortimer's epithet?," the simple theoretical answer is most commonly "Ambrosius Aurelianus." Before probing this as a probability other than the one proposed in the preceding chapter, it must be remembered that Gildas, as the original source, does not name Vortigern, Vortimer, Hengist, Horsa, or Arthur; he was very stingy with proper names, as though he were deliberately plotting to confound future generations. He writes of the *superbus tyrannus*, which was later translated as Vortigern, an epithet that has been dealt with in Chapter 3.

In *King Arthur's Avalon,* Geoffrey Ashe makes a general observation that epithets are rampant in Arthurian history. In reference to this commonplace occurrence, he writes,

> Very possibly Nennius has lumped together several separate items under the single evocative name of Arthur. But the likelihood of a certain correspondence to fact can scarcely be dodged.[11]

In *The Discovery of King Arthur,* Ashe raises questions about the confusion between proper names and epithets, rhetorically inquiring about Riothamus and Vortimer.[12] In light of all that has been written in Chapter 1 of this text, it is more accurate to state that "Nennius has lumped together several separate items under the single evocative name of *Ambrosius.*" Riothamus has fallen into the category, and it is worth a check to see if it applies to Vortimer.

There are several conditions which must be retained in order to effectively speculate about the Vortimer/Ambrosius equation. For one, the emendations in Chapter 1, including the misleading headings provided by translations of the *HB,* must be considered as accurate. The battles attributed to Vortimer in Chapter 43 are listed incorrectly under the title of "The Kentish Chronicle, Part 3." Rather than starting his battles as the beginning of a new section, the *HB* must be considered as a continuation without headings. And to view it in this perspective leads to several oddities which must be re-thought.

Chapter 42 is the section about Ambrosius defying Vortigern's wizards. It ends by Ambrosius identifying himself and Vortigern becoming so intimidated and terrified that he gives the fortress and all of the kingdoms of the western part of Britain to Ambrosius. The king then flees to the northern part of Gwynessi, where he will build a city called by his name, Caer Gwrtheyrn. Chapter 43 begins with the word *interea* (Latin), which has been translated by John Morris as "meanwhile," and by J. A. Giles as "at length." Extracted from *Nennii: Historia Brittonum* by Stevenson,[13] the passage I've translated is a key factor in pursuing Vortimer's identification.

> [Interea], Vortigern's son Vortimer fought vigorously against Hengest and Horsa and their people, and expelled them as far as the aforesaid island of Tanet, and there three times shut them up

> and besieged them, attacking, threatening, and terrifying them. So they sent envoys overseas to Germany to summon keels with a vast number of fighting men. And afterwards they used to fight against the kings and chieftains of Britannicæ, sometimes victoriously advancing their frontiers, sometimes being defeated and expelled.

After a great deal of deliberation, *interea* is most accurately translated as "in the interim" rather than "meanwhile," "at length," "later," or "afterward." This gives rise to the question of "In the interim between what and what?" Viewing Chapters 42 and 43 as a continuation of the same narrative, it would have to be interpreted as "the interim between Vortigern granting Ambrosius his fortress plus all of the kingdoms of western Britain *and* the king's building a new city in northern Wales."

Because of the striking similarity of wording, Chapter 43 can be directly related to the *DE* of Gildas. After the Britons have rallied under the banner of Ambrosius Aurelianus, Gildas records in Chapter 26 that

> From then on victory went now to our countryman, now to their enemies ... right up till the year of the siege of Badon Hill....[14]

Chronologically, this would have been set, then, somewhere between the end of Vortigern's reign and victory of Mount Badon. This is a fairly wide time span, even for Dark-Age history, but a combination of clues from several sources help to narrow down the range.

Gildas's account is highly compacted and sometimes vague, but does list the three Saxon *Adventi* as proposed by Alcock, who sets the respective general dates as 428, 440, and 450. In Chapter 23 Gildas writes that Vortigern and his council invited the Saxons into Britain but does not name his ally's leaders. In the same Chapter, Section 3, he writes in a parabolic sentence that a pack of barbarians burst forth from their own country and came in three keels, first seizing lands on the east side of the island. That would have been the first wave. In Section 4, the second wave, larger and more aggressive, arrives after learning that the previous contingency succeeded. According to Gildas, when the second wave arrived, they asked for supplies, which were granted and "for a long time 'shut the dog's mouth.'"[15] The third *Adventus* occurs at the end of Vortigern's reign and the beginning of Ambrosius's leadership, when the Welsh once again challenge the English Saxons

In the *HB*, Book 31 does too much compacting; only one sentence is devoted to the first *Adventus:* "Then came three keels, driven into exile from Germany."[16] The very next sentence erroneously names Hengist and Horsa as the leaders of the first *Adventus* rather than the second. However, then, Chapter 3 correctly records the second invitation, allowing in "sixteen keels, with picked warriors in them, [and] in one of the keels came Hengest's daughter, a beautiful and very handsome girl."[17] Out of sequence contextually but chronologically correct, the *HB* also records, similar to the Gildas manuscript, that the English Saxons were encamped at the island of Thanet (after the first Adventus). Vortigern promised to supply them with food and clothing in return for the Saxons fighting against the Picts and Irish. But the Saxons "multiplied in numbers [probably during the second and third waves], and the British could not feed them."[18]

Vortigern bargains for Hengist's daughter in return for British kingdoms, which precipitates the third wave, and Hengist "invited Octha [his son] and Ebissa, with forty keels."[19] Material here is not as compacted as in the Gildas narrative, and tells three stories, one of Hengist's treachery and the massacre of the Council of the Province; a second of the life of Saint Germanus, including some of Vortigern's genealogy; and a third of the life of Saint Patrick. The narrative finally focuses upon the campaigns of Arthur; Horsa has been killed, Octha has come down from the north to rule jointly with his father, Vortigern has been deposed, and Arthur (i.e., Ambrosius incognito) has assumed leadership to fight the Saxon dogs, which is where Gildas left off his story about the third wave.

Once the point is reached where Arthur is named, it then becomes necessary to view that term as the epithet *Arthus,* the High King Ambrosius. Changing the emphasis of what has already been quoted earlier, Gildas writes this of *Ambrosius:*

> Under him our people regained their strength, and challenged the victors to battle....
>
> From then on the victory went now to our countrymen, now to their enemies....[20]

And Nennius copies this of *Vortimer,* who is interestingly spliced between the tale of Ambrosius and the campaigns of Arthur:[21]

> And afterwards [the Saxons] used to fight against the kings and chieftains of Britannicæ, sometimes victoriously advancing their frontiers, sometimes being defeated and expelled.[22]

The preliminary indication is that there does seem to be a substitution of the title Vortimer for the proper name Ambrosius Aurelianus, who precedes him, and Arthur, who follows him. Graham Phillips and Martin Keatman cite a translation of Eliseg's Pillar (an Ogham stone) by the Welsh antiquarian Edward Lhuyd in 1696 in an attempt to verify the historicity of Vortimer. In part (because the ellipses indicate the illegible segments on the stone), Lhuyd's translation has been deciphered as

> ... Maun, Annan: Britu[23] [Brittu, Brydw] moreover ... the son of Vortigern whom Germanus blessed and whom Severa bore to him, the daughter of Maximus, the king, who killed the king of the Romans....[24]

The co-authors are theorizing a host of items: first, that there were *two* Vortigerns, one who came to power in the mid–420s and the other in the late

440s, partially based upon the *Historia's* alleged reporting of two distinctive deaths for Vortigern; two, that because Pascent's name appears as a bona fide son in the *HB* and on the pillar of Eliseg that Vortimer is likewise a historic figure, even though his name does not appear on the stone; three, that a linking verb can be inserted between "Britu" and "Vortigern's son"; and four, that "Britu" is the proper name connected to the epithet "Vortimer."[25]

The theory that there were two Vortigerns has been proposed before, mainly based upon Chapter 49 of the *HB,* specifically the genealogy which follows the second "son of Pascent" listing. Some translations interpret the passage *Pascent, filii Guorthigirn, Guortheu, filii Guitataul* as "Pascent, son of Vortigern the Thin, son of Vitalis," while others interpret it as "Pascent, son of Vortigern, [son of] Guortheneu, son of Vitalis." The difficulty lies in the original manuscripts omitting *filii* (son of), thus either omitting a generation, or supplying a descriptor for Vortigern. There have also been postulations of two Ambrosiuses, but most scholars and researchers don't ascribe to either.

That Vortimer is Vortigern's son, and that Vortimer had two brothers named Cateyrn and Pascent, are viable propositions and must be seriously considered even though no other sources, such as the *DE,* the *Historia Ecclesiastica,* or the *ASC,* record anything about Vortimer. Nevertheless, Phillips and Keatman present a credible case that Britu could be the proper name behind the "Vortimer" epithet.[26] Britu is listed as the grandson of Magnus Maximus, and judging from his association with Germanus, the authors estimate Britu's reign commencing about 447, based upon the assumption that "Vortimer" was Britu's title before he followed his father as the successive overlord to the throne.

Earlier in Chapter 3 of this text, three separate genealogical lines allowed some interesting comparisons. In the explicit sense of the word, new and innovative parallels can be drawn showing a marked likeness in the development of several individuals in separate written contexts. One parallel—Cunedda and Vortimer (Brydw)—reveals matching characteristics. For one, Cunedda's floruit/life span as given in the *HKA* and Brydw's floruit as proposed by Phillips and Keatman are remarkably similar, especially when one considers that they were devised independently of each other and for different purposes. Based upon Cerdic's triadic roles in the histories (as Cunedda's son, Vortigern's interpreter and the West Saxon king), Cunedda's floruit was deemed to be 435 to 465, with a life span estimated as 420 to 480. If Phillips and Keatman's date of 447 for the beginning of Brydw's reign is accepted as a median, then Brydw's floruit would be 432 to 462, almost identical to Cunedda's. Secondly, both Cunedda's and Brydw's floruits fit well with Hengist's arrival in Britain, since Hengist's floruit/life span was calculated as 428–458/413–473. These leaders would all have been contemporaries.

Similarly, Vortigern would then become a match with Æternus, the

Roman name for Cunedda's father. The vast majority of scholars agree that "Vortigern" is an epithet, commonly translating to something like "over-king,"[27] suggesting that Æternus could be the proper name behind the title. Vortigern has been identified as a Briton with Roman ties, and Æternus is an excellent Romano-Briton candidate appointed as Protector by the Roman emperor of the West. If viewed from the perspective of the *ASC,* Æternus would be the parallel of Esla, Cerdic the Saxon's grandfather. Hence (spanning the *HB,* the Welsh genealogies and chronicles, including the inscription on Eliseg's Pillar, and the *ASC),* Cunedda, Elesa, and Vortimer would have been generational contemporaries preceded by Æternus, Esla, and Vortigern, who also were concurrent historical figures.

Moving away from the narrower view of British happenings and concentrating upon a broader scheme of history, a chronological set of events can be devised based upon an amalgam of the ancient existent sources. In the *DE* Gildas writes of the *superbus tyrannus* (a reference used only twice) accepting the *Saxones* as allies to protect the island against invasion and aggression by the *Scotti* and the Picts. Bede taints the history for all the succeeding generations by misidentifying the *superbus tyrannus,* a term which is applicable to a *supreme* ruler—that is, the supreme ruler of the Western Roman empire—not a sub-king on a smaller scale limited to just the island of Britain. In his history Gildas has just described the Roman withdrawal from Britain and a respite of attacks from the *Scotti* and Picts; he then writes that the Briton scars are healing over and that the island is being flooded with an abundance of goods, creating a growth of luxury. This occurs at the end of Honorius's reign, in Constantius III's interim just before Valentinian III's succession, during a period when the barbarian invaders were successfully contained or resettled according to Honorius's policy of partially-autonomous mercenary kingdoms. When Valentinian (or more accurately Galla Placidia) acquired the throne, the Roman policy of allowing some autonomy to the barbaric mercenaries was still in effect. Gildas is referring to this policy: The short-sighted *superbus tyrannus* (i.e., Valentinian) of the weakening Western empire had the temerity to invoke this policy in an attempt in Britain to "beat back the peoples of the north"[28] by inviting the ferocious German Saxons into the island.

On a more localized scale, a tribal "over-king," Vortigern, was in command on the island to enforce the policies of the *superbus tyrannus.* That over-king, although a Briton by birth, had Roman ancestry, identical to Cunedda's ethnology through Æternus, Paternus, and Tacitus. When Vortigern lost control of his allies and the *Saxones* were no longer submissive, he had to recruit the help of his son, who was an over-king but in a diminutive sense—perhaps an over-prince. Unlike his weak and ineffective father, however, this son, Vortimer, was a capable military leader who not only stemmed the flow of the *Scotti* and the Picts in the north, but also drove the *Saxones* back to their homelands. But Vortimer died shortly thereafter. The account in the

HB records that the Britons ignored Vortimer's burial request designed to deter future continental invasions. Unlike this display of disrespect, however, a Welsh triad demonstrates the Britons' love for Vortimer: The "bones of Gwerthefyr the Blessed (Vortimer) are [buried] in the chief ports of this Island"[29] and the locations are concealed so that his remains cannot be disinterred.

Vortimer is listed as having two other brothers, Categirn and Pascent. Categirn's name is recorded on Eliseg's Pillar and also in the *HB* and Monmouth's *HKB.* The *HB* relates that both Horsa and Catigern were killed in battle at Agælsthrep. The *ASC* also records the battle at Agælsthrep at entry 455, thus giving a year for the conflict, and recording Horsa's death but not Catigern's. Monmouth, though, elaborates upon the battle, writing that "Horsa and Katigern (the second son of Vortigern) met hand to hand and both died, for each was mortally wounded by the other."[30] Pascent is likewise memorialized on Eliseg's Pillar, and his name appears twice in the genealogies of the *HB.* Pascent, too, fought against the English Saxons, and afterwards "ruled in two countries called Builth and Gwerthrynion after his father's death, by permission of Ambrosius, who was the †great† king among all the kings of the British nation."[31] Pascent also appears in the *HKB,* but Monmouth's account is much different. Pascent, portrayed as pro-Saxon, stirs up the German Saxons against Ambrosius, fights with the Irish against the Britons, and is killed by Utherpendragon.[32]

This synopsis of Vortimer's two brothers serves a singular purpose. Understandably, Vortimer is an enigmatic, controversial figure, and it is hotly debated whether he was a bona fide historical figure, a confusing composite of Vortigern/Vortimer or of Ambrosius/Vortimer, or, lastly, whether he was Irish, Briton, or Saxon. Glancing at the milieu of the period, it seems highly unlikely that Vortimer was an invented character in the histories. One of his other brothers could have easily carried the role of a Vortimer, rather than perpetrating a hoax that was bound to be uncovered. Both Categirn and Pascent were heroes in their own rights, and their associations with verified characters such as Horsa, Hengist, and Ambrosius would have been much more easily verifiable than it would have been through a "manufactured" character. As a pro-Briton character, Categirn would have functioned well; if one had preferred Monmouth's version of Pascent, then a pro-Saxon hero would have worked well.

To follow up on what seems to be a probable connection between the epithet "Vortimer" and Ambrosius Aurelianus (Arthus Ambrosius), a re-check of the chronology from Chapter 1 is in order. Whenever pondering a chronology, it is important to keep uppermost in mind that dates from ancient history should never be viewed as chiseled in stone. When a certain year is catalogued, it should be understood that there can be a deviation, based upon the precision and extent of the evidence. A deviation can sometimes be a decade either side of a specific year, but if there are several reliable sources—even though they are variant or do not express an actual year—a collation of all the facts might lead to only a one- or two-year deviation. Charles Plummer, for example, doesn't express concern with a one-year variant, but he does convey more serious consternation about a six-year or more differentiation. This is why the reconciliation of the *ASC* and its Genealogical Preface as presented in Table 2 of Chapter 1 is so astounding; of the eight entries analyzed, five were exactly the same, and of the three remaining, only one had a deviation of three years (i.e., 1.5 either side of an average).

Hence, when viewing charts and genealogies as those supplied in Table 3 of Chapter 1 and Table 4 of Chapter 2, there will be a ±2-year deviation, except in instances where the calibration was either a Dionysiac/Victorian miscalculation, or when the 19-year lunar cycle was not factored into the calibration. In Appendix A (A Century and a Half of Dark-Age History) the period known as the Ambrosius Aurelianus era covered about 40 years, from approximately A.D. 422 to some time around the end of the sixth decade in that century. Gildas praises the victories of Ambrosius and applauds his integrity. The Riothamus era began around 459-460, a time marked by the second migration to Brittany, when some survivors settled in lands across the ocean. Riothamus's span—about ten years long—ended at the close of the sixth decade and beginning of the seventh.

Then, traditionally, the beginning of Arthur's reign is marked in the mid-years of the seventh decade of the fifth century, during the time when Hengist died and his son Octha succeeded to the leadership as the sole ruler. Legend picks up on the name Arthur and records that he was coronated at the age of fifteen, which by curious coincidence is fifteen years after the first mention of Ambrosius's victories. The *HB* is the only source which records Arthur's battle list against the English Saxons, and with the exception of the last battle listed—Mount Badonicus—no other work, including poetry and "non-fiction" antiquarian material, makes more than just a mere passing mention of the previous twelve battles. Arthur's last fatal battle at Camlann does not appear in the battle list; its notice is very brief in the *AC* and it, like the Badon conflict, is only glossed over in other works. This is why Geoffrey of Monmouth's work is considered such a major contribution to Arthuriana; he does give details about the Battles of Badon and Camlann, plus wars at Kaerluideoit and Caledon Wood, before indulging in flights of fancy about a great many other unsubstantiated battles.

The *ASC*, in conjunction with other works, such as those by William of Malmsbury and John of Glastonbury, provide fill-in information for the tidbits which do exist for the great Briton king under the name of Arthur. Once the emendations are made for the *ASC* entries between the alleged beginning of his reign about 475 through the battle at Camlann in 518 when he is mortally wounded (at ninety-six years of age, which is itself a point to ponder!), the entries in that source offer other details for verification recorded elsewhere.

One emendation is proposed by Charles Plummer in his comparison of entries 519 and 527. Those two entries, with no intervening accounts, read as follows:

> 519—In this year Cerdic and Cynric succeeded to the kingdom; and in the same year they fought against the Britons at a place called *Cerdicesford.*
>
> 527—In this year Cerdic and Cynric fought against the Britons in the place which is called *Cerdicesleag/Cerdicesford.*

In the 527 entry, the Parker Chronicle (Ā) uses the name Cerdicesleag, while the Laud Chronicle (E) uses Cerdicesford. About this entry Plummer writes,

> "Cerdices ford" for "Cerdices leag" is peculiar to E. It is followed by H[enry of] H[untingdon] but not by Fl[orence of] W[orcester]. It is due to the influence of the preceding annal 519, of which in truth this looks very like a doublet.[33]

Plummer's identification of doublets heightens suspicions by other researchers, especially his comments on an "artificial system of chronology"[34] for entries in the *ASC* during this period. His identification of this as a doublet means that it should be stricken, and in addition, the entry for 519 as shown in Table 3 of Chapter 1, which was borrowed from the *HKA,* should be modified to read "*Creoda* succeeded to the kingdom."

That suspicion led to a suggestion in the *HKA* that there is another pair of entries which would fall into the doublet category. Consider the following two entries:

> 495—In this year two ealdormen, Cerdic and his son Cynric, came with five ships to Britain at the place which is called Cerdicesora, and they fought against the Welsh on the same day.
>
> 514—In this year the West Saxons came into Britain with three ships at a place called Cerdicesora; and Stuf and Wihtgar fought against the British and put them to flight.

There are two intervening entries between the above, one dated 501 and the other 508. The curiosity, however, lies in the year differentiation between 495 and 514—nineteen years, which is the same span as a lunar adjustment. Likewise, if the cultural/tribal term of "West Saxons" is replaced by proper names, or vice-versa, the entries become synonymous.

Four other peculiarities also surface. The first has to do with the term "West Saxon," which is set typically near the Southampton Water in south-central Britain. One of the theories proposed by the *HKA* is that a distinction must be made between *Cerdicesora* and *Cerdicesford,* Cerdicesora being somewhere in Wales and Cerdicesford near the south-central coast. The entries for 495 and 519 therefore makes sense: In the first the English Saxons land at Cerdicesora and fight the *Welsh,* and in the second they land at Cerdicesford and fight the Britons. But the 514 entry is spurious: Stuf and Wihtgar land in *Wales,* but they are fighting the *British.* The second is that Entry 495 should name Cerdic and his son *Creoda;* Creoda appears in the genealogical tree, but Cynric, Cerdic's *grandson* and Creoda's *son* appears incorrectly in the *ASC.* The third is the absolute necessity of distinguishing between the Welsh and the British; the Welsh were settled mainly inland from the west coast of what is now known as Wales and spilled over extensively into the western and northwestern midlands, while the British—a more generic term—referred to those Celtic people who inhabited the southern heartland. And last but not least, is the added peculiarity in Entry 514, which Plummer objects to on etiological grounds. Stuf and Wihtgar are two alleged West Saxon chieftains, but unlike Creoda, their names do not appear in any of the West-Saxon genealogical trees.[35]

Anchored in this milieu, Vortimer would historically appear just prior to Hengist's massacre of Vortigern's Council of Elders and therefore also prior to the second migration to Brittany, in the waning years of the sixth decade of the fifth century. This matches the ebbing years of Ambrosius's era and the waxing years of Riothamus during the second migration, the time in British history about fifteen years prior to the advent of a king termed Arthur. Not only is Vortimer's era a match, but likewise his enemies are identical to those of Ambrosius, Riothamus, and Arthur: Generally he is warring against the English Saxons. Specifically, to use the words in the *HB,* he fought "valiantly against Hengist, Horsa, and his people,"[36] and after Horsa's death, he fought against Octha, who then came down from the north to rule with his father. The narrative is also clear that the English Saxons sent envoys overseas to recruit German Saxons to fight against the princes and kings of Britain The events are given not only by the *HB* but verified by the *ASC,* although Vortimer as a historical figure does not appear in the latter work.

One contradictory condition, however, prevents the acceptance of Vortimer as an epithet for Ambrosius. That circumstance is Vortimer's death. The wording and arrangement of events are vague. Book 43 of the *HB* relates that Vortimer fought against the English Saxons and expelled them to Tanet, where three times he attacked them. The English Saxons sent for and enlisted German Saxon reinforcements from the continent, and the English and German Saxons subsequently fought against the princes and kings of Britain, sometimes being victorious and sometimes being defeated and expelled.

Chapter 44, translated from Stevenson's Latin, begins with the statement that Vortimer fought against the "them" at Thanet, blockading them and terrifying them on three separate occasions.[37] A list of three battles follows: Derguentid, Ægælesthrep, and the Inscribed Stone. Stevenson easily resolves the issue of the word "four" in the first sentence by explaining that Manuscript *a* indicates that the first battle was the one already mentioned in

Chapter 43.[38] However, the word "them" in that first sentence is not as easily interpreted; it implies battles against both the English and the German Saxons *if* the events are assumed to be sequential. Assuming that is the case, then Vortimer is successful three times against the English/German Saxon alliance, but soon after that he died.

And therein lies the controversy. For those proponents who believe 1) that Vortimer is a distinctively separate, factual figure, even though he appears in no other historical manuscript; 2) that Vortimer was in fact Vortigern's son; 3) and that he died in the early-to-mid 450s, there would seem to be no problem or contradiction. Simplistically, he can be explained as a prince since he is son to the Over-King, but that leaves a flood of questions unanswered. If he is only a prince, why does his epithet also imply that he, too, is an Over-King, the same rank as his father? How would it be possible for Vortimer and Vortigern to be joint rulers, particularly when considering their opposing views toward the Saxons? Why would Vortigern step down in the middle of his reign only to return again after Vortimer's death? Why doesn't the *ASC* identify Vortimer and his demise, since it would add great glory to their cause?

Furthermore, a belief that Vortimer is an epithet for Ambrosius, as suggested by several researchers already mentioned, would necessarily negate the belief that Vortimer (i.e., Ambrosius) was Vortigern's son. It would also disavow Vortimer's death, for if Ambrosius died at that time, who could the mysterious Riothamus—the powerful High King from across Ocean—be? Ambrosius is the obvious individual of the period who had direct ties to Rome and who could wield enough power to attempt to lure the Romans back to the island for protection. Neither would Ambrosius's reign have split Vortigern's reign; more than likely, Ambrosius would have been an apparent heir to the throne based on his Roman ancestry, but because of his age, Vortigern would have been an interloper.

Hence it is difficult to formulate a judgment about Vortimer and his historical role as reported in the *HB*. If his name is accepted as an epithet for Ambrosius, then not just one but several statements in the *HB* must be rejected: He is not Vortigern's son, his reign was not flanked on both sides by Vortigern's rule, and he did not die in the 460s. Logistically, then, he must be accepted as a bona fide historical entity, and the identity of that figure must be drawn from a small, finite field of possibilities. As the limited evidence from the existent sources suggests, Brydw—alias Cunedda, alias Elesa—is the only feasible choice available.

Chapter 1 of this text reinforced what *The Historic King Arthur* had originally proposed about Vortimer's battles having taken place not in Kent, but in the Cornovii territories of the midlands, bordering Mercia on one side and Wales on the other. The battle on the River Derwent was identified as the river just southeast of Manchester, along the borders of the Cornovii territories. However, at that point, there was still not enough evidence to verify that "Derwent" location as *Derguentid* with certainty.

In Chapter 4 of the *HKA*, at the end of the section on Vortimer, the germination of a theory which linked the epithet "Vortimer" with the name Cunedda was touched upon but then passed over. In the succeeding chapter, a strong suggestion was given that Cunedda might be the bona fide historical figure behind the epithet "Vortimer," but once again the theoretical possibility didn't advance anywhere. Chapter 7 repeated the pattern of strongly proposing that Vortimer and Cunedda were the same individual, since "Vortimer" could not be an epithet for Ambrosius and there were no other probabilities. Later in that same chapter, because Vortimer's and Cunedda's activities were matched in the same vicinity with Arthur's, the intimation was again made that "Vortimer" must have been an epithet for Cunedda.

In my experience, a theory typically takes a circular meandering path, which has happened in this case. It was the bond of kinship among Vortimer, Cunedda, and Maglocunus which led to something more substantial than simple conjecture. While pursuing a different train of thought about Maglocunus's important role in Arthurian history, another study of the Roman map, perhaps for the fiftieth time, drew my attention once more to the core of the Midlands—Viroconium and its vicinity. It is commonly held that if an enigma has been studied and researched for literally centuries by a train of scholars but the mystery has not yet been solved, it is because seemingly minor or trivial details have not been delegated their proper significance. Sometimes, however, the case might be that the enigma hasn't been explained because the obvious—by the very fact that it *is* so obvious—has been overlooked and therefore the solution has been delayed for a ludicrously interminable time.

In my first book the search for the geographic location of Vortimer's battle on the River Derguentid led through an intricate maze of terms. Eilert Ekwall's dictionary provided the cognate base of *Derventio.* From this, the River Darwen in Lancashire was derived, with its accompanying towns of Lower Darwen, Over Darwen, and Darwen near Blackburn. Similarly, the River Derwent in Cumbria comes from the same root, probably giving rise to the town of Derwen near Ruthin. Furthermore, there are three other possible sites: One is the River Derwent in Yorkshire and the accompanying villages of Derwent Fells and Derwentwater; a second is the River Darent in Kent, which gave rise to the town Darenth on its bank; and the third is the River Dart in Devonshire. All of these sites can be located on a modern ordnance map, but a more precise location for Vortimer's second battle couldn't be pinpointed because, among other reasons, some rivers take confusing courses. One example is the River Derwent in Derbyshire, which meanders southeasterly from its origin in the Howden Moor for about fifty miles before it joins with the River Trent.

However, the study of a map of Roman Britain drastically changes perspective and makes one realize that one need go no further than the original base of the word *Derventio.* What wasn't resolved in *The Historic King Arthur* can now be clarified here. In one of his footnotes, Josephus Stevenson gives a specific geographic clue by writing that *Derguentid* is "said by some to be the Derwent in Derbyshire,"[39] but unfortunately he then turns too quickly to the River Darent in Kent, most likely because he was following the erroneous leads of scribal headings interpolated in the *Historia Brittonum.*

Based upon solid, documented evidence, *The Historic King Arthur* weaves a pattern of events into a comprehensive milieu of the period so that Viroconium emerges as the site for Arthur's twelfth battle at Badon, a locale that had been famous for its Roman baths in addition to being adjacent to a hill fort with an extensive defensive view. There are six other specific conditions gleaned from the early histories and later Welsh tales which also point to Viroconium, a legionary fortress in the heartland of the Roman Cornovii territory, as the Badon site. This arena, separating the Cymry (Welsh) from the English Saxons in Mercia and East Anglia, was a constant battleground after the Roman withdrawal.

What is hidden during study of a modern ordnance map hits the researcher like a cold slap in the face after a glance at a map of Roman Britain. The importance of Derventio—or Derguentid and its many variations, including Derwent—in Roman insular history cannot be overstated. Derventio, in modern times known as Littlechester, is directly on the banks of the River Derwent. Only twenty-five miles southwest, along the Roman road known as Ryknild Street, lay Letocetum (Wall-by-Lichfield), an important fort and way-station with a large *mansio* and baths, the location proposed in *The Historic King Arthur* where Octha settled when he came down from the north. At the intersection there with Watling Street, Viroconium was about thirty miles to the west. In the opposite direction from Letocetum, Watling Street traversed the southeastern section of the island for 160 miles to Canterbury, Kent, where it fragmented into several different Roman roads to the coast.

Derventio was not only a fort, but was likewise adjacent to a major town. In the immediate vicinity were temporary military camps for training, practice, and drills. Dotting the landscape less than a half-mile to the north were pottery kilns, so that, in addition to Derventio's importance militarily, it was also a center for the production of ceramics. At Crich, only nine miles due north was a vital lead mine, which ranked just below bronze in Roman use. In a radius of fifteen miles, there were fourteen forts, two legionary fortresses, four vexillation forts, three military camps, five of the nine *burgis* on the island, two tribal cities, one *coloniae,* two major settlements, three iron mines, and two stone quarries. All of these attest to the crucial importance of the area in Roman and post-Roman Britain, a significant place to defend against enemies.

The impact of this is evident *and* simple. The previous Roman fort itself, *Derventio,* which is directly on the banks of the River Derguentid, is where Vortimer's crucial second battle was fought. It is impossible to substantiate any other locale on the River Derguentid which would be so significantly crucial for an emerging kingdom. In comparison, the site of Darenth on the River Darent in Kent pales to an insignificance. Although Vortimer's battle at Agælesthrep is too obscure for positive geographic identification, the other two, besides Derguentid, are not. Whereby a battle at Derventio would have been along the north-eastern borderlands, the battle at Tanat would have been approximately seventy miles away on the southwestern border, and the battle at the Inscribed Stone would have been about the same distance away directly west. Substantial evidence, events, circumstances, chronology, and personages unquestionably point to the Cornovii midlands as a major arena of Welsh/English Saxon/Welsh mercenary conflicts.

Also of interest here is Vortimer's initial conflict with the Saxons. Tanet (translated most commonly as Thanet) is mentioned three times in the *HB*—Chapters 31, 36, and 43. In Chapter 43, where some details are given about Vortimer's battles, there's an obscure clue about where Tanet might be located, but although the *HKA* followed its weak trail, no definitive information came to light. Chapter 36 is even less helpful; it records the name and offers no variables. Translations of the *HB* have placed misleading headings in the most damaging positions imaginable. Ironically, just prior to Chapter 31 is the heading, THE KENTISH CHRONICLE, PART 1; Chapter 36 is immediately preceded by the heading, THE KENTISH CHRONICLE, PART 2; and Chapter 43 is introduced by the heading THE KENTISH CHRONICLE, PART 3. It is almost as if some fiendish scribe interpolated these headings to mislead researchers for all times; every successive reader would unquestionably accept that all the geographic sites mentioned thereafter would be associated with Kent.

But close readings cast grave suspicions on Kent as a major focus. One of those suspicions slithers out in Chapter 31. The last sentence of the *narrative* segment relates that

> Vortigern welcomed the *Saxones* and handed over to them the island that is called Tanet, in British it is called Ruoihin.[40]

The first thing to arouse doubt is that in the twenty extant versions of the *HB,* not one single manuscript gives "Thanet" as a variation for "Tanet," which is highly unusual. The pure form "Tanet" still exists on modern maps as the River Tanat, originating in the mountainous region of Berwyn in central Wales and flowing eastward to join River Severn only six miles southwest of Old Oswestry, a hill fort re-occupied during the Dark Ages and the alleged home base for Guinevere's father, Gogyrfan. The river-name, meaning "brilliant river" derived from *Old Welsh,* [41] is in the border region between Wales and Cornovii territory of the Roman period, adjacent to all the sites associated with Vortigern and Ambrosius. On the other hand, "Thanet," which Bede uses in reference to Ethelbert in the mid-eighth century, is a derivative from the Greek word *thanatos,* "death," akin to Latin "smoke," perhaps a reference to fog.

The real key, though, is the British word "Ruoihm." Unlike Tanet, there are several variations of Ruoihm in the manuscripts: Ruichin, Rouichim, Ruoichin, Ruithina, Rudithin, Ruithon, Ruoithin, and Roihin. No site by one of these names exists today, and a scrutiny of the area around the River Tanet will not uncover such a place. However, "Ruoithin" is a cognate very close to Ruthin, approximately twenty miles due north of the River Tanet. A historical check shows that Ruthin was one in a string of hill forts extending from Moel Hiraddug on the coast, to Pen y cloddiau and then from Moel y Gaer and Foel Fenlli to Ruthin. The chain parallels not only the Clwydian Range, but also Offa's Dyke of a later age, a demarcation and protective shield between Wales and the barbaric northern interior of the island. In *The Age of Arthur* John Morris writes that

> The hill fort of Moel Fenli [Foel Fenlli as listed above, in ordnance maps] in Ruthin in northern Powys preserves the name of Benli, or else inspired it. An exceptionally large late Roman coin hoard there buried argues that it was in the fourth or fifth century the residence of a powerful ruler.[42]

A philological check is even more revealing. "Ruthin" comes from the same stem as "Ryther," and though obscure, Ekwall believes that its root is Old English, from *hryther-ea* or *hryther-eg.*[43] In and of itself, that is not astonishing, but *hryther-eg* leads to the root of Ripon, *hrypis, hripis.* This root took on great significance in the *HKA* to delineate boundaries of the ancient Hrype tribe, whose kingdom was Hwicce, or Gewissae, and whose heritage was English Saxon during the Arthurian period. The root *hrypis, hripis* dates back to documents in the early eighth century, and links Ruthin with Ripon, Ribble, and Ribchester. Even more notable is that in the root *hyther-eg* the *-eg* ending signifies an "island." That term, as *insulam,* can be figurative, an isolated or surrounded position. What Vortigern gives, then, to the Hrypingas is a province encompassing the River Tanat just to the south of Ruthin, which is a territorial boundary marker.

In Morris's translation of the last segment of Chapter 31 from Nennius is a Mommsen addition, marked by daggers (†). The proper noun, *Ripum,* emerges as a crucial item of interest. As a proper noun *Ripum* is a Latin word in this instance applied to *civitate,* a Roman city which was the seat of administrative function. Ekwall does not list Ripum in his dictionary, but under the entry Ripon, he writes,

> Hrypis, Hripis ... OE Bede *Hrypsætna* ... *Onhripum* ... *Hryopan* ... Ripun. Ripon is the dative plural of OE Hrype, a tribal name, found also in Repton.[44]

In tracing this further, under the entry Repton is the following information:

> *Hrypadun ... Hreopandune ... Rapendune ... Rependun ... Repedon.* "The hill of the *Hrype* tribe." The same tribe gave its name to Ripon and probably some places near Ripon (see Ribston, Ripley). The etymology of the tribal name is obscure.[45]

Bede uses *in-Hrypum* only once (page 187) and all of these possibilities except one led to a dead-end. However, because an intervocalic change of *p* for *b* is found in other names, the interesting revelation comes from the history of the word *Ribston:*

> No doubt *Hrypa stān* "the stone of the *Hrype.*" The stone may have been a boundary stone marking the territory of the *Hrype* tribe, or a stone at the meeting-place of the tribe.[46]

Photograph 3—The River Tanat, a possible site for Vortimer's first battle against the English Saxons.

This intervocalic change is also the root for the River Rib, the River Ribble, and Ribchester. The River Ribble in Lancashire, for example, meanders southwesterly from its source to the Irish Sea, and this, too, could have been a boundary marker for the *Hrype* tribe. This presumption for Ribchester is even stronger. Morris, even though he writes about this fortification in a different set of circumstances, contributes influential information. Ribchester was a principal fortified town in Lancashire shortly preceding Cunedda's migration to the south, where the territories of this region remained intact just prior to the end of the fifth century, Arthur's period.[47]

Archaeologist Peter Clayton also makes an indirect contribution. About Ribchester, he writes:

> This was a small cavalry fort in the territory of the Brigantes tribe. When a group of Sarmatian cavalry veterans were given land to settle here on their retirement about 200 it was Brigantian land taken from the tribe.[48]

Historically, Ribchester was not only a *civitas* but was a demarcation point and could have functioned as such for future divisional boundaries.

However, the most interesting thing which emerges from the *Hrype* affix is not just each *specific* location bearing this tribal identification, but also the *general* pattern which manifests itself. Ekwall claims that the etymology of the tribal name *Hrype* is obscure, but it is suspiciously similar to *Hwicce*. The Old English transcription would be *Hryppe,* where the "*pp*" is pronounced as a voiced "th-" sound, *Hrythe.* To map-plot only those place-names positively associated with the root *Hrype* splits Britain in half, from the mouth of the Ribble on the west to the River Humber on the east. Ribble, Ribchester,

Photograph 4—The River Darwent near Derby, the site of the Roman fort Derventio, where Vortimer's second battle against the English Saxons took place.

Ribble Head, Ripley, Ripon, and Riplingham form a jagged boundary across the country, in themselves a testimony to the borders of the *Hrype* tribe. The same is true down the center of the country to the south coast: Ripponden, Ripley, Repton, Ribberford, Ripple, and Ripley could be border markers for *Hrype* territories.

Some scholars and historians do not equate *Hwicce* and *Gewissae*. Morris, for example, labels the Hwicce territory mainly in the present province of Gloucestershire, and Geoffrey Ashe sets the Gewisse territory mainly in Dorset and Hampshire, with the later empire of the West Saxons superimposed between the two to show the eventual combined kingdom of the West Saxons. Yet there are clues within their own work to show that the two synonyms refer to the same kingdoms. Ashe cites Geoffrey of Monmouth as reporting that Vortigern was "the ruler of the Gewissei,"[49] Morris writes that "Gewissae was the earlier name of the Middle Thames Saxons,"[50] adding in footnotes that these Saxons were "probably" *confederates* "of the Berkshire English of the middle Thames about Abingdon."[51]

On a map showing the *seventh*-century English kingdoms,[52] Morris not only errs chronologically on the ancient nature of the Hwicce people, but he concentrates the Hwicce tribe solely in the area of Gloucestershire, rather than having the kingdom extend eastward as far as Abingdon in Oxfordshire. Ashe is trying to prove his point that Arthur is a fifth-century figure by interpreting Geoffrey of Monmouth, and sets the Gewisse in Dorset and Hampshire, even though Vortigern (of Dementia) is labeled as their ruler and has no historical associations with the south.

Very early in the Dark Ages, Hrype/Hwicce/Gewisse was a massive territory granted to, or perhaps taken by, the Saxon compatriots invited in by Vortigern. It extended from the River Ribble to at least Ripon and Ripley in the north, bounded roughly by Offa's Dyke to the west, all the *Hrype* place-names on the east, and two similar place-names in Hants and Surrey to the south. This massive kingdom germinated sometime after Vortigern's succession to kingship in the fourth decade of the 400s. The West Saxon conquests of fifty years later play an important role in the development of these kingdoms from their inception to Arthur's death in the second decade of the 500s. Vortimer's first battle helps define the boundaries of these territories.

Vitalinus

Another equally enigmatic figure is Vitalinus, and trying to track his name in the genealogies is like trying to maneuver through a maze. Because both Vortimer and Vitalinus are seemingly tied to Vortigern's lineage, the first task was to trace Vortigern's ancestral tree. Dishearteningly, though, the probe led to a labyrinth of dead-ends, so that the final results remained only

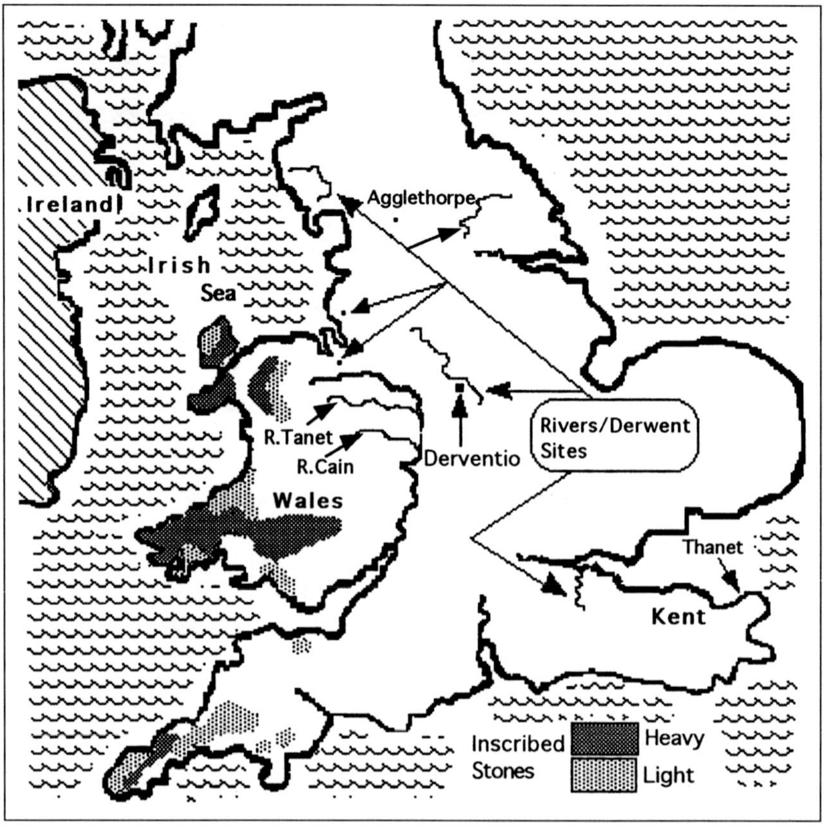

Map 5—Vortimer's battle sites. Commonly depicted as taking place in Kent, this map not only shows the location of the River Darent in Kent but the other possibilities, including the strategic location of Derventio. Tanat is confused with the Isle of Thanet, and Agglethorp is the closest name to Æglesthrepe in the original document. Note also that there are no inscribed stones in the vicinity of Kent.

inferences, implications, deductions, and probabilities. It is, nevertheless, a meandering path which had to be taken not only to reveal the complexity of the problem posed by genealogies, but likewise to separate the wheat from the chaff to help the next Arthurian quester.

The best launching point is Vitalinus's name in the original Latin manuscripts. In Chapter 49 the *HB* records the name of Guitolin and its variant Guitolion in Manuscript a, which reads differently from the others:

> ...Guitaul [is the son of] Guitolion; Guitolion [is the son of] Glouida; Glouida [is the son of] Paulmerion. [Moreover, Glouida

> is the one who built the great city on the banks of the River Severn, which is called Cair [Caer] Gloui in the British tongue and Gleucester in English.][53]

The name appears only once more, in Chapter 66, which mentions the discord between "Guitolini et Ambrosii."[54]

Similar to the profound differences about Pascent between the *HB* account and the one by Monmouth, Monmouth gives an entirely different rendition of the etymology for Gloucester. He writes that Kaerglou, or Gloucester, was founded on the River Severn between Wales and Loegria by Arvirargus to commemorate the name of his wife Genvissa who was the daughter of Claudius.[55] If true, this suggests a much earlier period in the history of the island. Monmouth does, however, in the same passage go on to explain that "Some ... say that [the city Gloucester] took its name from Duke Gloius, whom Claudius fathered in that city and to whom he granted control of the duchy of the Welsh after Arvirargus." Even so, the time-frame would remain approximately the same, suggesting that this particular Duke Gloius would have preceded Vortigern, Guitolin, and Ambrosius by several centuries.

Surprisingly, Peter Hunter Blair offers a clarification, even though at first what he writes seems to be totally unrelated. As a lead-in to his contribution, one common piece of information is that a legionary fortress of Roman times was Glevum, known now by its modern name Gloucester. Linked to this piece of information, Blair writes,

> "Fortress" is the word normally used to translate the Latin *castra* when used of a legionary base. At present the sites of six such fortresses are known in Britain, three of them, those at Lincoln, Gloucester, and Inchtuthil, having been occupied only for a short period in the first century.[56]

What this suggests is that Geoffrey of Monmouth knew quite a bit about early Roman history. When reconsidered very carefully, Monmouth's passage conveys that Gloucester was founded to commemorate the name Genvissa, the daughter of Claudius and wife of Arvirargus. By writing extracts such as these, Monmouth is guilty of a heinous sin, one committed inadvertently by every researcher of ancient history, the present writer not excepted. Monmouth's passage should, in fact, be interpreted as "*Glevum* was founded to commemorate the name Genvissa, the daughter of Claudius." This leads an individual to explore the possibility that "Glevum" might be an eponym for Genvissa, while "Gloucester" would be an eponym based upon Gloiu, accurately reflecting a later period when the Saxon incursions had contributed their eponymic influences of changing the name of that city from Glevum to Gloucester.

But this, however, is yet another example of Monmouth creating shadows for researchers and historians to chase. Michael Curley writes that

> Arvirargus is another Gaulfridian creation whose grandiose deeds were invented by Geoffrey almost out of thin air. Actually, Geoffrey culled Arvirargus's name out of Juvenal's Fourth Satire against the Romans in the time of Claudius, and for his daughter Genvissa.[57]

Based upon Arthur Hutson's *British Personal Names in the Historia Regum Britanniae,* Curley continues in a footnote that Genvissa's name is apparently based upon the term for an inhabitant of Gwent, "Gwenhwyss," or that her name could possibly be related to the Gewissei, a tribe and territory in the vicinity of Gloucester.[58]

Hence, after meandering through that eponymic maze, the only other association is the one provided by the *HB,* that later in the island's history, the name Glevum had been replaced by the Welsh term Gloucester, based upon the proper name Gloui. In some versions of the *HB* Caer Gloui appears as one of the thirty-three important cities of Britain. In his etymology, Ekwall lists the emergence of the name Caer Gloui around the year 800, appearing as Gleawecestre in the *Cartularium saxonicum* in about 804, modified as Glowecestre in the *Domesday Book* in 1093, and changing once again to Glouchæstre in version E of the *ASC* in 1205. He continues by adding,

> Brit[ish] *Glevum* belongs to O[ld] W[elsh] *gloiu,* Welsh *gloew, gloyw* (from *glevo-)* "bright" and means "bright, splendid place" or the like. This was adopted at an early date in a form that gave O[ld] E[nglish] *Gleaw-*, and later in a form that gave late O[ld] E[nglish] *Glowe-*. To the original name was added O[ld] E[nglish] *ceaster* "Roman fort."[59]

There are basically three genealogies which have an association with material on Vortigern, and therefore with Vortimer and Vitalinus. One of those is called the Harleian Pedigrees, so named because they occur in the Harleian 3859 folio, a miscellany which includes the *Historia Brittonum* attributed to Nennius; Leslie Alcock refers to this folio as The *British Historical Miscellany,* and John Morris labels part of it as the *Chronographer.* The second is the pedigree appearing in the *Jesus College 20* manuscript used by Thomas O'Sullivan and A. W. Wade-Evans. And the third which must be considered is an Irish manuscript titled The *Expulsion of the Dési,* analyzed by O'Sullivan, Wade-Evans, and Leslie Alcock. Each of these will be viewed separately.

As O'Sullivan writes,

> The Harleian and Jesus documents both trace the Dyfed Line from Magnus Maximus, the Roman general in Britain who assumed the purple in 383 … and was killed [in Gaul] in 388 … but they substantially diverge three or four generations above Vortiporius….[60]

Vortigern is of the Dyfed line, meaning that his lineage is associated with Magnus Maximus, the historical Roman emperor who was a usurper in the

Western Empire. He proclaimed himself as Emperor during his command of troops in Britain. After defeating Gratian in Gaul in 383, he was recognized by Theodosius, Emperor of the East, the same Theodosius who later divided the Roman empire into the East and West, granting the east to his son Arcadius and the west to his other son Honorius. When Maximus sent his troops to invade Italy, he was defeated and beheaded by Theodosius.

The segment which records Maximus covers three generations in only six words: *Maxim guletic map Protec map Protector*. There has been a great deal of speculation in previous research of who "Protec" and "Protector" might be,[61] but because of the purpose here, this controversy can be bypassed. The single question which has to be answered is, "Was Magnus Maximus actually part of the Irish lineage?" After careful and deliberate consideration, and not an off-handed snap judgment, the answer is "No." O'Sullivan, for one, observes that several Early Medieval genealogies, referred to commonly as the Dark-Age period of medievalism, link British ruling families with Magnus Maximus, known also in Welsh tradition as Maxen Wledig. He then cites Tolstoy, whose research indicates that families in Dyfed, Strathclyde, Man, and Glamorgan traced their roots to this usurper, and that "a purely political connection is therefore indicated."[62] The basic foundation in the Preface of the *HKA* agrees with Tolstoy's observation as proposed, which is why the analysis and judgment must be made here on the reliability or the weaknesses of genealogies as they appear in the existing manuscripts.

What holds true for Magnus Maximus is equally valid for Agricola in the pedigrees. In his role, Agricola—with variants of Calpurnia, Sextus Calpurnius Agricola, and Cnaeus Julius—is recorded in the line of Dyfed as "Guortepir (Vortiporius, Vortiporix, Vorticingas) map Aircol" by Wade-Evans.[63] His genealogical history is spurious because it blends with Agricola Longhand as it appears in the Harleian and Jesus manuscripts, but Julius Agricola's presence is undeniable; his rule can be traced along Hadrian's Wall and in Corbridge, Carvoran, and Ribchester. Graham Webster presents an effective capsule of his history: Agricola was first associated with *Legio* XX in Gloucester, troops which took part in the subjugation of Brigantium[64]; he then helped to consolidate the north with *Legios* IX and XX under his command, and was strategic in moving the major Roman fortress from Wroxeter to Carlisle;[65] and under his leadership Chester later became a legionary base in his northern progress.[66]

Although the historical material on Magnus Maximus and Agricola seems to meander pointlessly off course, it certainly doesn't, particularly in light of its effect on later tradition which has survived. For example, the ancestry listed on Eliseg's Pillar might be considered as untainted truth without the prerequisite knowledge of solidly based history. This monument in Valle Crucis has greatly suffered the ravages of time, but fortunately, the Welsh antiquarian Edward Lhuyd translated that part of the inscription which was still legible.[67]

The inscription was divided into at least ten phrases, but there are many ellipses because so much was indecipherable to Lhuyd, even in 1696. The eighth grouping lists Maximus, and the skepticism about the legitimate appearance of his name in an Irish lineage is heightened by the spurious inclusion of other names in that cluster. Brydw is listed as one of Vortigern's sons, but the name of Brydw doesn't appear elsewhere in any of the ancient manuscripts. Severa, listed as Vortigern's wife and Maximus's daughter, is likewise not recorded in any other document. And additionally, the name of Germanus appears in this section, someone whom Josephus Stevenson has already shown was not in the early manuscripts of the *HB* but was interpolated later.[68]

Two names of Vortigern's sons, Catygern and Pascent, appear on Eliseg's Pillar as verification of the names as they are recorded in the *HB*, but the remainder of proper names are difficult if not impossible to align with other sources. For example, the name Brochmail appears both on the pillar and in the *AC* in entry 662, but he is unconnected to other names that match. Similarly, Maugan (or Maun) from the Pillar may have a relationship to Mauron, but because of the placement of his name in the inscription, he would, if indeed they were synonymous names, be displaced by three generations. However, because this is outside the quest for Vitalinus's historicity, there is no need for a more profound analysis.

The inscription on another pillar, the circled cross of Vortiporius's gravestone, is equally relevant. It contains a bilingual inscription in Latin and in Ogham, which lends a great deal of credence to it. In Latin the inscription reads "*Memoria Voteporigis protectoris,*" and transliterated from Ogham, "*Votecorigas.*"[69] This indicates that according to the Roman style he was proclaimed "protector," an official rank which functioned as an imperial bodyguard. As with the Maximus claim, this is a delusive reference which cannot be taken literally. About this Alcock writes,

> There can be no doubt that Votepor never served in this way, but there is evidence that his dynasty maintained a hazy memory that one of his ancestors had been a *protector*, and the title may have been appropriated as though it were a hereditary one.[70]

This doesn't negate, though, the invaluable history provided by the third genealogical manuscript, *The Expulsion of the Dési* which traces the Dyfed pedigree. The presentation of the lineage in this source omits the Roman emperors entirely and instead concentrates upon the Irish origins. In this version, an ancestor of Gartbuir (contrasting to the name of Gordeber in the Jesus manuscript) in the fifth generation

> went over sea [sic] with his descendants into the territory of Demed and it is there that his sons and grandsons died.[71]

This is a meaningful kernel of history. Alcock, who is excellent in his calibrations of this early period, concludes that the most recent evidence places the migration of the Dési from Ireland to Dyfed at the very end of the fourth or beginning of the fifth century,[72] very much in alignment with upheavals in the Western Roman Empire associated with the abandonment of the island.

In giving a geographic overview of the area in question during the reign of Arthur—that is, from the mid-fifth century to its end—William Skene writes,

> We find the sea-board of Wales on the west in the occupation of the *Gwyddyl* or Gael, and the Cymry confined to the eastern part of Wales only, and placed between them and the Saxons.[73]

In essence, the division of territory shows that the Irish settled along the coast in earlier times, but there was also continuous intrusion from the Gaels. The Roman territories from Dementia northward along the coast through the Ordovices and Decangi provinces had been settled partly by the Irish who had migrated there and had become assimilated during the earlier part of the Roman occupation. But once Roman control had been eroded, new and more frequent tribal forays assailed the western shores. The Welsh occupied the eastern part of present Wales and part of the midlands, sandwiched in between the Irish and the Cornovii region just recently vacated by the Romans. The eastern territory—Coritani, which was later to become Mercia—was occupied by the Angles (Anglians). Gildas made reference to these incursions and civil wars at the end of the fourth century and into the fifth. After Maximus seized the empire, Gildas writes that all of Britain's resources were depleted, and the country was trampled under the invaders' feet, the *Scotorum* (Irish) from the western arc, the Picts from the north, and the *Saxones* from the east.

The arenas of warfare, then, are outlined quite well by scraps of information from difference sources once the debris has been cleared away. The "Old Irish" settlers—that is, those who had been settled in a crescent of Wales from Dememtia to Decangi—were not only condoned by the Romans, but utilized to protect the western flank of the Empire. The area was already heavily populated with Irish who had intermingled with Celts of the island, and as a matter of policy, the Romans used these local tribes to prevent further Irish attacks. This procedural tactic worked well while the Romans occupied the island, but once they left, the natives were again subjected to attack from the Irish across the sea. The Brigantes area to the north was no longer secured from the Picts, and the Coritani province was pushing its boundaries westward.

Two of the manuscripts, the Jesus College pedigrees and *The Expulsion of the Dési*, therefore offer an informative background of the history during this era. However, because neither records any specific information about Vitalinus—the target of the inquiry—all attention must now be concentrated on the Harleian manuscript. In the *HB* Vitalinus's name appears as Guitolin. Six centuries later Geoffrey of Monmouth supplies quite a bit of detail about a Guithelinus, who plays a key role in Ambrosian/Arthurian history. Among modern researchers, R. H. Fletcher refers to him only as he appears in the *HB,* but John Morris offers significant comments, and Leslie Alcock, who records this name as Vitolinus, contributes some insights about his role.

The name of Vitalinus appears only twice. The first reference occurs in Chapter 49, which is a genealogy on Vortigern. Already mentioned above, there is confusion about the possibility of two Vortigerns (a Vortigern and a Vortigern the Thin), and about halfway through the genealogy, Vitalinus is listed as either Vortigern's grandfather or a great grandfather, depending upon the translation of the passage. Alcock is justified in not simply rejecting the possibility of two Vortigerns during this period because "we know at least two Irish Vortigerns, one of them buried in Co. Cork, the other in Co. Waterford,"[74] and hence to dismiss the possibility without deliberation would be rash.

Temporarily setting aside that confusion, though, one translation of Chapter 49 furnishes this information:

> ...son of Vortigern the Thin, son of Guitataul [Vitalis], son of Guitolin [Vitalinus], son of Gloui. Bonus, Paul, Mauron and Guitolin were four brothers, sons of Gluoi who built the great city on the banks of the River Severn that is called in the British Caer Gloui, in English Gloucester. Enough has been said about Guorthigirno [Vortigern] and his clan.[75]

It has already been shown that in and of themselves genealogical trees are not an infallible gauge of authenticity, especially when a name cannot be matched in another source. Although there is not much which can be deciphered from this passage, one important item does emerge. Separate from the line of ancestors, Vitalinus, a name interchangeable with Guitolin, is listed as one of four brothers, the sons of Gloui.

This places Vitalinus in the proper geographic area, at a major city within the Hwicce/Gewissae territories and a hot-spot of Welsh/English-Saxon conflict. This is the area, too, which was identified for Agricola when he was commanding *Legio* XX during Gloucester's heyday as a legionary fort.[76] Originally known as Colonia Nervia Glevensium (shortened to Glevum), the city has a history as one of the major cities on the Severn because of its strategic importance.[77] Typical in an Arthurian search, however, there are long, silent periods, such as the one here for Gloucester in the fifth century, during the time when there was a switch from Roman to British power plus the adoption of the name Caer Gloui in lieu of Glevum.[78]

The only other significant passage which not only names Vitalinus but connects him directly to Ambrosius is in the *Chronographer* of the *HB.* It relates:

> And from the reign of Guorthigirni [Vortigern] to the discord between Guitolini [Vitalinus] and Ambrosii are twelve years. Guorthigirnus (autem) held empire in Britain in the consulship of Theodosius and Valentinian, and in the fourth year of his reign the English came to Britain.[79]

This passage conveys some amazing information which is helpful not only in establishing the relationship between Ambrosius and Vitalinus, but also in giving chronological and geographic clues. Before delving into that, though, there is a need to compare the two entries. In the lineage of Chapter 49, Vitalinus is identified as either a grandfather or great-grandfather to Vortigern. The former does not stretch the "reasonable age" concept, but the latter would, when viewed in conjunction with chapters 48 and 66.

One issue of Chapter 66 is the use of the word *discord* (discordiam). The word conveys some kind of disharmony between Ambrosius and Vitalinus; there was some incident between the two which caused some disagreement, but it was not as grave as *bellum* (a war) or *proelium* (a battle). In degree, the word implies an argument over contentious opinions.

There is no *historical* source which explains the root of this argument or disagreement. Most scholars identify it as a war or battle in locales as widely separated as Shropshire and Cornwall.[80] Of much more interest is that Geoffrey of Monmouth provides a motive for the discord. In Part Eight titled "The Saxon Domination," immediately after Arthur's mortal wounding at Camalnn, Monmouth writes "The Bishop of Gloucester was promoted to be Archbishop of London."[81] He does not supply a particular name for this Archbishop, but after some retrospective investigative analysis, the full set of circumstances can be pieced together. Initially, though, the name of the city Gloucester establishes the first vague and tenuous connection between the Bishop and Vitalinus's father. In order to make a solid connection, the reader has to backtrack to Part Four, "The House of Constantine." In the first sentence of that section, Monmouth has written that "The Britons took counsel, and Guithelinus, the Archbishop of London, then crossed the sea to Little Britain, called at that time Armorica or Letavia, to seek help from their blood-brothers."[82]

The connection is thus made that the Archbishop of London was once the Bishop of Gloucester, and his name was Guithelinus, strongly averring that the Bishop of Gloucester was Gloui's son, appointed to that position in that particular city because of parental power and influence. Bearing in mind that there is a common translational interchange of names in these earlier histories, Vitalinus (the name being substituted for Guitolin) ascended through the ecclesiastic ranks to Archbishop of London and was given the important mission of recruiting armies from Aldroenus, King of Britanny, because the pleas to Aëtius had been ignored. Monmouth refers almost verbatim to the Gildian manuscript, thus making the assertion that the Archbishop's voyage took place *after* the Roman evacuation but *before* the Saxon rebellion against the British, which would have been during the period when the Britons were being driven first into the sea and then into the hands of the "barbarians" (the Irish and the Picts). In plainer terms, then, whether Monmouth was cognizant of it or not, he is relating that Vitalinus, son of Gloui, made a trip from Britain to Britanny as an emissary to recruit armies to repel the invaders. Inherent in this, too, is that Aldroenus and Vitalinus are both part of the pro-Roman faction, those who wished for a Roman return to protect the island.

This lays the groundwork for the relationship between Vitalinus and Aurelius Ambrosius. In Monmouth's account, Aldroenus sends his brother Constantine and armies back to Britain with Vitalinus. As soon as they land in Britain, the armies attack and defeat the enemies, whereupon Constantine is given the kingship of the realm. The historical figure of Constantine as Ambrosius's father has already been addressed in chapters 2 and 4 of this text. This is a prime example of why it is so absolutely essential for any anyone researching the historic King Arthur to continuously scour old manuscripts for new approaches. To the casual reader, Tables 4, 5, and 8 (in this chapter) probably look identical, yet they provide very different information as the viewpoint changes. Basically, at the root of the genealogical tree which is of consequence in Ambrosius's ancestry and therefore Arthur's by extension, is someone who is in some way connected to the House of Constantine. As already explained, first in the chain is Constantius I, followed by Constantine I, Constantine II, Constantius II, and Constans I. Following these bona fide figures is a usurper known as Constantine, whose full name was Flavius Claudius Constantinus. Next, even though he was only identified in the existent histories as a member of a noble Roman family, Constantius III was given his designation by Honorius, who appointed him as a co-emperor. Suffice to say, Monmouth does not—because he cannot—clarify *Constantine* as Ambrosius's father. Hence, as suggested, the only possibility who chronologically falls into the Ambrosian time-frame is Constantius III. There is no evidence, no clue, no logistic inference which helps identify the father of Constantius III.

Monmouth, therefore, either as a copyist or a creator, has forged a spurious link in Ambrosius's chain of ancestry when naming Constantine II. Yet the background which follows it isn't necessarily bogus. According to the narrative, Ambrosius's father—whatever his name might be—is given a Briton wife of noble birth who bears him three sons. The new Briton king

> handed Constans his first-born over to the church of Amphibalus in Winchester, so that he might enter a monastic order. The other two, Aurelius and Utherpendragon, he gave to Guithelinus, so that he might bring them up.[83]

The more important issue now is to focus upon the connection which establishes Vitalinus as Ambrosius's guardian and, if possible, clarify any other figure named in the genealogy.

Even excluding the Constantine fiasco, Monmouth's worst weakness is his chronology. His other three major *faux pas* are his placements of the Aëtius letter, the death of Guithelinus, and Vortigern's encounter with Ambrosius Merlinus. The first of these, the Aëtius letter, is chronologically verifiable from several other historical sources, and because it has been a hotly debated topic by modern scholars, agreement has emerged as to its date. Cutting to the quick of the matter and ignoring Gildas's confusion of the name and Bede's perpetration of that error, the most widely accepted date for this correspondence is 446.[84] In determining the span of time characterizing the gradual Roman evacuation, Collingwood writes, "The last phase of Roman government, therefore, began in or about 417 and ended some years before 429."[85] The second date which can equally be fixed with a great deal of confidence is the year in which Vortigern succeeded to the kingdom, A.D. 425. Without giving the elaboration accorded to the calibration for the Aëtius letter, this second date shows that Monmouth anachronistically places the Aëtius letter at least thirteen years *before* Vortigern's ascension.

The death of Guithelinus—or more accurately the parallel of Guitolin from the *HB*—is another of the displacements in the Monmouth manuscript. Sandwiched between the bickering among the leaders after the death of Constantine and Constans being made the puppet king, is a single sentence which reads "Archbishop Guithelinus was dead by this time."[86] This, too, is *prior* to Vortigern's crowning himself as king, in direct opposition to the more reliable *HB* account, which states, "And from the reign of Vortigern to the *discordiam* between Guitolini and Ambrosius there are twelve years ... ."[87] Determining calibration typically from the beginning of a reign, this indicates that adding twelve years to the onset of Vortigern's reign would place the discord between Vitalinus and Ambrosius in the year 437 rather than several years prior to 425.

The third of Monmouth's transgressions is of a more serious nature, deviating completely from history and moving into creative fantasy; this deals with his version of Vortigern's encounter with Ambrosius Merlinus. Monmouth begins innocently enough with his borrowing material from chapters 40, 41, and 42, "The Tale of Emrys," in the *HB*. Because the narrative is well-known, it will not be detailed here, but the most profound change is that Monmouth substitutes the name Merlin for Ambrosius. First he writes of a "Merlin who was also called Ambrosius," and later the translation is given as "Ambrosius Merlinus."[88] Monmouth then abandons his story line about the history of the kings of Britain and inserts the lengthy section titled "The Prophecies of Merlin." When he returns to the continuation of "The House of Constantine," Merlin has emerged as a separate character, now a prophet for Aurelius Ambrosius. Interestingly, in Monmouth's account Merlin has contact with Aurelius Ambrosius and later with Utherpendragon, but he never meets or associates with Arthur.

The genesis of this new character named Merlin creates two parallel scenarios which are very interesting when compared. The Ambrosian tale begins when Vortigern commands his wizards to find a child without a father. The youth's blood must be sprinkled at the site of the king's future fortification in order for the stronghold to be built, so the wizards search the provinces of many countries before they find the lad in a country called Glywysing. When the wizards question the boy's mother, she swears that she doesn't know how she conceived because she had never been with a man. However, when the boy is taken to the fortification's site, he confounds the king through prophecies. Because the boy's powers frighten the king, he asks who the boy's father is. The boy responds that his father is a consul of the Roman people, meaning that Ambrosius himself is Emrys, the Overlord.

Contextually inserting this text's contention that Ambrosius's father is Constantius III, the tale takes on this flavoring: Ambrosius would be the rightful heir as High King through his father, Constantius III, who was actually Galla Placidia's husband. However, when Constantius III crossed the Channel to quell the uprisings in Britain, he acquired a concubine, whose name was not recorded in the histories. From that union, Ambrosius was born. But because of fear of retribution, the concubine, when asked about her young son, attempted to protect herself by saying that the boy had been conceived by an incubus. In great fear of Ambrosius, Vortigern gave the young boy vast tracts of land in Wales and fled to the northern regions, to a country now called Gwynedd.

The interesting parallel is the different perspective of the Arthurian tale. The beautiful Ygerna is married to Gorlois, King of Cornwall. When Utherpendragon, the powerful, rising king who is about to become Overlord of the Briton tribes, sees the beautiful Cornish queen, he is overcome with desire for her. Realizing Utherpendragon's intent, Gorlois and Ygerna flee to their stronghold at Tintagel to avoid Uther's lustful advances. In a rage, the rising Overlord, whose passion cannot be subdued, wages war with Gorlois and solicits Merlin to help him win the Cornish queen. Knowing that Tintagel is impenetrable by direct assault, Merlin wraps Utherpendragon's identity in a magical mist. Disguised as Gorlois, Utherpendragon gains entry into Ygerna's bedchamber and seduces her. From that union, Arthur is born.

Weaving these two strands of narrative together produces a very interesting result: Constantius III, bearing the insignia of the Roman purple dragon, was widely acclaimed as a hero for the conquest of Gaul. Upon summons to Britain to quell the uprisings there, he ordered that tribal kings hold council with him, as was the Roman policy. Gorlois, King of Cornwall, and his beautiful Queen Ygerna were in attendance. When Constantius III, known as Utherpendragon because of the insignia of the Great Caesars, saw the beautiful Cornish queen, he wished to possess her. Although he was married to the powerful regent Galla Placidia, he was across the sea from her and unable to resist the tempting beauty of Igerna. He seduced Ygerna and Ambrosius was conceived. Ygerna, aware of Utherpendragon's power and possible repercussions of consorting with this great man, claimed that the baby's father is enshrouded in mist; the father was an incubus, and Ambrosius has no human father. Yet in reality, Ambrosius's father is a Roman consul.

This scenario directly equates Ambrosius with Arthur. Table 8 gives not only that information, but a great deal more. In an enumerative format, it can be listed as follows:

1. Constantine II was not Ambrosius Aurelianus's father, as recorded by Geoffrey of Monmouth. Instead, if based upon historically accurate information, Ambrosius's father was Constantius III. This means that the heretofore-held belief that Monmouth created the word "Utherpendragon" out of thin air or as an anagram for Arthur is null and void. Therefore, contrary to the common belief that the word "Utherpendragon" was just creative fantasy, the word is a bona fide epithet referring to Constantius III.
2. Hence, Ambrosius Aurelianus is the progeny of Roman royalty and through his mother Ygerna would be linked to Welsh royalty. Likewise, he is Cador's half-brother, Valentinian III's half-brother (not forgetting the Roman genealogies), Constantine the Briton's uncle, and (keeping in mind that the word "Arthur" is an epithet) Mordred's uncle.

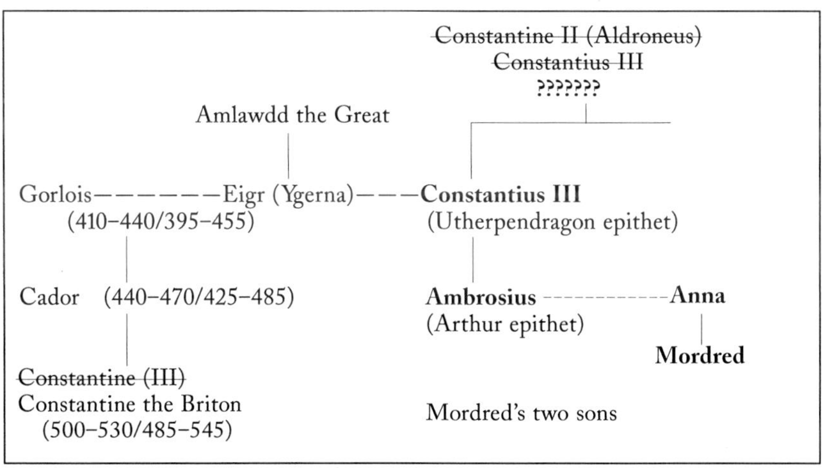

Table 8—The final revision of the House of Constantine.

3. Ygerna has two sons, Cador and Ambrosius, but because Constantius III is a higher authority than Gorlois was, Ambrosius (i.e. Arthur) was the rightful claimant as king among kings, or the Overlord.
4. Gorlois's line is associated with Cornwall, but the geographic locale should be the Cornovii territories, based upon Ambrosius's (i.e., Arthur's) Welsh heritage. Ambrosius is discovered by Vortigern's wizards in the Glywysing province (the more-modern Dyfed territories). When Vortigern discovers Ambrosius's heritage, he gives the boy all kingdoms of the western part of Britain and flees to Gwynessi (Gwynedd) in the north. Additionally, the encounter between Vortigern and Ambrosius takes place at the site which was to have been Vortigern's stronghold, identified as Dinas Emrys (named after Ambrosius the Overlord) near Beddgelert in Wales. Cornwall, during Ambrosius's time, was still known as Dumnonia.
5. Based on kinship, it's obvious why Cador and Ambrosius are allies and why, in the romances of eight hundred years later, Cador and Arthur are allies. Along these same lines, it explains why Constantine the Briton (Cador's son) would slay the two sons of Mordred to take over the kingdom.
6. Monmouth writes that Ambrosius's sister Anna had two sons by Loth, Gawain and Mordred. Accepting Monmouth's statement as true, that "Mordred was the son of Aurelius Ambrosius's sister Anna and Loth,"[89] then he would be Ambrosius's nephew. Perceiving him as Arthur's bastard son conceived through incest would be a moot point, because "Arthur" is an epithet (or homolog) for Ambrosius.
7. Although not identified by name, Gildas's passage about Constantine slaughtering two innocent royal youths might very well parallel Monmouth's narrative of Constantine slaughtering Mordred's two sons. Constantine the Briton would be in contention for the throne of the High King, and he would want to eliminate anyone who might have claims. Had Monmouth been fictionalizing the account from Gildas, there would have been no point for him to separate the massacres, one at Winchester and the other at London. Probably the most credible validation as to the truth of his narrative (or at least his accuracy as a copyist) is Monmouth's claim that he does not want to write about the matter of Mordred adulterously living out of wedlock with Guinevere.

The information in Table 8 has a crucial bearing on the chronology of the Arthurian period. In the *HB* version of the Emrys Ambrosius, when Ambrosius identifies his father as a Roman consul, Vortigern panics. The word "consul" is akin to the modern word "magistrate," but the best modified definition would be "a high-ranking commissioned official representing the interests of the appointing country and exercising administrative and judicial functions of the foreign nation." Hence, Ambrosius's father was not a king in the true sense of the word, but he would have been a powerful and influential individual who exercised a great deal of control even over the tribal sub-kings. Ambrosius says, too, that his father *is* a consul, which means that the meeting between Vortigern and Ambrosius takes place prior to the "shock of the notable storm"[90] when the Saxons turned against the Britons.

Both the *HB* and the *HKB* record Vortigern's fear of Ambrosius. The opening section on the fifth century in the *HB* recounts that "...during his rule in Britain [Vortigern] was under pressure, from fear of the Picts and the Irish, and of a Roman invasion, and not least, from the dread of Ambrosius."[91] There is no reason given why Vortigern might be so fearful of Ambrosius, but Monmouth provides a contextual rationale:

> Ambrosius and his brother Utherpendragon ... had fled to Little Britain because of [Vortigern]. [Vortigern's] ears were filled with a constantly repeated description of how they had come to man's estate and were planning to launch an enormous fleet against the kingdom which really belonged to them.[92]

Monmouth's assertion, coupled with what transpires in chapters 40, 41, and 42 between Vortigern the Emrys Ambrosius, explains why Vortigern became alarmed and sufficiently subdued to grant the fortress and all the kingdoms of western Britain to the young boy and then flee farther to the north. The word used to describe the boy is *puer*, meaning an adolescent, or someone between twelve and seventeen years of age, a median of about fifteen. This is what ostensibly gives rise to Arthur being coronated as a young lad fifteen years of age in the romances of 800 years later.

Unlike the historical account given by Gildas, Monmouth's narrative relates that ten years after Vitalinus's guardianship had been granted, a Pict stabbed Constantine to death, whereas Gildas writes that Ambrosius's parents were slain by the *Saxones*. The result, however, was the same: Upon Constantius' death, many leaders try to claim the throne, including Vortigern, whom Monmouth identifies as the leader of the Gewissei. Vortigern treacherously slays Constans in order to seize the throne, and the entire government of the kingdom is turned over to him.

All the bickering and the fear of assassination could be the reason behind the discord between Vitalinus and Ambrosius. Through Vortigern, Monmouth indicates that with Constans dead and the other two brothers too young to be made king, Vortigern realized that there was no one in the realm who was his equal. From this, discord could have arisen between Ambrosius and his guardian, the former wanting to avenge his father and become the rightful king although he was young, and the latter fearing another assassination. As a consequence, this discord provides the motive for the flight to Brittany. Monmouth writes that "those in charge of the upbringing of the two brothers Aurelius Ambrosius and Utherpendragon fled with their charges to Little Brittain, just in case the two should be murdered by Vortigern."[93]

The series of factual historical events, however, are different from what Monmouth suggests. In Monmouth's sequence, after Constans is killed and Ambrosius is described as still being in a cradle, the protectors of the infant flee immediately to Brittany, which seems a logical result or reaction. But in the intervening time between this event and Ambrosius's encounter with Vortigern, Monmouth inserts all these things into his narrative: 1) the first, second, and third Saxon *Adventi* into Britain 2) Vortimer's rebellion, rise to kingship, and death; 3) Vortigern's restoration to the throne; 4) the slaughter of the Council of Elders by the Saxons; and 5) Vortigern's flight to the north. Once again, verifiable history shows that the first *Adventus* was in 428 at the invitation of the *superbus tyrannus,* the second in approximately 440 under unknown circumstances, and the third in approximately 450, when the *ASC* picks up on the events.[94] Following that chain of events, the slaughter of the Council and Ambrosius's rise to kingship has been postulated as 458 for the former and the decade of the 460s for the latter. Vortigern's encounter with Ambrosius Merlinus, therefore, would be a gross displacement on the tail-end of all those other events.

Because of the wording about the discord between Vitalinus and Ambrosius in Chapter 66 of the *HB,* most scholars have inferred that Ambrosius was aligned with a pro-Roman faction while Vitalinus was allied with a pro-Vortigern faction; that is, they have interpreted the passage to mean that Vitalinus was one of Vortigern's subordinates who fights a battle against Ambrosius in 437. In opposition to this, Alcock writes,

> ...it is not possible to construe this particular conflict [the "discord" between Ambrosius and Vitalinus] in terms of nationalists versus Romanophils, for Vitolinus, unlike Vortigern, bears a name that is as Roman as Ambrosius.[95]

After the Roman withdrawal from the island, there were indeed two groups of dissidents, those of Celtic/Irish descent who inhabited the western and northwestern shores of Wales and had intermarried with tribes who had crossed the Irish Sea, and those of Celtic/Romano ties who encouraged Rome's return to the island. Ambrosius was part of this latter group; it is just as sensible to infer that because Guitolini was likewise of Roman origins and not Irish, these two would be allies and not enemies.

Yet it is not quite as simple as that. During this period of upheaval, allegiances were as changeable as the weather, which is why Gildas lamented the civil conflicts which were annihilating his country, and why, in a self-condemning mood, he apologized for not writing his epistle ten years earlier. He realized the senselessness of kin against kin when he inveighed against a murderer killing someone whose victim's face was very much like the perpetrator's.

Based upon names, Ambrosius and Guitolini were both of Roman ancestry, but their fealty could have easily led them along separate paths; Ambrosius's hopes might have been Rome's eventual return to the island, whereas Guitolini might have sensed the futility of relying on a crumbling empire, thus seeking to mold an empire of his own. The only "proof" to the contrary is Monmouth's narrative.

I recently became aware of a grave marker, termed the Vitalianus Stone by the vicar, churchwardens, and parishioners of the Church of St. Brynach in Nevern, Pembrokeshire. In eight years of reading, writing, and scouring England and Wales, I encountered no reference to this stone. It stands so unobtrusively just outside the door of the church that the magnitude of its impact and importance is casually ignored by a novice. But for those steeped in history and trying to decipher a piece of Welsh resplendence in creating the Arthurian legend, this stone permeates the fibers of the soul. In the preview of over two hundred sources of Arthuriana, this stone has not been mentioned. And even though it cannot resolve an issue or clarify a detail, it is like touching a holy relic.

This bilingual stone, dating from the fifth century and one of the oldest examples of this type of monument, stands to the east of the church's entryway. A modest pamphlet announces the stone and carries an elementary, humble epitaph:

> A sketch in the British Museum made about 1698 by Edward Lhuyd [the same individual who translated Eliseg's Pillar], Keeper of the Ashmolean Museum, Oxford, shows there has been no change in either the size of the stone [or] the legibility of the faint lettering since that date. The inscriptions are:
>
> *Latin.* VITALIANI EMERETO
>
> *Ogham.* VITALIANI.

In Latin and Ogham alike the meaning is "(THE MONUMENT) OF VITALIANUS." EMERETO is unexplained, but is conceivably a

> territorial adjective. Alternatively it may be a corrupt and ungrammatical derivative of Emeritus, "discharged with honor."[96]

Because the stone carries both a Latin and Ogham inscription, there is no way to determine where Vitalinus's allegiances lay. Fittingly, though, the location of Nevern is a very short distance north of Fishguard, along the western coast of Wales, in the crescent where the Irish settled, and thus in an area—that of Dementia which was later called Dyfed—which is geographically precise. The gravestone has also been judged to be from the fifth century, meaning that the chronological timeframe is also accurate.

Independent of the marker, but devising a chronological framework paralleling the dates given above, John Morris speculates that there are two leaders instead of just one named Ambrosius when he compares the Ambrosius from the *DE* to the leader of that name in the *Historia.* He writes that

> Ambrosius, who was Vortigern's enemy in the 430s, was too old to be identical with Ambrosius Aurelianus, the resistance leader of the 460s; but the elder Ambrosius may well have been father of the younger, and the father of Ambrosius Aurelianus ruled for a while as emperor, either in Vortigern's time, as his rival, or before him. Nennius' Chronographer reports that the elder Ambrosius made war on Vortigern in or about 437, and one late tradition exiles him [Ambrosius] to Gaul and brings him back with an army from Europe.[97]

The date (437) is of course based on the assumption that Vitalinus was Vortigern's subordinate who fought against Ambrosius, and that's why Morris makes the statement that Vortigern and Ambrosius "made war." The "late tradition" he mentions is Monmouth's narrative of Guithelinus sending him (perhaps "exiled" in the sense of being expatriated) to Little Britain (much more specific than Gaul) as a precaution, but it is Guithelinus and not Ambrosius who returns with the army. The major point, however, is that if Ambrosius was fifteen years old in 437, he would have been only thirty-eight years old in 460, easily within the "reasonable age" range without having to invent a second Ambrosius. The postulation of only one Ambrosius still remains possible under the Ambrosius/Arthur theory, assuming the premise that Arthur was "well-nigh one hundred years old when he died." Even if that postulation is not accepted, the contention of only one Ambrosius is still the most workable, since there is no evidence whatsoever which warrants the assumption that there were two.

Photograph 5—The fifth-century Vitalianus Stone at St. Brynach's Church, Nevern Wales.

Based, then, upon what can be gleaned from the various manuscripts and sifting through that information for a different perspective, the *HKA* has focused on several key elements. One is the word "discord," accepted at face value of its denotative and connotative meaning: Some kind of disharmony arose between Ambrosius and Vitalinus, but it did not result in a war or a battle. And if indeed there was a resultant battle, there is nothing to suggest that Vitalinus must be aligned with Vortigern and opposed to Ambrosius. A battle as the outcome of the discord between Vitalinus and Ambrosius might well have been that, as Ambrosius's protector, Vitalinus made war on Vortigern, the usurper of the throne. Perhaps this could even explain the words "Protec" and "Protector" included in the genealogical tracts, though this is just speculation.

Viewing the connection between Ambrosius and Vitalinus in this new light, there is no need to invent a second, older Ambrosius, assumed to be the father of Ambrosius Aurelianus. Morris's suggestion that Vitalinus might be an epithet for Vortigern would likewise be senseless because there would again be a need to invent another Vortigern in the genealogical line in order to create another Vitalinus as brother to Bonus, Paul, and Mauron, sons of Gloui.

Even without all this manipulation, cardinal years can be established for Ambrosius Aurelianus and his association with Vitalinus.

1. *The* Vortigern—with a proper name of Æternus still possible—rises nefariously to the kingship in 425 after the Roman withdrawal.
2. In 428, the *Saxones* were initially invited in to fight the people of the north, namely, the Picts. The alliance between Vortigern and the *Saxones* began favorably, but as more and more *Saxones* encroached upon the island, a split developed.
3. During the first couple of decades after the Romans abandoned the island there was a deep rift between those historically labeled as the *Romanophils* and the *Barbaria.* The first, epitomized by Ambrosius Aurelianus, sought help from the Romans on the continent and advocated their return; the second, exemplified by Vortigern, had more aboriginal ties and wanted to establish their own form of rule.
4. Because of a series of circumstances, including Ambrosius's age, Vitalinus, in the capacity of mentor or guardian, was responsible for urging Ambrosius, who was an aspirant of Roman royalty, to leave the island and seek refuge in Brittany until the lethal scramble for the throne had abated. Ambrosius, as a fiery youth, wanted to assume leadership and immediately confront all opposition—Pict, Irish, Saxon, or Briton. Cooler, more rational minds prevailed, and Ambrosius was granted asylum under Budicius in Quimper.

6

The Breach of Colors: Cunedda's Role in Civil War

Introduction

The historic King Arthur has been perceived as the most elusive hero in literary history to be traced as a factual figure. Based upon the very few existent manuscripts which mention King Arthur by name, this is true. His name appears twice in the *AC* in very short entries, one which praises his greatest victory against the Saxons at Mons Badonicus, and the other which records his death at the Battle of Camlann. The *HB* is the only other early manuscript which provides some information about this figure called Arthur; that manuscript gives details of Arthur's twelve battles against the Saxons, the last of which is echoed in the *AC*. Yet because of evidence that both the terms "Arthur" and "Riothamus" are epithets pointing directly to Ambrosius Aurelianus, a more expansive grasp of characters leads to a more comprehensive vista of historical events. An even more detailed picture is given about Ambrosius than of Arthur in the *HB;* Monmouth provides a more in-depth delineation of Arthur, but he does not ignore Ambrosius; and literary tradition devotes several tales to Arthur. Hence, when combined there is more detail about the great king than one would anticipate, and much of the history is set in Wales and directly tied to Roman sovereignty.

The symbol of the dragon (and its color) is one example of ties not only to Ambrosius Merlinus and Arthurian origins, but to Wales itself and even earlier, to the four centuries of Roman influence.

Wade-Evans writes,

> Here we find an intelligible explanation of how the Red Dragon became the symbol of Wales. Ammianus Marcellinus, the last Roman historian, describes in one place [xvi, 39] how Caesar was recognized in battle by the purple standard of the dragon, being

> the Roman imperial standard. As the one and only Roman emperor, known to have started out of Wales was Maxim Wletic, the origin of the Welsh dragon cannot but be ascribed to this event. In which case it may be regarded as a sign that the inauguration of Welsh national history (if it may be so termed) towards the close of the fourth century was attended by an ebullition of Roman feeling, *Romanitas,* which persisted among the Britons of Wales. In this case, it was the Red Dragon, that of Maxim Wletic, which led the way.[1]

The color purple is recorded in the earliest known work of Gildas Badonicus and correctly carries through to the tales of *The Mabinogion;* the red dragon is recorded in the tale of Emrys of the *HB* as an important emblem and accurately carries through to Geoffrey of Monmouth's narrative; the fictional name of Utherpendragon is derived from this symbol but changes colors again from red to gold and literarily becomes the representation of entwined serpents on Arthur's sword, Excalibur.

After "The Tale of Emrys" and "The Campaigns of Arthur" in the *HB,* there is an extended chasm of silence until Geoffrey of Monmouth writes about Aurelius Ambrosius, Utherpendragon and Ygerna, and the rise of Arthur in his *History of the Kings of Britain* during the third decade of the twelfth century. Thankfully, however, in addition to the Gildas and Nennius manuscripts, there are several other historical sources and a fair amount of literary tradition which paint a panoramic picture of the historic Arthur. There have been many speculations about the great king's origins—so many, in fact, that a spoof such as *Will the Real King Arthur Please Stand Up?* pokes fun at the scholarly attempts to prove that Arthur was an authentic character. Yet a serious pursuit of the real Arthur, delving into the right places, gleaning selective and precise details from the sea of information, and interpreting the age-old information in a proper perspective, shows that Arthur not only existed but participated in and influenced the historical milieu at the end of the fifth century and beginning of the sixth.

The history of the Arthurian era seems blurred by conflicting reports, or at least separate histories which, if compared, seem contradictory. Independent of King Arthur, Gildas Badonicus, writing of a time period just forty-four years before his own birth, chronicles the history leading up to the battle of Mons Badonicus, though he does not name Arthur as the Briton leader in that siege. After that victory he is writing of his own time, recording that external wars had stopped, but the aftershock of civil wars were still shaking the *Britanni* foundations. For literally centuries, the misplaced emphasis on what Gildas wrote has been on *external* wars rather than appropriately applied to the *civil conflicts* which tore Britain asunder.

There is a substantial body of evidence to support Gildas's lament that the generation immediately following Britain's glorious success had cast the nation into profligacy. The proof of this civil strife is founded upon the sketchy material provided on Cunedda in both the Welsh genealogies and the *Historia Brittonum.* Shortly after the Roman withdrawal from the island, Cunedda, the name which derives from the archaic spelling of Cunedag dating back to at least the seventh century,[2] came down with eight of his sons from the northern country of Manau Gododdin for the express purpose of driving the renegade Irish from Wales. According to the *HB,* Istorith and his clan prevailed in the country of Dementia and were expelled by Cunedda and his sons from all the territories of Britain.[3] The *HB* also gives a date for his migration,[4] linking him to Maelgwn, one of the later kings of Gwynedd, but the time frame has created a great deal of controversy, even though the years are written out and not given numerically.

In conjunction with other historical events and figures, however, Cunedda most likely migrated to the south at the request of a post-Roman authority "like that which brought in the Anglo-Saxons as allies."[5] The only intervening king between the withdrawal of the Roman empire from Britain and the leadership of Ambrosius Aurelianus was Vortigern, and his treasonous invitation to the Saxons is well-posted not only in the *HB* but also under the epithet of *superbus tyrannus* in the *DE.* During Vortigern's reign, his domain stretched the length and breadth of what is now called Wales, from Dementia (Dyfed) to the northern reaches of Gwynedd.

The Welsh genealogies record that Cunedda first settled in Carlisle near Hadrian's Wall upon his migration from the north. He was promised the vast territory from the River Dubr Duiu (Dee) southward to the River Tebi (Teifi), and upon driving out the *Scotti,* he was granted this dominion. In the history of Wales, the kingdom was divided, and several of those territories bore the names of his fourth son Dunaut—Dunodin; of his fifth son Cerdic—Ceredigion; and of Cerdic's son (Cunedda's grandson) Creoda—Creuddyn. Gwynedd later became Maelgwn's kingdom, inherited from his grandfather Enniaun Girt, Cunedda's seventh son. The floruits for Cunedda (435–465), Cerdic (465–495) and Creoda (495–525), who have such an important pivotal bearing upon King Arthur, fit into the milieu of the period.

Cunedda: a Pivotal Figure of History

This historical data attached to Cunedda's crucial role in insular history is not based upon unfounded assumptions or exaggerated episodes because of legendary or mythical offshoots. The histories portray Cunedda and his clan as unadorned, untainted figures of the Arthurian period; his role is not simply to resist *Scotti* encroachment but to expel them permanently from Welsh soil, and as a reward he is to receive the vast territory between the rivers Dee and Teifi. His invitation to migrate to the south occurs either shortly before the Roman withdrawal or shortly after the beginning of Vortigern's reign, and almost simultaneously he finds himself at war not only with the *Scotti,* but with the rebellious Saxons who were ostensibly allies with the Welsh tribes.

Cunedda's northern origins, the territory labeled the Manau Gododdin, offers another lesson in interpretation and translation; one of the fundamental directives of research stresses that only primary sources should be used, and only as a last resort should secondary sources be considered as acceptable. Even so, the snare is ever-present. Although Manau Gododdin plays an important role in the history of the period, its borders are normally and nonchalantly accepted as embracing the Gododdin general boundaries, or in Roman terms, the general parameters of the Votadini territory. With the exception of a few astute scholars, this locale has been traditionally accepted as authoritatively correct.

To accurately identify the Manau Gododdin, one must go beyond the translations of the *Historia Brittonum.* A different perspective develops from Chapter 62 after analyzing the original manuscript. One common translation, for example, relates that

> King Maelgwn the Great was reigning among the British in Gwynedd, for his ancestors, Cunedda, with his sons, to the number of eight, had come from the north, from the country called Manaw Gododdin, 146 years before Maelgwn reigned....[6]

A different translation of the same segment provides a meaning tinged with both subtle and literal differences. It reads:

> The great king, Mailcun, reigned among the Britons, i.e. in the district of the Guenedota, because his great-great-grandfather, Cunedda, with his twelve sons, had come before from the left-hand part, i.e. from the country which is called Manau Gustodin, one hundred and forty-six years before Mailcun reigned....[7]

Normally, the procedure is not as easy as simply looking at the original, because in the case of the *HB* there are at least seventeen variants. Comfortingly, however, Josephus Stevenson does not list any variants for this particular segment. The second translation makes a much more objective attempt at accuracy by using one technique only: The translator uses each form of a proper name as it appears in the original. And yet there are two glaring differences. One specifically states eight sons while the other lists twelve. Additionally, one expresses a time-frame in numerals, but the second spells out the number of years. These might at first seem like insignificant variations, but particularly with the latter, if the original manuscript had used numerals, there would have been a much higher probability of scribal error in recopying throughout the succeeding centuries. In Roman numerals, "146" was written in one of two ways, either CXLVI or CXXXXVI, the same type

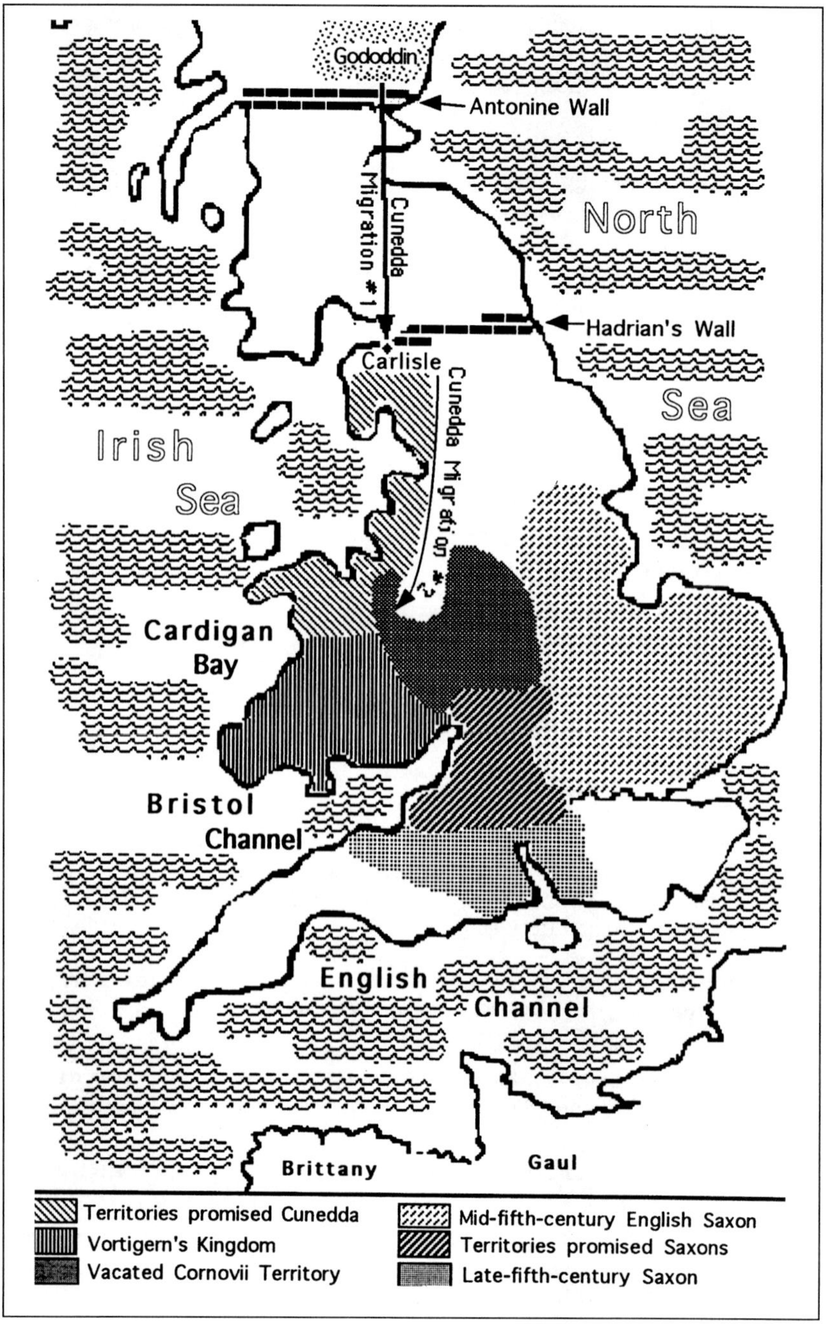

Map 6—Cunedda's path of migration.

of variation as CD and CCCC to represent four hundred. An error, therefore, of CXXXVI instead of CXXXXVI could much more easily occur in transcription rather than the expression *centum quadraginta sex.* A check of the original Latin resolves both problems immediately: The number of years are written out, and in accordance with the genealogies there are eight sons, not twelve. To be more historically accurate, Cunedda had nine sons, but the eldest died in Manau Gododdin prior to the southern migration.

Nevertheless, the difficulties of translations are not with the obvious differences, but with the subtle, seemingly insignificant variances. One of those suggested above and revealed by the *HKA* was the use of numerals in one commonly used translation as opposed to the Latin original, where it is written. In relation to a difference such as this, Leslie Alcock claims, logistically and statistically, that scribal error is much less likely to occur when numerals are written. In that same vein, Alcock explains that the word *atavus* in Latin can mean two different things: "ancestor," as interpreted in the first passage, or "great-great-great-grandfather," a much more specific concept, as used in the second passage.[8] The definition of this word points to another very common problem, which is called "scribal" or "transitional" errors when referring to ancient manuscripts, or "typographical errors" in modern terms. Alcock writes of "great-great-great-grandfather," while J. A. Giles writes of "great-great-grandfather," a difference of one generation, or approximately thirty years. "Mailcun" (or Mailcunus) is the older, original name for Maelgwn, which means again that the second translation is more historically accurate, but even so there should have been consistency because the original manuscript uses "Cunedag" for Cunedda, "Guenedotæ" for Guenedota or Gwynedd, and "Manau Guotodin" for Manau Gustodin or Manaw Gododdin.

Homeland

Prior to his move, Cunedda's homeland was Manau Guotodin, sometimes spelled as either Manau Gododdin or Manaw Gododdin, and sometimes incorrectly assumed to be the entire area of the Votadini tribe or the entire area named simply the Gododdin. As Alcock professes, there is no real dispute or controversy that Cunedda came from Manau Guotodin, not from Manaw, the Isle of Man. He then gives specifics about its location:

> a small district around the head of the Firth of Forth, on the northern limits of the tribal region or kingdom of the Guotodin, Gododdin, or Votadini.[9]

Scattered throughout his book, Wade-Evans also gives a specifically accurate locale as Cunedda's homeland, which he initially describes as "a little district to the west of Edinburgh ... on the southern shore of the Firth of Forth."[10] Using different landmarks, he describes Manau Gododdin as being to the west of Eiddyn, which is near Edinburgh and north of the Antonine Wall, [11] and becomes even more specific to clarify Collingwood's error when the latter individual describes the area as the country of the Otadini near Berwick-on-Tweed. Wade-Evans points out that

> [T]his contains at least two errors, for Manaw is known to have been a small portion beyond the Wall of Antonine facing Fife of the old (second century) territory of the Votadini (i.e., Gododdin in later Welsh), contemporary with the Selgovae, Novantae, and other "tribes"; and though Brewick-on-Tweed may be a mere slip for North Berwick, this too is not known ever to have been in Manaw.[12]

The erroneous identification of the ancient Manau Gododdin territory requires a closer analysis of this kingdom. A map[13] by William F. Skene shows The Manau Gododdin inland, a separate and distinctive kingdom to the *west* of the Gododdin, pictorially depicted as a large area to the south of the Firth of Forth. One translation of the *HB* relates that Cunedda came from the north, but a different translation more vaguely relates that Cunedda came from the left-hand part of the country.

This meant, of course, another etymological search, one which Cassell's Latin dictionary handled superbly. The original (Latin) manuscript narrates that Cunedda came from the *sinistral* part of the country, that is, from the region which is called Manau Guotodin.[14] The clarification is that "sinistral" means "from or on the left side." The Greeks, similar to the modern technique, faced north for a left versus right direction, thus orienting west to the left and right to the east. However, "...the Romans, who turned to the south, had the east on the left,"[15] which means that a modern-day researcher using a Roman-oriented map would be looking in the wrong sector if he were searching for Manau Gododdin in the sinistral part of the island. This error in orientation might explain why Skene devised his map the way he did. He probably knew, from all his prior research, that Gododdin was in the eastern part of the island, and tried to compensate by locating Manau Gododdin *a sinistra* (to the left, or west) of Gododdin.

Most researchers, however, are not confused by this, even though they might not realize the Roman mode of orientation as opposed to the Greek or modern one. Leslie Alcock correctly locates Manau Gododdin on "the *eastern* half of the Wall to the Firth of Forth,"[16] and the Votadini kingdom in "*eastern* Britain [near] the Firth of Forth and beyond [italics added]."[17] Similarly, those cartographers who depict the Gododdin in the same vicinity as Manau Gododdin and Votadini are correct in their placement, since the Gododdin name replaced the Roman one after the empire abandoned the island. Later divisions of Gododdin/Votadini were named Bernicia and Lothian, along the eastern coast and inland just to the west.

The issue, however, is specifically the location of Manau Gododdin, distinctive from Gododdin or Votadini. The province of Manau Gododdin appears only once in the *Historia,* in Book 62, and judging from Stevenson's commentary on all the manuscripts, the spelling remains constant throughout. The Isle of Man is recorded twice in the *Historia* (books 8 and 14) and twice in the *Annales Cambriae* at entries 584 and 684. In all instances except in Book 8, the Isle of Man is expressed in its Roman term, Eubonia. In that one instance, there are three variables which show up in the manuscripts: Manay, Euboniamanay, and Mana. Hence, it should be clear that Manau Gododdin is not a reference to the Isle of Man.

Aside from Cassell's dictionary, Sir Ifor Williams specifically focuses upon the Slamannan and Clackmannan areas near the mouth of the Firth of Forth, citing John Rhys as confirmation;[18] he later draws a comparison between Manau, Manaw, and Manann, which he relates to the Edinburgh district, and culminates with a reference to Mynyddawg Mwynfawr's court in Manaw Gododdin.[19] But by far the most comprehensive approach is supplied by Kenneth Jackson in (appropriately) the appendix of *The Gododdin.* The core of his explanation relates that Manau Gododdin is a narrow plain on the south side of the Firth of Forth, bounded by hills,

> ...but it extends from Grangemouth just east of Falkirk north-west to Stirling and round the head of the Firth, south to the Ochils, and eastwards past Alloa and Clackmannan to Kincardine opposite Grangemouth.[20]

He emphatically stresses that Manau Gododdin is a small province on the far north-western boundary of Gododdin and it cannot be assumed that it was the entire kingdom of Gododdin. One of the accurate maps which depicts this (also reflected in Map 14 of *The Historic King Arthur)* is in Barber's book, *The Figure of Arthur,* page 10. He encircles the area of Manau Gododdin and shows the Saxon kingdom of Bernicia, which would have been a segment of the earlier territory of Gododdin.

Motive for Cunedda Migration

Cunedda claims lineage from a Roman background: a father named Æternus, a grandfather named Paternus, and a great-grandfather named Tacitus. This heritage partially aids in uncovering the heretofore buried history of the period. Paternus, Cunedda's grandfather, was known as Patern Pesrut, Paternus of the Red Robe. And the Red Robe provides an indispensable key in structuring the events which followed in the decades during the abandonment by the Roman empire. It is commonly accepted that the color purple signified royalty for the Caesars; a direct offshoot is that those authorities with Roman heritage who remained on the island assumed the royal banners of color.

Maxim Wletic, a bona fide historical figure from the Roman empire, was the only Roman leader to emerge from Wales. After he was killed, the Picts, *Scotti,* and *Saxones* viewed his death as an opportunity to once again begin their incursions. The island, weakened by the Roman withdrawal, was dealt an even worse blow as the *Britanni* attempted to defend themselves against the fresh onslaught of barbarians. Vortigern came to power in this period, and hence the cause for Cunedda's migration lies with the waning Roman leaders *and* with the rising new Welsh king.

At this point in research, Cunedda's move to the south is an uncontested fact, but scholars are split on who instigated his migration, with both factions able to amass evidence to support their particular view. Wade-Evans, for example, writes that Cunedda came down from the north shortly after Honorius became emperor of the West and Stilicho, his minister, began the pacification of Britain. He is specific in stating that

> Directed by Stilicho, Cunedda assembled forces of divers elements, mostly British, who under the name of Cymry, "compatriots," congregated around Carlisle.... Their object in coming was to turn out the recent intruders from Ireland (not, of course the Irish of older standing), which they would seem to have accomplished with great effect.[21]

Just as Cunedda's northern dominion is not contentious, neither is the belief that he came from the north to expel the Irish. Here, however, Wade-Evans takes the stand that the invitation was by Stilicho, sanctioned by Honorius. The belief that Cunedda settled at Carlisle after his move to the south is based upon a poem by Taliesin,[22] which records a site named Caer Liwelydd; John Morris, among others, also interprets Caer Ligualid (his translation) as Carlisle.[23]

Other researchers, although they accept Cunedda's migration from Manau Gododdin to Carlisle, do not as readily agree that it was by invitation from Stilicho. Alcock gives the range of possibilities. At one point he writes, "It is arguable that it was Maximus who took care of north-west Wales by moving Cunedda and his war-band from somewhere north of the Forth."[24] This would mean, of course, an earlier period than Stilicho, before Honorius became emperor. Concentrating upon the time period, Alcock writes a few pages later that Cunedda's migration was an act of Roman policy if it took place around A.D. 380, but it (the migration) may have been organized by some sub-Roman authority associated with the Anglo-Saxon alliance if Cunedda's movement south occurred around 450. Alcock considered one other possibility, that if Cunedda's migration was "as late as 490 it was certainly an act of private enterprise."[25]

By the "sub-Roman authority which brought in the Anglo-Saxons as allies," he is referring to the *superbus tyrannus* of Gildas Badonicus and the Vortigern of Nennius. A previous chapter of this book questions the belief that Vortigern is the *superbus tyrannus*, but instead proposes that this title—*superbus tyrannus*—identifies someone with supreme power who is not answerable to anyone higher. This book also suggested the possibility that Cunedda might be the figure behind the title of "Vortimer," in which case Vortigern would be his father, making the motive behind Cunedda's migration strong blood-ties rather than a mercenary payoff. The key factor, of course, in determining which of the three possibilities is most likely depends upon chronological calibration. Attention must therefore shift to the time-frame of Cunedda's migration.

The Chronological Computation of Cunedda's Migration

In aligning Cunedda's migration to Stilicho's bidding, Wade-Evans writes "...doubtless as part of Stilicho's policy Cunedda Wledig and his sons arrived (401) in Wales...."[26] which sets the date of Cunedda's transit in 401. Wade-Evans determines this particular year by calculating the difference between *Ida's* reign in 547 (which he thought was mistakenly labeled as *Maelgwn's* reign) minus 146 years. The same calculation based upon the combined information from the Maelgwn obit in the *Annales Cambriae* and the *Historia Brittonum* nets the same result. Thus, Wade-Evans assumes the veracity of Cunedda's migration date as 401. However, as the material in Chapter 1 of this text suggests, establishing an accurate calibration for Cunedda's migration is not that simple.

The book *The Historic King Arthur* established that the obit as posted in the *AC* for Maelgwn's death was reliable, but of course the 146 years recorded in the *HB* raises an immediate disavowal. Even if the conjecture proposed in Chapter 1 is rejected—that 146 years must be subtracted from the beginning of Outigern's reign to determine the year of Cunedda's movement—then historical events of the period still support a date four decades later than Wade-Evans projected. One of the quotations which Wade-Evans points to in support of his conjecture is the *Chronica Gallic a. CCCCLII.* Unlike Alcock, who more accurately supplies the year such as "16[th year of joint rule of Theodosius and Valentinian],"[27] Wade-Evans simply records "A.D. 409," and then gives the information that, "At this time the strength of the Romans [was] exceedingly enfeebled by weakness, Britains [were] ravaged by an incursion of *Saxones*."[28] His interpretation is that there was an invasion of barbarians from the continent by those whom the Romans indiscriminately called the *Saxones*. Yet this interpretation is not necessarily accurate; the Roman term *Saxones* was a generic term for Germanic Angles (sometimes written as Angels) and Saxons who had arrived from the continent, but they had been settled on the island for several generations. In other words, the *Saxones* invasions were *not* from the mainland but were *internal* attacks, and furthermore, the Empire was simultaneously being attacked by the Germanic Saxons on the continent, in addition to the Visigoths, Franks, and Huns. It was these severe attacks in 410 on the mainland which caused the sacrifice (abandonment) of Britain in hopes of saving the West.

Once the Empire shrank its borders by concentrating on the mainland at the expense of the territories on the island, Honorius extended a token grant sanctioning the local kings and tribes to bear arms against not only the English Saxons, but against the Picts, the Irish, and the invading German Saxons who might venture across the Channel. This Rescript legalized political self-government for defense and protection. The *Lex Julia Majestatis* according to Zosimus, vi, 10, MHB lxxix, was relaxed in their favor, and Honorius "monished them to protect themselves," words used later in 440 when Genseric the Vandal was threatening with his fleet the coasts of the Empire, suggesting that the words were a technical relaxation of the standard policy. It was under these conditions, after Rome had withdrawn from the island, that Cunedda was enticed to the south. In the only two segments which name Cunedda, the *HB* specifically limits Cunedda's task as driving out the Irish "from all the countries in Britain,"[29] which again it specifically lists as Dementia, St. David's Head, Carmarthenshire, Pembrokshire, Cardiganshire, and the domain which was to later become Gwynedd. These are the same territories Vortigern was attempting to protect.

In discussing archaeological finds of hoards, which he claims was a widespread occurrence among the tribes on the fringes of the Roman Empire, Alcock indirectly points to the motive behind Cunedda's migration. There was a rich hoard found at the hill fort of Traprain Law, in the province of the Votadini, which Alcock felt would have been allied to the Romans. He further conjectures that this hoard was not loot but Roman payment in bullion "for the services of Votadinian mercenaries."[30]

The importance of this discovery hinges upon Traprain Law in the Votadinian territory and its proximity to Cunedda's original northern homeland. If in truth finds such as this can be interpreted as mercenary payments, then it is judicious to accept what I. A. Richmond suggests in his text. When the Romans initially withdrew from the island to protect their boundaries on the continent, the action was viewed as a temporary one; for several decades after their abandonment, no one believed that the Romans would not return. Having been entrenched in Britain for over four centuries, no empire as powerful and pervasive as that of the Romans could ever be in serious jeopardy of defeat or annihilation. In addition to Vortigern's fear of Ambrosius and his fear of Pictish and Irish invasions, his other real fear was the return of the Romans to the island.

The basis of this fear stemmed from what was typical Roman policy. Honorius as well as his predecessors

> had adopted for Britain the policy of settling folk of the outlands, in this case Saxons, in the border territories of the Empire which they had once come to rob, giving them lands in exchange for military service.[31]

Vortigern, then, might have been acting under a direct suggestion of the Roman emperor (the *superbus tyrannus)*, or had adopted the common policy which the Romans had followed in encouraging the Saxons to become allies. Perhaps Gildas Badonicus was too harsh in the condemnation of the *superbus tyrannus;* this new emperor of the West was more than likely simply following the age-old policy of hiring local mercenary tribes. And Bede, who assumed that the *superbus tyrannus* was Vortigern, new Briton king, was undoubtedly too harsh on a tribal sub-king under an obligation to someone who far exceeded his own localized powers.

This policy applicable to the Saxons could likewise have been the typical impetus behind the Cunedda migration from the north. As an interim king, Vortigern could have been directed to seek allies the way the Romans had done, or on his own volition.

> Vortigern's action can be seen as forming part of the pattern of devolution rather than as a new remedy by a desperate and inexperienced native prince.[32]

Under these circumstances, the outcome would have been the same. In the transitional phase of Rome's withdrawal and the *Britanni* kings fending for themselves during the second through fourth decades of the fifth century, the purpose was to repel the barbaric invaders from the north, from the west, and from across the Channel.

Cunedda's Ancestry and Progeny

The name of Cunedag—Cunedda in the later manuscripts—gives some amazing insights into his genealogy. Both Rachel Bromwich and Thomas O'Sullivan[33] give some sketchy information about the etymological significance of Cunedag's name, but those particulars are much more profoundly consequential than they first seem. In his castigation of the five tyrants, Gildas Badonicus supplies a great deal of information about Cunedda's clan. The first, Constantine, is referred to as "leænæ Damnoniæ tyrannicus catulus,"[34] translated as "the tyrant cub of the filthy lioness of Dumnonia." The Latin term "catulus" refers generically to a young animal, but here, because it attaches to a lioness, the translation of "cub" is more appropriate. Michael Winterbottom uses the term "whelp,"[35] but although that term is a generic reference to any young carnivorous animal, it is specifically used to identify a dog's young, not a lion's.

Gildas uses the expression "catule leonine"[36] to describe Aurelius Caninus. As with Constantine, this is a reference to a "lion's cub," a more accurate term than a lion's whelp. Then, continuing his comparison, Gildas calls Vortipor "pardo similis,"[37] like a panther, or more generally, like a leopard. Cuneglasus is ascribed the most interesting but the most interpretive attributes. He is called in "*Romana lingua lanio fulve.*"[38] The first two words are, of course, "In the *Roman language.*" O'Sullivan defines "lanio" as "butcher," "executioner," or "one who mangles."[39] In addition to the noun form, however, this particular word is also a verb declension which could connote a slashing, ripping, lacerating predator. Combined with "fulvus," meaning "tawny," which in turn most commonly suggests the color of a lion, Gildas is categorizing the four tyrants as belonging to the same clan or tribe, associated with Cunedda.

Maglocunus is the only tyrant who is described differently; he, unlike the others, is referred to as "insularis draco,"[40] the dragon of the island. Gildas writes of Maglocunus as having a face in battle not much different from the faces of the lion's cubs. What he means by this cryptic observation is difficult to decipher. Maglocunus, Cuneglasus, and Cunedag all have the same affix base, "-cunos-." Bromwich labels this as a genetive form meaning "dog," but based upon Gildas's writing and the references in the *Pa gur* poem in which Llachau and Kei are fighting "lions," a better interpretation for the affix "-cunos-" seems to be "lion," a reference to the northern tribes bearing this symbol. To compound the mystique of Maglocunus, it is interesting to speculate why Gildas Badonicus calls him dragon of the island, especially in combination with Monmouth's fictitious character Utherpendragon of almost six hundred years later, and its filtration likewise through the *Pa gur* poem as "Uthyr Pendragon."

Perhaps no more than a coincidence but still of interest, Gildas, the *Pa gur* poet, and Monmouth could all have been suggesting a connection between Cunedda's northern royalty and the standard of the Roman Caesars, the purple dragon. As Rachel Bromwich suggests, there is a strong case supporting the contention that much of the Welsh heroic tradition stemmed originally from the "Old North,"[41] and that the quest for Arthur's identity must take into account this movement of oral tradition from the earlier northern *Cymry* territories southward and westward to what became known as Wales. Cunedda's original homeland, Manau Gustodin, was at one point in early history a strategically important locale, adjacent to the Antonine Wall when the Roman Empire expanded its northern perimeter, a locale where the Roman military would have practiced its typical policy of inducting local tribes as allies to protect its newly set borders. That local chieftain might well have been Æternus, Cunedda's father, and Cunedda would have inherited the powers of that local chieftain. Once the Empire's borders were relocated again to the south at Hadrian's Wall, Cunedda, based upon his father's successful record in the north, would have been enticed by an authority to migrate south as a mercenary contingency in return for grants of territory between the Rivers Dee and Teifi. This movement would also explain the transit of oral tradition from the Old North to Wales.

Logistically, an inspection of Cunedda's forefathers does, in fact, bear out a connection to Roman royalty. As continuously pointed out, Cunedda claims Roman lineage from a father named Æternus, a grandfather named Paternus, and a great-grandfather named Tacitus. In commenting upon Cunedda's three immediate predecessors as being Roman, Alcock suggests that this northern family had strong ties to the Roman influence in the south. He writes that "[i]n particular ... Paternus' red robe or cloak was a mark of some romanized authority or office, or at least of recognition by the Romans."[42] Just as Arthur's (inferring also Ambrosius's) contingency is associated with the color purple as a rank of royalty, Cunedda's ancestry could also have been granted authority, though of course, a lower rank than the *superbus tyrannus*.

Not many scholars comment upon Cunedda's heritage, but Wade-Evans does convey the following:

> That *Romanitas* prevailed in the country between the Walls is shown by the tradition of Cunedda Wledig (son of Eternus, son of Paternus, surnamed Pais rudd "red tunic," son of Tacitus) in Manaw Gododdin on the Forth, and of Ceredig Wledig at Dumbarton....[43]

Hence, whenever the color purple (or red) or the symbols of dragons, lions, ravens, hawks, and bears appear, it is worth in-depth exploration to look for connections. The significance of the insignia of a red dragon on the Welsh national flag is not widely publicized, although the "Tale of Emrys" in the *HB* offers a very plausible explanation. Ambrosius, who can interpret the symbols, tells Vortigern in essence, "The red serpent is *your* [italics added] dragon." In addition to the color purple, red is also notable in the Arthurian material. Not only is Vortigern's symbol a red dragon, but the Welsh flag carries on the tradition. Additionally, Cunedda's grandfather was known as *Patern Pesrut,* or *Pais rudd),* Paternus of the Red Tunic.

A syllogism shouldn't be constructed for the parallels between various characters and the color red, because syllogisms can be valid or invalid, correct or incorrect, depending upon the relationship between premise and conclusion. But a paradigm is certainly in order; when side-by-side parallels are drawn, a pattern emerges which seems to be more than just coincidence. Using the color red as a connector between Vortigern, Paternus, and as extensions of bloodlines Æternus and Cunedda, several conclusions can be drawn. For one, Vortigern is correctly perceived as having connections with Wales and the kingdoms there, not in Kent or other parts of Britain. Additionally, it implies that Vortigern, Paternus, and Cunedda are all of the same tribe.

Third, it adds validity that Vortigern is an epithet for Æternus, Paternus's son. Last, by extension, it infers that if Vortigern is Æternus, then Vortimer is an epithet for Cunedda. This would then align symbology with authentic history. Borrowed from the purple dragon of the Roman Empire, the red dragon[44] became the symbol of Welsh insular history. It carried with it nationalistic pride and patriotism from Paternus through Æternus's and Cunedda's generations, but it was defiled when it reached Cunedda's progeny, specifically Cerdic and Enniaun Girt, and then spilled over into the succeeding generational kings, Creuddyn, Cyneglassus, and Maglocunus. Gildas Badonicus characterized the desecration of the symbol when he assigns to Maelgwyn the deprecating epithet of "dragon of the island." The color red, then, initially bound Vortigern/Æternus, Cunedda/Vortimer, Cerdic, and Ambrosius as fellow-countrymen with *Romanophil* leanings until Cerdic switched allegiance and embroiled the island in civil war.

One other item must be mentioned before focusing further upon Cunedda's progeny. One of Taliesin's poems provides several key words about Cunedda. In part, it is as follows:

> There is trembling from fear of Cunedda the burner,
> In Caer Weir and Caer Lliwelydd [Caer Liwelydd].
> There is trembling from the mutual encounter.
> A complete billow of fire over the seas,
> A wave in which the brave fell among his companions.
>
> ....
>
> The death of Cunedda, which I deplore, is deplored.
> Deplored be the strong protector, the fearless defender,
> He will assimilate, he will agree with the deep and shallow,
> A deep cutting he will agree to.
>
> ....
>
> A chief of lion aspect, ashes become [Cunedda's] fellow-countrymen,
> Against the son of Edern [Aeternus], before the supremacy of terrors,
> He was fierce, dauntless, irresistible,
> For the streams of death he is distressed.[45]

Although impossible to identify without qualification, the geography and history of the era suggest that Caer Weir could be a reference to Viroconium (Wroxeter), a major Roman fortress during the era, located in the central midlands, a base that would have been strategically crucial once the Romans abandoned the Cornovii territory. Unquestionably, Caer Lliwelydd (Luilid, Ligualid) identifies Carlisle, Cunedda's initial base once he migrated to the south from Manau. A "strong protector, fearless defender" carries overtones of Æternus's role passed on to his progeny; Cunedda's poetic title of a "chief of lion aspect" tends to confirm, like the *Pa gur* poem cited earlier, that Cunedda's clan, the Lion clan, was later in opposition to Arthur's forces, which is reinforced by the remainder of the poetic line: Cunedda's fellow-countrymen have become ashes. To put the same idea into Gildas's words,

"External wars may have stopped, but not civil ones."[46] The next line—naming his father as Æternus—re-confirms Cunedda's Roman connections.

Cunedda and his ancestry laid the foundation for the major Welsh role in insular history; it is now time to analyze the major role which his progeny plays in the Arthurian saga. After his migration to the south, and by the time Cunedda passes through history, the stark reality that the Romans will never return to Britan is finally driven home. The Britons, the Welsh, the English Saxons, the German Saxons, and the Bretons, upon recovering from the shock waves of independence which reverberated throughout the island for literally decades, had to begin rebuilding new kingdoms upon the old ruins of the Empire. The all-powerful Roman Protectorate was a thing of the past; the tribes and kingdoms were forced to govern themselves.

7

The Breach of Colors: *Romanitas* Versus Cunedda's Progeny and the Saxons

The Interfusion of Arthur's Personality

Before one can formulate the essence of Arthur's adversaries, one must continuously attempt to extract feelings or notions pervading the milieu of the fifth and sixth centuries in Britain. Just as important, one must explore the singular most influential figure to emerge as Britain's heroic, evanescent savior, Ambrosius Aurelianus, prior to his assuming the epithet "Arthur." Both the *Historic King Arthur* and several earlier chapters in this volume have concentrated intently upon Ambrosius, and yet persistent reinforcement is essential, since it is impossible to understand Arthur without understanding the history which molded him.

The histories of both Gildas and Bede do not identify a hero named Arthur. Even the *Historia Brittonum* of a later century is sparse in the praise of Arthur, recording his name only four times, one of which is in the *Mirabilia.* The *Annales Cambriae,* of a century later than the *HB* and even further removed from Gildas and Bede, gives Arthur's name in two laconic entries. Shortly after the turn of the millennium Welsh chronicles and genealogies record Arthur's name more heavily, and by Geoffrey of Monmouth's time an elaborate mystique had emerged about Arthur, King of Britain. Some tales from *The Mabinogion* sprang up about Arthur; his name was recorded in bardic poetry; and both Wace's and Layamon's *Bruts* embellished Arthur's fame. All these opened the floodgates of the romances several centuries later. What can be gleaned from this transformation is that Ambrosius Aurelianus was the historical Briton hero-king, and as time passed, an exaggerated chimera of Arthurian escapades evolved.

The only early manuscript which records both Ambrosius's and Arthur's names is the *HB*, but in this source the two are not linked in any general or specific way; there is no suggestion of their being companions, contemporaries, or military associates, and there is no implication that the two are blood-relations. Alcock considered the historical credibility of Ambrosius and Arthur, additionally adding Vortigern to his list. By citing various manuscripts which record the names, he concludes that both Vortigern—knowing of course that this term is actually an epithet and not a proper name—and Ambrosius have stronger claims to historicity, but "much of the widespread skepticism about the historicity of Arthur stems from the undoubted fact that his name became attached to unhistorical tales, to fabulous wonders, and to places which can never have been connected with him."[1]

After the very brief notices of Arthur in the *HB* and later the *AC*, the name does not resurface again until its advent in the Welsh tales and chronicles reflecting a much earlier oral tradition than its written word. Whether appropriated or invented, Monmouth's manuscript provides the most comprehensive information about Arthur. Upon the appearance of his work, there is a distinctive separation between Ambrosius and Arthur. From what seems to verify the *liber vetustissimus*, Monmouth indelibly records for all the future generations that Ambrosius was one of the sons of a vaguely identified Constantine. Arthur is designated as the son of Ambrosius's brother, the "fictitious" Utherpendragon, and henceforth Monmouth gives confusing and conflicting information about the kinship between Ygerna and Aurelius Ambrosius, between Aurelius Ambrosius and Cador, and most commonly between Ambrosius (or Arthur) and Mordred, each of the contradictory kinships appearing several times throughout Monmouth's manuscript and further suggesting a borrowed source.

Arthur's advent as a separate figure is as bogus as Merlin's emergence as a historical individual. Toward the end of Monmouth's segment on "The House of Constantine," most of the material is directly borrowed from the *HB* but at one point Monmouth substitutes the name Emrys (that is, Aurelius Ambrosius) for Merlin, referring to this figment of his imagination as "Merlin, who was also called Ambrosius" and later "Ambrosius Merlin."[2]

Alcock realized the importance of this tenet when he wrote,

> Even the fables about Vortigern's citadel and the conflict of Ambrosius and the magicians may contain truth about Vortigern's sphere of influence in north Wales, and about a real conflict, partly political and partly religious, between Ambrosius and Vortigern himself.[3]

At this point, the political implication should be evident. Upon the Roman evacuation, the *Britanni* no longer had the assurance of adequate protection; after having relied upon Roman guardianship for literally centuries, the *Britanni* were admonished to set up their own government and their own defenses. In a state of panic, Vortigern attempted to do just that, and after failing miserably, he fled to the distant reaches of his kingdom. Alcock believed that evidence of this type of scenario was clearest in Wales; among several notable sites, he lists Dinas Emrys, where Ambrosius confronted Vortigern, as yielding pottery and other finds of the Arthurian period.[4]

Alcock becomes even more explicit about some of his finds and concludes by focusing upon the archaeological finds at Dinas Emrys, the fortress of Ambrosius, in northern Wales near Beddgelert. This is the famous fortress where Ambrosius, as a young boy, confronts Vortigern and his wizards. Alcock cautions that the artifacts found there cannot be specifically linked to Vortigern or Ambrosius, but he does conclude that "a sherd [shard] from a Class E cooking pot, fragments of Biv amphorae, an amulet with *chi-rho* and *alpha-omega* symbols, and evidence of metalworking … point to Dinas Emrys as a prince's stronghold."[5]

He elaborates even more. He writes that at Dinas Emrys, local Glamorgan iron ores were smelted and forged into weapons, knives, and other tools. Additionally, excavation of the site disclosed the casting of bronze and gold jewelry.[6] This range of metal-smithing once again indicates that the citadel was occupied by an important chieftain. Alcock then turns to the work done by Dr. H. N. Savory of the National Museum of Wales who excavated the hilltop fortification of Dinas Emrys, and although his discoveries did not prove that Ambrosius built the citadel at this hill fort, he did show that a British chief had a fortress there toward the close of the fifth century, "enjoying a measure of luxury and wealth."[7] But historically this British chief did not know a separate individual named Merlin; instead, Merlin must be viewed as an alter ego of Ambrosius.

This is suggested after Monmouth injected "The Prophecies of Merlin" into his manuscript and then continued Part Two of "The House of Constantine." Monmouth inserts Merlin as a separate character, who predicts Vortigern's downfall at the hands of the two brothers Ambrosius and Utherpendragon. Once Ambrosius is anointed as king, Merlin, identified as the "prophet of Vortigern,"[8] is summoned by the new king to erect a special monument which entails moving Stonehenge from Mount Killarus in Ireland to Mount Ambris in Britain. From that point onward, Merlin is interwoven into the story as a distinctive new personality, just as Arthur becomes a separate figure who retains all the characteristics attributed to Ambrosius. Transferred to Arthur are: 1) the color purple signifying Roman royalty, 2) direct ancestry to Constantine (more accurately Constantius), 3) the title of king among kings or emperor, 4) kinship with Mordred as his son, 5) links to Amlawdd the Great and thus to Ygerna and Cador, and 6) continental connections with both Gaul and Brittany. There is also a parallel of adversity with Vortigern as a usurper, ongoing wars with the Saxons, several battles against Cerdic, and a Cornish affinity.

Excluding Arthur's portrayal in the *Saints' Lives,* because these picaresque tales are biased in the saints' favor, Arthur becomes almost godlike. Carried over from history as Ambrosius, he is the most honorable man to survive the onslaught of barbarians; he saved the island from annihilation after the storm, and he is beyond compare as a magician confronting Vortigern's wizards, which suggests his powerful druidic background.

In "How Culhwch Won Olwen" (one of the earliest tales of *The Mabinogion* set in northern Wales) the emphasis shifts from Ambrosius to Arthur. The main character, Culhwch, states that the "daughter of the ruler Amlawdd is my mother."[9] Although he does not name his mother, she would be Ygerna according to the *Tysilio,* thus identifying Arthur as Culhwch's first cousin. The oddity given previously in the tale is the description of Culhwch's mantle: "[He] wore a four-cornered purple mantle with a red-gold apple in each corner; each apple was worth a hundred cows."[10] This instantly draws attention to the color purple recorded by Gildas Badonicus as a symbol of Roman royalty for Ambrosius Aurelinaus's parents and hence for Ambrosius himself, since according to Roman law, authority transferred from one generation to another. These connections, coupled with the passage in "The Dream of Rhonabwy" that Arthur's mantle had "a red-gold apple in each corner"[11] signify the Roman royalty of the two ancestral lines. This parallel of Roman authority evinced by the color purple for both Ambrosius historically and Arthur literarily is one of the reasons underlying the theory proposed in *The Historic King Arthur* that "Arthur" is an epithet for the proper name "Ambrosius Aurelinaus."

Of Arthur's mantle being named Gwenn, Jeffrey Gantz translates that word as "white."[12] This interpretation allows objectors to deny the theory that Culhwch's and Arthur's mantles are the same color and logo. However, for those who do indeed believe that both mantles are purple, Gantz mentions in his introductory remarks that the evolution of Welsh words has led to multiple and sometimes diverse definitions, so that "it is not always clear which [definition] is meant."[13] "Gwenn" is one such example; it can literally mean the color white, but it can likewise connote purity or chastity. The name "Gwenn Alarch" in the Culhwch tale, for instance, does suggest the color white; "arlarch" means swan, so it logistically follows that her name would translate to "White Swan." But the name "Gwenn Lliant" is not as clear-cut; "lliant" means flood, so that her name could more likely be translated as "Foamy Flood."[14] For Arthur's mantle, the translation for "gwenn" which makes the most sense is "invisible" or "transparent," particularly since one of its magical properties is that "a man wrapped in it could see everyone but no one could see him, nor would it allow any other colour on it but its own."[15] The suggestion, therefore, is that only those of royalty would be allowed to wear the mantle or could use its power.

By unraveling the jumble of history and intertwining the strands with more care and logistics, an orderly design of Celtic weave magically discloses the heretofore hidden intricacies of character and sequence of events. Ambrosius Aurelianus/Emrys/Merlin/ Aurelius Ambrosius/Utherpendragon/Riothamus/Arthur under the initial protection of Vitalinus/Guitolin/ Guithelinus is threatened by the usurper Vortigern/Æternus/Esla who is following the orders of the *superbus tyrannus/* Valentinian III. Cunedag/ Cunedda/Vortimer/Elesa comes down from the north to help drive the Irish and the Picts from Britain. His fifth son, Cerdic/Ceretic/Chelric/ Cheldric/Chedric turns against his own Welsh heritage and treacherously casts his allegiance with the English Saxons, notably Octha/Octa/Osla Big Knife/Æsc, in fighting internal wars for supremacy on the island. All the variable names induce a certain confusion, but if each name is selected individually, the story is both coherent and short.

Cunedda's Progeny as Arthur's Adversaries

The threads of Cerdic's relevance tie together two disparate sources. The first is, of course, Welsh. The name Cerdic appears in the Welsh genealogies as Cunedda's fifth son, of Welsh royalty, who migrated with his father from Manau Gododdin or at least was born in Wales shortly after the migration. Additionally, the name Cerdic appears in Chapter 37 of the *Historia Brittonum.* Hengist, an Angle *(Saxone)* mercenary recruited by Vortigern to fight the Picts and the Irish, is bargaining his daughter Renwein for territories through an interpreter "whose name was Ceretic."[16] Because of the confusing grammatical structure, most translations, such as that by J. A. Giles,[17] indicate that Cerdic is *Hengist's* interpreter. But scholars invariably agree that Cerdic is a Welsh name. Richard Barber directly lists Ceretic as Hengist's interpreter, writing that this interpreter "and no other Briton among the Britons knew Saxon except this man...."[18] Hence, he correctly identifies Cerdic as Briton, but doesn't clarify Cerdic as Cunedda's son, a young boy who would have had close ties with Vortigern.

The other source is *The Anglo-Saxon Chronicle.* From out of nowhere, Cerdic makes his appearance in the entry of 495: "In this year two ealdormen Cerdic and Cynric his son came to Britain with five ships [arriving] at the place which is called *Cerdicesora,* and the same day they fought against the Welsh."[19] Among others, Charles Plummer, one of the most respected scholars of Anglo-Saxon history, confirms that Cerdic is not a Saxon name: "It is curious to find the traditional founder of the West-Saxon kingdom, the source to which all West-Saxon pedigrees are traced, bearing a name Cerdic, Certic, so like the Welsh Ceredig, Ceretic. (It is worth noting that in Nennius, § 37, Ceretic is the name of Hengest's interpreter.)"[20] He, too, incorrectly assumes that Ceretic is Hengist's interpreter, but more significant is his confusion of seeing the Welsh name Cerdic in the West-Saxon genealogies.

It becomes more than just a curiosity; it becomes the rock-bottom premise for the history of the era. In answer to the fundamental question of why the Welsh name Cerdic appears in a Saxon chronicle, the answer is ludicrously simple: Cerdic the West-Saxon king is not Saxon, he is Welsh.

The next question of how that can be is much more serious, but it is answerable, offering not only proof that he is *not* Saxon, but also confirming that he *is* Welsh. A comparison of the entries prior to Cerdic's appearance in the *ASC* allows a different perspective. The entry of 449 parallels the information provided by the *HB;* it links the Welsh (in the *persona* of Vortigern) and Hengist, one of the leaders of Saxon *Adventus* #2. Both the *HB* and the *ASC* report that the Saxons entered Britain by invitation. By the years 455, 457, 465 and even into 473 it is evident from both sources that the alliance had disintegrated, and there was war between the Welsh and the *Saxones. None* of these entries from the *ASC* even remotely imply that there were invasions from across the Channel. The *Saxones* had been living in eastern Britain for generations, and the ensuing conflicts are *internal* to Britain, meaning that for nearly two decades the battles do not involve the *Britanni* trying to repulse the *Saxones* as they crossed the Channel from the continent, but that the battles themselves are being fought *in Wales,* a vastly larger territory known as *Cymru* during that particular era.

Then in 477 Ælle, from the bona fide *Angle* house of Deira, intruded into Britain from outside its borders. The most common postulation is that he and his three sons landed on the southern coast of the island, near Selsey Bill. But there are three grating discrepancies in the entry. One peculiarity is that he is a *German Saxon* fighting the *Welsh* on the southern coast of Britain in *Sussex.* Second, one of Ælle's three sons is called Cymen, a name suspiciously like Cymru. And third, even more spurious, Ælle and his sons landed at *Cymenesora,* a *Welsh* location interpreted as The Owers off the *southern* coast of Britain. Only after these bizarre events does Cerdic, a *Welsh* name, appear in the *ASC* as the founder of the West Saxon royal house. The number of inconsistencies are so outrageous that they're humorous.

If sanity is to be restored to the histories, Cerdic's lineage as listed in the *ASC* must be viewed in a *Welsh* context. Entry 552 contains Cerdic's ancestry: Cerdic was the son of Elesa, the son of Esla, the son of Gewis...."[21] Geoffrey Ashe initially made a connection between the name Eliseg on a genealogical pillar in Wales and the name Elesa in the Saxon chronology. The word "Gewisse" figures into early medieval Welsh and also attaches to the name of Gewis as one of Cerdic's forebears.[22] Cerdic's father is known as Cunedda in a Welsh context, but it would not be uncommon for his father to have a distinctive name such as Elesa in a Saxon context. Ashe reaches the conclusion that the similarity between the Valle Crucis pillar and the genealogy in the *Chronicle* suggest a "phase of British fraternisation and intermarriage in the fifth century, before the debacle."[23]

The name "Gewis" (Cerdic's great-grandfather in the *Chronicle)* is the same cognate as the term "Gewisse." It is a Welsh reference to the West Saxon people, meaning "allies" or "compatriots." A lengthy search through Eilert Ekwall shows that the words Gewisse, Hwicce, and Hyrpe are also variants of the same cognate, suggesting territories settled by the Saxons who had lived on the island for several generations. If Gewisse place-names were plotted on a map, the boundaries would match almost identically the division between the Welsh territories and the old domain of the Roman Cornovii province. Although the tendency is to label the Saxon genealogy as bogus because it fades into mythological fantasy, the similarity between "Gewis" and "Gewisse" is too obvious to ignore. The similarity gives rise to evidence that the connection between Cerdic the West-Saxon king and Cerdic of Welsh heritage is much more solidly based than expected. John Morris is not attempting to make a correlation, but in *The Age of Arthur* he discusses the name of "Gewissae" being defined as *federates* (or confederates) who eventually adopted the name "West Saxons." He writes that the term Gewissae "was ... probably the earlier name of the Berkshire English ... known to the British as Saxons, as were all other English.... Thereafter "West Saxon" was the common and usual national name...."[24]

Following a similar pattern, the Romans themselves used the term "Britanni" generically to refer to all peoples and all tribes who were settled on the island of Britain; that is, "Britanni" included all the provincials of the Roman empire who settled as natives and therefore fell under the protectorate of the empire. The term most commonly referred to the pre-Roman inhabitants called the Ancient Britons used by Gildas, but the term also applied to Welsh and Saxon settlers alike. Before the advent of the term "Welsh" or the common use of the phrase "English Saxons" (as opposed to "German Saxon," who were considered foreigners from across the Channel), the term "Briton" meant those settlers *west* of Cornovii as opposed to the English Saxons of East Anglia to the *east* of Cornovii. In Roman terms, that meant "English Saxons" referred to those Britanni who occupied part of Britannia Secunda and Britannia Maxima, and "Britons" referred to those native inhabitants of Britannia Prima. The Roman buffer between East Anglia (part of the English Saxon settlement) and the Cymru was the territory of Cornovii. Once the Romans left, war developed between the Welsh and those *Saxones* who were once allies in an attempt to grab the vacated province.

The parallel between the names of Elesa and Eliset (or Eliseg) is not particularly difficult to corroborate. For one, the *location* of the inscribed stone bearing Eliseg's name is ideal for establishing a connection between the Saxon and Welsh names. It is one of the most famous of the Ogham stones, erected in the old kingdom of Powys near Llangollen in northeastern Wales. Dating from the ninth century and bearing an inscription now nearly illegible, it was dedicated in honor of Eliseg, King of Powys. The pillar, mentioned above and most commonly known as Eliseg's Pillar, is the shaft of a broken cross that gave the valley and the neighboring abbey their names, Valle Cruis (Valley of the Cross) and Valle Crucis Abbey. Fortunately, the inscription was copied and translated by a foresighted Welsh antiquarian named Edward Lhuyd in 1696,[25] but even in his day the stone had weathered so badly that much of inscription was illegible and Eliseg's ancestry was obscured. However, two entries in the *AC* carry Eliseg's name for the years 814 and 943. The 943 entry is traceable back to the Clonmacnoise Chronicle, which adds that Elizeg and his father Idwal (Iudgual) were killed by the West Saxons.[26] Even though the name Idwal isn't traceable, Elise ab Idwal is the closest similarity to Elesa of the *ASC*. Hence, because there is the name Elise as a parallel to Elesa, it logistically follows that Cunedda might have been known as Elesa by the English Saxons who had once been mercenary allies of his father, Æternus.

These assertions also lead to other positive correlations supporting the contention that Cerdic son of Cunedda, Cerdic the young interpreter for Vortigern and Hengist, and Cerdic the eventual king of the West-Saxons are all references to one individual. The following premises are beyond reproof:

1. Cunedda came down from Manau Gododdin in the north at the invitation of some post-Roman authority;
2. the purpose of his migration was to drive the Irish from Wales;
3. he re-settled south of Hadrian's Wall in the province of Clwyd, in the vicinity of where Eliseg's Pillar was eventually erected;
4. his fifth son was named Cerdic;
5. Cerdic is a Welsh and not a Saxon name;
6. Cerdic was the name of Vortigern's interpreter;
7. because of historical conditions, Cerdic had very close contact with English Saxon allies in defending the territories against Irish and Pict invaders;
8. Gewisse, Hwicce, and Hyrpe are synonymous terms describing the lands bordering the Cornovii territories;
9. continuous conflicts developed between the Welsh and their former allies, the East Anglians;
10. Cerdic the West Saxon king as described in *The Anglo-Saxon Chronicle* emerged out of nowhere at the height of these conflicts;
11. Cerdic the West Saxon king does not have a bona fide Saxon lineage;
12. Cerdic the West Saxon king fights against the Welsh during the last decade of the fifth century;
13. Cerdic succeeds to the kingdom of the West Saxons during the second decade of the sixth century.

All of this historical background seems far removed from the colors of King Arthur, but in truth it is intricately and inextricably tied to historical connections during this particular era. Based upon available historical and literary sources dealing with the famous king, then, it's necessary to determine Arthur's role according to these conditions.

John of Glastonbury is another source who links Cerdic and King Arthur. In Chapter 32 of his manuscript he writes that the West-Saxon kingdom began about the year 495 under Cerdic and his son Cynric, material which John evidently borrowed from *The Anglo-Saxon Chronicle*. But in the next sentence he adds different material: "In the eleventh year of Cerdic, when Utherpendragon, the brother of Aurelius Ambrosius, had been killed with poison, his son Arthur, a youth of fifteen years, began to reign over the Britons."[27] The bulk of this second sentence is obviously borrowed from Geoffrey of Monmouth, but there are several items which are not. One is the time-reference which is very rare in the older manuscripts, the eleventh year of Cerdic. This can be interpreted that Cerdic was eleven years old when Arthur was fifteen, or it could mean that Cerdic had been reigning for eleven years when Arthur was crowned. Overlooking the allusion to the enigmatic Utherpendragon, and linking the statement with other historical events of the period, more than likely it means the former.

A second item not borrowed from Monmouth is the indirect link established between Cerdic and Arthur. Geoffrey writes about a Cherdic, a Chelric, and a Cheldric, but he does not tie them together or assume that the three names identify one singular individual. Either John of Glastonbury perceptively bound all three of these characters into a homolog, or he was using some unrelated source.

John's second mention of Cerdic forms a *direct* link with Arthur. He writes, "Often [Arthur] struggled with Cerdic, who, if one month Arthur vanquished him, rose up the next [month] the fiercer for the fight. Finally, when Arthur tired of the conflict, he accepted Cerdic's fealty and gave him Hampshire and Somerset, which Cerdic called Wessex."[28] This gives a different perspective from *The Anglo-Saxon Chronicle* (entry A.D. 519) and its Genealogical Preface (A.D. 500), both which state in translations that Cerdic "obtained the kingdom" or that Cerdic "conquered" the kingdom of Wessex. John's account relates that Arthur *gave* Cerdic those territories in return for a pledge of fealty.

The third reference to Cerdic by John occurs in Chapter 36 of his manuscript: "After Cerdic had reigned in Wessex for fifteen years he died...."[29] Similar to the Æthelweard Chronicle, this assertion shows that John is accepting the viewpoint of the Genealogical Preface, that Cerdic acquired the kingdom in 500 and died in 516, very near the *Chronicle* entry of 519 which claims that he was just succeeding to the kingdom. In a structural chronology including Arthur, the viewpoints of Æthelweard, John, and the Genealogical Preface are the most accurate. Accepting Alcock's contention that the *Annales Cambriae* entry for Arthur's victory at Mount Badon must be modified from 518 to 499, and that the entry for Arthur's defeat at the battle of Camlann must be changed from 537 to 518,[30] a comprehensive account emerges from the mists.

Cerdic, a Man of the North who had royal ties to Rome through his father Cunedda and his ancestors Æternus, Paternus of the Red Robe, and Tacitus, established himself as a co-chieftain with his father in driving out the Irish from the Welsh provinces. Through his father's pact with *his* father, he earned the kingdom of Ceredigion as his part in the bargain. Through the *superbus tyrannus* and through Vortigern, he fraternized and became comrades with the English Saxons, helping as an interpreter to establish an alliance between the Welsh and the *Saxones* to protect the frontiers against the Picts from the north.[31] As the alliance decayed and disintegrated, leading to civil strife on the island and deeper political division between the Welsh and those with Roman affiliations, Cerdic, motivated by reasons known only to him, sided with the English Saxons against both Vortigern and the *Romanophils.*[32] By aligning himself with the English Saxons in this way, he forsook his national heritage and fought alongside Octha at the battle of Badon, where Octha was ultimately killed.

The pact which had been made between Arthur and Octha at Badon also bound Cerdic, but Cerdic betrayed his pledge to Arthur, and even after Arthur granted territories to him as a newly arisen leader of the West Saxons, Cerdic continued to create internal havoc. The new king of Wessex called upon the German Saxons for further support, and incursions from the continent began again. These clashes erupted intermittently for two decades, until the fatal battle of Camlann, in which both Cerdic and Arthur were slain.

But the West Saxons still held kingdom after Arthur's death. With the passing of their hero, the *Britanni's* resolve rapidly deteriorated and disappeared. On the island, the void created by the shattered *Britanni* kingships was filled by marauding bands of barbarians from the north, the northeast, and the mainland. On the continent the Roman empire of the West also was in its death-throes. Barbarian tribes led by chiefs such as Euric the Visigoth and Attila the Hun were overrunning what had been considered impenetrable Roman foundations, and eventually Rome itself was sacked several times. After decades of desperate struggle against enemies on all fronts, the candle of hope lit by King Arthur was extinguished.

With the passing of the great Welsh king, Cerdic's son Creoda—the generation so often ignored in the West-Saxon histories—established his main court in the province of Creuddyn in Wales, and maintained his kingdom with the help of his son Cynric, who has most often been depicted as Cerdic's son instead of his grandson. Creoda ruled until his death in 534, and thereafter the Welsh heritage of Cerdic and his son faded from island history, and the established kingdom became known as the House of the West Saxons.

Octha's Invitation into Britain

The effort spent so far in certifying the location of Manau Gododdin is consequential in interpreting critical passages in the *Historia Brittonum* dealing with Octha's role once he is invited to the island by his father Hengist. One translation relates that Hengist tells Vortigern,

> I will invite my son and his cousin [Ochta and Ebissa] to fight against the Irish, for they are fine warriors. Give them lands in the north, about the Wall that is called Guaul.[33]

A different translation interprets this with some crucial variations, giving an entirely different contextual message. Hengist informs Vortigern that

> I will send for my son and his brother, both valiant men, who at my invitation will fight against the Scots, and you can give them the countries in the north, near the wall called Gual.[34]

The difference between cousin/brother doesn't really carry with it any important ramifications in Arthurian history, but the variants between Irish/Scots, wall/Wall, and Guaul/Gual make it mandatory to scrutinize the original manuscripts to determine where Octha is sent, especially since it ties directly to Cunedda's original dominion and the motive for his migration to the south.

Josephus Stevenson, whose replications of originals are authoritative, reveals how the original text could be misconstrued. By translating his passage verbatim and using the original Latin words (boldfaced) dealing with kinship, locations, and nationalities, the segment relays that Hengist tells Vortigern

> I will invite my son along with his **fratrueli**, both truly virile and pugnacious warriors, to battle against the **Scottos**; give them lands to the north, near the **wall** called **Guaul**.[35]

Although not important, the word *fratrueli* points out the difficulties of translations. Cassell's dictionary indicates that this word can mean a brother or—based upon citations from Cicero, Ovid, and Tacitus—sometimes a cousin, or even a brother-in-law as used by Livius.[36] However, *Scotti* or *Scottos* does not mean "Scots" or "Scottish" as Giles implies. In both the *DE* and the *HB*, *Scotti* is a reference to the *Irish*, those tribes which settled along the western and northwestern coast of what later became Wales. Some *Scotti* also crossed the narrows of North Channel to Argyll and Strathclyde, but that area—particularly Strathclyde—was mostly inhabited by Romanized *Britanni*. During the Roman occupation and shortly thereafter, the far northern territories were not called Scotland; beyond the Antonine Wall were the barbarians and even to the south of it—in the northern segments of territories the Romans called Dumnonii, Selgovae, and Votadini—the tribes were known as the Picts. The Antonine Wall was a very temporary Roman border, and when it was abandoned in favor once again of Hadrian's Wall, the Picts began settling along the strip of land just south of Antonine Wall.

The last segment of Chapter 38 in the *HB* unfortunately creates havoc when attempting to accurately ascertain and resolve Octha's location. That segment narrates Octha and Ebissa sailing around the country of the Picts and laying waste to the Orkneys, which can be construed as undeniable proof that Octha was sent to the *far* north. This might be true, except for some contradictory circumstances. Octha had been invited over for the express purpose of helping his father and Vortigern stem the invasional flow of Irish which was moving from the west to the east, not from the north to the south nor from the east to the west. If Octha had been that far north, in hostile Pictish territory, his mission would have been useless; instead of resisting invasions on one crucial front, he would have been instigating wars on a different one. This perspective leads to a germane piece of information proposed by Wade-Evans, entangled and almost hidden in an extravagant tale he weaves about Octha being commissioned by Roman Britain against the northern nations. His purpose is to show that the latter part of Chapter 38 in the *HB* (among other sections) is tainted by Welsh bardic storytellers *(cyfarwyddiaid)* [37] whose interpolations were incorporated into Bede's work and thus passed on to the *HB* as historical truth.[38]

The last item to address in the above quotation from Stevenson focuses on the terms "wall" and "Guaul." The spelling differentiation of Guaul and Gual between the two translations is not significant. Among all the different versions of the *HB*, Stevenson lists the spelling variants as Guahle, Waul, and Gual. What *is* off-base is Giles's suggestion of Gual being along the Antonine Wall. What becomes very important is the difference between one translation indicating "wall" as a proper noun while the other lists it as a common noun, particularly in its connection with "Guaul." When capitalized, the understood suggestion is that it is a reference to Hadrian's Wall, hence near (Hadrian's) Wall at a place called Wall.

Once again, however, as is so common when attempting to pinpoint a geographic area associated with Arthurian history, a dilemma arises. There is a Wall near Hadrian's Wall in the same vicinity as Hexham, and there is likewise a Wall just west of Lichfield near an extensive wall. The choice, then, of which Wall is being identified in the *HB* requires a close look at the milieu of the period. Hadrian's Wall, of course, is a much more realistic setting than the Antonine Wall, but based upon events which have been tracked, it is still too far north. The *Scotti* (that is, the Irish) were making inroads into

Britain mainly from the western coast of Wales. There was some filtration across the North Channel into the Roman territory of Epidii, but it is not likely that the Irish were penetrating the island at this point, travelling parallel to Hadrian's Wall inland for a distance of about 130 miles, then turning southward to capture land which would still be about 165 miles away.

In relation to all the other historical facts related not only by the emended *HB*, but also by the *DE*, the *ASC*, and a wealth of literary tradition, it is much more conceivable that Octha was sent to Wall-by Lichfield, only about fifty miles farther north from where his father and Vortigern were fighting the Irish, which would have still been about 125 miles south of Hadrian's Wall. Wall-by-Lichfield is verified by both John Morris and Graham Webster as Caer Luit Coyt. This locale is known by two other names, one the Roman city of Letocetum, and the other Wall, near a wall. Webster describes this site:

> The modern name "Wall" appears to have been derived from a long stretch of masonry visible at least up to 1817 in the field known as Castle Croft, and which was presumably part of the late defence system discussed below.[39]

Part of the detail which Webster gives is that a civil settlement had developed along a two-mile stretch of the main road.

An impressive list of evidence supports why this Wall is the "Guaul" near a wall that the *HB* refers to:

1. Wall—i.e., Caer Luit Coyt, Caer Lwytgoed, Wall-by-Lichfield, or Letocetum—was listed in the *HB* as one of the twenty-eight most important cities of Britain. Graham Webster notes that "Wall, appearing as Cair Luitcoyt, and undoubtedly correctly ascribed, appears rather incongruously among such major towns and military depots as York, London, Chester, Wroxeter, Caerleon, and Caerwent,"[40] but nevertheless must have been a place of important consequence because of its inclusion as a strategic city.
2. Its importance is magnified by its also being a fortification. As its synonymous terms Caer Luit Coyt and Caer Lwytgoed indicate, "Caer" means a "fortified place." "Luit" or "Lwyt" attests to its Welsh derivation, coming from *leito-* or its Welsh form *llywd,* meaning grey,[41] and *-goed* stemming from Argoed, meaning wood, i.e., forest. Webster writes that Wall's "size and the character of the buildings suggest a legionary presence,"[42] and even more pertinent to why Octha would have been sent to this locale, he adds, "A legionary force here would also be available for any trouble either from the Welsh tribes or even more important from the north...."[43] Hengist, too, would have been aware of the critical relevance of this position, protecting his flanks against attack from the Picts, the Irish, or the Welsh.

3. Directly related to it as a fortification, it is mid-way on Watling Street, the most important Roman road running from the southeast of London for nearly three hundred miles to Carnarfan in northwest Wales. Hengist would also have realized how essential the control of Watling Street would be, based upon the remains of the Roman camps and forts along this thoroughfare, which functioned as a supply route. Graham Webster writes of the archaeological discoveries of the area, including finds that show Wall was a substantial community covering a larger area than is normally associated with a mere way-station. To date, a defense system, including three ditches and a wall backed by a rampart, have been unearthed, plus building and pottery debris, metal-working material, cemeteries, and cremation burials.[44]
4. At Wall, Watling Street intersected with Ryknild Street, the most important Roman road running northeast to York. This intersection also allowed land-contact to the south through present-day Birmingham, eventually connecting with Foss Way, which was the thoroughfare leading to Cirencester, Aquae Sulis, Axminster, and finally the southern coast.
5. Wall also had easy access—within three miles—to the River Trent, which formed a V from the northwest to the northeast;
6. It was an important way-station containing a *mansio* and an elaborate bathhouse for troops in transit. For literally centuries, Watling Street remained the principal route to North Wales and Ireland, which Webster indicates connected *burgi* along its entire course, from southeastern Caves Inn to Red Hill; Manduessedum (Mancetter) was only twelve miles from Wall, and Pennocrucium was only about sixteen miles distant.[45]
7. During occupation, Wall had been a strong-point for defenses set up by the Roman army in a deep zone of military control where "the Britons in the area of Wall would have had occasional visits from cavalry patrols watching for signs of potential hostility, but at the same time attempting to establish friendly relationships."[46] This would also have been Octha's mission, once he was directed to the north by his father.
8. Wall was in the borderland region of the Cornovii (i.e., Cornish) and the Coritani territories, the vast area vacated by the Roman abandonment which not only the Irish but the Welsh and the English Saxons were clamoring to conquer. Twenty miles due east was Leicester, the tribal capital of the Coritani, and thirty-three miles due west was Viroconium (Wroxeter), the tribal capital of the Cornovii, both which became administrative centers for their districts after the Romans had departed. Wall would have been an ideal site, so conveniently located between the two.

9. Viroconium (Wroxeter) takes on a significance of its own, not only as another major city, but also as a major fort in Roman times and the Cornovii tribal center, which since that era has produced massive archaeological evidence.
10. Within a couple of miles from Wroxeter is the Wrekin, a hill fort identified by *The Historic King Arthur* as the site for the Battle of Mount Badon, where Octha was killed in 497;
11. And last, Wall also had easy access to the River Severn at Buildwas for either northwesterly travel or southern travel to Gloucester.

Webster makes two other important conjectures about Wall's role in history, related to Arthur's period, but of course not adorned specifically with Arthur's name. One is that Webster theorizes, "At about the time of the building's destruction (at Wall), the Wroxeter Forum was also destroyed by fire, and it is possible that both events were connected with a revolt in Wales at this time."[47] This postulation seems to be attached to a earlier reference in the text about the poem "The Lament of Cynddlan," describing a pagan raid on Wall (Caer Luydcoed) under Moriael of Ercall:

> Here may be preserved in poetic form the memory of a clash between the Celtic pagan west and the remnants of the Romano-British Christian community in that twilight period in the fifth and sixth centuries before the advent of the Saxon Settlers.[48]

This puts Wall (the one in central Britain) as the focus of events just prior to the civil strife narrated by Gildas Badonicus.

Therefore, the small obscure village of Wall near Hadrian's Wall cannot amass such circumstantial evidence as this; it would not be a strategic place to send warriors as reinforcements. Octha, therefore, was not sent that far north to fight against the Picts; he was fighting against the same enemies Cunedda had been commissioned to fight—the Irish, who were continuously encroaching farther and farther inland toward the east, then fanning out northward toward Hadrian's Wall. Once the issue of Wall's location is laid to rest, its importance relates directly to Cunedda's migration to the south, to his ties with Maelgwn, and to Cerdic as one of the inheritors of the West Saxon kingdom, all of which link to Arthurian history.

Once Octha is placed at Wall, known also as Caer Luit Coyt, two tales from *The Mabinogion* in combination provide a surprising revelation of Octha's treachery. In the story "How Culhwch Won Olwen," one of Arthur's warriors and comrades is Osla Big Knife, a name which causes instant discord: Osla is the Welsh version of Octha, a name that is as out of place in Welsh tales as the name of Cerdic is in Saxon histories. His title, too, verifies him as Saxon; "Saxon" literally comes from *seax* as "broad sword." Osla's name first appears in this tale during Culhwch's invocation: "Osla Big Knife (who carried Bronllavyn Short Broad; when Arthur and his troops came to a cresting flood, they would find a narrow spot; the knife in its sheath would be laid across the flood and that would be bridge enough for the three armies of the island of Britain and the three offshore islands, with all their plunder)....”[49] Later in the story he appears as Arthur's *comrade* when he is hunting the boar Twrch Trwyth and crosses the river.[50]

Osla Big Knife is also a character in "The Dream of Rhonabwy," but in this tale he is Arthur's *adversary*. The reader is first notified that Arthur's huge army is on the move to be at Baddon by noon in order to fight against Osla Big Knife.[51] Later, near the end of the story, twenty-four horsemen come from Osla Big Knife to ask Arthur for a truce to the end of the month and a fortnight, which Arthur grants after a tribute is paid.[52] This switch in allegiance must logically point to the decay of the alliance between the Welsh and the English Saxons. One other enlightening piece of information emerges: Osla and Arthur are enemies at the Battle of Badon, where, according to the *HB*, Arthur wins a victory over the Saxons.

With this tale establishing Arthur and Osla as adversaries at Baddon, and Osla equated with Octha son of Hengist in the *HB*, one can now turn to another source—the *ASC*—to verify the connections. As mentioned earlier, the name Æsc in the *Chronicle* is synonymous with Octha, and likewise the entries for 449, 455, 456, 465, and 473 inherently show that Hengist and Octha were *English* Saxons, having been settled on the island for at least two decades. Only one other entry, for the year 488, records the name of Ochta succeeding to the kingdom. As an added perplexity, the Parker Chronicle recorded that Octha reigned for twenty-four years, while the Laud Chronicle lists his length of reign as thirty-four years.

Nothing in the search for the historic King Arthur is simple, and this last entry on Octha is no exception. Which chronicle might have recorded a scribal error is insignificant, since both stretch the "reasonable-age" concept. Using the Parker Chronicle for computation, if Octha began his sole reign in 488 and ruled for twenty-four years, his death-year would have been 512. Assuming that he had inherited the kingdom with his father in 455 in accordance with the entry in the *ASC*, and that he was eighteen at the time, his birth-year would have been 437, making him seventy-five years old at his death. Calculated according to the Laud Chronicle, he would have died at age eighty-five.

Octha succeeds to the kingdom twice, once when he shares the rule with this father, and then again as the sole ruler. The early chronicles commonly listed the succession to the kingdom simultaneously with the previous ruler's death, such as the entry of 534, which records that Cerdic died in this year and his son Cynric ruled for twenty-seven years. An equally common practice, however, was to list only the succession to the kingdom with the death of the previous ruler inherently inferred for that same year, as in the entry of 560, which relates that Ceawlin succeeded to the kingdom in Wessex but tells nothing of Cynric's death. If the entry for the year 488 is viewed as an example of this latter technique, then it would be logical to assume that Hengist died in that same year, which is the reason for listing Octha as the sole ruler. Yet if that is the case, Hengist at his death would have been about seventy-five years old.

What seems more plausible, therefore, is that Octha became the sole ruler in the year 473, the last entry in which Hengist is mentioned, allotting not only Octha but also Hengist reasonable life spans. This would mean that Hengist would have been about thirty years old when he was the leader of Saxon *Adventus II* and made an alliance with Vortigern, and he would have died at the approximate age of sixty. Octha would have been about twenty years old when he succeeded to the kingdom with his father in 455, about thirty-nine years old when he became sole successor, and approximately sixty-two when he died. Interestingly, if this sequence is accepted, Octha's twenty-four-year reign beginning in 473 would have ended in 497, almost identical to the time calculated by Leslie Alcock for the Battle of Mount Badon,[53] and precisely the figure as proposed in *The Historic King Arthur.* This would not only verify the information recorded in the *Historia Brittonum* that Arthur fought against Octha in those days, including the battle at Badon, but would also attest to the historical base of "The Dream of Rhonabwy" and further reinforce that Arthur and Octha were rival leaders at Arthur's twelfth battle. Furthermore, it attests to an original alliance between Arthur and Octha as reported in the earlier tale of "How Culhwch Won Olwen."

The strand of Cerdic's association with both Octha and Arthur would also be strengthened and substantiate this historical sequence, stressing even further Cerdic's key role during the Arthurian period. *The Anglo-Saxon Chronicle* makes no explicit connection between Octha and Cerdic, but the end of Octha's reign would have touched the beginning of Cerdic's, meaning that there would have been about a fifteen-year age difference between the two. Cerdic would have been approximately forty-seven when Octha died in 497. The only link in history or tradition between the two is given by Geoffrey of Monmouth, who simply records that Vortigern did what Hengist bade in having Octa and other mercenaries join the alliance, and "Octa and Ebissa arrived, and a man called Cherdic, too, with three hundred boats filled with a fully-equipped army."[54] The strands do, indeed, form an intricate but comprehensive pattern of history.

8

Arthur's Battles with the Saxons

Based upon the revelations of research in *The Historic King Arthur* and the explications in earlier segments of this text, the title of this chapter conveys three significant concepts which must be stressed. First, the word "Saxons" means not only "English Saxons" in the generic sense used by the Romans, but also includes the continental "German Saxons" because Arthur's endeavors to salvage Britain likewise took him across the Channel to fight in Gaul and Burgundy. As the "Briton king from across Ocean," Arthur (as Riothamus) risked this complicated undertaking in an attempt to systematically stem the flow of German reinforcements to the island.

Second, although the *Historia Brittonum* lists "Arthur" as the leader of the twelve battles against the Saxons, the battles should more accurately be attributed to Ambrosius Aurelianus/Riothamus/Arthur—or, using a homolog—attributed to Riardd Ambrosius as proposed in *The Historic King Arthur,* since these battles spanned several decades, fought under the banner of Ambrosius Aurelianus, who became better known by progressive epithets. Although most scholars attempt to place all of the battle sites listed in the *HB* on the island of Britain, there is no information in any of the ancient manuscripts which undeniably establishes this as fact. If a battle was fought by Ambrosius Aurelianus as Arthur, then the locale most likely would have been in Wales or the midlands just to the east, which were known at that time as Cornovii. If a battle was fought by Riothamus as a title referring to the Overking Arthur, then the locale would have shifted to the mainland, in Brittany or Gaul. Likewise, if a battle was fought by Arthur in the twilight of his career, the location would shift to the southern quarter of the island, nearer to his last and fatal battle at Camlann, one of the most significant of the Arthurian battles, and one which is not listed in the *Historia Brittonum.*

And third, from a historically reliable viewpoint, the geographic identifications of each of these sites are based upon sketchy, tenuous, conjectural information. The *Historia Brittonum* provides the format, but even it does not assure the chronological sequence by its listing, nor does it assist in determining a span of time.

Accepting the presumption that they are not part of the twelve battles listed in Section 56 of the *HB,* the four major battles attributed to Vortimer were enumerated and discussed earlier in Chapter 4. Available evidence indicates that the epithet "Vortimer" is not Ambrosius Aurelianus, but instead strongly suggests that it is it a title for Cunedda. Hence, these particular conflicts led by a spurious historical Briton figure against the Saxons would not connect with the "Riardd Ambrosius" homolog. The speculation that the words "Vortimer" and "Vortigern" are philologically identical and thus name the same individual is also weak, especially since Vortimer is fanatically anti-Saxon and Vortigern is unswervingly pro-Saxon. The two play diametrically different roles in the history of the period, in addition to one dying before the other, which effectively invalidates Fletcher's belief that the Nennius history reflects more oral and literary tradition while the Gildas history has post-Roman biases.

This milieu sets the stage for Arthur's battles against the Saxons. Preceding the battle list from the *HB,* Nennius writes that during Arthur's era the Saxons increased their numbers and grew in Britain. Together with the kings of Britain Arthur fought against the Saxons. Inherent in these lines from the *HB* is the understanding that Arthur was fighting not only the *English* Saxons but also the influx of *continental* Saxons, so-called in those days the *German* Saxons. Also, according to what is recorded—that Arthur fought the Saxons—the implication might be that he fought the *German Saxons* in their *native land.* Knowing, however, that Geoffrey of Monmouth is not a reliably accurate historian, there is also the possibility that Arthur fought the *German Saxons* in *Gaul* and not in their native land.

The purpose of *The Historic King Arthur* was to present an authenticated picture of this historic king as untainted as possible by wild guesswork. For this reason, the battles attributed to Arthur in the *HB* were acknowledged but not focused upon except for the battle of Mons Badonicus, even though research pointed to some suggestive clues for the less prominent of the conflicts. The omission of the battle list from the text's probe does not infer that the battles are not predicated upon fact but only that undeniable substantiation is impossible because of geographic uncertainties.

Now, however, because this book is more speculative, it is possible to concentrate upon the battles listed in Section 56 of the *HB*. In an attempt to be more accurate in the probabilities, the battles can be separated into three distinctive categories because there are three discernible stages of Riardd Ambrosius's career The first of these would be the "Ambrosius" phase under the actual *praenomen/cognomen,* Ambrosius Aurelianus, covering the earliest period from near 440 until around 460, or considering the events, from approximately the beginning of Aëtius's third consulship and the Saxon Revolt until the second migration to Brittany. The second would be the "Riothamus" decade (460–470), from the end of the second migration and the reign of Ægidius until the Battle of Bourg-de-Déols. The last span would be from the advent of "Arthur," whose reign is traditionally set in the opening years of the 470s until the Battle of Mons Badonicus, set by the cardinal year 497 in *The Historic King Arthur.* Although the battle at Badon marks Arthur's victory over the Saxons and Arthur's death isn't recorded until twenty-one years later, this is the terminal point since it is the last battle recorded in Section 56. A final note of caution: The battles listed in the *HB* are titled "The Campaigns of Arthur," but they should be taken to reflect any conflict fought under the banners of Ambrosius, Riothamus, or Arthur.

The three divisions aid at least to some extent by narrowing the sections of the island where certain battles might have been fought. Based upon a great deal of circumstantial documentation in *The Historic King Arthur,* the locale of the Ambrosian era focuses upon the early borders of Wales and the western midlands. Sir Ifor Williams coincidentally verifies this in his research of Welsh poetry. He proposes that the Llywarch Hen englynion are verse elements in stories, tales and sagas told in pre-Norman times in north-east Wales, in the eastern part of Powys bordering England, opposite to, and perhaps including portions of Shropshire and Hereford, and in doing so outlines the war zones for the Arthurian saga. He is using as his source *The Red Book of Hergest* (circa 1400),[1] and specifically names north-east Wales, Shrewsbury, and the border country. He relates, "The Saxons have advanced far from the eastern shores of Britain, the midlands are in the hands of the enemies, and the fighting is almost on the boundaries of modern Wales."[2]

The Riothamus phase is concentrated on the continent. Riothamus is a rather obscure historical figure, especially regrettable since he occupies such a monumental role in the Arthurian saga. He appears in the manuscripts of Jordanes, Gregory of Tours, and Sidonius, but continental as well as insular history is very sketchy at this point. During this era Europe was in pervasive turmoil, not only from conflicts between barbaric tribes and the decaying Roman empire, but with intra- and inter-tribal warfare laden with pacts, broken treaties, treachery, and almost daily switches of allegiance. From bits and pieces of information, the upheaval drags on for a decade, during which Riothamus aligns himself with Gaul in support of the Romans. Shortly after his victory against the Saxons at Angers, Riothamus suffers a defeat at the hands of Euric, the leader of the Visigoths. The accounts by both Jordanes and Gregory are very brief, and once Riothamus and the remnants of his army retreat into Burgundy, he vanishes. He is not acknowledged again in any histories.

Interestingly, the Arthurian era immediately succeeds the Riothamus phase; just at the time when Riothamus disappears in Burgundy, Arthur materializes on the island. Whereas Ambrosius's locus is Wales and the western midlands, and Riothamus's is the continent, Arthur's is typically southern

England. His inception is dated around 475 by John Morris in *The Age of Arthur*,[3] and Norris Lacy gives several spans based upon various documentations: 457–474, 468–474, and the narrowest, 469–470, by Sharon Turner, tied, however, to Riothamus.[4] The earliest literary reference to Arthur is in Aneirin's *The Gododdin*, but it is a mere dropping of the great king's name in a passage which reads "[Gwawrddur] glutted (?) black ravens on the rampart of the stronghold, though he was no Arthur."[5] The earliest extant manuscript which could be said to contain Arthurian poems not showing any obvious influence from Geoffrey of Monmouth is *The Black Book of Carmarthen*, compiled around 1250 by a southern Welsh cleric, possibly at Carmarthen.[6] Two versions of *The Book of Taliesin* survived, one (Peniarth MS 16) of the thirteenth century, and the other (Peniarth MS 2) dating to the first quarter of the fourteenth century.[7] Though appearing considerably later than the historic Arthurian period, the content of both Aneirin's and Taliesin's poetry suggest a much earlier tradition during the early 600s.

The name "Arthur" also made its way into Welsh prose. An early manuscript, *The White Book of Rhydderch (Llyfr Bwyn Rhydderch)* written around 1325, is preserved in two volumes, Peniarth 4 and 5, and is reposited in the National Library of Wales. Peniarth 4 originally contained the earliest complete text of the "Mabinogion" tales, but only fragments of the Culhwch tale have survived, and the Rhonabwy tale is missing altogether.[8] A later version, hailed as including "almost the whole of Welsh literature known to have been committed to writing before 1400,"[9] appears in *The Red Book of Hergest* around 1400 and contains complete copies of *The Mabinogion*.

"How Culhwch Won Olwen," according to Brynley Roberts, "is not only the earliest but the longest surviving prose tale written in medieval Welsh and based upon oral traditions."[10] Roberts also adds that this "is the work of a virtuoso, an author as knowledgeable in Welsh *cyfarwyddyd* as he was skillful in its modes of narration."[11] Compared to the laconic notices given of Arthur in the *Historia Brittonum* and the *Annales Cambriae*, this tale gives a wealth of information about Arthur the emperor, some of which has been given throughout the earlier chapters of this text. Characterized by Jeffrey Gantz as the last to have taken shape, another tale—"The Dream of Rhonabwy"—gives equally as much (or perhaps more) detail about Arthur than the Culhwch tale. It concentrates solely upon the last battle in the *HB* battle list, the clash at Mons Badonicus, and gives more clues and details about this particular conflict than any of the other sources combined, including material by Monmouth.

In summary, these three distinctive phases will aid in chronicling Arthur's battles as listed in the *HB*, in addition to limiting the feasible geographic locations. Unfortunately, the demarcations between the phases are not clearly defined. There are shades of grey and overlaps, and, of course, there are no guarantees that the battle list is recorded sequentially. Similarly, the geographic parameters are tenuous; the operations accorded to Ambrosius could have encroached further south, or the arenas attributed to Arthur might have extended deep into the midlands. Akin to this, there is no dictum that bars the possibility, for example, that Riothamus fought the first battle at the River Glein, the sixth battle at the River Bassas, and the eleventh battle at Agned on the continent. Historians commonly agree that there was fluid movement not only from one part of Britain to another, but also from the island to the continent. One other admonition should be reiterated: The suggestion of a geographic location for a battle site is speculative; for centuries historians and scholars have ventured suppositions about the campaigns of Arthur, a process which, although there might not be profound contributions, adds spice to Arthuriana. Admittedly, there are those of a more sober nature who view this endeavor as a frivolous waste of time and energy, but if nothing else it provides a break from the rigors of research.

The Cities of Roman Britain

Before exploring the geographic possibilities of the battle list in the *HB*, the important cities of Britain provided by some of the versions are included here for two reasons. For one, it provides a convenient reference for those who are interested in the contents and variations of the *HB*. More important, it allows comparisons with the actual battle list to determine if there are any connections between it and what were the most important cities in Britain during the Roman and early post-Roman periods. John Morris in *British History* lists twenty-eight cities by Nennius, giving first the Latin terms, then translating them into what he thinks are modern sites. Giles has done something similar, but he must have been using a version from *The Red Book of Hergest* since he lists thirty-two cities by name; Roberts explains, for example that whereby *The Red Book of Hergest* lists thirty-two cities and also describes twenty-seven of the thirty-four marvels, other versions such as *The White Book of Rhydderch* simply refers to the list of cities but doesn't identify them.[12] Likewise, there is a difference in translations between John Morris and Josephus Stevenson, in that Morris includes the "Cities of Britain" as Section 66a, and Stevenson inserts his at the end of Section 76, without a title. Each, however, enumerates twenty-eight cities; atypically, Stevenson makes no comment about other versions.

The cities are listed in an easy-to-use table. The cities listed in the left-hand column are from Giles, with the variations from Morris in parentheses underneath, if a variation exits. Most of the variant spellings are closely enough associated so that errors are unlikely to occur, but some of the similarities such as "Gurcoc," "Guorcon," and "Guricon," could easily be interpolated. Only one other example is needed to demonstrate a point. The site

Table 9—The largest cities of Roman Britain, listed in the *Historia Brittonum*

Giles / (Morris)	*Giles's Translation*	*Morris's Translation*
1. Cair Ebrauc	York	York
2. Cair Ceint	Canterbury	Canterbury
3. Cair Guroc	Anglesey(?)	————————
4. Cair Guorthegern (Guorthigirn)	unknown	Vortigern's Fort
5. Cair Custeint (Custoeint)	Carnarvon	Constantine's Fort
6. Cair Guoranegon (Guiragon)	Worchester	Canterbury(?)
7. Cair Segeint	Silchester	Caernarfon
8. Cair Guin Truis (Guinntguic)	Norwich/Winwick	Winchester
9. Cair Merdin	Caermarthen	————————
10. Cair Peris	Porchester	Llanberis(?)
11. Cair Lion (Legeion Guer Usic)	Caerleon	Caerleon
12. Cair Mencipit (Mincip)	Verulam	Verulamium
13. Cair Caratauc	Catterick	Caradoc's Fort
14. Cair Ceri	Cirencester	————————
15. Cair Gloui	Gloucester	————————
16. Cair Luilid (Ligualid)	Carlisle	Carlisle
17. Cair Grant (Grauth)	Cambridge	Cambridge
18. Cair Daun	Doncaster	Doncaster
19. Cair Britoc (Brithon)	Bristol	Dumbarton
20. Cair Meguaid	Meivod	Lindisfarne
21. Cair Mauiguid (Maunguid)	Manchester	Manchester(?)
22. Cair Ligion (Legion)	Chester	Chester
23. Cair Guent	Caerwent	Caerwent
24. Cair Collon (Colun)	Colchester	Colchester(?)
25. Cair Londein (Lundem)	London	London
26. Cair Cuorcon (Guricon)	Worren	Wroxeter
27. Cair Lerion	Leicester	Leicester(?)
28. Cair Draithou (Draitou)	Drayton	Draitou Fort
29. Cair Pensavelcoit (Pensa vel Coyt)	Pevensey	Penselwood Fort
30. Cair Teim	Teyn-Grace	————————
31. Cair Urhahc (Uranarc)	Wroxeter	Urnarc Fort
32. Cair Celemion	Camelot	Celemion Fort
33. Cair Loit Coit (Luit Coyt)	Lincoln	Wall-by-Lichfield

"Caratauc" is translated by Giles to mean Catterick, which is located near the North Sea, close to Hadrian's Wall. A person might be led to believe that Morris's translation, listed as Caradoc's Fort, suggests the same locale of Catterick, but Caradoc wrote about the Life of St. Gildas, and his location was Llancarfan, in Wales, almost on the coast of the Bristol Channel, near Cardiff.

Surprisingly, there is agreement on thirteen of the cities out of the twenty-eight possibilities, almost a fifty-percent average. One city listed by Giles, Cair Guorthegern, is oddly listed as unknown, although Giles, in Chapter 23 of the works of Gildas refers to Vortigern as Gurthrigern, unless he was claiming that he was unsure where Vortigern's Fortress was located. Others, such as Cair Guoranegon, Cair Guin Truis, Cair Peris, and Cair Guorcon are quite varied. And two, Cair Segeint and Cair Britoc, are widely dispersed. One site listed by Giles elicits special interest. Caer Gloui is identified as Gloucester, which in itself is not interesting or surprising. However, what does make it noteworthy is that Geoffrey of Monmouth must have had as one of his sources some version which made its way into *The Red Book of Hergest*. Had he not had this version, the association he made with Duke of Glouis would have sprung from his own imagination. It restores, perhaps, a little bit of faith that Monmouth used and was loyal to some of his sources.

Another site worthy of note is the one which Giles lists for Cair Celemion. His full listing is Camalet, in Somersetshire, a clear reference to South Cadbury Castle as Camelot in Somerset. Morris doesn't hazard a guess but hedges by saying that the site refers to Celemion's Fort, giving no hint where it might be located. Caer Luit Coyt is identified by Morris as Wall-by-Lichfield, in agreement with most of the other scholars. Contextually, that is important here because it aids in confirming the importance of that site as a strategic location where Octha would have been sent upon his entry into Britain. Finally, there is general interest (as apart from battle-related interest) in the city of Caer Ligualid. Both Morris and Giles identify it as Carlisle, important because it signifies the location where Cunedda initially settled after his migration from the north.

Geographic Possibilities of the *Historia Brittonum* Battle list

The *Historia* battle list is one of the most written-about topics in Arthurian lore. On the one hand, of all the miscellany of this material which legitimately can be called "history," the battle list has been labeled as sheer fantasy and has been molded, revised, and imagined as whim dictates. On the other hand, those who consider it as a coveted source of history feel that if used properly it can be a ring of keys to open doors to the past. The battle sites on the list are symbolic latches, and casual readers will not be able to unlock them. Some, like Glein and Dubglas, seem as if they would be easy to locate; others, like city of the Legion and Celyddon Forest are deceptive because the locales seem self-evident although they are not. No single name on the list is easily identifiable, even to avid readers and researchers who have studied the names for years.

The battle list has been contentious for centuries. Not only have *all* the geographic locations been problematic, but as suggested earlier in this chapter, chronology has also been an issue. With the former—geographic location—several scholars have speculated, with excellent reasoning, that perhaps some of the battles were not fought in Britain but on the continent. Additionally, sites on the island have ranged from forests in Scotland to the Badbury hill fort on the southern coast. With the latter, there is no indication, other than the consecutive enumeration, if these battles are listed in a chronological order; furthermore, there is not the slightest bit of evidence in Nennius what the lapse of time is from the first battle to the last; there is no solid evidence, other than Nennius saying so, that any or all of these battles are attributable to Arthur. The one exception is the last entry listed as the Battle of Mons Badonicus, which is verified by another source, the *Annales Cambriae*.

Excluding Camlann, which isn't listed, there are actually only nine battle sites, since four battles were fought in the same locale. The river sites are Glein, Dubglas (where four battles were fought), Bassas, and Tribruit. Two—Agned and Badonis—were fought on hilltops; Celidonis is a reference to a forest; Urbe Legionis is a city of legions; and Guinnion is a castle or fortress, depending upon translation.

The First Battle: At the Mouth of the River Called Glein

Part of the difficulty in tracing geographic names are all the etymological variations. The River Glein is a case in point. According to Stevenson, just in the copying of the versions there are two other differences, Gem and Glem in manuscript E; he adds that the Lun in Westmoreland and the Leven in Cumberland are the most probable.[13] J. A. Giles cites listings of the River Glein as the Glem in Lincolnshire or the Glen in the northern part of Northumberland.[14] Alcock traces these two possibilities philologically because they are derived from the word *glein,* meaning pure or clear.[15] Yet based upon theoretical proposals on englynion, Sir Ifor Williams unknowingly asserted that the conflicts with the English Saxons were on the boundaries of modern Wales. This bonus, touched upon above in a slightly different context, does indeed show that the River Glen in Northumberland is too far north and that the River Glen in Lincolnshire is too far east.

A site, therefore, in or near Wales is the place to look for the first of Arthur's battles at the River Glein. Because the reference here is to a river and not to a valley (though sometimes the etymological distinction is impossible), there are fewer possibilities, but *glein* as a root meaning clean, holy, pure, or beautiful still has many variants: *glano-* (British), *glania* (Welsh), *glanio* (Welsh), *cainos* (Gallic), and *cain* (Old Irish). These can lead to additional place-names of Great Glemham/Little Glemham/Glemsford in Suffolk, River Glen in Lincolnshire, Glen Magna/Glen Parva in Leicestershire, Glencoyne/Glenderamackin/Glenderaterra in Cumberland, Glendue in Northumberland, River Glyme/Glympton in Oxfordshire, Glynch Brook in Gloucestershire/Herfordshire/ Wocestershire, and Clydach in southwestern Wales.

Most of the above sites can be eliminated because of their remoteness, or their protected stability away from the centers of conflict: Great Glemham, Little Glemham, Glemsford, River Glen, Glencoyne, Glenderamackin, Glenderaterra, Glendue, and the three Clydachs. Based upon their etymologies, Glen Magna and Glen Parva are both possibilities but not probabilities. But the remaining two—River Glyme and Glynch Brook—are strong contenders.

Glyme, a river in present-day Oxfordshire, was first recorded as *Glim,* meaning "bright stream."[16] in 958 in the *Cartularium saxonicum.* It is associated with *Glen, Gleni,* and *Glene* which mean "clean, pure, beautiful," and thus a cognate of Glein, meaning "pure or clear water." It has, however, other, even more important claims. It is only nine miles from Bicester, once a strategic Roman fort and a crossing of the two most important roads in Britain. As a hub, there was one spoke leading northeast to connect with

Photograph 6—The River Glyme, a possible site of Arthur's first Battle against the Saxons.

Watling Street and Northampton, another pointing southeast to connect with Watling Street and eventually St. Albans, a third going directly southward toward Roman Town (Silchester), and the last, another major route, Akeman Street, going southwest across the River Glyme and on to Cirencester. Ambrosden, a stone's throw from Bicester, testifies to the importance and influence of Ambrosius Aurelianus, the powerful enemy of the *Saxones,* in the area. And, probably most important, this site is on the very borders of the West Saxon territories and part of the Cornoviian no-man's land left after Rome withdrew from Britain. Conflict here would have been a common occurrence.

For similar reasons, Glynch Brook is another probability. Its variations are *Clenc* and *Glench,* derived from *glano-* and also tied to *Glen,* meaning "pure" or "clean." This site is a focus in the triangular area of Gloucester, Herford, and Wocester. It is deeper into the Cornovii territory, approximately forty miles south of the Roman center of Wroxeter, with easy access to the River Severn and a river-crossing at Bewdley, plus one farther north at Buildwas. Roman roads criss-cross the region, including Ermin Way from Roman town, through Gloucester, to Hereford, and beyond. Intersecting Ermin Way is Foss Way, coming from the southwest at Lyme Bay and heading to Lincoln in the distant northeast. Like the area of the River Glyme, Ambrosius's influence is reflected in place-names such as Ombersley and Amblecote. Additionally, it is on the very fringes of the Gewisse territories, the stronghold for Vortigern and his Saxon allies.

Either locale, River Glyme or Glynch Brook, would be a better probability than anything that has ever been proposed. The *Historia Brittonum* devotes only one sentence to the battle site: "*Primum bellum fuit in ostium fluminis quod dicitur Glein*"[17] ("The first battle was at the mouth of the flowing waters called Glein"). However, from the amassed evidence, philologically and historically, the identification of the River Glein as either the River Glyme or Glynch Brook is tenable, especially since on an east-west axis, the two sites are no more than thirty-five miles apart.

One other river as a possibility must be mentioned, one whose variant form is the Old Irish *cain.* The location of this river is shown on Map 5 in Chapter 5, no more than a mile from the River Tanat, one of Vortimer's battle sites. The Old Irish *cain* is interesting in another aspect, too; it is a cognate of *cæint,* which might be part of the reason why Hengist's kingdom was misidentified as "Chent" or "Kent." This site would be farther west into Wales, but would still be close to the borderlands.

The Second through Fifth Battles: A River Called Dubglas in the Region of Linnuis

For the site of these four battles, Stevenson gives only two variations; one is "Duglas" for Dubglas in manuscripts *a* and E and the other is "Lindsey" for Linnuis in manuscript D.[18] Alcock refers to several philological variables for Dubglas/Douglas but doesn't follow through. *Dulas, Dulais, Dawlish, Dowlish, Divelish,* and *Devil's Brook* all stem from the root *Dalch,* which Ekwall lists etymologically as "a compound of Brit *dubo-* 'black' (Welsh *du)* and OW *gleis,* Welsh *glais* 'stream.' Hence 'black stream.'"[19] Dulas, City Dulas, and Dulas Bay, however, are on the northeastern shore of Anglesey and therefore outside the realm of Arthur's milieu; Dawlish is on the southern coast of Devon and likewise outside Arthur's sphere of operations during what would have been his earlier period. Giles identified the Dunglas River, which is the southern boundary of Lothian, but Whitaker identifies the site as the Duglas in Lancashire near Wigan.[20]

Alcock bypasses the river-name and instead concentrates his efforts on Linnuis. He reasons that this region and its variants in spelling suggests two major locations, either Lincoln and the surrounding district called Lindsey, or Lindum to the north of the Clyde estuary in Dalriada. He lists "Dubglas" as dubious for two reasons: First, there is no known river called Dubglas or its variants in the region, and second, Lincoln was a strong, long-established Anglo-Saxon area.[21] He rejects Lindum because it is too far north for conflicts between the Britons and Saxons during the Arthurian era.

S. G. Wildman, however, in his 1971 book *The Black Horsemen,* which lamentably has sunk into obscurity, focuses simply and directly upon the river-name Dubglas. He postulates that the Saxons, coming from the Lincoln area, penetrated the Briton area of Elmet down the River Ribble, turned south to occupy south Lancashire, but were defeated on the bank of the River Douglas.[22] This, of course, sets the battle at a more logistic location.

Correctly, the focus of any battle should be upon Wales and the midlands. Whereas the battle at the River Glein is on the *southern* fringes of the Welsh/English Saxon borders, the River Dubglas occurs on the *northern* borders between the warring factions. Chester, the legionary fortress sometimes listed as the Arthurian battle site of Caer Legion, lies about thirty miles south of the River Douglas, on the outskirts of the Cornovii territory. But more significant are the sites which were just to the north, where the River Douglas is a tributary to the mouth of the River Ribble.

The name *Ribble* is one of the many keys to unlocking the secrets of the area. It is associated with the words *Ripus* and *Ripon,* both which are dative plurals of *Hrype,* an Old English tribal name.[23] Ekwall adds information about the Hyrpe tribe in two successive places; at one point he writes that "The [Hrype] tribe gave its name to Ripon and probably some places near Ripon (see Ribston, Ripley)."[24] For the name Ribston, he adds that the word has an intervocalic change of *p* for *b,* relating that Ribston is "No doubt *Hrypa stan,* 'the stone of the *Hrype.*' The stone may have been a boundary stone marking the territory of the *Hrype* tribe, or a stone at the meeting-place of the tribe."[25] This intervocalic change is significant because it is also the root

Photograph 7—The Douglas Valley, the possible site of Arthur's second through fifth battles at a river called Dubglas in the region of Linnuis.

for the River Rib, the River Ribble, and Ribchester. The River Ribble meanders a hundred miles or so through Lancashire to the River Douglas, where both join and then empty into the Irish Sea.

Ribchester was one of the principal fortified towns of Lancashire just prior to Cunedda's migration to the south. With his initial movement to Carlisle, Ribchester once again became an important stronghold. This site and its surrounding regions remained focal points just prior to the end of the fifth century, evidenced by other geographic sites in the area appearing in the histories. In an arc just nine miles northeast of the River Douglas, near Preston, is the large village of Darwen (and Ryal Ford, a parallel to Ryhd yr Fael in the *Historia Brittonum),* the River Darwen flowing near Lower Darwen. Additionally, the Roman road from Manchester runs through Lower Darwen to Ribchester, only six miles distant, where the road splits, one branch going almost directly northward to Penrith and eventually to Carlisle, and the other northeastward. During early conflicts, then, between the English Saxons and the Welsh, the River Douglas just north of Chester would be a logical placement.

THE SIXTH BATTLE: ON THE RIVER CALLED BASSAS

For this sixth battle Stevenson lists the variant as Lusas in manuscript *a.* Something which he doesn't frequently do is speculate on the battle sites, but in this instance he gives information which is not cited, but which might be his own observation. He writes,

> Probably in Hampshire, near Basingstoke and Basing, near which is Cherfield, preserving the name of some battle in which Cerdic, Arthur's great opponent, was concerned.[26]

The connection between Basingstoke/Basing and Bassas is logical; the eponymous link between Cherfield and Cerdic also makes sense based upon the text from John of Glastonbury and the inferences in Geoffrey of Monmouth. However, there are no indications or inferences in either source which can be drawn from manuscripts, such as the *Annales Cambriae,* that Arthur and Cerdic were enemies dating back as far as this sixth conflict, once again assuming that the battles are listed in chronological order in the *Historia Brittonum.* Cerdic first appears in the Genealogical Preface in 494, and in *The Anglo-Saxon Chronicle* in 495, closer chronologically to Arthur's twelfth battle, the Battle at Mount Baddon. Additionally, the 495 entry in the *Chronicle* claims that the two Saxon leaders fought against the *Welsh* and not the Britons, perhaps somewhere in eastern Wales or the western midlands, but not in southern Britain.

Although most scholars do not comment upon this site because of its obscurity,[27] besides the River Lusas in Hampshire there have been several other locales suggested by various writers. One other postulation, by J. A. Giles, has been an isolated islet called Bass Rock in the Firth of Forth near North Berwick,[28] more than seventy-five miles farther north and east than Camboglanna on Hadrian's Wall. This is one of the most northerly sites proposed, and except for the most steadfast proponents of a "northern" Arthur, this locale is inconceivable, particularly when considering the conflict here was between Arthur and the English Saxons. There seems to be nothing strategically crucial about this isolated Rock to warrant a momentous battle.

On the other hand, one of the most perceptive proposals is offered by Graham Phillips and Martin Keatman, associating Bassas with the *Churches of Bassa* and therefore at Baschurch, very logistically in the kingdom of Powys.[29] Indirectly, Rachel Bromwich supports their contention by writing,

> [Of the 114 englynion, there is] a series of dramatic monologues declaimed by Heledd (or *Hyledd),* sister of Cynddylan, lord of Pengwern. She stands on one of the neighboring heights, and looks down on the blazing ruin of her home. In chain on chain of englynion she laments the destruction of Pengwern, of *Eglwysau Bassa* (or Baschurch), and the white homestead in the valley.[30]

Bromwich, of course, is writing of something in an entirely different context, but she does make the connection of Bassa and Baschurch. This site would be in much stronger contention than an obscure islet in the Firth of

Forth, almost 250 miles farther north. Baschurch is almost in the heart of Cornovii territory, the huge expanse of Roman territory which acted as a buffer between the Welsh and the English Saxons. After the Roman abandonment of the island, this territory would have been a no-man's land, ripe for the taking. Baschurch is within a thousand yards of the River Severn; it is only twelve miles to the northwest of Viroconium and the Wrekin, locations which were archaeologically shown to have been occupied by various tribes after the Roman withdrawal; it is six miles to Old Oswestry, previously known as Maes Cogwy, meaning "Cogwy's Boundary," the legendary court of Guinevere's father, Gogyrfan, on the borderlands between Wales and Cornovii; it is ten miles due west of the confluence of the Rivers Tanet and Severn; it is also within a twenty-five-mile radius of Darwen, Eliseg's Pillar, Powis Castle, Breidden hill fort, and Caerenion, one of the possibilities as a site for Arthur's eighth battle.

There is another interesting possibility for the locale of Arthur's sixth battle, one which has never been proposed before. An enticing variation, based upon the word *Riothamus* being an epithet for Arthur, plus comments that Riothamus protected the coasts of Gaul and Brittany, is that the Bassas battle was fought on the shores of Brittany. Because of the migration in the fifth century, the territory was called Little Britain and the inhabitants became known as Bretons to distinguish them from Britons. A synonymous Latin term is *Armorica*, referring to the Atlantic coastal region of northwestern France between the Seine and Loire Rivers. Its derivation is from *ar-*, meaning "on" and *mor-*, meaning "sea."

This new kingdom was geographically divided into two areas. Haute Bretagne (Upper Brittany) is characterized by scrub trees on its interior plateau, the section of the country which lies closest to France. Basse Bretagne, or Lower Brittany is the territory which lies along the ocean. The coastline is rugged, with numerous bays, inlets, and capes. Nennius uses the word "on" (interestingly, not "at" or "near") the river called Bassas, meaning that the battle took place on water. However, the water (or the shore) might not have been a river, but instead the coastline of Basse Bretagne, shortened through familiarity to Basse and later configured to "Bassas." Riothamus's voyage, the alliance between Ægidius and the Bretons, the continuous wars with marauders, and the geographic location meld with the events and chronology of the period more than an isolated rock in the Firth of Forth or a river in Hampshire.

Unlike the geographic proposal of Bass Rock but similar to the Phillips/Keatman chronological proposition, this postulation fits better into a general scheme. In the earlier section on Ambrosius Aurelianus, a general chronological span for the Nennius battle list was suggested as 453 to 497. Based upon the events occurring on the continent, the Battle of Bassas—if it were based upon this contention—would most likely have been fought after

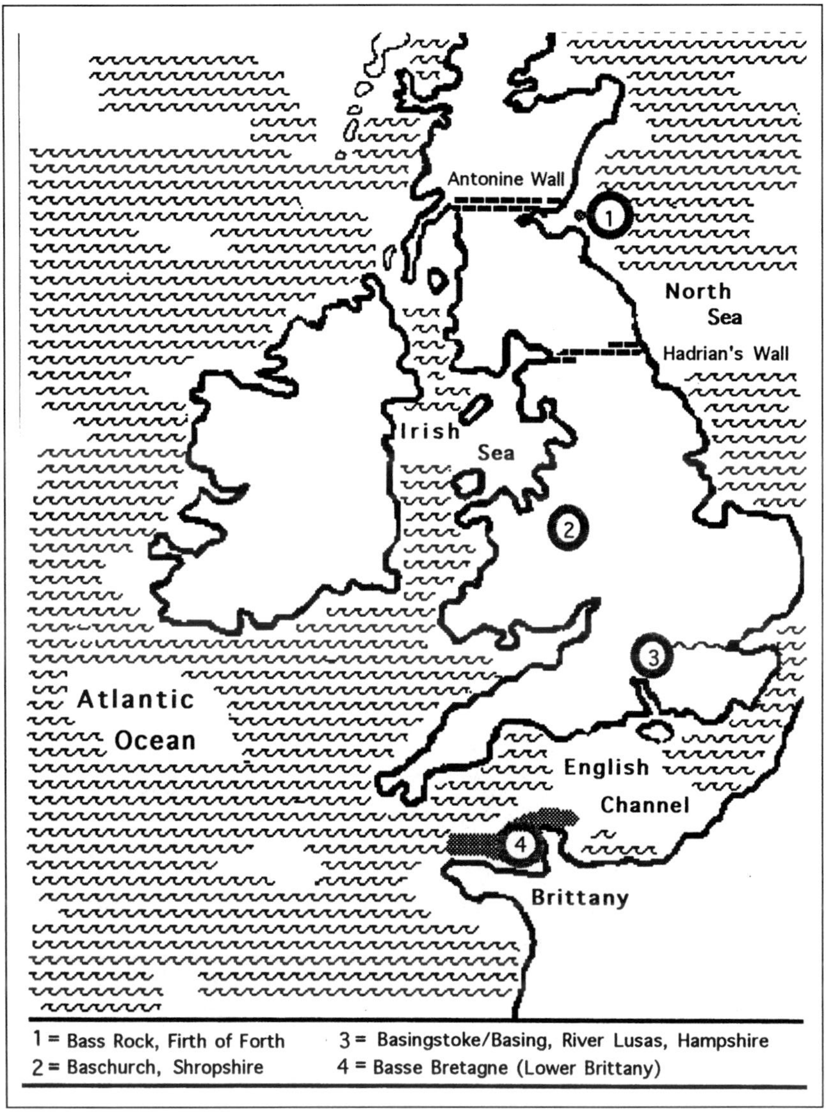

Map 7—The possible sites of Arthur's sixth battle, the Battle on the River Bassas.

the second migration to the continent and during Ægidius's reign, between perhaps 460 and 464, with a median date of 462. Several historical sources indicate that when Riothamus, along with his army and all the other people of the second migration, came to Gaul, Ægidius welcomed them openly and gave them land (significantly supportable of this proposal) in *Lower Brittany,* another name for Basse Bretagne. Conditions were unstable in Europe, just as on the island, and as Morris described, there were so many conflicts among the tribes that allegiances were changed almost daily. The Bretons, with their name just recently changed from "Britons," had to defend their territories from marauders, including Saxons. Part of what they were protecting was Basse Bretagne, or the Basse, the shores of their peninsula, mistakenly recorded in history as the banks or the shores of a *river,* not the shores of a sea. Riothamus, the "Briton king from across Ocean," would have been continuing the battles against the Saxons as a reciprocal pact with the Romans, offering his aid against the barbarians on the continent in trade for renewed Roman support on the island once the continental uprisings were quelled. As an interesting citation which can be used to support this contention, Ashe writes, "Jacques [de Guise] speaks of Arthur as having been King during the rule of General Ægidius in northern Gaul, that is, in the years 461–464."[31]

One other benefit from this proposal about the Bassas battle is that it would resolve—at least in part—the chronology of the battle list, which in turn locks it more securely into place. Except for Badon, none of the battles ever hinted at a time-frame. Now, based upon the battle of Bassas, not only could location be given—the Bretons and Britons protecting their shores of Basse Bretagne—but a date could be established. Keeping in mind Morris's tenet that no date can be precise, there is a range that is possible within a framework, so that when a singular date is ascribed, it is with full knowledge that it must be fluid. The time span for the Bassas battle would be the middle part of the sixth decade in the fifth century, shortly after the Briton migration to Gaul. Conflicts undoubtedly started almost immediately, with the enemies trying to prevent the migrants from establishing a stronghold, and the primary target would have been the coastline.

The Seventh Battle: In the Forest Celidonis, That Is, Cat Coit Celidon

From two sources giving information about the *Historia's* seventh battle in its original Latin—Josephus Stevenson's *Nennii: Historia Britonum*, and Morris's *British History*—there is a difference of only one comma. The passage reads, "*Septimum fuit bellum in silva Celidonis, id est(,) Cat Coit Celidon.*"[32] In footnote 8 Stevenson gives two variants in spelling, "Catoit Celidon" in manuscript E, and "Cacoit Celidan" in manuscript *a.* He also adds that Usher believed the site to be near the city of Lincoln, and Carte imagined it to be in Cumbria (south and west of Hadrian's Wall). Morris translated the passage to mean "The seventh battle was in Celyddon Forest, that is, the Battle of Celyddon Coed,"[33] which, obviously, is very vague. An answer that Morris gives in *The Age of Arthur* is not only vague, but also sounds conflicting. He first identifies Celidon Wood as "being in the north."[34] Later he writes that Gwendoleu's bard Myrddin hid "in Celidon forest," but identifies Gwendoleu's territory as the Carlisle region,[35] which seemingly agrees with Carte and J. A. Giles. Giles translates this passage of the battle as "The seventh in the wood Celidon, which the Welsh call Cat Coit Celidon,"[36] which is a more accurate translation because it retains the original Latin names. Giles proposes in a footnote that the site of this battle is the forest of Englewood (Inglewood) extending from Penrith to Carlisle, which would, of course, be part of the vast area Carte unproductively generalized as Cumbria. Attempts at identification have become circular.

Leslie Alcock and Geoffrey Ashe break from orbit and identify *Celidonis* as "Caledonia." Alcock writes that "There is full agreement that this [battle site] was in Scotland, but if we attempt greater precision, dispute begins."[37] The first part of this statement is a confident oversimplification. Even though Alcock iterates that "Catcoit Celidon, the battle of the Caledonian Forest was fought in southern Scotland,"[38] and reinforces that concept later when he writes "Cat Coit Celidon was in Scotland,"[39] available historical evidence of the period shows that this as the site for the battle is an impossibility or, allowing some leeway, nearly so.

Caledonii, the Roman name for this Scottish terrain, is a massive region, about forty miles beyond the Antonine Wall. It is bordered on the south by the Domnonii territory on the other side of the Antonine Wall, on the west by Epidii and Creones, on the north by Vacomagi, and on the east by Taexali and Venicones. With no exaggeration, there are at least two dozen forests listed by name, two of the largest being Mamore Forest and the Forest of Atholl almost directly to its east. There are several minor points which do not actually refute this area as Arthur's seventh battle site, but more accurately render this possibility as useless. The first is that there is not *a* Caledonian Forest; that is, the word "forest" in the *Historia Brittonum* is listed as a *common* noun, thus asserting that this site is *a* forest in the province of Caledonii. Because this vast expanse probably covered 450 square miles, it is impossible (and it would be ludicrous to try) to pinpoint with any degree of accuracy a single battle site here. The second fallacy is that the translation of "Celidonis" as "Caledonii" is not uncontested fact.

One of the benefits which this battle-entry in the *Historia* offers is that it gives not only the term "Celidonis," but also the Welsh rendition of it, "Cat Coit Celidon" and its variables. This latter translates generally as the "Wood" (or "Forest") of Celidon, and surprisingly (because he is so meticulous and skeptical), Alcock immediately equates "a Caledonii forest" with the "Wood of Celidon." To continue one of the extracts given above, Alcock writes, "Cat Coit Celidon was fought in Scotland against *uncertain enemies.*" [italics added][40] This is not an accurate statement. The introduction to "Arthur's Campaigns" in the *Historia Brittonum* leaves no doubt as to whom Arthur's enemies were:

> At that time the *Saxones* increased in number in Britain. Upon *Horsa's* death [emended by *The Historic King Arthur* from Hengist's], Octha came down from the north.... Then Arthur

> fought against them in those days, together with the kings of Britain, but he was the leader in battle.[41]

The list of twelve battles follows, and then the summary adds that when the *Saxones* were defeated they sent for reinforcements from Germany. The *Historia* is so implicitly and explicitly definitive that it is impossible not to accept its recording as truth.

The surviving histories of Caledonii bear this out. Collingwood provides a succinct but effective background.[42] Once Gnaeus Julius Agricola succeeded to power in Britain, he advanced beyond the Forth-Clyde line to begin his assault on the Caledonian territory. For some reason not explicitly stated in the histories he stopped in the summer of 83, but then advanced again into central Scotland, camping in various places to be supplied by his fleet. His objective was to establish himself in central Caledonii before the summer of 83 ended. A Calenonian attack on the Ninth Legion didn't deter the local tribe even though it was defeated, but it did slow the Roman army. In the summer of the next year (84) Agricola fought and destroyed the armies of the Caledonian tribes while simultaneously having his fleet ravage the coast to the north.

However, in 85 Agricola was recalled, according to Tacitus, because of Domitian's jealousy, although in actuality the recall might have rationally been based upon a sense of futility in subduing the northern tribes while additionally depleting Roman resources.

This was the extent of Rome's offensive in the far north; for the remaining two and a half centuries of Roman occupation of Britain, the border of the empire to the north, stopped for a short while at the Antonine Wall before receding to Hadrian's Wall. The invasion into Caledonii was the deepest penetration ever made into the far north, but it was also short-lived, lasting no more than three years in the latter half of the first century. It is totally unrealistic to believe that Arthur was on the *offensive* in fighting a battle in Caledonii; in relation to the far northern reaches, history shows that during the entire Roman occupation *and* the immediate post-Roman period the *Britanni* continuously took a *defensive* stance. Beyond the Antonine Wall there are only a few fortifications to attest to Rome's invasion, and, more important, because the Romans' stay was so short, there wasn't even the beginnings of the famous Roman roads which made military travel so easy and far-flung areas so accessible, which was true in all the areas south of Hadrian's Wall.

The best approach to pursue other geographic possibilities for Arthur's seventh battle is through the Welsh name for the conflict, Cat Coit Celidon. Alcock also suggested that "in Welsh tradition Coit Celidon (in modern Welsh, Coed Celyddon) lay not far north of Carlisle, most probably the Southern Uplands."[43] Yet he doesn't pursue his own lead, nor does he look farther south of Hadrian's Wall. The area north of Carlisle is vaguely described, but it sounds as if it is the same locale which John Morris records, although Morris is even more anomalous. Morris refers to a "Nennius poem [which] gives Arthur several battles in the Cheviot region north of Hadrian's Wall,"[44] and claims his source as Chapter 56 of the *Historia.* He is obviously designating Chapter 56 as evolving from a battle-poem, which is a common contention among researchers, and then he is evidently further singling out Arthur's seventh battle, but how he is able to deduce that the battle of Cat Coit Celidon was fought in the Cheviot area is a mystery. Under other circumstances he explains the significance of the Cheviot sector, but he never justifies his selection of this particular site for Arthur's battle.

Three weak possibilities as the Battle of Coed Celidon can be extracted from the jumble of information. The weakest starts in the far north, and the other suggestions become progressively stronger as they move to the south. Caledonii is definitely *not* an unquestionable site, but is in fact the most impractical. As tribes were expanding they were seeking better lands and environments which made survival easier, not the contrary; the native kingships which had flourished under Roman rule for several centuries were not eager to accomplish the opposite by acquiring hostile territories. The Cheviot Hills as a possible battle site is a shade stronger, but it likewise is too far north. The Romans had already relinquished the Antonine Wall as the northern border, so that by Arthur's time, Hadrian's Wall had become the perimeter of territory worth fighting and dying for. The Englewood Forest just south of Carlisle is the best possibility of the three; this area already has a niche in Arthurian history through Cunedda, who settled there upon his initial move to the south. As a reward for clearing the area of the *Scotti* and the Picts, he was granted the territory between the Rivers Dee and Teifi.

There are, however, two other possibilities which have never been proposed or explored. The first is the Clun Forest in north-central Wales, near the present village of Kerry. It is necessary to emphasize once again that the *HB* is a *Welsh* manuscript and that Arthur springs from a *Welsh* source, not a Dumnonian or Cornwallish one. Although this is commonly acknowledged by antiquarians and later historians, Wales and its original extensions into the midlands has not been the primary focus when considering Arthur's historic perspective. It is necessary, therefore, to re-set sights to this area and concentrate upon Welsh influences and characteristics.

To take the original passage from Nennius and add an explanation for more clarification, the term for "woods" or "forest" goes back to the early Celtic word *argoat,* with a variant of *argoed.* The first affix of the word, *ar-*, the same affix which occurs in the Celtic word for Brittany, *Armorica,* means "on" or "in." In the term "Armorica" it means "on the sea"; in the term "argoat" it would more logistically mean "in the woods or forest." Put into context, then, the Nennius passage would be Argoed Celidon, in the Forest Celidon. Morris concurs, but transmutes Argoed by dropping the initial two letters and changing the "g" to a "c," with "Argoed Celidon" becoming "Coed Celidon," a natural etymological transmutation in the development of the language. Using the Old British, the term for this battle is Cat Coit, the origin of which is Cat (Ar)Goed. Ekwall explains that *cat* is from *catu-*, an Old British affix meaning "war" or "battle."[45] The entire phrase would literally translate into "battle in the woods." The term is a specific one—that is, a proper noun—because it is capitalized in the original, translating therefore to the Battle in the Celidon Forest.

The next step is to track the term Celidon, Celidonus, or Calidon for this particular battle. Rather than typically accepting the proposition that Celidon is equated with Caledonia, however, this new supposition assumes that Celidon is associated with a proper place-name built eponymically upon its geographic characteristics. This, of course, will still not allow the identification of a specific setting, but it does allow latitude for a more realistic site than Caledonii. "Celidon" can etymologically be broken down into two affixes, *celde-*, with its variations of *celdi-* and *celda-* plus the suffix of *-don* or its variant *den*. The former means "a cold spring (of water)" and the latter means "a valley." Ekwall does point out the possibility that there is an Old English affix *ceole-* meaning "throat," in the sense of a gorge, valley, or a neck of land. If the first is used for identification of locale, then "Cat Coit Celidon" would be interpreted as "in the valley of the forest where there is a cold spring." If the second is used, then its description would be "in the forest's narrow gorge."

Chambers correctly indicates that "Celidon might be any forest; perhaps Chiltern, not claimed as a Saxon name, may represent it."[46] In the same sentence, however, he hazards a guess of a forest in the Chiltern Hills, about thirty-five or forty miles slightly northwest of Central London. In an entirely different context, however, Argoed (or Ar Coed) does seem to point to the Clun Forest. When Sir Ifor Williams lectures about Welsh poetry, he cites one poem which seems relevant here. It is "The Song of the Old Man" and he translates it as literally and faithfully as he can. The important line is the third one in the extract:

> Before my back was bent, ready of speech was I.
> What is wonderful is praised.
> The men of Argoed have always fed me, etc.[47]

He uses the word "Argoed" as a proper name, and therefore, as a specific site. He does not elaborate upon the site, but Bromwich makes an interesting contribution in a footnote, again not in a specific reference to Arthur's battle, but applicable here. Of Argoed she writes,

> Not the northern locality, but Powys, or a part of Powys; Cynddelw also uses *Argoedwys* as equivalent to "men of Powys," RBP

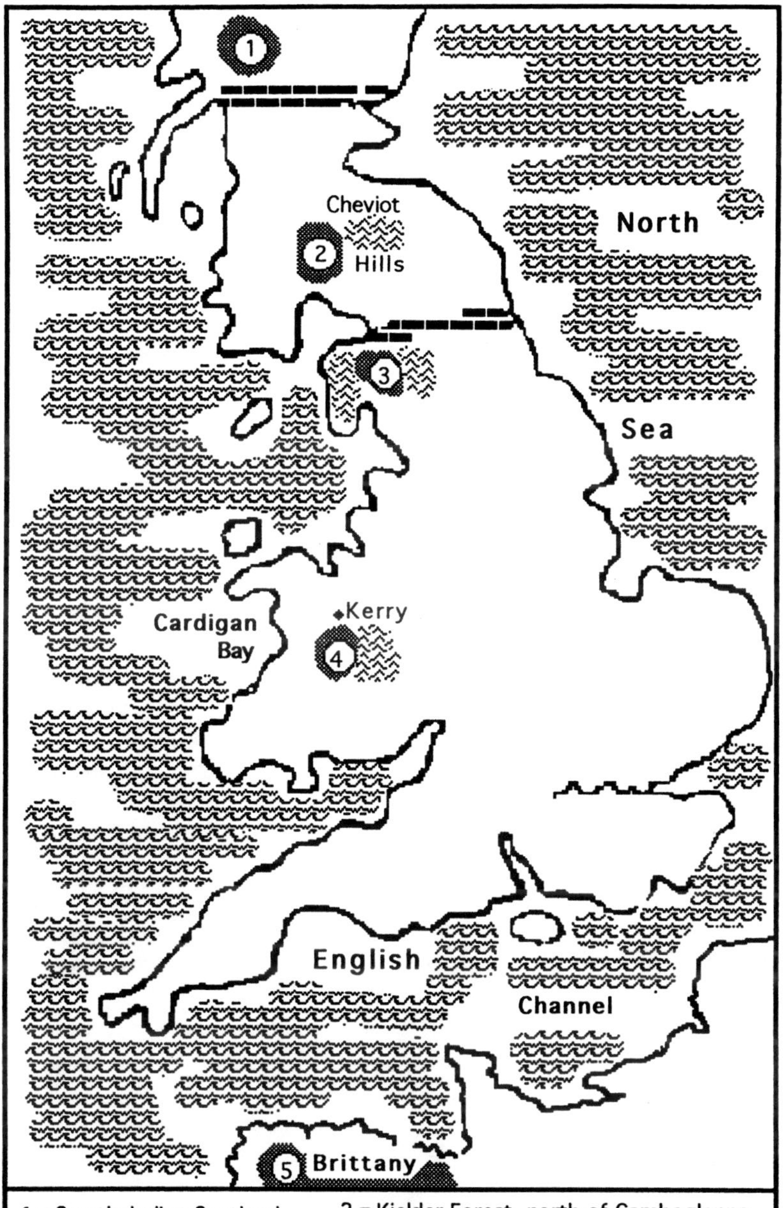

1 = Strathclydian Scotland 2 = Kielder Forest, north of Camboglanna
3 = Forest of Englewood between the Cambrian and Pennine Mountains
4= Clun Forest, near Kerry 5 = The Argoed, Haute Bretagne (Brittany)

Map 8—Arthur's seventh battle at silva Celidonis, Cat Coit Celidon.

> col. 1396, *ll*.30–1; 1398, 27 (where *argoetwys* is paralleled by Powys in the succeeding stanzas) 1399, 34 *Argoedwys bowys*. Further, cf. RBP 1421, 15-16; 1391, 12; 1399,4; 1400, 36. There are several places called Argoed near Kerry, and round Clun Forest.[48]

The above extracts link Kerry and Argoed as synonyms. One other extract by Williams strengthens this connection. He claims that "During this transitional period, Powys and Llanfor are forgotten in favor of the more popular Arthurian cycle, and over the span of time, Celliwig [Kelliwic] and Carleon are substituted for the earlier Argoed and Llanfor."[49]

These passages take on much greater significance when viewed from the perspective that the *HKA* theorized in passing that Kelliwic (or any of its variants) as it appears in the *Mabinogion* tales could possibly be Kerry. Based upon supposition, Kelliwic (Celliwic) was initially viewed as a scribal error for Kerriwic, the "village of Kerry," rather than "the village in a forest." Or, from a different perspective, "Celliwic" and "Cellidon" could be synonymous. -*Wic* from the Latin word *vicus* could mean village, *or* it could refer to an estate or fortified country manor. That Kelliwic evolved as a fortification is an even better supposition, since Kelliwic was identified in tradition as Arthur's Camelot. This possibility was further supported when the Battle of Badon was so convincingly established as the Wrekin near Wroxeter. Approaching Badon from the east, Caersws, because of its strategic importance by the Romans, was at first considered as a possible location of Arthur's court. But "The Dream of Rhonabwy" relates that Arthur, who wanted to be at Baddon by noon, had to cross the River Havern (Severn) only once, not twice. Had he been coming from Caersws by the most direct route using Roman roads, he would have crossed the river first near Newton and later near Buildwas. Because the Severn makes such a wide northerly loop, the options of coming to Baddon from Wales were quite limited. Within the arc, Arthur could have been traveling from Montgomery, Forden, or Middletown in order to reach the battle site. However, if he were traveling from Rhydycroseau or Old Oswestry farther north there would be no need to cross the River Severn. He could have conceivably been traveling from a point of origin further *south* than Kerry, but it would have been impossible for him to travel from Caerleon or Caerwent—two of his most commonly listed courts—in a morning's ride, especially when moving with such a massive army. Similarly, his ride from South Cadbury/Camelot would have been extremely far for a morning's ride, and it wouldn't have required crossing the River Severn. Under these conditions, the battle of Coit Celidon in this place (at Clun Forest near Kerry) and during this time would be more sensible than a conflict approximately 350 miles to the north.

There is one other possibility for the site of this battle, also based upon circumstantial developments. Intriguingly, it is aligned with Arthur's sixth battle at Bassas, and similarly, it is associated with Brittany and therefore with Riothamus's sojourn there while fighting in league with the Romans to try to salvage the empire. The inhabitants of this area between the Seine and the Loire came to be called Britanni during Sidonius's lifetime, owing to the settlement there of many Britons who crossed the Channel fleeing from the influx of the Saxons. Because of this migration in the latter half of the fifth century, the Britons who had migrated to the northwestern section of the continent named the territory "Little Britain," Brittany, and they themselves became know as Bretons, distinguishable from Britons.

As already mentioned above, in the discussion of Arthur's sixth battle, Armorica divides naturally into two geographic areas, Basse Bretagne and Haute Bretagne, the latter also called Upper Brittany, which is characterized by scrub trees on its interior plateau, the section of the country lying closest to France. In accord with three attributes, this interior of Armorica, Haute Bretagne, could be the site of the seventh battle. Some scholars surmise that several Arthurian battles were fought on the continent, specifically in Brittany, because it was considered as a "continental homeland" to the Britons, based upon the several migrations there. As suggested by previous scholars about different battles, ascribing some of the Nennius battles as taking place in Brittany is not unusual. Second, the battle of Cat Coyt Celidon immediately succeeds the battle at Bassas, suggesting that once the coastal areas of Armorica were secured, attention focused upon the interior to drive barbaric tribes, including the Angles and Saxons, out of the borders. And third, the back-to-back battles of Bassas and Cat Coyt Celidon fit into the time-frame for Riothamus, the Briton King who traveled across Ocean with twelve thousand men to fight alongside Ægidius and Syagrius.

Brittany's interior is commonly called the Argoed—the land of the woods—by the Gauls, and though there are mainly isolated villages on this plateau, Brittany's previous administrative capital was Rennes, one of the most important inland cities. True, this setting gives a common reference instead of a specific one, but the Caledonian Forest of the far north is based upon the same generality. Even from a general perspective, then, Haute Bretagne is a better probability, based not only upon the likelihood of Saxon opposition but also upon a reasonable chronological calibration; it follows the Bassas battle but *precedes* Riothamus's defeat at Angers and his re-appearance on the island and his later success at Badon.

If these battles are viewed as part of Riothamus's ten-year tenure on the continent, Ægidius and his son Syagrius as the leaders of the Gauls were strong, especially in the first half of that decade. Euric was dealing with internal struggles, and the Goths did not pose a serious threat until the second half of the 460s. If the date set for the Battle of Bassas is two years either side of 462, then the Battle of Cat Coed would be some time between then and 468.

The Eighth Battle: In the Castello Guinnion

The entry for this eighth battle as it appears in the *HB* is longer by far than any other entry. Whereas, for example, the first battle is recorded simply as the battle "at the mouth of the river called Glein," the eighth battle is listed as

> in castello Guinnion, in which Arthur carried the image of Saint Mary Ever Virgin upon his shield (shoulder) and the pagans were put to flight during that day, and there was great death upon them because of the virtue of Our Lord Jesus Christ and Saint Mary his virgin mother.[50]

Before concentrating upon the geographic components of this particular battle, attention must first be directed to the blazon on his shield, particularly because it points to a Christian conversion. The story—perhaps more accurately, the legend or traditional tale—furnishing the background comes from John of Glastonbury's description of Arthur's vision of the Virgin Mary. Chapter XXXIIII of the *Cronica* includes a long account of Arthur's stay on Glastonbury, the Island of Avalon. One night, while Arthur was at Wearyall in the monastery of the holy virgins, he was awakened by an angel of the Lord calling his name and telling him to arise at dawn and go to the hermitage of St. Mary Magdalene's of Beckery. Arthur tells Gawain about the vision, who tells him to ignore it. Arthur is visited a second time by the angel, but does nothing until a third vision.

John interrupts his narrative at this point and inserts a confusing passage about Arthur's servant having a dream—which turns out to be a reality—of going to the hermitage.[51] At any rate, the squire dies at the hermitage because of his misdeeds, and Arthur visits the site at dawn alone. He is barred entrance and is terrified because he does not know what prevents him from entering the holy place. Kneeling, praying and meditating, he humbly begs pardon for his sins and finally is able to enter.

The king observes the sacrifice of mass, and afterward sees the vision of the Holy Mother and her Son. The old priest who had recited the mass explains the vision, and the king vows to believe firmly in the holy sacrament and will do anything asked of him for love of the glorious Mother and her Son. John then inserts into his account that the glorious Mother, in testimony of Arthur's conversion, gave to the king a crystal cross. Arthur changes his shield in their honour, and in lieu of his blazon being three red lions on a silver background, turning their heads over their backs, it becomes a silver cross on a green background, and upon the cross's right arm is an image of the Virgin Mary holding her Son in her arms.

One interesting peculiarity of this story is more than just Arthur's association with Glastonbury, the "Isle of Avalon." In this story, Arthur is at Wearyall and Beckery rather than at the Abbey itself. Perhaps, as Philip

Rahtz suggests, Arthur was uncomfortable at the Abbey and did not like to resort to the companionship of the monks, therefore residing during his sojourns at a more scenic and serene spot. Of even more interest, however, is the explanation that this story provides about the reference in the *HB* to Arthur's insignia in the eighth battle. There seems to be some intervening source, no longer available, between John's explanation of Arthur's insignia and the mention of it in the *HB*. If indeed there is no explanation from an independent unbiased source during the intervening centuries, then John's account is evidently an interpolative attempt at deceit, especially since Arthur's new blazon is almost identical to the one which in later years was adopted by the Abbey. Without that intervening source, it would be very easy for any monk familiar with Nennius to supply a story explaining in detail Nennius's entry in order to extricate the Abbey from its political and/or financial straits by identifying it with the great king.

Two major authors address Nennius's passage of Arthur carrying the image of the holy Mary, the everlasting Virgin, on his shield/shoulders. Robert Fletcher touches upon it and comes up with an intervening legend of sorts. He labels Nennius's statement as clumsy and repetitious, reports that Monmouth restores some sentence sense, and explains that William of Malmsbury (he probably means an interpolator of Malmsbury) reports that Arthur sewed the image on his arms. Geoffrey of Monmouth is not the intervening unbiased source; although he reports and restates the passage, he does not explain the story behind it. Malmsbury is not that source because Malmsbury, in his original *De Antiquitate*, prior to the later tampering, does not specify Arthur. Unfortunately, Fletcher then sidetracks to an error in translation between "shoulder" and "shield."[52] He quickly redeems himself, however, by giving an explanation of the Cambridge edition of Nennius, which states that Arthur went to Jerusalem, where he made a model of the true cross and had it consecrated. For three days Arthur fasted and prayed that the Lord would make him victorious over the pagans. The Lord listened, and Arthur carried back with him an image of the Holy Mary,

> whose fragments are still kept at Wedel in great veneration.[53]

The thrust, however, of Fletcher's inquiry has to do with the Badon entry in the *AC*, including the cross, and the confusion with the Guinnion entry and its mention of the Holy Virgin. What Fletcher's conclusion leads to is that at least as early as the tenth century Arthur had become a heroic legendary figure for the Welsh. In answer to the question, "Is this Jerusalem myth the intervening unbiased legend which explains Arthur's blazon mentioned by Nennius?" there isn't, as usual, a simple yes or no. The answer is elusive. Yes, this myth is disassociated with Glastonbury; yes, it is twelfth century and unattached to Cambrensis, Adam, or John; and yes, it does explain why Arthur would change the blazon on his shield.

Yet even this explanation is shrouded in skepticism. Fletcher indicates that the legend which is recorded might be from the "genuine" Nennius, and perhaps might be even older than the time of Nennius. But the specificity of the blazon on Arthur's shield is the image of the Holy Virgin and not the cross. And of course there are some claimed relics at the Abbey, but nothing has ever manifested itself. Lastly, what is most difficult to accept is Arthur's pilgrimage to Jerusalem. There is no historical or literary record, by inference or implication, that Arthur journeyed to Jerusalem. The answer to the question doesn't enter the realm of possibility; it is neither likely nor probable nor convincing that this story offers a logical explanation of why Arthur changed the blazon on his shield.

Richard Barber, the other scholar who deals with this passage, is much more thorough and therefore more convincing. In *The Figure of Arthur* he attacks the Guinnion passage head-on. He demonstrates the difficulty of dealing with the major details in Nennius and cites specifically the image of the Virgin on Arthur's shoulders. He, too, briefly points out the mistranslation of "shield" and "shoulder" but then moves quickly to the more compelling aspects of the entry. He candidly declares

> A detailed device on a shield of this date has yet to be found, and even in the eleventh century, devices were still extremely simple.... On the other hand, there is a long tradition of bearing crosses into battle, though even this is rare enough in the west.[54]

Barber then specifically addresses Arthur's choice of the Virgin Mary as "patron saint." In essence, he writes that Mariolatry developed in Eastern churches and didn't spread to western Europe until perhaps the seventh century. Of Nennius's title for the Holy Mother, *sanctae Mariae perpetuae virginis,* he writes that it would have been rare before the ninth century.[55] His opening remarks about the simplicity of design in Arthur's day is logical; it was not until the thirteenth and fourteenth centuries that the heraldic arms became more elaborate. For example, the emblem of the rampant lion on the shields of Sir Tristram, Sir Pellinor, and Sir Brunor were quite detailed, varying only in color. The two-headed falcon on the shields of Mordred, Gareth, and Gawain are equally artistic, though some of the romance shields are simpler in design. Lancelot's blazon is diagonal lines of alternating gray and red; Arthur's of this romance period is three gold crowns on a red background.

This leads to an insupportable inference: There is no physical evidence, archaeologically or otherwise, and there are no intervening legends to verify that Arthur changed his blazon because of what happened to him at Glastonbury. A similar question can be asked about the Fletcher material, "Is there an intervening legend which explains why Arthur changed his blazon between the Nennius entry and John of Glastonbury's account?" And the answer is still "No." The only conclusion to reach, then, is that the story of

Arthur's vision which appears in the Glastonbury manuscripts picked up on Nennius's cue and was invented, probably for the aggrandizement of the Abbey.

Yet accepting this conclusion does not mean that any association of Arthur and Glastonbury is automatically non-existent, nor does it necessarily mean that the entire entry of the eighth battle is bogus. A generalization which can apply to this as well as other instances is that interpolations, scribal errors, and deliberate deceptions and deceits are commonplace in Arthurian material. In spite of it all, though, Arthur could have fought a battle in *castello Guinnion,* but his shield Wynebgwrthucher did not have Saint Mary or her Son emblazoned on it.

Rather than the extra material about this battle aiding in deciphering its locale, just the opposite has happened. Flagrant, deliberate distortion has caused confusion not only between the eighth and the twelfth battles, but also between entries in the *AC* as opposed to the ones in the *HB*. The heinous interpolater of Malmsbury's *De Antiquitate* twisted two entries almost beyond recognition when he wrote,

> Finally, at the siege of Mount Badon, relying upon the image of the mother of the Lord which he had sewn on his armour, rising alone against nine hundred of the enemy he dashed them to the ground with incredible slaughter.[56]

The expression "mother of the Lord" does not appear in either Badon entry of the *AC* or in the Badon listing of the *HB*. The *AC* entry simply records that at the battle of Badon Arthur carried the Cross of our Lord Jesus Christ on his shield but does not allude to Mary, and the *HB* is devoid of any religious references. The "mother of the Lord" does, however, appear in the entry for the eighth battle in the *HB*.

After all this preliminary confusion, to try to determine the geographic location of this eighth battle seems anti-climactic; it lies between the shadows and a dark place. In the oldest of the manuscripts, it is fought adjacent to a *castellum,* which means a castle, fortress, fort, or elevated dwelling-place.[57] One supposition is that it refers to Binchester, in Durham, just south of the eastern end of Hadrian's Wall.[58] Naturally, however, it is much more difficult (well-nigh impossible, actually) to try to locate.

Not many researchers have speculated about this site. Alcock's stance is that there are three battles which are impossible to locate because their names cannot be identified with modern place-names; he enumerates these as the sixth battle on the river Bassas, the eighth in castle Guinnion, and the tenth on the shore of Tribruit.[59] An obscure clue, however, comes from Graham Webster's book[60] *The Cornovii,* which offers a tenuous connection between a site and Arthur's eighth battle. As in other cases, Viroconium as a substitute for Wroxeter was a transference from a nearby place; in this instance the name was borrowed from the Wrekin, whose inhabitants resisted the army. Starting with the old Welsh name of Wrekin, Caer Guricon, and the later Anglo-Saxon form (Wreocen), Kenneth Jackson has suggested that the Roman term *Uriconon* evolved with a proper Latin ending to *Viroconium* for ease of pronunciation. Giles translates this battle as "near Gurnion castle," but then in a footnote writes, "Variously supposed to be in Cornwall, or Binchester in Durham, but most probably the Roman station of Garionenum, near Yarmouth, in Norfolk."[61] Giles includes "Cair Guorcon" in his list, but then suggests Worren or Woran in Pembrokeshire as possibilities,[62] evidently not equating the city with his interpretation of the Guinnion battle as Gurnion castle.

There are five reasons why the Wrekin comes to mind as a possible locale for the eighth battle. First, it was the originally named site for Caer Guricon. Second, its inhabitants resisted the Roman army there in earlier times before the evacuation. Its importance is stressed by Peter Clayton,[63] who writes of its heavily fortified system, its extensive view for defensive purposes, its importance as the tribal center of the Cornovii territory, and its reorganization in later years. Third, that reorganization might have stemmed from warring Cymry or Hrype tribes in the area, scrambling for power after the Romans vacated the territories. Fourth, as suggested by Graham Webster,[64] the Wrekin controlled the crucial intersections of Roman roads connecting all points of the island as far away as Lincoln, London, Axminster, and Chester. And last, this center is in the same vicinity as Vortimer's battles against the treacherous Saxons and Cunedda's activities following his southern migration, once again strongly suggesting that Vortimer is an epithet for Cunedda. Of further consequence, Arthur's twelfth battle at Badon is in this same significant locale.

Based upon even more reckless speculation, and perhaps as rash as Morris's assumption that the battle of Guinnion took place at Winchester or Giles's belief that it was at either Norwich or Winwick, there are gossamer filaments attached to two other possible locations. One is Castle Caereinion, because it contains the word "Castle" in its name and because of its close approximation with Gurnion. Even more logistically intriguing, however, is its location near the heartland of Welsh/English Saxon conflicts: It is within twenty miles of Wroxeter, near major Roman roads to the northwest, the northeast, the southwest and the southeast, adjacent to the Rivers Tanat and Caint, and in the vicinity of inscribed stones. The second possibility is attached to the assumption that, since the battle occurred during Riothamus's era, it was fought not on the island but in Brittany. The name Guinnion Fort is a very close parallel to the name of Guingamp on the continent, a fort (or camp) which is a very short distance west from St. Brieuc, on the coast of a shallow bay. The voyage from Southampton Water to southwest Brittany, sailing past the islands of Guernsey and Jersey, would be short indeed. With the Britons and the Bretons both trying to stave off the Saxon attacks, Guingamp would be just as logical a site as Winchester, and even more logical than Norwich or Winwick. This spot might afford the connection between Guinnion Fort = Guin Fort = Guin Camp = Guingamp.

In spite of all the rhetoric, Arthur's eighth battle still remains an enigma. A single location cannot be identified beyond a reasonable doubt. Like other battles, it hangs in an immutable void.

The Ninth Battle: In the *Urbe Legionis*

Similar to the seventh battle at Cat Coit Celidon, the ninth battle at *Urbe Legionis* seems easy to identify, yet it, too, is illusory. When contemplating the possible location, what immediately comes to mind is Caerleon. Manuscript D of the *HB* has recorded in its margin "Qui Britannice Kairliun dicitur,"[65] meaning "which the British call Kairliun," commonly translated as "Caerleon." Typically, the City of Legions is identified as either Caerleon-on-Usk or Chester-upon-Dee, but the oversimplification comes from interpolations scrawled in the margin in Manuscript D. The more reliable manuscripts, such as *a* and *A*, record only the term *Urbe Legionis,* which, of course, is generically interpreted as "a city where Roman legions were stationed." Hence, in addition to Carleon and Chester, there were a number of other "Urbe Legionis" in Britain. In the eastern midsection of the island was York, and Lincoln was only a short distance south; to the southeast between the Rivers Stour and Blackwater was Colchester; at the mouth of the Thames was Londinium, and to the west at the mouth of the Severn was Gloucester. All of these were "cities of legions" during the Roman occupation.

One of the most significant *urbe legionis* was Wroxeter, the heart of the Cornovii territory. Graham Webster and Philip Barker write that "Wroxeter would have been the obvious site for a legionary fortress."[66] By Arthurian times Viroconium as a legionary fortress would—like Colchester, Lincoln, and Gloucester—have been converted to civil and administrative posts, which in turn became *coloniae,* settlements for retired legionnaires. Wroxeter was even more exceptional because it became a tribal center with local autonomy; it was patterned in grids after the Roman cities, governed by laws and courts, and contained a forum, bath house, water supply, and drainage.[67]

There is no need to go into more detail about *Urbe Legionis,* since it has been thoroughly covered in a host of reliable sources. Caerleon is listed as Arthur's court by Geoffrey of Monmouth; Chester-upon-Dee is where the legionary fortress was moved after leaving Wroxeter; and Wroxeter as a highly significant site in Roman and post-Roman Britain has been well documented, in addition to its being the site proposed as the Battle of Badon in *The Historic King Arthur.*

The Tenth Battle: On the Bank of the River Tribruit

Tribruit is one of the sites which Alcock deems impossible to locate, a condition which seems to be holding true for many of the battle sites. No unshakable facts have been established; instead, all that can be proposed are sites which seem to be the most logistic given the circumstances of events and chronologies. Some seem well-founded in circumstantial evidence, while others range from Hadrian's Wall southward to the interior of Brittany. For Arthur's tenth battle, there is quite a bit of information to be gleaned from literary tradition, aiding in clarifying Arthur's milieu and the events of the period; for this reason, Tribruit should not simply be discarded because it defies specific identification.

Manuscript D of the *HB* internally records the name of this battle site as Ribroit instead of Tribruit, and additionally, added in the margin, is the name Trathtriuroit; Manuscript E is similar to D, but its internal word is "Robroit," varying only in the second letter.[68] Unlike the eighth battle at Guinnion, this one is skimpy in its information and provides only the name. John Morris translates this term as "Tryfrwyd"[69] in *BH,* but unfortunately he does not define or identify the term there or in his earlier work, *The Age of Arthur.* More than likely, however, he picked up that spelling from an Arthurian poem (commonly termed the *Pa gur* poem) in *The Black Book of Carmarthen* appearing in lines 22 and 48.[70]

Ekwall provides several important clues of what two place-names from the *Pa gur* poem might be. Based upon the word "Tryfwrd" as it appears in the poem, rather than the word "Tribruit" from the *HB,* there is one locale, Treyford, on a modern map which is an English rendition of the Old Welsh spelling for determining the possible location of the battle. Ekwall's etymology for this word gives the following information:

> Tree ford, ford marked by a tree or provided with a tree trunk to assist in crossing. Second element = *fryde,* found often in *twyford.* OE *treo(w)* "tree" … as a first element the word is not so common.

He goes on to explain that

> Names of this kind refer to some prominent tree, sometimes one with religious associations, … some times one remarkable for its size. The first element is frequently a personal name. In these cases the tree was probably one marking a meeting place, and the first element may well be the name of a lawman.[71]

Ekwall's *Twyford* is close to the *Tryfrwyd,* which in turn suggests a village called Treford, located approximately eight miles north of Chichester, a very short distance off a major Roman road running from Chichester to Roman Town. It is the general vicinity of what is called the heartland of southern Britain, although it is farther east than where the normal boundaries are set. In its favor are its adjacency to the River Rother, its accessibility to a major Roman road running north and south, and its nearness to Chichester Harbor and Portsmouth. It is within the arena of conflicts between the Britons and German Saxons from across the Channel, and also near the southern heartland.

Contrary to this locale, the word "Ribroit" offers interesting support for a more likely site in the Midlands. An analysis of ancient tribal borders, towns on the fringes with names such as Ripon and Ripley, plus those with intervocalic changes such as Repton and Ribston, and Ruthin (based upon Ryther), suggest instead a Midlands location, verified by references in the *Pa gur* poem. A northern demarcation, approximately fifty-five miles south of Hadrian's Wall running east from Ripon near York to Ribchester in the west in the midlands, indicates what would have been the borders of the ancient Hrype territories. The *Pa gur* poem stresses the impact associated with this information. A segment of this poem reads:

> 17 Stout were my servants
> 18 defending their rights.
> 19 Manawydan son of Llyr,
> 20 whose counsel was weighty;
> 21 Manawyd brought
> 22 shattered spear (or shields) back from Tryfwyd.[72]

In Welsh, line 22 actually reads *eis tull o tryvruid,* and Sims-Williams makes these comments about its reference:

> *O tryvruid* could be a misspelling of another adjective which describes a shield elsewhere in the Black Book. On the other hand the verb and its tense (preterite) suggests that Arthur is referring to a particular incident rather than to Manawydan's habitual bravery.... *[O]tryvruid* is best taken as an allusion to the "battle ... called *Tribruit,*" the tenth in the list of Arthur's battles in the *Historia Brittonum....*[73]

A reference to Arthur's tenth battle is made again in line 48:

> 46 they fell by the hundred
> 47 before Bedwyr the Perfect (or Perfect-Sinew),
> 48 On the shores of Tryfwyd,
> 49 fighting with Rough Grey,
> 50 furious was his nature
> 51 with sword and shield.[74]

The important addition in the above extract is that Arthur's enemies at the battle of Tryfwyd are the "Rough Grey." Sims-Williams views Rough Grey as singular, an ellipsis for Gwrgi Garwlwyd based upon the word *garvluid,* a figure whose murder is listed in the Triads' "Three Fortunate Assassinations." The assassin is Diffydell, son of Dysgyfdawd, who appears in a different triad, "The Three Chieftains of Deira and Bernicia," which leads Sims-Williams

Photograph 8—the Wrekin, the possible site of Arthur's twelfth battle, on Mount Badonicus.

to conjecture that the battle was fought somewhere in the north.[75] These two kingdoms were parts of the old Roman territories of the Votadini north of the Antonine Wall and the Parisii south of it. By extension, this means that Arthur's enemy referred to as "Rough Grey" was a contingency of the Gwyr y Gogledd, the Men of the North, who migrated south to initially defend against encroachment from the *Scotti* and later from attack by the rebellious English Saxons.

Hence, the tenth battle can be viewed in one of two ways. If based upon Tryfrwyd and therefore associated with Treyford, the sequence would indicate that this particular battle was fought in southern Britain against the *German* Saxons who had been recruited by the English Saxons. These reinforcements would have crossed the Channel and engaged the Britons in this southwest section. On the other hand, if the battle is based upon the word "Ribroit" and therefore associated with the Hrype tribe, then the sequence would indicate a battle fought in the northern midlands against the rebellious *English* Saxons, who would have allied themselves with the traitorous northern Britons who were trying to eke out their own kingdoms after the Roman abandonment. In either case, it is difficult to correlate this battle with Arthur's eleventh battle if Geoffrey Ashe's proposal is accepted that the Battle

Photograph 9—The baths at Wroxeter (Viroconium) near Mount Badonicus.

of Agned was fought on the continent, although that proposal is logistically sound.

The Eleventh Battle: On a Hill Called Agned

As is typical, the eleventh battle is beset by controversy and must be judged by its role in conjunction with other events, figures, and circumstances of the era. What makes this task even more difficult are the number of variants. Agned is labeled as "Agned Catbregomion" in manuscript D of the mid-twelfth century and as "Agned Thabregomion" in manuscript E of the early thirteenth century. In the margin of the former is the name Bregnion, identifying it as Cathbregyon in Somersetshire; in the margin of the latter is the name Agned Cathregonnon, which Camden lists as Cadbury in Somersetshire. [76] E. K. Chambers offers a comment, although it creates more confusion rather than offering clarification. He writes,

> Others give Bregion or some variant as a second name for Agned, and it has been suggested that both names [Bregion and Agned] stood in an original list of twelve, and have been compressed to make room for an intrusive Badon. The Celtic names, as known to Nennius, may not be quite fairly represented by his manuscripts. Most of them are difficult to fix to the West Saxon area, even if we conceive of Arthur as operating north as well as south of the Thames.[77]

Photograph 10—Solsbury Hill, a possible site of Arthur's twelfth battle on Mount Badonicus.

Chambers doesn't clearly define "the West Saxon area," but more than likely he visualized it in its traditional sense as south-central Britain along the coast. Similarly, when he writes of Arthur operating north of the Thames, he is not suggesting even as far north as the midlands, but probably a line no farther north than a Gloucester-Aylesbury boundary.

The most recent theory, though—proposed by Geoffrey Ashe—clinches the likelihood that some of these battles moved across the Channel but still took place between the Celts in the general sense of the word (whether they were Britons or Bretons), and the Saxons. In *The Discovery of King Arthur,* Ashe speculates about the possibility of any of these battles being on the continent rather than in Brittany. He cites a book, *Will the Real King Arthur Please Stand Up?* (a spoof taken as such) by Ronald Millar, which locates all twelve battles in Brittany. But Ashe then focuses on the eleventh battle, the Battle of Agned, as worth studying. He postulates,

> [Agned] ... could find a place in Arthur-Riothamus's Gallic enterprise. Moreover, ... [s]everal copies of Nennius have "Breguoin" instead. This is a much-modified version of Bremenium, the name of a Roman outpost north of Hadrian's Wall. A battle was indeed fought among its abandoned buildings, but by a northern British King in the late sixth century. It looks as if someone thought Agned didn't count, struck it out, and made up the twelve by crediting this other battle to Arthur. Was the name Agned suspect as being no longer known in Britain?

Photograph 11—The baths at Aquae Sulis (Bath), possible Badon site.

> ...A startling possibility is that Agned is Angers, where the Loire Saxons were beaten, probably when Arthur-Riothamus was in the neighborhood.... Gregory of Tours in the sixth century gives Angers the Latin names Andegavi and Andegavum. When writing of the Saxons and their collapse he uses both these spellings. Given either, in Gregory or elsewhere, scribal contraction and corruption would have been quite equal to producing Agned. This explanation could not compete with a known and confirmed Agned in Britain, but none exists, and even the possibility is exciting, in a place where a major Saxon defeat is on record and the King of the Britons may have played a part. To judge from *Goeznovius*, he was believed to have done so.[78]

Ashe's allusion to the "Arthur-Riothamus Gallic enterprise" pertains to his belief that "Riothamus" is an epithet (a Gallic designation) for Arthur. His theory is the foundation which gave rise to the theory in *The Historic King Arthur* that not only was the term "Riothamus" an epithet, but the word "Arthur" was, as well, both of which pointed to the bona fide historical figure Ambrosius Aurelianus. Riothamus's encounter with the Saxons at Angers is documented in historical sources by Jordanes and Gregory of Tours, as well as in sources such as Goeznovius's manuscript, plus by Sidonius in a letter to Riothamus.[79] In addition to this evidence, what makes the likelihood of the eleventh battle as occurring on the continent so plausible is that right after this victorious encounter against the Saxons, Riothamus is defeated by Euric and the Visigoths at Bourges de Déols, and disappears with fragments of his army into Burgundy. It is only after this time period that the name Arthur is recorded in insular history, paralleling Arthur's famous victory at the Battle of Badon fought against the English Saxons on the island.

The Twelfth Battle: On a Hill Called Badonis

Because the Battle of Badon is discussed in such depth in *The Historic King Arthur*, it will not be reiterated here.[80] What should suffice from this source is a nine-point précis explaining why the site was deemed to be in the vicinity of Wroxeter and its neighboring hill fort, the Wrekin, as opposed to Bath and its hill fort, Little Solsbury Hill, its closest contender. For those not familiar with the background, Badon is based upon one of two etymological possibilities. The first is Badbury, hill fort sites which point to Badbury, Badbury Hill, and Badbury Rings. The second focuses upon Roman bath-sites, based upon Baddon, in which the doubled "d" is pronounced as an unvoiced "th-" sound, rendering the site as "Bathon." The traditionally accepted site has been the city of Bath, or more precisely, Little Solsbury Hill just outside the city. *The Historic King Arthur*, however, settled upon the bath-site at Wroxeter because of overwhelming evidence pointing to it. The major considerations which elevated Wroxeter over Bath as the probable site for Badon were these:

1. The city of Bath was not known by that name until the 700s. During the Arthurian age, this area was known by the Roman term Aquae Sulis, named after a Roman goddess.
2. Aquae Sulis was not the thriving metropolis which it is today, whereby Wroxeter, in the Roman and early post-Roman period, was listed as the fourth-largest city in Britain. Wroxeter had been the site of a legionary fortress, and once the Romans moved their legions to Chester-upon Dee, Wroxeter became a *civitate,* a civil and administrative post, while Aquae Sulis was more famous as a spa.
3. In the post-Roman period, Wroxeter retained its importance as the tribal center for the Cornovii tribe. Detailed archaeological information shows that it was a hub for those in the area and was actively inhabited at the end of the fifth and beginning of the sixth centuries. On the other hand, excavations at Aquae Sulis have not yielded the versatile finds that were discovered at Wroxeter.
4. Unlike Little Solsbury Hill and Aquae Sulis, Wroxeter, at the base of the Wrekin, has been extensively excavated, relinquishing artifacts which attest to the area's crucial role and extended occupation during the Arthurian age.
5. In addition to a tor, the adjacency of the River Severn to Badon plays a crucial role in determining Badon's geography. Whereby Aquae

Sulis lies fifteen miles east of the river, the fortified walls of Wroxeter literally touched its banks.

6. Carrying this rationale even further, the Mouth of the Severn near Aquae Sulis would be impossible to ford, because it is approximately four miles wide as it empties into Bridgwater Bay and eventually the Bristol Channel. In contrast, immediately outside its protective wall, Wroxeter had access to the navigable river for commercial, political, or military purposes.
7. According to literary tradition, Arthur approached Bathon from Wales. Assuming that Aquae Sulis was the Bathon site being approached from the west, Arthur would have been barred a crossing unless he detoured to the north, where he would have crossed the River Severn approximately thirty miles away, near Gloucester. Assuming, however, that Wroxeter was the Bathon site being approached from Wales, Arthur would have traveled a Roman road due east, with two accessible fords in the vicinity of Wroxeter.
8. Also from literary tradition but very important, Arthur crosses the River Severn at a ford located *at the base of the hill fort.* No such place exists when considering Aquae Sulis as the Badon site, but the Wrekin lies only about a thousand yards from a ford across the river.
9 The last major consideration which must be taken into account is how Badon fits into the scheme with all the other battles listed in the *HB*. Aquae Sulis is perhaps a reasonable choice, but the underlying question which has the most pertinence upon each and every battle must centralize upon Arthur's adversaries. The *HB* unequivocally states that Arthur's enemies were the Saxons, and this extends not only to the English Saxons, but the German Saxons and the traitorous *Britanni* who sided with them as well. Under these conditions, Wroxeter literally and figuratively would be the hub of activity. Discounting any battles which might have been fought in Gaul or Brittany but including those fought by Vortimer, those battles (based upon the logistics of the most probable sites) would be in a radius of thirty-five miles from Wroxeter. Only if Arthur is considered a Welsh figure can this be possible.

9

The Strife of Camlann

Arthur's last battle at Camlann is recorded in the *Annales Cambriae,* but it is not mentioned anywhere in the *Historia Brittonum* and is glaringly absent from Arthur's campaigns listed in Chapter 56. That the battle list does not conclude with this momentous conflict provides a polarity of usefulness. On the one hand it suggests three things:

1. The Battle of Badon and the Battle of Camlann were fought chronologically close together, perhaps six years apart rather than nineteen;
2. there were no intervening battles between the Badon and the Camlann wars against the English Saxons; and, if these first two conditions are true, then it would follow that
3. the Battle of Camlann was likely fought in the northern Midlands, near Hadrian's Wall.

At the other end of the continuum, the inclusion of the Camlann battle might mean

1. that there were other battles between the Battle of Badon and the Battle of Camlann, based primarily on the nineteen-year span between the two as recorded in the *AC;*
2. that the battles fought subsequent to the one at Badon, including Camlann, were fought in southern Britain against German Saxons, judging from information provided by the introductory paragraph of Chapter 56 in the *HB;* and
3. that the end of the list—i.e., from perhaps the sixth battle to the twelfth—were more than likely fought in the midlands and/or in Gaul, not in southern England.

Because *The Historic King Arthur* addresses the issue of Camlann's chronology and geography in great detail,[1] it will be only briefly summarized here. The first set of three conditions point to Camlann being fought to the southwest of Hadrian's Wall, based upon several premises. The first has to do with the etymological connection between Camboglanna and Camlann. When Cunedda and his sons migrated from the north, their first settlement was near Carlisle, only a short distance from the Roman fort of Birdoswald, which would have been in good repair during this migrational period. The Battle of Camlann could have been so named because of its association with the word *Camboglanna,* a reference to the area overlooking the Irthing Valley at the southwestern end of Hadrian's Wall. The meaning of *Camboglanna,* "crooked bank," would link to the Middle Welsh word Camlann, and could easily be a descriptor for the meandering River Irthing.

Alcock accurately writes that this rationale marks Camlann "as a battle not against invading pagan Saxons, but as an internecine strife of Briton against Briton, and the terse entry of the [*Annales Cambriae*] would not contradict this."[2] The intense conflicts in the midlands were fought by a triangle of enemies from alliances gone sour. There were the Welsh to the west and the Anglians (known more commonly as English Saxons) to the east, in addition to those seditious *Britanni* from the North (known in Welsh as the Gwyr y Gogledd), who had aligned themselves, for a variety of reasons, with the English Saxons in a power-play to grab the Cornovii territories vacated by the Romans.

The bulk of circumstantial evidence points to a midlands site for the Camlann battle, based mainly upon translocations, scribal errors, and inconstant translations, not only in the ancient manuscripts prior to the end of the millennium, but also from sources such as *The History of the Kings of Britain,* which borrowed extensively from earlier manuscripts. Geoffrey of Monmouth's account of the battle (termed by him "Camblam") is unrealistic on four counts. First, he misinterprets *Cæint* for the southeastern territory of Kent, a common error for Arthur's milieu made because of interpolations in the *HB.* Second, Monmouth's battle unrealistically spans the entire width of southern Britain. Third, he assumes that the word "Camlann" is based upon the word Cam or Camel. And last, he misidentifies Cornwall as the site where the battle ends. In Arthur's era and up to the 700s the southwestern peninsula of Britain was known as Dumnonii and wasn't called Cornwall until much later, after people from the Cornovii territories in the midlands had migrated to the peninsula after the Roman abandonment of the island.

Most noteworthy among misinterpreted passages is the introductory paragraph to Chapter 56, partially translated in Chapter 8. It reads as follows:

> At that time the English Saxons gathered strength and increased in size in Britain. After [Horsa's] death, Hengist's son Octha came from the northern part of Britain to the realm which up to this time had continuously been called Cantiorum, and he was the origin of the kings of Cantiorum. Then the warlike Arthur fought against them accompanied by the kings of Britain, but he was the

> commander of the battles. And though there were many who belong to families which had held the official seats of consuls, he was nevertheless the battle-leader and victor of the twelve battles.[3]

This is undoubtedly one of the most difficult and controversial passages in the *Historia Brittonum.* My first text, *The Historic King Arthur,* addresses several of the issues. One has to do with the importance of distinguishing between the *English* Saxons and the *German* Saxons. My postulation, supported by several other scholars, including Wade-Evans, shows that the term "English Saxons" is a generic reference to those Angles, Saxons, Jutes, and Frisians who had migrated to the isle of Britain while it was still occupied by the Romans, and who had been there for a couple of decades or several generations. Because these settlers fell under the protection of Rome's policy, they were considered as part of the *Britanni,* the provincials of Britain. This in itself has led to confusion among modern scholars because the writings of Gildas Badonicus are so often misinterpreted. The wars tearing Britain apart after the Roman withdrawal were *internal* conflicts between the Welsh and the English Saxons, not, as some conjecture, conflicts between the Britons and the continental Saxons. Those continental Saxons, also called the German Saxons, on the other hand, were tribal relatives who had remained on the continent and who were later to ally themselves with the English Saxons.

A second common scribal error in this passage is marked by the brackets. In the original *HB* manuscript, Nennius records that Octha comes down from the north after *Hengist*'s death, when in reality it should identify *Horsa*'s death. Once again, through careful calculation, the *HKA* shows that several chronological entries in the *ASC* must be emended. In a battle against Vortimer's forces, Horsa was killed in 455, along with Vortimer's brother, Catigern. Hengist's reign, however, did not end until 473; prior to that time, Hengist and his son Octha were co-rulers, and after Hengist's death, Octha was the sole successor until 497.

The third problem lies with the translation of the geographic location identified as Cantiorum in the original Latin. In Manuscript *a* of the *HB,* which seems to be one of the most reliable, its spelling is *Cantwariorum.* Stevenson explains that, because of the spelling of Cantwariorum, the scribe must have been using a manuscript which preserved the Saxon character *w,* indicating that Kent must have remained an independent kingdom.[4] The problem, however, lies in the misidentification of the kingdom of Cantiorum. Once again, as the *HKA* points out, the *internal* conflicts between the Welsh and the English Saxons were located in the Cornovii territories of the midlands, and *not* in the southeastern corner of the island. The *Cæintish* territory in Cornovii was still an independent kingdom because the Romans had just recently evacuated the buffer zone between the Welsh and the English

Saxons. The conflicts were originally between Vortigern, a *Welshman,* and his rebellious allies, the English Saxons of the Mercia territories, for the vacant lands between the two realms.

Last, but by no means minor, is Arthur's role in these battles against the English Saxons. What lies at the base of confusion is the age-old issue of translation. Scholars have spent literally decades debating the uncertainty of Arthur's rank during these conflicts, and the dilemma is how words should be defined when translated from Latin into modern English. Commonly, there are at least a couple of alternate definitions, and the necessity to choose must be based upon predilection tempered by objective judgment.

The above extract, from Manuscript *a,* is different from the others, in that there is the addition of the adjective "warlike" to describe Arthur, but one major emphasis should be on "*sed ipse dux erat bellorum,*" where *dux* could mean, literally or figuratively, "guide," "conductor," "leader," "ruler," or "military commander."[5] Because *bellum* means "battle," the best choice seems to be "military commander," which infers that Arthur is the chief commander, or in modernistic terms, the commander-in-chief, the supreme leader or ruler of military forces.

Likewise peculiar to Manuscript *a* is the addition of "*Et licet multi ipso nobiliores essent, ipse tamen duodecies dux belli fuit, victorque bellorum.*" The key word in this segment is *nobiliores* because its precise definition is absolutely essential in determining Arthur's rank. Its possibilities are much more complex: In Cassell's terms, it can *literally* mean "celebrated," "renowned," "well-known," or it can be *transferred* in suggesting "noble," "of noble birth," or "belonging to a family which had held the office of consul."[6] Those scholars who translate *nobiliores* as "noble" are then faced with a paradox: Although Arthur is traditionally described as the leader of battles, he's not normally deemed a king. Hence, if Arthur is not a king, he therefore cannot possibly be viewed as High King or the King of Kings. Accepting his father as a consul and selecting the proper definition of *nobiliores* resolves the issue. Arthur is elevated to a powerful, prominent position because he is from a royal line of consuls, born during an era when it was traditional for a king to lead his warriors into battle. Because he has joined with other tribal chieftains, he has become the High King, or the King of Kings at tribal councils.

Fortunately, there is a clue indicating which translation is undeniably buried in the earlier Chapter 42 of the *HB.* To extract that clue and apply it to the appropriate translation here, the main theory of *The Historic King Arthur* must be iterated once again. Concisely, it is this: The word "Arthur" is not a proper name, but an epithet, or substitution for a proper name. It is not, as some scholars claim, a namesake based upon Lucius Castus Artorius of the second century, but instead is derived from the Welsh prefix *Ardd-* (pronounced Arth-) meaning "high," and the Roman root *-us* added to the word to make it a noun and to give it prestige in the newly developing Welsh language. This means that *Arthus,* or *Arthurex,* is a composite of three figures of that era: Ambrosius Aurelianus, which *is* a proper name; Riothamus, which is another epithet meaning "Overking;" and Arddurex (pronounced Arthurex), which is a different epithet meaning "High King."

To trace Arthur's forebears, then, one must work through Ambrosius Aurelianus and Lucius Domitius Aurelianus. The proper name Ambrosius appears in Chapter 42 of the *HB.* When Vortigern and his magi are confounded by the boy wizard, Vortigern asks who the boy's father is, and the boy responds that his father is one of the consuls of the Roman people. The word *consul* becomes highly significant when combined with Arthur's description in Chapter 56. Hence, Arthur is, in fact, of royal Roman heritage, belonging to a family which had held the office of consul before Rome's evacuation of Britain. This perception is verified in the *DE* by Gildas Badonicus, who writes that Ambrosius Aurelianus "alone of the Romans, had survived the shock of [these notable battles with the Saxons]: certainly his parents, who had worn the purple, were slain in [these conflicts]."[7] There is no dispute among scholars that "wearing the purple" signifies Roman royalty, and because of the application of terms after the Romans withdrew from Britain, the Welsh rallied under the banner of Ambrosius and accepted him as the only surviving heir to Roman sovereignty. Ambrosius, therefore, as Arthurex, is rightfully a king leading other kings and their warriors into battle against the English Saxons.

The only other necessary clarification in the introductory extract of Chapter 56 is also detailed more thoroughly in the *HKA.* That clarification focuses upon the kingdom of Cæint. Both implicitly and explicitly inferred in the *DE,* the *HB,* and the *ASC,* the largest number of conflicts are between the *Welsh* and the English Saxons and *not* the Britons and the English Saxons. The realm of Cæint is misidentified as Chent (Kent) and therefore was displaced from its accurate locale in the central midlands, which was part of Wales (Cymry territories) in the southeast section of the island. As a *Welsh* king, Vortigern had no suzerainty in a territory (called in those times "countries") over two hundred miles away. Vortigern gives his kingdoms in the *western* part of Britain[8] to Ambrosius, but the lands on the southeastern coast are *not* his to give to Hengist.

All this information at first seems tediously detailed and pointless in establishing the Battle of Camlann as a midlands site, especially since many theories list the Camlann battle in the midlands or Cymry territories near Hadrian's Wall. Yet in spite of this mass of information, several nagging clues prevent the rejection of a southern Camlann, the first being the information in the *concluding* passage in Chapter 56, which gives an enlightening possibility of Camlann's geographic location. After listing the twelve battles in which Arthur is victorious, the last segment by Stevenson relates,

> And when he himself [Arthur] had defeated the English Saxons and the traitorous Britons in all the battles, the English sought assistance from Germany, and their numbers multiplied without interruption, and the kings from Germany were commissioned to rule over them in Britain [my translation].

What this suggests is that German Saxons began infiltrating Britain as reinforcements. The German Saxons might very well have penetrated the island up the River Thames to the midlands, but invasion from the southern coast is a stronger possibility because of a specific entry from the *ASC* which corroborates a crushing defeat of the Britons twenty-one years after the Battle of Badon. In this context the emendations of the date from 519 to 518, and of the name from Cynric to Creoda, aren't significant, but the entry in the *ASC* is:

> In this year [518] Cerdic and [Creoda] obtained the kingdom of the West Saxons, and the same year they fought against the Britons at a place named Cerdicesford. And from that day on the princes of the West Saxons have reigned.[9]

There are two key words in this extract which favor a southern site for Arthur's fateful battle at Camlann. One is the word "Britons." G. N. Garmonsway is meticulous in his translations of entries, and he is explicit in pointing out that the *Saxones* (a generic term not differentiating between the English and the German) sometimes fought against the Welsh, and at other times warred against the Britons. Those entries recording battles against the Welsh, therefore, would have been fought in the midlands or the west-central part of the island, while other entries indicating battles against the Britons would have taken place farther south or along the southern coast.

The entry for 518 would fit the characteristic pattern of Saxon incursions, if clarification is gleaned from the 449 entry. Separating the chaff from the wheat, the passage of Vortigern granting southeastern land in exchange for fighting the Picts can be discarded. The Picts were several hundred miles to the north, just beyond Hadrian's Wall, and Vortigern would not have recruited mercenaries from Ebbsfleet, Kent. Heopwinesfleot cannot be properly identified, but most certainly it was not Ebbsfleet, Kent. The Old Saxons more than likely did penetrate the island from the River Thames and settle along the northern shores of the river in what is now Essex, but the Angelns (or Angels) settle a bit farther north, in what is now East Anglia. As the 449 entry explains, more and more Angelns filtered across the sea, pushing further inland into Mercia and touching the borders of Cornovii while the Romans still occupied Britain. These Anglians, who were associated with Vortigern as mercenaries, were part of the second and third *Adventi,* led initially by Hengist and Horsa.

Five decades later, near the end of the century, when the westward and northward expansion had been stemmed, John of Glastonbury writes that

> Often [Arthur] struggled with Cerdic, who, if one month Arthur vanquished him, rose up the next fiercer for the fight. Finally, when Arthur tired of the conflict, he accepted Cerdic's fealty and gave him Hampshire and Somerset, which Cerdic called Wessex.[10]

This fits well with Garmonsway's translation of entry 519 (emended to 518 in *HKA)* which uses the wording that Cerdic and Cynric (emended to Creoda in *HKA)* "obtained the kingdom," verifying that the Saxons did not *conquer* the territories by battle, thus confirming what was recorded in the Genealogical Preface. The important variance which must be duly recognized is that John of Glastonbury identifies Cerdic's newly acquired territory as "Wessex," but Garmonsway's translation conveys that Cerdic obtained the kingdom of the "West Saxons." This difference is easy to gloss over as two synonyms, but more realistically, Cerdic's West Saxon kingdom is his *entire* realm, including Ceredigion in Wales, to which he adds the segment of Wessex.

One last characteristic which points to the Battle of Camlann as a southern site is the most common translation of *Cerdicesford.* Dorothy Whitelock doesn't use the original proper nouns when translating from the Latin manuscripts, but instead supplies the geographic site of Charford instead of the primary name Cerdicesford in the 519 entry. The locale of Charford is commonly accepted as the modern substitute for Cerdicesford, and etymologically Charford conforms to the meaning of the word Camlann. As already explained, *Camlann* is associated with the word *Camboglanna,* which means "crooked bank," and Charford, on the meandering banks of the River Avon, would be a likely choice. This area, too, is the center of the southern heartland, directly on the River Avon and within striking distance of Old Sarum as the hub of Roman roads in the area.

The Historic King Arthur leans theoretically toward the Battle of Camlann being fought at a southern location, especially when considering other historical events and bona fide personages whose genuineness has never been questioned. Coupled with Cerdicesford and the word "Britons" identifying the Saxons' enemy, a southern site seems the most probable.

However, as with so many Arthurian aspects, my continuing research has uncovered an intriguing different potential for Camlann's locale. In the summer of 1995 while touring various Welsh sites as prospective Arthurian connections, I stopped at Fishguard for rest and relaxation at the Manor House Hotel. As a break from the rigors of research, the owner, Mr. Ralph Davis, recommended an afternoon visit to St. Brynach's Church at Nevern, just a short distance up the coast. This site turned out to be a treasure-trove of links to King Arthur beyond my wildest expectations. Surprisingly, it has never surfaced in other works dealing with Arthuriana. A compact booklet, its authors identified only as "The vicar, churchwardens, and parishioners," focuses upon several astounding relics directly associated with King Arthur and research centering upon chronological and geographic verification of his authenticity. Why these relics have not appeared in the quest for the real Arthur is mystifying.

One such relic is a stone slab discovered by the Cambrian Archaeological Association in 1906 along a passage leading to the priests' chamber over one of the transeptal chapels. The stone is now embedded as a sill in one of the windows, and has a bilingual inscription. One is in Latin, which reads "*Maglocuni fili Clutor*," and the other is in Ogham script, translated to "*Maglicunas maqi Clutar.*" The first word in the Latin inscription was miscut and reads "Maglocuui," and the slash-style Ogham must be read from right to left, but both mean "(THE MONUMENT) OF MAGLOCUNUS (MAELGWN) SON OF CLUTORIUS."[11] The Ogham script is the Irish branch of Celtic, the Goidelic (the earliest form), as opposed to the Brythonic, which spread to Britain and later replaced the earlier Goidelic form. "Maqi" and its variants "mab," "mac," "map," and "ap," plus the Latin "fili" mean "son of."

The name Maglocunus is a crucial cornerstone in establishing a reliable chronology beginning during the Roman occupation and extending to Gildas Badonicus's lifetime. For instance, *The Historic King Arthur* uses the death of Maglocunus map Catgolaun Lauhir (also commonly spelled Cadwallon Lawhir) as a pivotal cardinal year for the Arthurian chronology. Maglocunus map Clutar, as named on the monument at St. Brynach's, would therefore be a solid piece of evidence that he was an ancestor. That is, according to calculations, the memorial stone at St. Brynach's dates to the fifth century.[12] As a comparison, the death-date of Maelgwn map Catgolaun Lauhir is 547.[13]

Several corollaries can be determined from this piece of information:

1. Maglocunus map Clutar became a king of Welsh realms shortly after the evacuation by the Roman legions.
2. Using the beginning of Vortigern's reign as a reference point, the ancestry for Maglocunus map Catgolaun Lauhir can be traced back at least 122 years.
3. The realms ruled by the Maglocunus line were Dyfed/Gwynedd, formerly the Dementae/Ordovices/Decangi Roman territories.
4. Cunedda is a bona fide ancestor of Maglocunus map Catgolaun Lauhir as recorded in the *Historia Brittonum*, and would have been a contemporary or near-contemporary of Maglocunus ap Clutar.
5. It follows that Cunedda's new homeland just south of Hadrian's Wall after his migration would have been at Carlisle, in the Gwynedd territory.

Saint Brynach's Church is a propitious find for another reason. The booklet about this site objectively reports in a segment headed as "A Walk Round Outside" that

Photograph 12—The Maglocunus bilingual stone of the fifth century, located in St. Brynach's Church in Nevern, Wales.

> Celtic Chieftains and Priests were of similar status and it was customary for the chieftain to grant to the Priest a piece of ground as a sacred enclosure, or "Llan," a rill of water forming a convenient boundary between them: the water was used also for both sacred and secular purposes. This seems to have been the arrangement at Nevern, with the Chieftain's stronghold on the hill to the west,... a boundary provided by the brook Caman, and the "Llan" comprising the ground within the wall of the old graveyard.[14]

There is no elaboration upon this piece of information, and hence no hidden agenda or ulterior motive, but any Arthurian scholar will be immediately intrigued by the term "Caman Llan." No matter which geographic site for the battle of Camlann is being considered, the evidence hangs by a gossamer thread. The southern site along the River Avon attaches its credibility to the word *camboglanna*, "crooked bank," and rationalizes the choice on three counts: 1) its access to the southern coast by any German Saxons who infiltrated from across the Channel, 2) its proximity to Badbury Rings as a look-out and a hub for Roman roads, and 3) its simplicity of ingression into Britain's heartland. The site just to the south and west of Hadrian's Wall accomplishes the same purpose under a different set of criteria: 1) Carlisle was Cunedda's southern base after his migration, 2) from the abandoned

Photograph 13—A heretofore undiscovered possibility of Arthur's last battle at Caman Llan.

Roman fort of Birdoswald the site of Camboglanna was a look-out surveying the winding Irthing River and its valley, and 3) German Saxons could have penetrated to the central part of the island to help their kindred English Saxons conquer new domains.

The heretofore undiscovered possibility of Caman Llan can offer similar defenses. For one, a covenant between chieftain and priest was a time-honored Celtic tradition. Although there were secular-ecclesiastic ties, there was a literal and figurative separation of their lands; the sacred, ecclesiastic land was an enclosure onto itself. That this particular brook is named "Caman" seems beyond coincidence. An even stronger defense for Caman Llan is its general and specific locale. Generally, it is on what would have been the early borderlands between Dyfed and Gwynedd; specifically, it is in the area not only of Welsh/*Scotti* conflict, but what would later develop into Welsh/English Saxon conflict and Welsh/Briton conflict. Interestingly, attached to this aspect is the area's role in traditional Welsh lore. Some tales of *The Mabinogion* are set in Penvro (Pembroke), Dyved, Gwynedd, and Powys, not surprising because they were such large domains. Nevertheless, Strumble Head was one of the most populous areas.

Furthermore, only a short walk from the churchyard and up a slight rise is a stronghold atop the tor to the west. Although there are some claims that the chieftain of this stronghold was Maglocunus's father, Clutor (perhaps a cognate of Clether or Clechre), the possibility is obscure. What *is* known, however, is that the stronghold was occupied by a Celtic chieftain of some stature, and it would not be unreasonable to assume that the chieftain was a tribal leader who had been bequeathed power by Roman authority, since this was a common Roman practice; in return for fealty and mercenary support, the Romans granted privileges to selected chieftains. The Roman withdrawal from Britain was initially deemed as temporary, so that when they left and endowed power to certain domains, that power was taken very seriously. Roman civilization which had dominated the island for almost four centuries didn't just disappear; it gradually deteriorated over a period of several decades. Someone, therefore, like Vortigern or Maglocunus or Cunedda would have been a logical successor of the emerging government.

One of the most important verifications of this site as a strategic area in the post-Roman/Arthurian age is another stone monument in the same churchyard at Nevern. The Vicar, et al., label it as the "Vitalianus Stone." Once again, this label contains a name which captivates the Arthurian researcher: The name Vitalinus (a slight variation in spelling) appears twice in the *Historia Brittonum,* once in Chapter 49, where it appears in a garbled genealogical passage, and again in Chapter 66, in a segment which reads, "And from the reign of Guorthigirn [Vortigern] until the discord between Guitolin [Vitalinus] and Ambrosi [Ambrosius] are twelve years, which is Guoloppum, that is, Catguoloph."[15]

This monument in the churchyard at Saint Brynach's is, like the Maglocunus Stone, bilingual, etched in both Latin and Ogham. The booklet claims that the Latin inscription reads "Vitaliani Emereto,"[16] based upon a sketch in the British Museum dating to 1698 by Edward Lhuyd (the same individual, incidentally, who translated the inscription on Eliseg's Pillar). A close look at the monument itself, however, doesn't seem to show the second 'I' between the 'L' and the 'A,' and the final two letters are blurred by lichen. In spite of the circumstances, though, the inscription would be a cognate of Vitalinus or Vitalianus; in fact, Leslie Alcock spells the name V-i-t-o-l-i-n-u-s,[17] and if "Vitalianus" is considered acceptable, it echoes the suffix of Ambrosius's Roman ancestor, Lucius Domitius Aurelianus, who was Emperor from 270 to 275.

Traditionally, the single sentence about Vitalinus in Chapter 66 of the *HB* is translated to mean that Vitalinus and Vortimer are allies and, conversely, that Vitalinus and Ambrosius are enemies. Leslie Alcock, among others, though, addresses the paradox that the name of Vitalinus is "as Roman as Ambrosius's" but is inconsistently aligned with Briton nationalists rather than Romanophils once the Empire withdraws from Britain.[18] *The Historic King Arthur,* however, takes the contrasting viewpoint that Vitalinus is indeed Ambrosius's mentor and guardian protecting the young boy against possible

Photograph 14—The Vitalinus Stone at St. Brynach's. This is a close-up view of Photograph 5 in Chapter 5.

assassination by Vortigern. This perspective is based upon Monmouth's narrative about Vitalinus.

Pieced together, Vitalinus (known in the earlier manuscripts as Guitolini and appearing in Monmouth's book as Guithelinus) is first introduced by Monmouth in Part Three, "The Coming of the Romans." As Archbishop of London, Vitalinus encouraged the Britons to begin fending for themselves after the Roman withdrawal, but the enemy devastated the Britons, forcing them to once again appeal to the Romans for intercession. With no help from the Romans forthcoming, Vitalinus crossed to Brittany and was granted help from Constantine. Upon their return to the island, the Britons won an immediate victory and Constantine was raised to the kingship. The new king married, and from the union three sons—Constans, Aurelius Ambrosius, and Utherpendragon—were born, the latter two given in safekeeping for Vitalinus to raise. After Constantine's murder and Constans's deposal, Vortigern seized the throne and Vitalinus's two wards were taken to Brittany to prevent their possible assassination.

In Part Eight, the last section, which is similar to an epilogue, Monmouth writes, "The Bishop of Gloucester was promoted to be Archbishop of London."[19] The full impact of this statement at first escapes notice, and would be something too subtle to be labeled as characteristic of Monmouth's brilliant ploy of irony. Upon reflection, this statement turns one's attention to the last segment of Chapter 49 in the *Historia Brittonum,* which relates that four brothers, Bonus, Paul, Mauron, and Vitalinus, were

> sons of Gloui, who built the great city on the banks of the river Severn that is called in the British Caer Gloui, in English Gloucester.[20]

Throughout his book, Monmouth identifies Vitalinus as the Archbishop of London, and only at the end is the reader able to deduce that Vitalinus, the son of Gloui, was the Bishop of Gloucester before being elevated to the Archbishop of London, meaning that Vitalinus indeed played a significant role directly linked primarily to Ambrosius (i.e., Arthur) and only secondarily to Vortigern. At the time when Monmouth recorded Vitalinus's role in the Arthurian saga, he was either unaware of the parallel in the *Historia* because he was simply copying text, or he was aware of it and thought that it was inconsequential; the former seems the most likely, suggesting, therefore, that Geoffrey was not cognizant of the connection nor its impact.

Combined with details about Vitalinus in the *HB,* therefore, material in Chapter 5 of this text is more comprehensive than it first seems. As suggested in the *HKA,* Vitalinus, like Ambrosius, is empathetic to the Roman cause and not only wants the Romans to return to Britain, but is also directly responsible in trying to entice them back. When Constantine is assassinated and Vortigern seizes the kingship, Vitalinus, as a guardian, wisely resolves to take the two brothers to Brittany and consigns them to the care of Budicius.

The Vitalianus Stone at Saint Brynach's affirms three things:

1. Vitalianus would have been an overlapping contemporary with Maglocunus map Clutar, Vortigern, Vortimer, and Ambrosius Aurelianus;
2. Wales and a segment of the eastern midlands would be the correct locale for the battles against the *Scotti,* in addition to the later internal conflicts which erupt;
3. The culminating conflict, the Battle of Caman Llan, realistically could have been fought in this vicinity.

As with the Badon battle, an entire chapter of the *HKA* was devoted to Arthur's fateful battle at Camlann. Yet because of its uniqueness, the Battle of Camlann must be allotted an extraordinarily special niche in Arthuriana. First and foremost, this singular, most important battle portending the end of a golden era for Britain is curiously and remarkably omitted from the *HB,* a source which is truly the only extant repository of detailed but still meager insular history. The victorious conflict at Mons Badonicus is surprisingly at the *end* of the battle list in the *HB,* although it marks the *beginning* of a respite from Saxon incursions. The *DE* of Gildas Badonicus is saturated with despair and gloom because the descendants of the golden age have become shamelessly corrupt, but there is no specific reference to the battle of Camlann or the devastation which led to such consequences. Gildas writes only that "all the controls of truth and justice have been shaken and overthrown, leaving no trace, not even a memory,"[21] but he gives no hint of a specific event which reversed the recovery and prosperity of the island. He does not elaborate, but relates that external wars "have stopped, but not civil ones."[22]

If indeed the German Saxons had caused these changes in the fortunes of war, then the *ASC* should be brimming with lavish detail about the magnitude of such a glorious victory. But it, too, is silent about a specific naming of the Battle of Camlann. Fortuitously, however, parallels can be drawn between the Battle of Mons Badonicus as described in the *HB* and entries recorded in the *ASC* because of a specific chronological fix. Similarly, parallels can be drawn between the history in the *DE* and an entry in the *ASC*, but instead of vague references, this latter success of the Saxons over the Britons should have been heralded from the hilltops. Therefore, it was the *civil* war—that is, the war between the English Saxons who had for generations been settled on the island and the Welsh—that caused the "ruin of Britain," leading to the brief notice in the *ASC* that in 519 the West Saxon kingdom reigned from that time onward.

The Welsh version of the battle is equally as laconic and cryptic. The *AC* relates that in the year 93

> *Gueith Camlann in qua Arthur et Medraut corruerunt, et mortalitas in Britannia et in Hibernia fuit.*[23]
>
> The Battle of Camlann, in which Arthur and Mordred fell, and there was death [i.e., plague] in Britain and Ireland.

Paradoxically, even though this is the only annalistic source which specifically mentions Arthur's final battle and is not traceable back to parent Irish annals, Alcock writes that "Despite this, even the most cautious of scholars has been inclined to accept the reference to the deaths of Arthur and Modred at Camlann as authentic, whether or not the date is accurate."[24] Additionally, in spite of the word *gueith* instead of *bellum*, Alcock indicates that

> Camlann is far from being the only battle entered as *gueith* rather than *bellum*.... The expression *gueith Camlann* does nothing, therefore, to weaken the authenticity of the entry.[25]

In the Introduction to *The Arthur of the Welsh*, the editors refer to Thomas Jones's article in the *Bulletin of the Board of Celtic Studies* and write that "For Jones the allusion in the *Annales [Cambriae]* to *Gueith Camlann* was 'perhaps the most authentic historical reference to Arthur.'"[26] Parts of the testimony which support his belief are the frequent references in Welsh poetry to the Battle of Camlann and its seal of doom for Britain.

Welsh literature generally and Monmouth's the *HKB* specifically more than make up for the brief allusion to Camlann in the annals, and histories elaborate upon Camlann in surprising detail. The annal entry on Camlann does not allow any leeway for deduction or inference; on its information alone, it is difficult to determine a general geographic locale for the battle, whether Arthur and Mordred died or were just wounded, or whether Mordred was an ally or adversary.

The tale of Culhwch in *The Mabinogion* tells us that: Morvran, son of Tegid, was not struck at Camlann because he was so ugly that the enemy thought he was the devil; that Sanddev Angel Face was not struck at Camlann because he was so handsome that the enemy though he was an angel; that Saint Kynwyl was one of the three men to escape unharmed from Camlann; and that Gwynn Hyvar, Steward of Devon and Cornwall, was one of the nine men who planned the Battle of Camlann.[27] Another tale, "The Dream of Rhonabwy," reveals that Iddawg was one of the messengers at Camlann and that it was he who stirred up bad feelings between Arthur and his nephew, thus weaving the Battle of Camlann.[28]

Although there is no definitive clarification about Camlann's geographic location other than the word *gueith* suggesting Wales, there are two pieces of salient information which emerge from these sources. One is that Mordred is Arthur's nephew, and the second is that they were adversaries at the Battle of Camlann. Monmouth gives a great deal of background on Mordred and on the description of the final battle,[29] claiming at various times that this information was not of his own creation but came from the *liber vetustissimus*. It is now necessary to turn to Mordred's role.

Mordred, Arthur's Nemesis

When writing *The Historic King Arthur,* all of my effort was focused upon proving that Arthur was an authentic historical figure by closely analyzing many different sources, both factual and literary. Because of the intensity of that focal point, I decided to avoid the individual Medraut and his link to King Arthur in one of the most crucial historical sources, the *Annales Cambriae,* naming the great king. In relation to this source, the singular most important purpose was to verify beyond mere speculation that the *date* for this particular entry was displaced by one lunar cycle, thus establishing what was termed a cardinal year for a comprehensive and accurate milieu for Arthur's era. In addition to verifying 518 as the year in which the Battle of Camlann was fought, that book also substantiated several other years as either cardinal or ordinal years. It determined that the Battle of Badon was fought in 497, that Gildas penned the *De Excidio* in 541, and that Maglocunus map Catgolaun Lauhir died in 547.

Now, however, with that work satisfactorily completed and the base

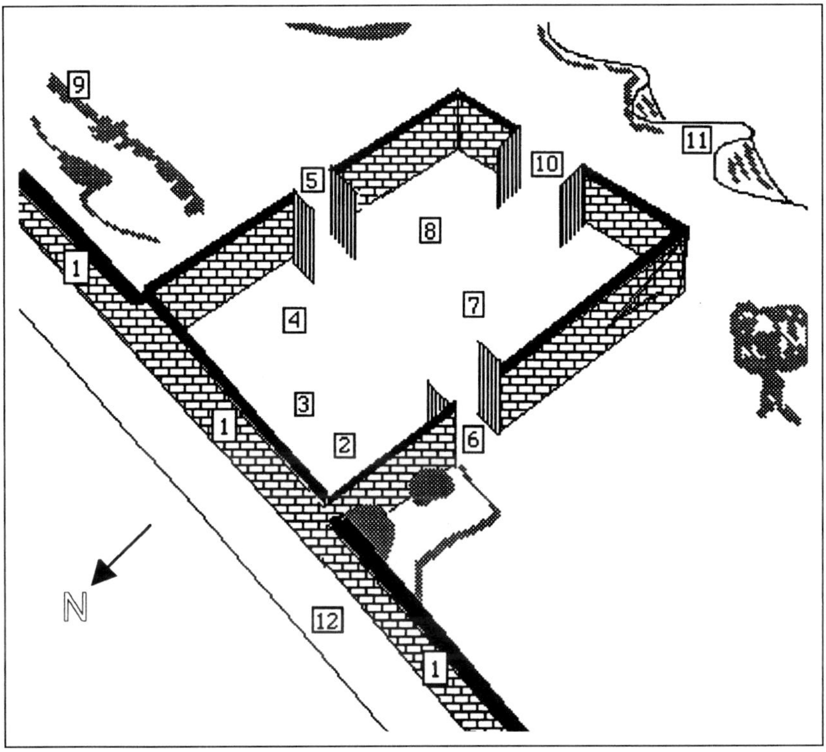

Map 9—Birdoswald, Roman fort near Camboglanna. Although not to scale or representative of existent walls, this sketch accurately shows the characteristics of the Birdoswald Roman fort on Hadrian's Wall. Each aspect is given a number. The east and west subsidiary gates (to the south of each double-portal east/west gate) are not shown, nor is the north double-portal gate, buried under the modern road.

1=Hadrian's Wall; 2=Exercise Hall (buried under farmhouse buildings); 3=entrance to visitor center; 4=*via principalis*; 5=east double-portal gate; 6=west double-portal gate; 7=two fort granaries; 8=buried headquarters building; 9=original turf wall; 10=south double-portal gate; 11=drop-off to valley and Irthing River; 12=modern road

established, the gnawing enigma of Medraut's identity has returned. Medraut—variants are Mordred, Modred, and Mordreth to name just a few—is not mentioned in any other *historical* source, meaning that after he appears just once in the *AC* during the second decade of the sixth century, there is a silence of more than six centuries before he again makes an appearance, this time in a manuscript by Geoffrey of Monmouth. Once the six centuries of silence prior to Geoffrey is broken, a veritable torrent of material pours forth about Mordred, the name Monmouth uses.

In a passage where Monmouth refers to himself in third-person, he

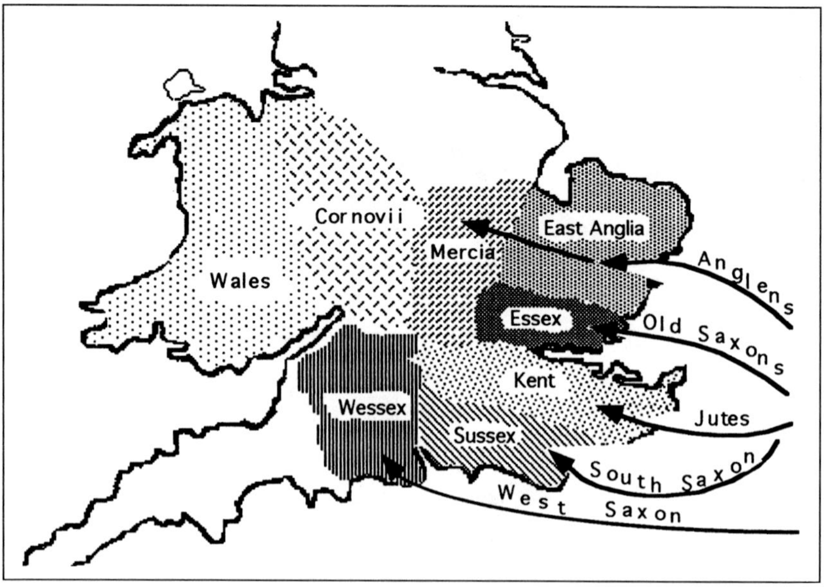

Map 10—The traditional theory of *Saxones* incursions.

claims himself innocent of inventing Mordred. Interpolated, after addressing his patron the Duke, he writes,

> About this particular matter [Mordred, the treacherous tyrant, living adulterously and out of wedlock with Queen Guinevere] ... [I] Geoffrey of Monmouth prefer to say nothing.... I will, however, in [my] own poor style and without wasting words, describe the battle which our most famous King fought against his nephew, once he had returned to Britain after his victory; [because I] found [the story] in a British treatise ... and heard it, too, from Walter of Oxford, a man most learned in all branches of history.[30]

By shifting outside his own narrative and directly addressing himself to his patron, Monmouth claims that the Mordred story came from two sources: the notorious "ancient book"[31] which has created a flurry of debates for centuries, and Walter of Oxford, his close friend.

From the onset, the reader is provided with contradictory information about the kinship between Mordred and King Arthur. In itself, this too has created a flurry of debates. Mordred has come down through the ages and entered the period of the later medieval romances sometimes as Arthur's incestuous bastard son, and sometimes as his nephew. Geoffrey himself is confused on the issue, attesting to the belief that in truth there was an ancient book Monmouth was using as a source, from which he was simply copying the information.

Because of Monmouth's abstruse delineation of Mordred's mother, Anna, Monmouth has irreversibly propagated confusion about Mordred. In seven separate passages about Anna, she is listed as Arthur's sister three times, Ambrosius's sister once, and in a confusing noun-of-address sequence, as Utherpendragon's sister once. At one point she is listed as the Queen of Brittany, who bears a son, Hoel, to King Budicius; and in several instances she is labeled as the Queen of Lothian, who bears two children, Mordred and Gawain.

Listed sequentially, the passages are as follows:

page 208—With great love for each other, Utherpendragon and Ygerna lived together as equals, and had a son named Arthur and a daughter named Anna.

page 209—"...[Utherpendragon] had given [Loth] his daughter Anna and put him in charge of the kingdom while he himself was ill." (Five pages previously Monmouth had recorded that Aurelius had died from poisoning, and hence the common noun "king" must be a reference to Utherpendragon.)

page 214—Hoel was the son of Anna, Arthur's sister, and Hoel's father was Budicius, King of the Armorican Britons.

page 216—Because Arthur's cousin, Hoel, was seriously ill, Arthur left him behind in the city of Alclud.

page 221—"[Arthur restored the dukedom of Lothian] to Loth, who in the days of Aurelius Ambrosius had married that king's own sister [Anna] and had had two sons by her, Gawain and Mordred."

page 222–223—Arthur wanted to give Loth, who was his brother-in-law, the kingship of Norway.

page 237—When Arthur learned of a possible Roman invasion, he granted the task of defending Britain to his nephew Mordred and to his Queen Guinevere during his absence.

Because the book *The Historic King Arthur* sets forth a theory that the epithets "Utherpendragon" and "Arthur" are both references to the only historical figure of the era, Ambrosius Aurelianus, named Aurelius Ambrosius in Monmouth, the point as to whether Anna is a sister to Arthur or whether she is a sister to Ambrosius becomes moot. Monmouth could possibly have been transcribing from some material and gotten confused about the homolog of Arthur for Aurelius, particularly since he seemingly created Utherpendragon from his own imagination. Be that as it may, Arthur must be viewed as Mordred's uncle, eradicating the incestuous relation between the great king and his sister which lurks behind the romances of later periods.

Once the kinship between Arthur and Mordred is identified as uncle/nephew, it becomes possible to identify at least tentatively the phantasm of Mordred, so long hidden in the shadows. The *AC* supplies only the information that Arthur and Medraut "fell," implying that they were wounded, presumably killed, in the battle. Phillips and Keatman cite "Welsh poems" relating that Medraut was Arthur's opponent,[32] but don't list the context of the specific poems. Later, the co-authors suggest that Medraut is a *Welsh* name, more specifically a Cornovian Welsh name, of an individual who might have established some kind of alliance with Cerdic.[33] But the real inspiration was what they wrote still later:

> ...[W]as Maglocunus' uncle the warrior who gave rise to the Arthur legend? A similar story of internecine struggle does occur in several later works: Geoffrey of Monmouth and the subsequent Romances portray Modred bringing about the death of *his* uncle, Arthur, in an attempt to seize the throne. What can be made of this?[34]

This sparked a twist in thinking patterns (lateral thinking), which in turn led to a closer scrutiny of material on Maglocunus map Catgolaun Lauhir, since the name Medraut was a dead-end. The outcome was the formation of a null hypothesis by rewording the Phillips/Keatman proposition: Independent of the later Romances, the name Medraut in the *Annales Cambriae* is a homolog for Maglocunus.

A segment of Chapter 3 in the *HKA* is devoted to the verification of Maelgwn's death in 547, as it is recorded in the *AC*. There has been a great deal of controversy on the entry, some focusing on the date, much dealing with the possible connection between the name Maelgwn and Maelchon, and perhaps even more controversy about the word "plague" as opposed to "Yellow Pestilence."[35] The *HKA* also establishes an ordinal year for the Battle of Camlann in 518, the year in which Arthur and Medraut are killed. In order to verify or nullify the equation of the null hypothesis about Medraut as a synonym for Maglocunus, it is necessary to stay within the parameters of those two dates without manipulating information.

Temporarily putting aside the variance between the *AC* date of 537 and the *HKA* date of 518, it's important to compare the two dates for any similarity in order to determine if deeper analysis is warranted. My translations read as follows:

> 537—The battle of Camlann, in which Arthur and Medraut fell; and there was death in Britain and Ireland.
>
> 547—The great death in which Mailcun, king of Gwynedd died. †Hence it is said the long sleep of Wailgun in the court of Ros. Then there was the Vad Velen.† [Last sentence suggests an interpolation.]

Of course, no interpretation is simple. O'Sullivan devotes five full, heavily-documented pages analyzing the meaning of "death," "the great death," and

"Vad Velen." Most commonly "death" and the "great death" referred to the Bubonic Plague, but "Vad Velen" referred to the Yellow Pestilence. Another complication is the insertion of daggers in the entry, meaning that the material between them is an interpolation in at least one of the extant manuscripts. Nevertheless, at face value they both mention a plague or pestilence, which can be used as historical validation. Interestingly, William P. MacArthur verifies that in the mid-sixth century the Yellow Pestilence struck both Britain and Ireland, as recorded in the un-interpolated entry of 537.[36] This alone warrants that there should be a deeper probe.

As a general rule, the *AC* is an accurate and reliable historical source. Nora Chadwick writes that "The evidence [which would include material from the *Annales Cambriae]* as a whole points to the conclusion that genuine historical tradition and genuine genealogies in Celtic Britain began to be preserved shortly after the close of the Roman period."[37] And the time period under scrutiny would be from approximately 410, the beginning of Roman abandonment, to 547, the established date of Maelgwn's death. Of the same time frame, P. H. Blair writes, "...the Welsh genealogies can be checked at a sufficient number of points to suggest that they are reliable at least as far back as the beginning of the sixth century."[38]

From a variety of sources, an accurate genealogy can be structured for Maelgwn,[39] delineated as follows:

Tacitus
|
Paternus of the Red Robe
|
Aeternus
|
Cunedda
|
Enniaun Girt
|
Eugein Dantguin —————— Catgolann Lauhir
| |
Cinglas Mailcun

O'Sullivan himself writes that "It is clear that these pedigrees were not manufactured to authenticate the *De Excidio*."[40] The genealogy written therefore in the *Historia Brittonum* can be deemed accurate. There is only one basic piece of information, but it is crucial: King Maelgwn the Great of Gwynedd traces his ancestry back to Cunedda and his eight sons who come down from the north to expel the Irish raiders from the country.

In contrast, the *De Excidio* is a repository of information on Maelgwn; Gildas's castigation of him flares across four pages. From Michael Winterbottom's edition and translation,[41] these are the most relevant pieces of information on Maglocunus:

1. he is called Dragon of the Island (Section 33, page 32);
2. he is higher than almost all the generals of Britain (Section 33, page 32);
3. in his youth he killed the King, his uncle (Section 33, page 33);
4. the faces of his enemies in battle were not very different from those of the lions' whelps (Section 33, page 33);
5. afterward he vowed to be a monk forever (Section 34, page 33);
6. he fell back into his old ways (Section 34, pages 33-34);
7. his first marriage (after breaking his vow to become a monk) was illegal (Section 35, page 34);
8. he fornicated with the wife of his brother's son (Section 35, page 34);
9 he killed his wife and his brother's son (Section 35, page 34);
10. he married the other woman, claiming it was legitimate because she was a widow (Section 35, page 34).

In drawing a parallel between Medraut and Maelgwn, there are four pieces of information which immediately become evident. The first is his title, Dragon of the Island, which provides a great deal of information. Not only was the dragon a standard of the Roman Caesars, thus linking him to Roman royalty and heritage, but the symbol was later adopted for the Welsh banner, a red dragon on a green and white background. Additionally, the dragon ties to the fictional character, Utherpendragon or Uther, the Head Dragon, whose sign of kingship flashed in the sky as

> ...a star of great magnitute and brilliance, with a single beam shining from it. At the end of this beam was a ball of fire, spread out in the shape of a dragon. From the dragon's mouth stretched forth two rays of light, one of which seemed to extend its length beyond the latitude of Gaul, while the second turned towards the Irish Sea and split up into seven small shafts of light.[42]

The territories he was to rule over, then, included not only Gaul, but Wales near the Irish Sea and seven other smaller kingdoms. Even more important, though, is Arthur's inheritance of the Dragon's kingship; Arthur, too, is linked to Roman royalty, whether it be through the fictitious (yet perhaps symbolic) character of Utherpendragon, or through Aurelius, a bona fide historical character.

This kinship gives rise to the meaning of #4 above. The "lions' whelps" is a reference to Cunedda's offspring; Cunedda himself is the symbol of the lion, and those who spring from him (including Maelgwn) are his whelps. Earlier, Gildas also refers to Aurelius Caninus as a "lion-whelp," identifying Cunedda as his ancestor. In both instances Gildas uses the terms *catule/catulorum* to describe Cunedda's clan. In general terms, *catulus* is a reference to any young carnivorous animal; Horace used it to refer to a lion's cubs, Vergil used it for a wolf's pups, and Ovid used it for a bear's cubs.[43] In each of Gildas's instances, there is no doubt that this is the tribe of the lions, since he prefixed the term with the adjective "lion." The term "dog," then, so commonly used to identify Cunedda is a translation in a generic and not specific sense. Maelgwn's enemies are blood-kin, again leaving no doubt that in Gildas's time the country is torn apart by appalling civil wars, not foreign invasions.

This leads to the second important revelation: In his youth, Maelgwn killed the king, his uncle, to seize the province of Gwynedd. This would explain the rise of the tales in the later romances about Mordred. Monmouth was indeed confused about the kinships he was recording from a copy of some manuscript, and wasn't sure of the relationship between Mordred and Arthur. Even to any cautious modern researcher, the number of epithets are difficult to keep separate, and one of the crucial conditions is that the oldest available source must be used to dispel the confusion. The ancient Welsh chronicles such as the *Tysilio* suggest that Aurelius Ambrosius/Ambrosius Aurelianus (whose epithet is Arthur) is Mordred's uncle. This in turn explains why Gildas writes that Maelgwn (i.e., Mordred) is of higher rank that almost all the subkings of Britain: In his youth he traitorously killed his uncle the High King. After this there is silence about Medraut, which could be mirrored by Maelgwn becoming a monk and thus dropping (or falling) temporarily from view as a catalyst of internal warfare.

Unfortunately the comparison between Mordred and Maelgwn fades at this point. Maelgwn abandons the monastic life and arises once again as a war-leader who sinks into profligacy, which could be a parallel of Mordred's personality since Maelgwn is portrayed as licentiously abusing Queen Guinevere. There are no other specifics about Maelgwn's adulterous relationship with the wife of his brother's son, nor is there mention of his first wife's murder or that of his brother's son.

But the parallel does not end there. It is possible to either show or disclaim the link of the two as a homolog by examining floruits and chronological calibrations. As the above genealogical chart shows, Cunedda was Maelgwn's great-grandfather. After defining "floruit" as a thirty-year period and life span as sixty years, the *HKA* establishes the floruit of Cunedda as 435 to 465 and his life span as 420 to 490. This would in turn give Enniaun Girt a floruit/life span of 465–495/450–510, Catgolann Lauhir one of 495–525/480–540, and Maelgwn one, of 525–555/510–570.

A floruit/life span can also be devised for Mordred even though Arthur is considered an epithet for Ambrosius, since Arthur as a name appears in the sunset of Ambrosius's reign and is typically given the floruit of 475 to 505, with a life span of 460 to 520. Mordred as a nephew would be the succeeding link, with a floruit/life span of 505–535/490–550. Even as a loose generalization—which is no more than can be expected—Maelgwn's and Mordred's floruits and life spans reasonably overlap. Accepting two dates as correct—the lunar adjustment for the Battle of Camlann in the year 518, and the death of Maelgwn in the *AC* as it is given in the year 547—Mordred might have been somewhere around the age of twenty-eight at the Battle of Camlann, and he could have died at an age around fifty-seven of the Yellow Pestilence. Maelgwn might have been around eight in the year of Camlann and died at around thirty-seven from the epidemic.

Arguably, when Gildas writes that Maelgwn was youthful when he killed his uncle, the age twenty-eight might not seem "youthful" but the age eight might be too youthful. That is one of the risks of simplification and generalization, yet it is a risk worth taking. Viewed in a different perspective, the two comparable life spans have a twenty-five-year overlap, which is in the realm of possibility that either separate individual (Mordred or Maelgwn) might have been young when the battle of Camlann was fought, and died before his time, a ± variation of only one decade, which is within the realm of reason when a researcher is looking retrospectively at a life span from fifteen centuries earlier.

The hypothesis that Mordred and Maelgwn are synonymous names therefore leans toward acceptance. Re-enumerated, the similarities far outweigh the differences: both are in *AC* entries known for their reliability, which record a plague; both have ancestries of Roman royalty; both are of high rank; both are fighting kinsmen in a civil war; both slay an uncle; both mysteriously drop from view for a segment of their lives; both are portrayed as profligates; and both exist within an overlapping time-frame. Mordred might not have been killed at the Battle of Camlann; the entry indicates only that both he and Arthur "fell." If he were a young man of eighteen or so and he survived Camlann, his death-year in 547 would be realistic. Yet nothing, of course, can be listed as undeniable fact. The circumstantial evidence, though, offers an intriguing story which neatly—albeit fancifully—resolves Arthur's last battle.

Epilogue

Narrative History

When *The Historic King Arthur* came to fruition, there was not a deliberate plan to write a sequel. There is always something, of course, which can be written about the historic Arthur, and although there is still a great deal to be discovered about Arthur's authenticity and his impact on insular and continental history, there was no intent to develop another installment continuing the quest for Arthur's origins, particularly so soon after the distribution of the first book. A supplement might be a normal outgrowth, an addition to the original—something, perhaps, focused upon correcting errors or making modifications to theories, or even filling out a few details. But over the period of a year, further discoveries have come to light, not invalidating the tenets of the first book, but instead gratifyingly reinforcing what had been proposed. These further confirmations validating several proposals additionally opened the door for other speculations which had been omitted from the earlier work. Because the first book had to construct and validate a great deal of basic information largely independent of Arthur—including methods of chronological calibrations, relevant historical events contemporaneous with each other, verification of bona fide historical figures, and inaccuracies or interpolations in the ancient manuscripts—only the later chapters interrelated the impact of these circumstances upon Arthur's role. The result is that this second book is able to more intently focus upon Arthur's milieu and those who directly affect him in his environment.

In retrospect, there are a surprising number of new concepts presented herein, and hence there are two primary objectives of this epilogue. One is to point out these other viable probabilities that have manifested themselves, and, closely aligned to that, to relate their significance as a whole, not only to this book but to the conjectures and theories presented in *The Historic King Arthur.*

Beginning with the oldest existent manuscript, Gildas Badonicus perhaps was too harsh in the condemnation of the *superbus tyrannus,* who came to be identified as Vortigern. Britain's entire army was despoiled, her military resources were depleted, and many of her faithful and honorable supporters were annihilated. Gildas writes that the Britons, ignorant of the ways of war because they had for centuries survived under the protection of the Roman Empire, struggled for many years after the abandonment, trying to repulse the savage attacks from tribes to the north—the Picts—and to the northwest—the *Scotti.* Histories relate that the Romans began their process of withdrawal around A.D. 410 and Vortigern rose to power in 425, thereafter recruiting the help of the English Saxons about three years later, in 428. Further, the Saxon Revolt occurred around 442, Riothamus fought on the continent during the 460s, and the name of Arthur appears about 475. All of this indicates that the Roman withdrawal from Britain was not a cataclysmic event.

When the Empire began evacuating the island to protect its continental holdings, the measure was considered as a temporary state of affairs. Roman leaders themselves, in addition to the barbaric tribes functioning as mercenaries on the island, expected a full-force return of the Romans after the uprisings on the continent were squelched. Rome had been the *supreme* power for five hundred years on the continent, and had directed all of Britain's affairs for nearly four centuries. That a power of this magnitude could be vanquished was unthinkable. The Gallic tribes on the continent had discovered the bloody way that Roman power could not be denied; Rome's conquest had been inexorable and methodical until no tribe in western Europe could resist the Empire's expansion.

Hence, when Rome filtered out legions from the island, the general expectation was that those legions would return. There were too many camps and retirement villages, villas and civic centers, fortresses and military establishments to be simply and permanently deserted, in the true sense of being abandoned. The *Historia Brittonum* specifically relates that Vortigern was in dread of three things: attacks by the Picts and the *Scotti,* the return of the Roman legions, and most of all, Ambrosius Aurelianus. The full impact of these statements must be considered. Vortigern was one, perhaps two, generations removed from the Dési migration from Ireland to western Britain, or more accurately, to the coastal regions of Wales. Based upon Roman policies of the period, he was one of the native Briton kings who was used by the Roman military to help protect the borders of the Empire in return for other favors, including land grants. When the Romans began their emigration back to the continent, Vortigern was one of the native kings who had been bestowed with the power to rule in Rome's absence. He, like the entire populace, believed that the Roman absence was only temporal, and that the power granted to him was an interim condition.

In the past, Rome had granted these same provisos to the English, those Saxons who had migrated from the continent and been settled on the island for several generations. It was therefore expected, or at least not uncommon, that Vortigern, acting as an interim king, would seek to maintain an alliance with the English Saxons. However, whereby the English Saxons succumbed to their role as mercenaries under the awesome power of the Romans, these same Saxon leaders were not intimidated by the power of the new Briton King. Both the *Historia* and *The Anglo-Saxon Chronicle* tell of the Saxons' scorn of the Briton leader's weakness and advocated that the Saxons seize the prime heartland of Britain. Following the common policy of the Empire, Vortigern's intentions at the outset of his interim reign were honorable but were marred by the grave oversight that he, unlike the Empire, did not have the power to keep the subordinate Saxons in check.

A host of circumstances channeled Vortigern's fate according to the classic Greek definition of tragedy. Almost simultaneously with the Roman withdrawal, a famine gripped the island, civil strife kept rearing its ugly head, and immediately on the heels of those conflicts, another famine devastated the country. Gildas writes that any gentle and truthful king became perversely regarded as a destructive leader for Britain, and hence hatred, deceit, disrespect, and dishonesty were viewed more favorably. In this atmosphere and under these conditions, Vortigern was doing those things which were the only things he knew; he was keeping faith with the Saxons according the procedures he had observed under the Romans, and was granting them land and concessions to "shut the dog's mouth." Yet despite this trust, the villainous Saxons pretended allegiance only to treasonably massacre his Council and hold him hostage for ransom.

All of these conditions pushed Britain to the very brink of destruction. Vortigern was no longer in control of his own destiny or the destiny of Britain; he was a star-crossed leader whose path led directly into the chasm of a dishonorable death. Fear twisted Vortigern's sensibilities and his very soul became sullied, for if the Roman legions did return, they would condemn him as a miserable failure, which would lead to disgrace and undoubtedly death. Not only that, but the *Scotti* and the Picts launched a constant barrage against Britain's frontiers, and there was the nagging dread that Ambrosius, once he reached the age of accountability, would return from Gaul to lay claim to his rightful heritage because his parents had "worn the purple."

Vortigern thus became the scapegoat of Briton history; he has been reviled with a host of terms: naiveté, stupidity, egocentricity, greed, powermongering, amorality, insensitivity. In the histories he became an Oedipal ghost, hated by all his countrymen for his sins, wandering from place to place until he died without honor. His failure then sets the stage for his nemesis, the savior of Britain, Ambrosius Aurelianus. As one of the sole survivors imbued with Roman authority, Ambrosius restored sanity to the island through his excellence of military leadership. There was finally a reprieve from continuous defeat, and the nascent Briton kingdom enjoyed at least a transient period of peace and prosperity.

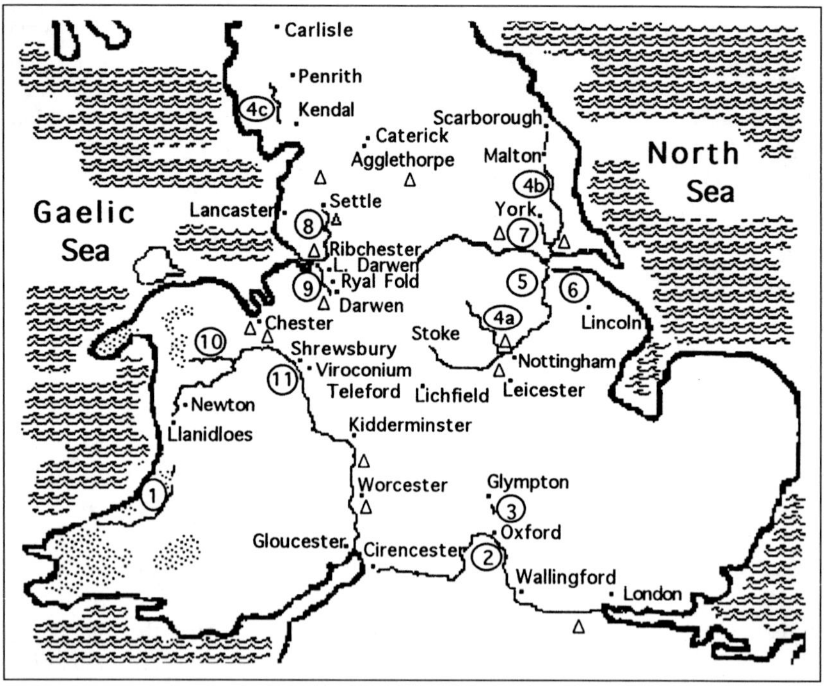

Map 11—Arthur's British military arena.

Important rivers: 1. River Teifi; 2. River Thames; 3. River Glyme; 4 a, b, and c. Rivers Derwent: Howden Moors to the Trent; Scarsborough to the Ouse; west of Penrith; 5. River Trent; 6. River Humber; 7. River Ouse; 8. River Ribble; 9. River Douglas; 10. River Tanet; 11. River Severn

· = Sites based upon the Hrype tribal name.

[dotted box] = Inscribed stones

Identification of Historical Figures and Locales

Almost two hundred years after Gildas wrote the *De Excidio,* Bede completed his own manuscript in which he supplied the epithet "Vortigern" for Gildas's descriptor, *superbus tyrannus.* And ever since the third decade of the eighth century, antiquarians, historians, scholars, and various other researchers have accepted that equation. Because my primary interest was from a slightly different perspective, I too ignored the analogue and glossed over it as indisputable. Only after careful consideration have I questioned this anomaly. Vortigern may well have been an epithet for a Welsh king who rose to high kingship after the Roman evacuation of the island, but evidence dictates that the title cannot be used interchangeably with *superbus tyrannus.*

Chapter 3 of this text presents plausible arguments, the most notable one being the uniformity of Valentinian's and Vortigern's reigns. Both rule from 425 to 455, which seems too anomalous to be coincidental. As detailed earlier, there are six translations for the term *superbus tyrannus,* any of which could be used: high king, supreme ruler, great king, over-lord, haughty tyrant, or proud tyrant. As an epithet, the word "Vortigern" is commonly translated as over-chief or over-king. Selecting the most similar definitions for the two terms combined would give the translations as over-lord, over-chief, or over-king. As with the lengths of reign, these three translations from the two different terms are indistinguishable from each other, further suggesting that this characteristic is too remarkable to be simply a coincidence.

Hence, Gildas Badonicus is writing about someone who is not merely the "overseer of Britain," but the *supreme* overseer of the western Roman Empire. Bede interprets that on a much narrower scale and obscures the identification of the *superbus tyrannus* by using another (and lamentably, incorrect) epithet; there is no purpose served or enlightenment advanced by defining one epithet with another—by doing that, the actual proper name behind the epithet becomes even more of a mystery. Furthermore, the *superbus tyrannus* didn't "invite" the Saxons into Britain; the *Saxones* (that is, the Angelns and the Saxons) had been settled on the island for several generations, and the *superbus tyrannus* was simply exercising the Roman policy of using local tribal mercenaries in exchange for special privileges, just as all the preceding Emperors had been doing for centuries.

If the *superbus tyrannus* is identified as Valentinian III, then the problem of identifying Vortigern remains. Somewhere in Briton/Welsh manuscripts, Bede encountered the term Urtigernus or Vortigern, a tribal chieftain who had been elevated to the rank of an over-king by Roman policy or edict, but his interpolation does not identify the historical figure behind the epithet. There are only a finite number of names from which to choose, and that, in conjunction with the inscription on Eliseg's Pillar, led through a series of intricate details and presumptions to the name of Cunedda's father, Æternus. Alcock obliquely attacked the problem, and even though he was working under the misguided assumption that Vortigern was indeed the *superbus tyrannus,* his process or procedure was on target when he stated that the emergence of the *superbus tyrannus* had to be explained "within the framework of Roman civil administration." As he should have done, Alcock analyzed the term *superbus tyrannus,* but because Bede had equated that term with the epithet Vortigern, Alcock didn't take the final step of identifying Vortigern without becoming circular in his definition.

The "framework of Roman civil administration" is, of course, the use of tribal mercenaries, and as Alcock himself pointed out, Cunedda's ancestors—Æternus, Paternus, and Tacitus—were Roman. They were associated with, or perhaps a contingency of, the Men of the North, *Gwyr y Gogledd,* who inhabited "the region between Glasgow and Edinburgh, and down to mid–Lancashire on the west and South Yorkshire on the east."[1] Among others, Alcock and Morris identify Paternus as "Patern Pesrut of the Red Robe." Of this individual Morris writes that during the 370s and 380s Paternus's dynasty was established "north of Hadrian's Wall a few generations before the emergence of the fifth-century kingdoms south of the Wall."[2] He explains, too, that the dynasty of Paternus transferred to Wales, and that Cunedda "was the grandson of the Paternus who had been appointed, probably by Valentinian, to rule the Votadini of the north-east coast, between Tyne and Forth."[3] Morris even goes so far as to write that "Men so named [such as Paternus] were not native kings to whom Rome granted recognition, but Roman officers placed over border barbarians,"[4] and summarized that

> In northern Britain, as in Europe, officers clung to their authority, and bequeathed it to their sons, founding hereditary dynasties.... [These] commanders appointed in a later age to Dementia, south-west Wales, also used officially the Roman military titles of Tribune and Protector, though contemporaries called them kings.[5]

Because there is such a great deal of crucial information compacted into these tiny capsules, it is better to concisely enumerate them so that the relevance of each is magnified, hopefully without being mired in detail.

1. Cunedda's ancestors can be viewed not simply as tribal mercenary chieftains elevated to authority, but instead as bona fide Roman officers.
2. These circumstances explain why the terms "Tribune" and "Protector" would be applied to the Cunedda clan and its ancestry, and thus be inscribed on Eliseg's Pillar.
3. The generic Votadini territories of the north can be viewed more explicitly as Manau Guodotin, Cunedda's (or at least Æternus's) homeland in the north before he migrates to the south.
4. Morris specifically mentions Dementia of southwestern Wales, precisely the area where Vortigern's domain of Dyfed is established one or two decades later.
5. Cunedda's authority would therefore have passed from his grandfather Paternus, through Æternus, to him.
6. The age-old question of the motivation behind Cunedda's migration would then be answered that it transpired by Roman authority—that is, his father Æternus—or perhaps even directly by the *superbus tyrannus,* Valentinian III.
7. The acceptance of Æternus as the proper name behind the epithet Vortigern also inherently explains why Vortigern (i.e., Æternus) was able to grant territories from the River Dee to the River Teifi to Cunedda.

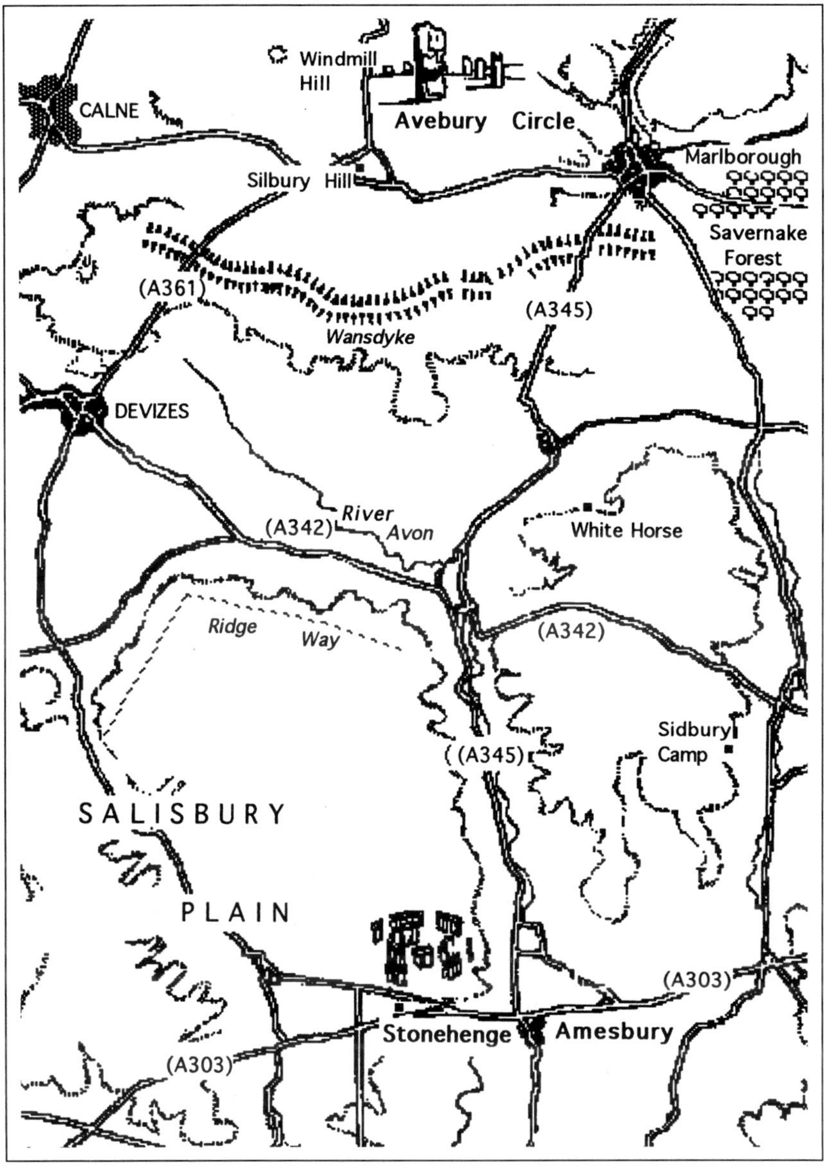

Map 12—Historic locales associated with King Arthur in Salisbury Plain and vicinity. Geoffrey of Monmouth writes that Merlin and Utherpendragon moved the Circle of Stones from Ireland to Mount Ambris. However, because Monmouth is so vague about the site, various scholars have recommended Avebury, Stonehenge, or Amesbury. Amesbury is the site associated with Ambrosius, and some scholars theorize that the Wansdyke was constructed by Ambrosius Aurelianus after the Roman abandonment.

The answer concerning Vortigern's identity is within Morris's grasp, but it slips between his fingers when he observes that Cunedda was a contemporary of Vortigern.[6] If Cunedda is considered to be Vortigern's son, then he is the key link between Britain's Roman past and its medieval future. In the true sense of Gildas's meaning, Britain would be in the throes of civil war, viewed traditionally as being based upon differences between *Romanitas* and the native Britons. But that would have been a condition which evolved; Vortigern (Cunedda's father Æternus) would have been simply following the protocol expected of him by Roman policy, but Cunedda (Vortimer) was evidently opposed to an alliance with the English Saxons. By the time Cunedda's heirs (his eight sons) succeeded to power, their political philosophy was different still; their motives were more personal than nationalistic, which gave rise to traitorous coalitions such as Cerdic's alliance with the English Saxons. Simplistically stated, it would have begun literally as *Romanophils* versus *Romanophils,* Vortigern and his clan "wearing the red," and Ambrosius and his clan "wearing the purple." After Vortimer's death, the fundamental principles unifying Britain deteriorated. Ambrosius came to represent the faction wanting to cling to the Roman past, while Cunedda's progeny envisioned their own glory in structuring the medieval future.

As shown by chapters 6 and 7 in this text, Cunedda is a pivotal figure of insular history during this era. He is a powerful leader who expels with great slaughter the *Scotti* from Dalriada, Cetgueli, and Dementia so that the enemy never again returned to inhabit these countries of Britain. And yet, as with Ambrosius Aurelianus, it is disquieting that an individual of such eminence is not granted his proper niche by records which recognize his influential impact on the internal affairs in Britain. Cunedda is accorded some of his deserved praise by linking his name with the epithet "Vortimer," but his contribution is even more profound than that. If this man expelled the barbarians by superior military might and in essence changed the course of British history after the Roman abandonment, then why is his name not echoed more loudly and clearly in the halls of history? An innate sense indicates there is more to this imposing figure, but still there are only two laconic passages about Cunedda in the *Historia Brittonum.* He is not recorded in the *De Excidio,* the *Annales Cambriae,* the *History of the English Church,* nor *The Anglo-Saxon Chronicle.* His name appears in the Welsh genealogies, but only in that capacity; his lineage is recorded and then ends with a brief passage that Cunedda and his sons hold many regions in western Britain. That is the extent of material about Cunedda; nothing more is given about his valiant and successful campaigns, first in Wales against the Irish and then against the English Saxons when they revolted.

The inscription on Eliseg's Pillar is the only other source available. It is an important aid—in fact the only aid—in linking the epithet "Vortimer" to Cunedda, but because of severe weathering spanning centuries, the inscription was never seriously considered as a source. *The Historic King Arthur* merely touched upon it because Geoffrey Ashe had suggested a possible connection between the name Elesa in the *ASC* and Eliseg on the monument, but scholars haven't considered Eliseg's Pillar as anything more than an interesting artifact with nothing unique to offer in tracing insular history. In spite of the enigma about Cunedda's history as seeming indecipherable, it is possible to extract details and thoughtful parallels from various sources, especially since so many links between epithets and proper names have been successfully made.

The consequences of those efforts are reflected in Table 10, and the results are more than gratifying, once again enforcing the value of "lateral thinking."

The floruits for Cunedda, Cerdic, and Creoda have been borrowed from *The Historic King Arthur* and function as a base for the other floruits and life spans in Table 10. Similarly, the Cunedda/Vortimer/Brydw/Elesa link is retained from earlier chapters in this text, along with the Vortigern/Æternus link. At first all these names attached to a single individual seems ludicrous, but during this era it has been continuously shown that epithets are common. The events and the people were also affected by the fading of some languages and the inception of others. Any singular individual could have names based in Breton, Briton, Welsh, Anglo-Saxon, and Latin, and any singular individual could have a nickname attached to any or all of those languages.

An additional consideration is that, during the intervening centuries between the histories and the chronicles, or the histories and the romances, there would more than likely be variants of the proper names, of the epithets, and of the nicknames.

There is no additional information to be extracted about Tacitus or Paternus, but there are accretions for each of the others.

I. The word "Gwylog" from Eliseg's Pillar is actually an epithet for Æternus; it is a cognate of Gwledic or Gwledig (meaning the ruler of a domain or kingdom) common, generic Welsh terms applied not only to Æternus but also to Cunedda. The word "Gwrtheyrn" is simply a variant of "Vortigern."

II. Earlier in this text Cunedda's Anglo-Saxon name Elesa was traced to Elise in the Irish annals, but interestingly and appropriately this ogham stone was dedicated in honor of Cunedda. The legible inscriptions on the Pillar are perfect appositives for Cunedda: He devastated not only the English with fire and sword, but expelled the Irish from Wales and united the inheritance of what was to become Powys. According to the Pillar he is the son of Gwylog, which in turn allows him to use the epithet Gwledig.

Table 10—Comparisons of genealogical sources for Cunedda's blood lines

Floruit—Life Span	*Common name or Epithet*	*In* ASC	*In* HB	*On Eliseg's Pillar*	*In Welsh ancestry*	*Comments*
345-375 330-390	Tacitus				Tacitus	
375-405 360-420	Paternus				Patern Pesrut	Paternus of the Red Robe
405-435 390-450	Æternus	Elsa	Vortigern	Gwylog/ Gwrtheyrn	Æternus	
435-465 420-480	Cunedda	Elesa	Cunedda/ Vortimer	Brydw/ Eliseg		United the inheritance of Powys Laid waste the English with fire and sword Blessed by Germanus (EP) Blessed by Germanus *(HB)* Son of Gwylog (EP) Son of Gwrtheyrn (EP, *HB*)
465-495 450-510	Cerdic	Cerdic	Ceretic	Brochwel	Ceredig	Son of Eliseg (EP)
495-525 480-540	Creoda	Creoda		Cadell	Creuddyn	Son of Brochwel (EP)
525-555 510-570	Cynric	Cynric		Cyngen		Great-grandson of Eliseg (EP) Erected the Pillar (EP) Son of Cadell (EP)
555-585 540-600	Ceawlin	Ceawlin				Second Bretwalda (*ASC*)

Similarly, a certain Brydw is recorded on the Pillar but nowhere else in the histories. Because he is listed as one of Vortigern's sons, one item which links Brydw to Vortimer is the inscription on Eliseg's Pillar which characterizes Brydw as being blessed by Germanus, while the *HB* characterizes Vortimer in the same way. Further support for this contention (that Vortimer, Brydw, Elise, Eliseg, and Cunedda are the same individual) is the *cunos-* affix as part of its designation on the Pillar, through the names Cyngen and Cynfarch, tribally linked to Cunedda. Otherwise, why would a leader of Cunedda's stature be omitted from the Pillar?

The kingdoms and "countries" into which Cunedda migrated were very different from what they evolved into. Skene writes that the seaboard of western Wales was occupied by Gaelic tribes known as the *Gwyddyl,* and the Cymry were confined to what is now eastern Wales, sandwiched between the Gaels and the Saxons. He further describes the demarcations: "A line drawn from Conway on the north to Swansea on the south would separate the two races of the *Gwyddyl* and the Cymry, on the west and on the east. In North Wales the Cymry [possessed] Powys, with the *Gwyddyl* in Gwynedd and

Mona [Anglesey]; in South Wales, the Cymry [possessed] Gwent and Morganwg, with the *Gwyddyl* in Dyfed; and Brecknock [was] occupied by the mysterious Brychan and his family."[7]

In addition to verifying Cunedda's expulsion of the Irish, Chapter 62 of the *Historia* also furnishes the genealogical link between Cunedda and Maelgwn (Maglocunus). The *cunos-* affix in both names is an obvious kinship link, but the adjacency of territories strengthens that tie. Maglocunus ap Clutor and Vortigern are contemporaries or near-contemporaries in the late first-quarter of the fifth century, and after Cunedda's migration the entire western coast of Wales is in the hands of blood-relatives: Cunedda's new home-base to the south of Hadrian's Wall is Carlisle, in the Gwynedd territories; Vortigern occupies Dyfed along the southwestern coast; Cerdic, Cunedda's fifth son, acquires the central section of coast known as Ceredigion; Meriaun, Cunedda's eldest son who migrates to the south with him, claims Meirionnydd just to the north of Cerdic's domain; Etern claims north-east Wales; and Maglocunus's realm becomes the northwestern coast, including the Isle of Anglesey.

III. Cerdic acquires only one other name, Brochwel, son of Eliseg according to the inscription.

IV. Creoda, the lost generation in the *ASC,* was known by the Welsh name of Cadell, and his inheritance in Wales, Creuddyn, was named after him.

V. Cynric, Creoda's son and Cerdic's grandson in the *ASC,* is the individual who erected the Pillar in honor of his great-grandfather, Cunedda.

VI. Ceawlin is especially interesting, because he is not memorialized by the Welsh, and the reason why is explained by the word "Bretwalda." Ceawlin did not remain on the island as an English Saxon, but instead returned to the continent. When the English Saxons were defeated in all their campaigns by Arthur, they sought help from the German kings. Caewlin was one of those German kings who allied himself once again with his father and the English Saxons, and because he became a German king ruling a domain in Britain, he acquired the title of Bretwalda.

VII. Two other items are inscribed on the Pillar, but were not included in the table because they are only of satellite interest. According to the inscription, Severa was Maximus's daughter, Vortigern's wife, and hence Brydw's mother. Her floruit would be similar to Vortigern's, creating a floruit for Maximus of 375–405. This is a perfect match with the bona fide Roman genealogies provided for Maximus: Maximus proclaimed himself emperor in Britain in 383, defeated Emperor Gratian in Gaul, and was eventually beheaded by Theodosius I in 388.

Eliseg's Pillar, therefore, is an extraordinary repository for the history of the Arthurian age, one of its most important contributions being Cunedda's bloodlines which properly emphasize the role of the northern tribes after their migration to the territories between the Rivers Dee and Teifi. Like the neglected Welsh chronicles which Griscom excoriates historians for ignoring, the Pillar also has been relegated to an obscure niche for literally hundred of years. Both exemplify how a new look at ancient material can provide accurate, innovative perspectives of history.

"Lateral thinking" also allows a more specific identification of Vortimer's battle on the River Derguentid as the Roman fort in modern Derbyshire; the location is ideal, since it was of such crucial importance both militarily and administratively, and it is in close proximity to the other three battles attributed to Vortimer. More has come to light, too, about Vortimer's battle at Tanet. Although the word "Tanet" appears several times throughout the *Historia,* only in Chapter 31 is it also called "Ruoihin," with eight variations scattered among the variant copies, including Manuscripts D, E, G, H, P, L, *b,* and *a.* As detailed in Chapter 4 of this text, Ruoihin is a cognate of Ruthin, an important site on the borderlands just fifteen miles southwest of the legionary fortress of Chester. Not only does Ruoihin link itself to Vortimer's first battle, but it also aligns itself with his fourth battle near an Inscribed Stone, which unconditionally must be set in the vicinity of Wales, since there are no known or discovered inscribed stones in Kent. Both battles, therefore name the *Hyrpe* tribe and territories, which further verifies the locus of Vortimer's battles as the heartland of the Midlands rather than the far-distant Isle of Thanet in Kent, obviously quite removed from the battles during the Arthurian era.

The Maglocunus and Vitalianus monuments also are useful finds. The "Maglocunus map Clutor" stone at Saint Brynach's Church in Nevern helps verify the tribal *cunos-* designation of Cunedda's bloodlines early in the fifth century, contemporary with Vortigern and the Roman evacuation. It provides a crucial link between this era and the reign of Maglocunus the Great, son of Catgolaun Lauhir, whose death is recorded in the *Annales Cambriae* in the year 547, verifying the continuation of the Maglocunus line which ruled in Wales for over a century and a half. The Vitalianus stone, also of the fifth century, provides a gratuitous parallel to the "Cunos clan" and Ambrosius Aurelianus's role in this same geographic area during the same time-span. Although there isn't any further solid archaeological evidence, if it is indeed a commemoration of the Guitolin from the *Historia,* it fits the correct chronological and geographic pattern; this is where those who "wore the red" would be in conflict with those who "wore the purple."

The Earliest Manuscripts as History

It is a lamentable fact that most twentieth-century historians do not grant proper credibility to pre-eleventh-century manuscripts that record the only available insular history of the fifth and sixth centuries. Even worse are those who not only discount credibility, but ignore or neglect any serious in-depth analysis of these old records. Without exaggeration, a typical seven hundred-page history of Wales will probably have no more than fifteen pages devoted to Welsh history between A.D. 400 and 550, which is, of course, the most crucial era in the molding of Wales as an emerging power in insular development. Some purists will undoubtedly claim that more material has been written about this period of Welsh history than anything before or after, and also deride the efforts of interpretations or translations as egocentrically motivated or lackadaisically inept.

However, there must be a deep and abiding sense of awareness that there is a crucial difference between *recording* history and *interpreting* it. Scribes of this early period—mainly ecclesiastics—were for the most part copyists, presumably just recording what had been written earlier. Difficulties arose when copyists of the early ages decided to interpret or elaborate upon material which they were only supposed to transcribe. Most probably they did not add material for self-gratification or public recognition, though there have been some notable hoaxes uncovered indicating the contrary. Faced with these circumstances, researchers—which include purist historians—must accept the only alternative available, and that is to extricate the original historical manuscript from the chaff of the later added interpolations. This is not interpretation in the strict sense of the word and should not, therefore, be chided as an unworthy or unrespectable endeavor. The likelihood of an untainted, purely objective history ever being unexpectedly discovered is more ludicrous than any attempt to piece together some detached and unbiased account from the existent records. This should be the goal of the historian, probably more accurately labeled not as *interpreting* history but as *explicating* history. Unraveling or untangling history is a much more noble intent, with a rewarding and gratifying outcome of filling a void in past events.

Gildas Badonicus can be more accurately described as a recorder rather than a copyist, but even so he is criticized for not being a classical historian, who, had he been such, would have filled the Dark Ages with light. Instead, Gildas was an ecclesiastic who viewed history as a contrivance for God to reward the faithful and punish the wicked. However, putting judgmental purpose aside, the point is that Gildas *did* view history, and in the process of castigating the wicked, he *did* relay a framework of events. He doesn't name Arthur, he doesn't identify the *superbus tyrannus,* he doesn't include Cunedda in his narrative, but he does give a general historical background. And contrary to what some modern historians attempt to devise, just because Arthur, the *superbus tyrannus,* and Cunedda are not recorded in the *De Excidio* does not mean that these figures must be viewed as invented characters. Gildas likewise does not mention Honorius, Valentinian, Anthemius, Ægitius, Syagrius, Euric, Attila, Hengist, Horsa, Octha, or Cerdic, but that does not mean all these individuals are figments of someone's imagination; *their* historicity has not been seriously questioned.

Gildas has also been denigrated for his portrayal of wars with the *Saxones.* Based upon Chapter 24 of his manuscript, he is accused of overexaggerating the devastation and destruction of the island. The reading of any translation shows this accusation to be true—on the surface. If one *explicates* Gildas's history, Chapter 24 demonstrates that the author is an undisguised, agitated zealot drawing comparisons with the Assyrian assaults on Judea, literally loaded with fire, brimstone, and death. What is more accurate from an objective point of view (and not Gildas's subjective one) is what he writes in Chapter 26:

> But the cities of our land are not populated even now as they once were; right to the present they are deserted, in ruins and unkempt. External wars may have stopped, but not civil ones.[8]

Unlike Chapter 24, which is a figurative, imaginative description of the times, Chapter 26 conveys a perceptive piece of history. In one brief passage Gildas is expressing two unquestionable pieces of history. The first is the desolation of the land after the Romans left. Historians such as R. G. Collingwood and J. N. L. Myres accurately indicate that from the first decade to the last quartile of the fifth century Roman society continuously deteriorated while the more barbarized Briton/Saxon settlements conversely grew. Collingwood writes,

> Some have thought that [Roman civilization in Britain after the evacuation] came to an end by the destruction of cities, the burning of villas, the massacre of the villagers, and in a word the extermination of the people.... The truth is too complex for such crude generalizations; if they are posited as the horns of a dilemma, the facts of history slip between them....
>
> In the case of the smaller towns, evidence of complete desertion is the rule rather than the exception.... These towns came to an end, not by fire and sword, but by decay and evacuation.[9]

That is exactly what Gildas conveys: The cities are and were deserted and decaying.

Gildas's second perceptive piece of history is that civil wars are tearing the country apart. Wade-Evans gives the specifics of what this actually meant. As common Roman policy, mercenary tribes were hired to protect the Romano-British borders, and some of the mercenaries were the *Saxones.* The Romans used this generic term and didn't distinguish between the Saxons, Angelns, Jutes, or Frisians who had been living for several generations on the island, nor did they distinguish between the *English* Saxons on the island or their counterparts, the *German* Saxons on the continent. When Gildas writes of civil wars, he is referring to those Britons (another generic term) wanting to salvage the Roman way of life conflicting with those who sided with the English Saxons. The external wars were against the Picts, the *Scotti,* and the German Saxons.

Explicating Gildas's historical contributions via the section of his manuscript commonly known as the "Complaint Against the Kings" would require a book in itself. It will suffice here to say that much valuable historical information can be harvested from what Gildas planted, and which some future enthusiast must take the time to analyze. A recent book which has begun a proper, serious study of the ancient manuscripts is a concerted joint effort by Rachel Bromwich, A. O. H. Jarman, and Brynely F. Roberts, all who are respected in their fields of endeavor. The Introduction explains that the purposes of *The Arthur of the Welsh* are to "supplement and revise" Loomis's earlier work from 1959, and to examine "the early Welsh poems which make allusion to Arthur."[10] This update approach accords with Acton Griscom's plea in 1929: Geoffrey of Monmouth and the Welsh chronicles which preceded him such as the *Tysilio,* plus other traditions and histories, should all be properly translated and interpreted so that the importance of Wales's role in insular history can finally and accurately be realized. And although Peter Beresford Ellis's book *The Druids* is focused on a different purpose, he grants the importance of Gildas's historical contribution and emphasizes the irreplaceable role of Nennius's *Historia Brittonum,* "which is a primary source for British Celtic history."[11]

Turning now to Nennius's invaluable contribution, we are faced with basically the same problems as with the *De Excidio,* except that the work ascribed to Nennius fills out the skeletal offering by Gildas. By his own admission in the Preface, Nennius questions his ability to compile this information about Wales, but readers shouldn't be too quick to jump on that bandwagon by labeling his efforts as the ramblings of an ignoramus. Thomas Charles-Edwards gives an interesting reaction which sums up how various people view Nennius's history. He writes,

> The curious mixture of boast and modesty found in this Nennian Preface has been seized upon, both by those who would portray the writer as an ignorant and incompetent compiler and also by those who see in his words a foreshadowing of modern historical attitudes to evidence.[12]

Unlike Gildas, Nennius is a copyist and realizes the formidability of the job ahead of him. John Davies accurately describes Nennius's work as "intractable"[13] because it is complex to explicate, but its intractability stems from the work Nennius was copying, not from Nennius himself. Nennius is putting together bits and pieces of a historical puzzle, and considering that, he comes up with a respectable (and accurate) aggregate. Of course, not everything in the *Historia* is reliable as fact, but the manuscript does reflect an attempt at objectivity. The value of the *Historia* is its age, with its earliest recension dating to 829 or 830,[14] from which comes priceless information not available in any other source. As Charles-Edwards states, the Preface of the *Historia* suggests that the manuscript traces back to the *Annales Romanorum*, and in turn to other parent English and Irish sources such as the *Collection canorum Hibernensis* and possibly the *Annales Hebraeorum* of the early eighth century.[15] The Preface gives prestige, therefore, to the main body of the work, which should *not* be labeled as a heap of what Nennius used.

Modern academic analysis of the *Historia* has created two general controversial approaches to the material, one labeling it as "synthetic history" and the other "synchronistic history." Synthetic history is defined as historical writing which stresses nationalistic patriotism, but because the historical aspect is so tenuous, it relies upon a legendary past. Synchronistic history, on the other hand, is more comparative in its nature and therefore more attentive to chronological interrelationships between the various histories of different peoples. As the basic difference between the two, the first emphasizes its legendary quality while the other concentrates upon the chronological aspect.

David Dumville is a proponent of the synthetic theory. In a way which many people have come to identify as Dumville's technique, his ascription of the *Historia* is that

> no historian would now place any trust in the literal truth of the narratives offered by such texts; they are interesting for the mentalities ... of the authors, not for the periods about which they proport to write.[16]

This condescending condemnation is typical of Dumville. Under a different set of circumstances regarding another ancient manuscript he wrote, "...it would be most unwise to rely too heavily on the entry in the *Annales Cambriae*,"[17] based upon his judgment that it, as information borrowed from an Irish text, might possibly or probably be derived from an oral source, which is evidently taboo from a purist's point of view. Under still different circumstances, Geoffrey Ashe at one point commented that Dumville thought the Welsh matter was worthless as history.[18] Each of these episodes reflects stances which are too harsh, going beyond the healthy hesitation of skepticism ingrained in any kind of scholarly pursuit. Clothed in that kind of philosophy, there is no possibility of experimentation or exploration, hence no space for expansion, progress, or discovery.

Thomas Charles-Edwards espouses the opposing viewpoint. On a more optimistic note, he sees the value of what the *Historia* offers and what its potential contributions are and can be. Dumville rejects other values of the

Historia based upon his definition of synthetic history, which has led Charles-Edwards to observe

> What has enabled Dr. Dumville to take a sceptical position with such confidence is not any rule of historical method, but the proposition that the *Historia Brittonum* is a work of synthetic history.[19]

What Charles-Edwards sees on the opposite side of the coin is synchronistic history which is not a quasi- or pseudo-historical rendition of a past buried in legend; he considers the *Historia* an integral part of records and traditions of indigenous peoples. He then further points out that

> ...if an interest in legends about the origins of peoples is to be enough to brand an entire text as synthetic history and thus as worthless evidence for the period of which it treats, Paul the Deacon and Bede will stand in the dock along with the author of the *Historia Brittonum*.[20]

Just because no history can be "pure," one doesn't throw out the proverbial baby with the bathwater. It would have been very convenient if Gildas, Bede, Nennius, and all the other unnamed and unrecognized scribes had had before them prescribed criteria defining history as judged by the researchers of the twentieth century. But because those antiquarians did not have those guidelines, what seems the most rational option is to accept the second-best—their work—and take the time to sift through it for the best possible view which can be molded and remolded by successive armies of scholars. The only other alternative is a black hole. Under these circumstances, Charles-Edwards's endorsement is by far the best: "The *Historia Brittonum* is in the grand tradition of early medieval history."[21]

The *Historia Brittonum* is a repository of Welsh information which exists nowhere else in early-medieval history. Gildas Badonicus offers the outline and Bede is the echo, but only the *Historia* gives the background of events centered upon Arthur and his contemporaries—both comrades and enemies—after the Roman withdrawal. The epithet "Arthur" appears in two of the early manuscripts, the *Historia* and the *Annales Cambriae.* Two others, the *De excidio* and *A History of the English Church and People,* use the proper name Ambrosius Aurelianus as a substitute for the epithet "Arthur," and it is only at the end of the millennium that the word "Arthur" emerges as the major identification for the High King who becomes the most well-known figure in British history and tradition. After the turn of the millennium Geoffrey of Monmouth records both Arthur and Ambrosius but severely clouds the issue by misinterpreting the manuscripts from which he was copying, and by adding his own creative imagination to history.

Because of Geoffrey's ingenuity and artistry, he had the capability to invent an "Arthur," but as Kenneth Jackson writes, "[Nennius] could hardly have invented Arthur himself for Nennius was no Geoffrey: he was not capable of creating a character out of nothing at all."[22] Although the main thrust of inquiry here is the Arthurian Matter, it is essential to heed Thomas Charles-Edwards's admonition lurking in the background when he cautions that any analyses of Arthur's battles must be judged in context to the structure and outlook of the entire *Historia Brittonum.* He suggests that the death of Hengist retrospectively focuses upon the central theme of the *Historia;* that central theme has to be the effect of the Roman withdrawal and the ensuing turmoil not only to involvement in continental warfare but likewise to internal conflicts. Charles-Edwards also writes that the significance of the content of the *Historia* can best be understood by comparing it with Bede's *Historia Ecclesiastica* because he perceives that both manuscripts were relying upon Kentish material, including the supposed ancestors of the kings of Kent.[23]

Taking into account the common misidentification of Kent for Cæint discussed in detail in *The Historic King Arthur* (which Charles-Evans would not know of), he presents an accurate history of the pre-Arthurian segment. For a proper geographic perspective, Hengist has to be localized in the Cæintish area, which was part of the ancient Cymru territories. The reason why Charles-Edwards believes that Bede combined two different sources is because this re-identification of Kent had not yet been made. Hengist's locus is the west-central part of the Roman Cornovii territory, and hence the account of Octha and the kings of *Cæint* is parallel to that of Hengist. *The Anglo-Saxon Chronicle* makes the same mistake in identification because it was largely based upon Bede's work.

J. N. L. Myres gives an excellent, detailed account of the extremely complex migrations to and from the island during the Arthurian period.[24] Attempting to identify tribal homelands and migratory patterns is well-nigh impossible, even though it is "fortunately possible to supplement that story from the results of archaeological excavation, and the character of Roman remains is such that a maximum of historical information can be derived from them."[25] Myres admits, though, that "On the Anglo-Saxon side there is indeed no contemporary evidence at all, for the very good reason that the invaders were illiterate."[26] Nevertheless, in spite of these obstacles, an accurate though sketchy history does emerge. Cutting a straight path through the maze of details, it's possible to use Bede's elementary summary, because after a close analysis of the refined specifics, "it is clear that Bede has unduly and perhaps consciously simplified the confused issues of the age of settlement."[27]

Condensed, then, from the "complexity of the continental situation as well as the specialized evidence,"[28] the basic history is as follows. Before beginning, there are three major conditions which must be considered uppermost. The first, as stated in *The Historic King Arthur,* is that in the recorded accounts in Britain, the Romans did not make definitive tribal distinctions; the generic Roman term was *Saxones,* which applied indiscriminately to the

Saxons, the Jutes, and the Frisians. The second, also mentioned in *The Historic King Arthur,* is that a distinction must be made between English Saxons, who had been settled on the island for several generations and had been accepted as part of a mercenary system by the Romans, as opposed to the German Saxons, who were based in the ancestral homeland on the continent. The third is that the *Historia Ecclesiastica* (Bede), the *Historia Brittonum* (Nennius), and the various versions of *The Anglo-Saxon Chronicle* all contribute to the history which emerges. Bede bases some of his material upon Gildas's *De excidio,* and in turn, Nennius and *The Anglo-Saxon Chronicle* base some of their material upon Bede. Although there is basic agreement among all the manuscripts, there are likewise some very interesting divergencies peculiar to each.

Bede's account furnishes the foundation. He writes,

> These new-comers were from the three most formidable races of Germany, the Saxons Angles [correctly the Angels or Angelns], and Jutes. From the Jutes are descended the people of Kent and the Isle of Wight and those in the province of the West Saxons opposite the Isle of Wight who are called Jutes to this day. From the Saxons—that is, the country now known as the land of the Old Saxons—came the East, South, and West Saxons. And from the Angles—that is the country known as Angulus, which lies between the provinces of the Jutes and Saxons and is said to remain unpopulated to this day—are descended the East and Middle Angles the Mercians, all the Northumbrian stock (that is, those peoples living north of the river Humber), and the other English peoples. Their first chieftains are said to have been the brothers Hengist and Horsa.[29]

The last statement in the above extract does not appear in Gildas's manuscript; it is Bede's addition, one that is responsible for almost all of the ensuing confusion. Bede identifies three distinctive tribes, capped by a statement that *their* (italics mine) first chieftains were Hengist and Horsa, which of course means that these two chiefs were leaders of *all* the various tribes.

Myres points out that the coastal Germanic tribes were, unfortunately and mistakenly, blended. As an example, he writes,

> Even Penda of Mercia, sprung, as it appears, from the purest Angles[correctly Angel] stock in England, from the old royal family of the Anglii of Angelen, appears in the Welsh annalists as "Panta the Saxon."[30]

This would have been normal in the course of events, since the victims, subjected to looting, killing, and rape, were indifferent about whether their attackers were Angles, Saxons, or Jutes. Nevertheless, these generic generalizations were the root of confusion. In spite of this, there are important pieces of information which can be extracted from Bede's insertion about the specific tribes.[31] One is that the Jutes, not the Old Saxons, were settled in Kent. Another is that the Angelns settled East Anglia, Middle Anglia, Mercia, and Northumbria. This locale is much farther north, near the River Humber and directly east of what is now Wales, or more specifically, the Midlands, which encompasses the old Roman Cornovii territories.

The Parker version of the *Chronicle* gives a similar account, yet varies in some crucial aspects. It provides this information:

> 449—...Hengest and Horsa, invited by Vortigern,... came to Britain at ... Ypwinesfleot at first to help the Britons, but later they fought against them. The king ordered them to fight against the Picts, and so they did and had victory wherever they came. They then sent to Angel; ordered (them) to send them more aid.... These men came from three nations of Germany: from the Old Saxons, from the Angles [correctly Angels or Angelns], from the Jutes. From the Jutes came the people of Kent and the people of the Isle of Wight, that is the race which now dwells in the Isle of Wight, and the race among the West Saxons which is still called the race of the Jutes. From the Old Saxons came the East Saxons and South Saxons and West Saxons. From Angel, which has stood waste ever since between the Jutes and the Saxons, came the East Angles, Middle Angles, Mercians, and all the Northumbrians.[32]

The Parker Chronicle retains Bede's identification of the chieftains as Hengist and Horsa, but three important new pieces of information emerge. One is that Hengist and Horsa are specifically identified as Angles; these two chieftains send for reinforcements not from Old Saxony or Jutland, but from Angulus or Angeln, depending upon which translation is used. This chronicle, like its sister chronicle the Laud, both identify Angeln as the province in Schleswig-Holstein between Jutland and Saxony on the continent. The territory of the Angelns in Britain remains the same in these two versions as in Bede's account, but the second important variation in the Parker Chronicle is that Hengist and Horsa are recruited to fight *Picts,* thus negating that they are in, or have associations with, Kent. The Picts were from the far north, and though there was some penetration to the south of Hadrian's Wall, there is no recorded history which indicates that the Picts ever threatened the territory of Kent. And third, the Anglia territories are further verified as parts of the Cornovii territory abandoned by the Romans, the buffer domain which formerly existed between the Welsh (or Brython) and the so-called English Saxons.

The Laud Chronicle slightly shifts viewpoints. It relates that

> ...Vortigern invited the Angles hither ... in three ships at ... Heopwinesfleot. King Vortigern gave them land to the south-east of this land on condition that they fought against the Picts. They then fought against the Picts and had victory wherever they came. Then they sent to Angel; ordered (them) to send more aid.... They then at once sent hither a larger force to help the others. These men came from three nations of Germany: from the Old Saxons,

> from the Angles, from the Jutes. From the Old Saxons came the East Saxons and South Saxons and West Saxons. From Angel, which has stood waste ever since between the Jutes and the Saxons, came the East Angles, the Middle Angles, Mercians and all the Northumbrians. Their leaders were two brothers, Hengest and Horsa; they were sons of Wihtgils.[33]

The Laud closely parallels the Parker, but it, too, has some interesting details, different from the other sources. Like the Parker, it identifies Hengist and Horsa as *Angles,* but does it with more assurance. From the Parker Chronicle the reader can only infer that Hengist and Horsa are Angles because they solicit aid from Angeln; the Laud Chronicle states outright that Vortigern recruits help from the Angles (not the Saxons) and that Hengist and Horsa were *Angles,* chiefs who rule over the East Angles, the Middle Angles, the Mercians, and all the Northumbrians. This places Hengist and Horsa in the *eastern Midlands,* not in Kent. The Parker Chronicle is explicit in stating that the people of Kent are descended from the *Jutes,* not the Anglens.

One other finer point clarified in the Laud Chronicle is misinterpreted by other sources. Similar to the Parker account, the Laud Chronicle indicates that Kent is *not* the appropriate locale as Hengist and Horsa's newly acquired land. Whereas other sources interpret lands given to Hengist and Horsa as the southeastern part of the island (hence Kent), the Laud narrative clarifies the misinterpretation of this identification by relating that Hengist and Horsa were given territories to the *southeast* of Heopwinesfleot. This site cannot be identified with any confidence, but it does suggest a locale which is *not* necessarily Kent. Hengist is an Angle who has been recruited to fight the Picts—a far northern tribe—and he would *not* be fighting them in the extreme southeastern section of Kent. Heopwinesfleot, then, would *not* be the modern village of Ebbsfleet, as it is so commonly translated.

Right after the Roman evacuation, the Angles began an increased infiltration on the island, moving farther to the north, so that by the 600s they were occupying Lothian along the eastern coast, just south of the Antonine Wall. Based on this influx, an area southwest of Heopwinesfleot in the mid-fifth century, using the River Humber as a northern limit, would be in the old Roman territories of Coritani, Iceni, and Trinovantes, which later became Mercia, Middle Anglia, and East Anglia. These territories—where Hengist and Horsa would have settled as Anglians after the "exile" from their country—were adjacent to the Cornovii territory which was left vacant when the Romans abandoned Britain. And it was for these vacated excellent lands that the Angles rebelled against Vortigern, as related in the Parker and Laud Chronicles.

The last source giving similar information is the *Historia Brittonum.* Under the heading of "The Kentish Chronicle, Part 1," which *The Historic King Arthur* has shown to be a later interpolation causing a millennium of confusion, the manuscript records that when Vortigern ruled in Britain, he was under pressure and feared the Picts, the Irish, a Roman invasion, and Ambrosius. It continues,

> [1]Then came three keels, driven into exile from [Germania]. [2]In them were the brothers Horsa and Hengest ... [3]Vortigern welcomed them, and handed over to them the island that in their language is called Thanet, in British Ruoihm.[34]

Vortigern is in fear of the Picts and the Irish, two tribes which direct the focus to the western and northwestern borders of the island. Additionally, he was in dread of a Roman return to the island, since their withdrawal was at first deemed temporary. Even more alarming was Vortigern's dread of Ambrosius Aurelianus, the symbol of *Romanitas,* who wanted to claim his right to the throne as high king. In sentence 1, the word used in the original Latin manuscripts is "Germania," a generic word similar to *Saxones.* As Peter Ellis suggests, the word "Germania" and all its forms was not incorporated into Roman history or the Latin language until 222 B.C.[35] and its meaning was "ancestors to the English and Franks." In turn, the word "English" is the generic translation for *Saxones;* that is, the singular word reflects the composite of not only the Angles, Saxons, and Jutes, but also the Frisians and the Franks.

Likewise, implied in sentence 1 by the word "exile," is the historical kernel that the vast area termed Germania, the barbaric territories outside the realm of the civilized Roman empire on the continent, was in a constant and shifting turmoil. J. N. L. Myres demonstrates the extreme complexity of the Germanic history,[36] but using oversimplification to express what the *Historia Brittonum* supposedly meant by "exile," the Angeln territory between Saxony and Jutland was being squeezed out of existence (or perhaps being assimilated), and some of the old Angelns, in an attempt to escape this pressurized absorption, fled to the island, as implied in both the Parker and Laud Chronicles, which recorded that Anglen stood as a wasteland between Jutland and Saxony. Later, these displaced Angelns headed by Hengist and Horsa, were the ones recruited by Vortigern to resist the invasions and incursions by the Picts. In sentence 3 of the above extract, John Morris compounds the ethnologic confusion by using the word Saxon rather than English, a culpability shared by several modern researchers, including Michael Winterbottom.[37]

A following section of the *Historia,* again under an incorrect, interpolated heading "The Kentish Chronicle, Part 2," ties in to sentence 3 in the above extract. Hengist recognizes Vortigern's spinelessness, barters his own daughter for territories, and then, according to Morris's translation, Hengist took counsel with the elders of Angeln to decide what the Saxons should ask of the king for the girl, and the council all agreed to ask for "the country that in their language is called Canturguoralen, in ours Kent."[38] Morris is not directly responsible here for the misidentification of Kent, but he is misleading because of his use of the term "Angeln." On the positive side, he is correctly identifying Hengist's homeland as Angeln instead of Saxony; however, the term *Insula Oghgul* is used in the Latin original, which gives an entirely different meaning to the passage. *Insula Oghgul* is an ancient term for the island of Ireland; hence, what should be conveyed is that Hengist is meeting with *Vortigern*'s council, migrants of earlier generations originally from Ireland who are now settled in Wales. The two sides bargain for territories called Canturguoralen, which some early antiquarian interpreted as Kent.

"The Kentish Chronicle, Part 3," provides the bulk of proof that Kent is an incorrect identification, focusing on Vortimer's (Vortigern's son) four major battles against the English.[39] As would have been normal, Nennius, like Gildas and Bede before him, was writing in Latin and hence used the generic term *Saxones,* which translated to "The English." Nowhere in any of the *Historia Brittonum* sections, including section 56, which recounts Arthur's twelve battles, does the manuscript use the specific word Saxon to refer to the tribes of Saxony. The more generic term "English" is used, specifically for English Saxons as opposed to German Saxons, and whenever a synonym is needed, it is translated as "heathens."

In summary, Myres relates that in a later stage of revision Bede added the three ethnological sentences about the Jutes, Saxons and Angels, an insertion which Myres felt was unfortunate because he thought it broke the thread of the narrative which contends (correctly, in Myres's view) that Hengist and Horsa were the leaders of the Kentish *foederati.* Myres also has reservations about following too closely Bede's distinction of three areas of tribal settlement in Britain. In spite of these extenuations, though, the four manuscripts still available to the modern researcher give quite an accurate picture in broad, general strokes. In an elastic sense, this reflects Thomas Charles-Edwards's observation that "the *Historia Brittonum* is in the grand tradition of early medieval history"[40]; these four discrete manuscripts give an adequate feel of Dark-Age events and circumstances.

That the *Historia Brittonum* is the single most important source available for structuring the history of the period cannot be emphasized enough. Only Gildas's and Bede's works are nearer to the fifth and sixth centuries, and although it is crucial to examine texts that are as close to the contemporary source as possible, this approach should not exempt the *Historia* on the grounds that it is further removed. Referring to a method of research which accepts only evidential testimony that is either contemporary or shown to be indisputably derived from contemporary sources, Charles-Edwards writes, "This rule seems to me to be too limited," and then explains that contemporary sources may have been be so constrained by political and social pressures that they couldn't tell the truth, "whereas a later text, being under less pressure, may be a more reliable source, even though we have no precise idea of the source from which it derived its information."[41]

As a reference, Josephus Stevenson's book is one of the most comprehensive and accurate. In his introduction, Stevenson clarifies three basic premises: that the *Historia* is ascribed to someone known as Nennius but that sometimes it is attributed to Gildas or Mark the Hermit; that the ascription to Nennius is based solely upon the two independent versions of the Prologues; and dependent upon the method of counting, that there are eighteen variants of the manuscript so that studying the *Historia* is no easy task. For the most objective analysis Stevenson has not selected those copies which contain the greatest number of additions or interpolated passages, but instead has concentrated his efforts upon those variants which have been least distorted by the interpolations.

He selects Manuscripts A and *a* as being the purest forms, thus minimizing incorrect assumptions and deductions which might have distorted the essential history. Of Manuscript *a* Stevenson writes,

> [This text] is particularly valuable, and seems to transmit the work in a purer state than it occurs in any other manuscript, especially in regard to its arrangement.[42]

This consideration expresses how badly distorted the truth can become through interpolation over the span of a millennium.

Because *The Historic King Arthur* gives a very detailed analysis of those interpolations which have distorted the historical truth for centuries, they need only enumeration here.

1. The insertion of headings within the *Historia* demonstrates the worst transgression of additions. Passing over the additions of title, contents, and ages of the world, the heading of "The Kentish Chronicle, Part I" sets up a series of headings which have lamentably been accepted as truth for eleven centuries.
    a. "The Kentish Chronicle, Part I" mistakenly identifies Hengist and Horsa as the Saxon (rather than Angle) leaders of the first *Adventus* rather than the second *Adventus,* and further errs by labeling them as *Kentish* Saxons.
    b. Following the lead of the first part, "The Kentish Chronicle, Part 2" confuses geographic locales.
        i. Tanet is misconstrued as Thanet and therefore misplaced in Kent.
        ii. "Insula Oghgul" is incorrectly translated as "Angeln," leading to the false assumption that Hengist is consulting his own council rather than Vortigern's Council of Elders.

iii. Guoyrancgono is listed as the deposed *Kentish* king but his name is obviously Welsh.

iv. Chapter 38 also provides a clue that Kent cannot be the proper setting. Hengist invited his son Octha into Britain to fight the *Scotti,* the **Irish**, who during this period were localized in Wales and the northwestern midlands. As mentioned, too, in Chapter 31, Vortigern feared attacks from the Picts and the Irish, and as a consequence, he hired the mercenary English Saxons to stave off those attacks. Raids from those barbaric tribes definitely would **not** have been farther south than the Dobunni/ Catavellauni/ Trinovantes provinces, or farther east than the Coritani kingdom.

v. Octha is sent "to the north," wrongly assumed to be Wall near Hadrian's Wall rather than Wall near Lichfield in the center of the Cornovii territories.

vi. Hengist's tribe migrates to the "regionem Cantorum," once more identified as Kent rather than the section of the Midlands which was once a part of Wales.

c. "The Kentish Chronicle, Part 3" continues the erroneous connection to the southeastern part of the island.

i. Vortimer's battle against the *Saxones* at Derguentid is set at Darenth in Kent rather than at Derventio in the Cornovii territories.

ii. Another of Vortimer's battles—by the *Lapidem Tituli* which is on the shore of the *Gallici maris*—gives two clues which cannot be overlooked. There are no "Inscribed Stones" in Kent, which leads to the obvious error that the "Gallic Sea" should have been translated as the *Gaelic* Sea. Alcock verifies this in reference to a Roman element in the ancestry of Group I inscribed stones when he writes that "their overwhelming distribution pattern is *away from the lowland heart of Roman Britain, and lies instead in the Irish Sea zone.* [italics mine][43]

iii. Still another of Vortimer's battles was fought at *Ruithod,* which can't possibly be translated as Episford in Kent. It is much more like a referent to the modern-day Ruthin and hence associated with the boundaries of the Hyrpe territories in Wales.

2. The heading of "The Campaigns of Arthur" falls into a hazy space between the alleged Kentish Chronicles and the so-called Northern Histories.

i. Once again, there is an inaccurate reference that the kings of the Kentishmen have sprung from the Angles Hengist, Horsa, and Octha, even though the Kentish kings come from the *Jutes,* according to *The Anglo-Saxon Chronicle.*

ii. Based upon chronological calibrations, rather than Octha coming down from the north after Hengist's death as recorded in the introduction to Chapter 56, it should read that Octha came down from the north after *Horsa's* death.

3. As a type of epilogue to the interpolated heading of "The Northern History, Part 1," another misleading heading ("Southern English Genealogies: The Genealogy of the Kings of Kent") introduces Chapter 58, once again erroneously directing the readers' attention back to the southeastern part of the island. Stevenson, however, explains in a footnote that "These titles are added in [Manuscript] A by a later hand, and are not found in the other MSS."[44]

Resolutions

In summary, if an individual takes the time to explicate the *Historia Brittonum* by very careful reading and objective analysis, just this single source will open the doors for proper explications and enlightening verifications in the other ancient manuscripts. As a cohesive whole, they provide the chronological framework which not only confers a historical reality upon Arthur, but sets geographic limitations. At one point Leslie Alcock wrote that "It would be interesting to know whereabouts these Saxons and Picts were marauding in 428-9."[45] Peter Hunter Blair's curiosity shifts in time about sixty years when he ponders, "Nothing could contribute so greatly to a better understanding of the Anglo-Saxon invasions than exact knowledge about the site, date, and consequences of this British victory."[46] Similar to Alcock but perhaps with more optimism, Blair expresses more faith in finding answers for the myriads of questions about this era in British history during which the *Saxones* (the broad, generic term) began a long, slow, occupations which spanned over three centuries.

Though the amount of information covering the Arthurian century from approximately 420 to 520 seems depressingly meager, Blair points to a host of resources which can be tapped. Once again, like Alcock, he has great faith in innovative reinterpretations of the old material, especially in light of continual archaeological finds. He doesn't minimize the value of early manuscripts or their trustworthy copies, and in addition to these sources, he points to the Easter Tables, chronologies, hagiographies, regnal lists, charters, codes of law, and oral tradition, the latter being decried by purists. Upon reflection, there is, then, more evidence than at first assumed. The resources which are available must be carefully and minutely contemplated, and Blair sets up a series of procedural steps—perhaps more accurately described as rhetorical questions—outlining a way to understanding the history of the period through the available information.

To arrive at a comprehensive narrative, he asks eight questions which must be resolved: 1) who was "the proud tyrant," 2) when did he live, 3) where in the "eastern part of the island" were the first Saxons settled, 4) who was Ambrosius Aurelianus, 5) where was Mons Badonicus, 6) what was the date of the battle fought there, 7) what was its outcome, and 8) how long-lasting was the age of peace which followed the battle of Mons Badonicus.[47] The essence of each question is crucial, but each needs modification or augmentation. Revised, they focus upon these aspects:

1. Who are the actual historical figures represented by all the epithets provided by the sources, specifically
   a. superbus tyrannus
   b. Vortigern
   c. Vortimer
   d. Arthurex
2. When did these four people live, and can they be chronologically pinpointed as contemporaries or overlapping a successive generation?
3. What were the interrelationships of these people?
4. Where was the homeland for the *orientalis sacrilegorum?*
5. Who was Ambrosius Aurelianus?
6. Where was the Battle of Mount Badon fought?
7. What was the date of the battle fought there?
8. What was the outcome and the effects of that outcome?
9. How long-lasting was the age of peace which followed the Battle of Badon?

Question 5 can be eliminated because it links to Question 1-d, and Questions 8 and 9 ask basically the same thing. A cursory examination also shows that this text and its predecessor, *The Historic King Arthur,* not only answer these questions but document the logistics underlying the judgments.

1. Who are the actual historical figures represented by all the epithets provided by the sources, specifically
   a. superbus tyrannus—the Roman emperor of the Western Empire, Valentinian III.
   b. Vortigern—Æternus, a Roman controlling the northern domains of the Empire on the island.
   c. Vortimer—Cunedda, son of Æternus.
   d. Arthurex—Ambrosius Aurelianus, High King of Britain after Æternus's reign.

Gildas wrote of a supreme ruler, a Roman emperor ruling over Britain as a part of the entire Western Roman Empire, whose common policy was to employ mercenaries to protect the Empire. Æternus was one of the individuals under his command to help carry out those policies. Gildas doesn't directly state, infer, imply, or suggest that the *superbus tyrannus* is a Briton, nor that the *superbus tyrannus* is living on (or ruling from) Britain.

Several centuries after Gildas's time, Bede identified the *superbus tyrannus* by using another epithet, "Vortigern," and thus set up an underling Roman commander in Britain as the scapegoat responsible for all the evils that engulfed Britain. When the majority of legions withdrew from Britain to protect the Empire's holdings on the mainland, Æternus, left behind as a commander of the local mercenary tribes, became known as Vortigern, or the Overking of those tribes he controlled. As a Roman he was still expected to carry out Roman policy in an attempt to maintain the borders of the Roman holdings in Britain. Vortigern's sons were expected to conform to and carry out those mandates as set forth not only by the temporarily absent Roman commanders, but by their father.

As the situation deteriorated in Britain and it became clear that the Roman withdrawal might not be just temporary, Vortigern began losing control of his mercenary army. In spite of this he remained loyal to the alliance, but his son drifted away, aware of impending catastrophe for his country if the mercenary allies were not kept in check. The *Scotti* were infringing upon the western coast of Wales and the southwestern borders of the Brigantian territory, plus the Picts were putting greater pressure upon the northern boundaries. When the alliance with the *Saxones* broke out into open rebellion, Vortimer was able to crush the uprising and drive the traitorous rebels back to their homelands.

Unfortunately, shortly afterward, Vortimer either died or was killed, and Vortigern reassumed command. The older king still felt ties to the *Saxones* and hoped to mend the split alliance. His grandsons, no longer able to look to their father for a united effort against the jealous sub-kings who wanted to snatch the land, selected what seemed to be the only option left: join forces with their grandfather and try to salvage what kingdoms they could from the Picts, the *Scotti,* and the infiltrators from the mainland. Once the Council of the Province was slaughtered, chaos reigned, and it was basically every man or tribe on his own It was a period of son warring against father, comrade turning against comrade, and loyalty or allegiance a whim of the day.

2. When did these four people live, and can they be chronologically pinpointed as contemporaries or overlapping a successive generation?

The process of establishing the island as a kingdom independent of Roman rule and free of invasions from all sides was a slow and laborious one.

The movement of legions from Britain began in second decade of the fifth century and continued for almost a century. Vortigern ruled for almost three decades, interspersed with the short interim reign by Vortimer. Pleas to the Romans during the fourth decade failed. The Saxon Revolt took a heavy toll, and there were back-and-forth victories and defeats.

3. What were the interrelationships of these people?

Tacitus, Paternus, and Æternus were Romans by heritage, and therefore Cunedda, the Vortimer of the northern tribes, assimilated their beliefs, ideals, traits, and thinking patterns. His sons conquered and pacified segments of Wales and the eastern midlands, and one in particular—Cerdic—became a king more powerful than the rest, and hence his kingdoms expanded as far as the south-central coast. His objectives and aims were different from those of Ambrosius, the Arthurex with Roman leanings who survived the holocaust and tried to unite Britain. Through sheer force, or sometimes by crafty subterfuge, Cerdic remained a prominent figure not only in insular history, but in continental chronicles. Both Cerdic's son Creoda and his grandson Cynric established kingdoms for themselves, and when the wars required that the dynasty seek aid from across their shores, Cynric called upon his son Ceawlin, who thus established himself as the second Bretwalda—the first Bretwalda from the West-Saxon house.

4. Where was the homeland for the *orientalis sacrilegorum?*

To correctly interpret certain segments of history, it becomes necessary to "compartmentalize" not only certain events but also specific ethnic distinctions. Once that is done, the histories of the period become amazingly accurate, supported by all the other facets of information, including oral tradition. The difficulties of compiling an accurate history arose because the ancient historians and antiquarians misinterpreted parts of what they read, and the modern historians perpetuated the misinterpretations.

The Anglo-Saxon Chronicle is a prime example of misinterpretation. The hyphenated word runs off the tongue with ease, and the idea behind the word has become so vague that most people—not even professional philologists or etymologists—explain it in enough detail. British history has especially allowed too much emphasis on the word "Saxon," and conversely in an inadvertent, deleterious way, ignore the "Anglo" part, thus creating subtle and unwarranted interpretations. Latin itself, as it was used on the island, is one of the contributing culprits, since it collectively classified the Angles, Saxons, Jutes, and Frisians as *Saxones.* As a clarification, reference to this particular chronicle—as it applies to British history at least—should be titled more accurately "The Angle and the Saxon Chronicle." When considering the history of Britain as related by Gildas Badonicus and Nennius, the mandatory emphasis for the Arthurian age must be upon what the *Angles'* role was in British history, not the *Saxons'* role. The *De excidio* and the *Historia Brittonum* focus upon the *Angles* as Roman mercenaries in the midlands just east of Wales, not upon the *Saxons* as mercenaries of Kent.

In Entries 443, 444, and 449 of the Parker/Laud Chronicles, *The Anglo-Saxon Chronicle* specifically lists Hengist and his offspring as *Angles,* not Saxons, but since time immemorial Hengist and his kinsmen have been labeled as Saxons, and hence erroneously placed in the kingdom of Kent. At one point the *ASC* relates that "[The Britons] sent to the *Angles* and made the request [for aid] to the princes of the *Angles.*"[48] Entry 448 narrates that "At that time [of Marcian and Valentinian] *Angles* came to this land [Britain], invited by king Vortigern, to help him overcome his enemies," and Entry 449 is similar in recounting that "In their days Vortigern invited the *Angles* hither, and they then came hither to Britain in three ships."[49]

What seems evident as common knowledge is that the Great Island was known as Albion, and in more modern times a segment of it became England, a cognate of Angleland or Engleland, with Britain once more used as a generic term referring to all of the United Kingdom. As Blair points out in the early histories, the East Saxons, the South Saxons, and the West Saxons were derived from the Old Saxons, stemming from the Old English as a cognate of *Seaxe.* The kingdoms which sprang from these settlements were Essex, Sussex, and Wessex, which dominated the south-central and southeastern coast. Conversely, the Roman territories in Britain settled by the Angles were parts of Iceni, Trinovantes, Coritani, Catavellauni, and Parisii, later becoming East Anglia, Mercia, and Lindsey. Just as Hengist, Horsa, and Octha should be translocated to regions *east* of the old Cornovii territories, so should Ælle's kingdom be associated with *Suthanhymbre,* the lands of the *Angles* south of the River Humber. Because Ælle was not a South Saxon, he must *not* be associated with Sussex. He fights battles at Cymenesora and Mearcrædesburna, and although these sites cannot be precisely pinpointed, the cognate of the first is Cumbrian and the second is Mercian, both which are borderlands of Cornovii. Ælle, therefore, is a South Angle and should be associated with the eastern midlands.

This comes full circle in answering the fourth question proposed by Blair: "Where was the homeland for the *orientalis sacrilegorum?*" The *Angles* (a more specific term than *Saxones)* were allowed to settle on lands in the *east* (not the south or the southeast) of the island by the *superbus tyrannus* (not necessarily Vortigern) in return for aid against the Picts and the *Scotti.* These enemies were viewed as plunderers, not invaders seeking to settle on the land, which is why they return *home* (to their lands in the east of the island and not on the continent across the sea). However, once the Romans began their evacuation and there was no authority separating the "westerners" from the "easterners," there was a scramble to conquer and settle the land. Civil wars continually erupted and when the *westerners* (the Welsh) scored a major victory, the *impious easterners* (the Angles) sought help from the German kings (Angelns).

5. Where was the Battle of Mount Badon fought?

As documented in *The Historic King Arthur,* of the several possible sites based upon the word "Badbury" and several different possibilities based upon the word "Bathon," a host of collective clues point to the Wrekin hillfort and the baths at Wroxeter on the borderlands of Wales as the correct site. This selection was based upon:

a. its cognation with the word "Baddon";

Several contenders based upon the word "Badbury" have traditionally been proposed for the site of the Battle of Baddon, the most notable being Badbury Rings and Liddington Hill. However, because of the Welsh cognition of the word "Baddon"—the doubled 'd' being a voiced "th-" sound producing the word "Bathon"—the most common contender has traditionally been Aquae Sulis. Closer scrutiny, though, points to Wroxeter because of

b. its proximity to the River Severn;

Because Aquae Sulis is located approximately twenty miles from the Mouth of the Severn, the site at Wroxeter is more logical, since the walls of that city actually touched the banks of the River Severn and there was easy access to the river itself for military, commercial or defensive purposes.

c. the fordability of the river at that spot;

Based upon the same rationale, any movement from southern Wales directly toward Aquae Sulis (or vice-versa) would be impossible because of the width and depth of the River Severn at that point. Conversely, near Wroxeter there were two fording places, one near Wroxeter itself and the other at Buildwas.

d. its prominence as a site of Roman baths paralleling or even exceeding the ones at Aquae Sulis;

Although the baths at Aquae Sulis have been better preserved over the centuries, the ones at Wroxeter would have been just as impressive. More important, however, the access to the baths at Aquae Sulis was limited; that is, it was more of a spa and religious site than a center for everyday use. Also, it was not known as "Bath" until the 700s, over two centuries past Arthur's time, and because it was in a settled civil district, it would not have been tactically significant from a military viewpoint, as Wroxeter would have been.

e. its adjacency to the Wrekin, a hill fort;

Aquae Sulis fits the condition of baths being adjacent to a tor (the condition doesn't stipulate a hill fort), yet Wroxeter not only meets but exceeds those conditions. There has been a great deal of archaeological activity not only at Wroxeter, but also at the Wrekin. Ivan Lapper has done a spectacular job of replicating the city of Wroxeter, depicting street scenes near the Market Hall and reconstructions of the interior of the Exercise Hall at the baths; he also re-creates the exterior of the Exercise Hall as it may have appeared in the fifth century (during Arthur's era) after the baths had gone out of use. Graham Webster and Philip Barker have given a comprehensive history based upon their archaeological finds, including the revival of the area.

They write that the rebuilding might have been carried out by a local chieftain who emerged from the chaos of the fifth century. Although the dates are not specific or certain, they contend that "The long sequence of buildings can hardly be fitted into the fourth century and is likely to have lasted well into, if not to the end of, the fifth."[50] They also point out that the Roman Empire selected groups of the barbarian tribes to settle on frontier lands on the condition that they acted as the defenders to prevent other barbarians from crossing Roman frontiers, which explains the Germanic settlers in Essex and East Anglia who "could have been allowed to settle there to protect the approaches to London and the South Midlands."[51]

f. its location in the western midlands;

Because the Cornovii territory was heavily occupied by the Roman military, it originally acted as a buffer zone between the Welsh on the west and the Anglians and Mercians on the east. Once the legions withdrew from the area, the Cornovii territories became a prime target for invasion and conflict between the two factions.

g. its strategic importance in regard to resources and defensibility;

This vast area was literally and figuratively the core of Britain. Although it might not be considered the cultural heartland, it was the hub of military strategy. Foss Way and Watling Street intersected near the core of this territory, giving access to the entire Roman empire in Britain. Only thirty miles northwest was another main intersection of Ryknild Street and the continuation of Watling street at Wall-by-Lichfield, the location of a major way-station and site of Octha's settlement. Coupled with the maze of Roman roads, the navigable rivers of Severn, Trent, Upper Thames, and Derwent allowed ingress to every segment of the territory. As pointed out earlier in this text, the number of legionary fortresses, vexillation fortresses, regular forts, and fortlets emphasizes the importance of this area in maintaining the security of Britain. The *colonia* of Glevuum was on the southwestern border; Ratae, Wroxeter, and Corinium were tribal cities dotting the area; there were over a dozen large towns in the province; Letocetum, Uxacona, Pennocrucium, Tripotium, and Bannaventa were *burghis* in the region; the three major settlements were at Mediolanum, Duston, and Magiovinium; there were numerous tile and pottery kilns, three iron mines, two lead mines, a stone quarry, a copper mine, and, at Aquae Arnementiae, a spa. From Magnis in the southwest and Magionivium in the southeast to Mediolanum in the northwest to Causinnis in the northeast, there were no fewer than seventeen villas. And last, to stress the importance of the area, within a radius of twelve toises (one Roman mile measured 1480 meters) from Irchester, there are too many Roman artifacts to enumerate.

6. What was the date of the battle fought there?

Based mainly upon Alcock's variables of chronological calibration but considering the two-year discrepancy between Alcock's and Morris's point of reckoning, the date calculated in *The Historic King Arthur* was a lunar adaptation pointing to 497.

7. What was the outcome and the effects of that outcome?

The ramifications are so far-reaching and profoundly intricate that no single volume—and indeed probably no series—could answer a question of such magnitude. Although my inquiry historically focused upon a span of only one century, the consequences of events and outcomes reverberated throughout the millennium and no doubt still continues its wave-effect. The Britons/Welsh won the battle, but the conflicts persisted, not only with the Picts, *Scotti,* and *Saxones,* but also with the Danes, Vikings, Norwegians, Normans, and others.

8. How long-lasting was the age of peace which followed the Battle of Badon?

Limited to just the Arthurian influence, the period between the Battle of Badon and the Battle of Camlann in which Arthur was killed was twenty-one years. Arthur was summoned from human activity in 518.

History is analogous to a hurricane; although the vortex creates a false sense of peace and security, the raging storm indiscriminately destroys everything in its path. During the first century, when Rome invaded the Isle of Albion, the legions of the Apocalypse wrought death and destruction wherever they trod. After the massacre of Boudicca and her rebellious army, the subdued tribes bowed to an uneasy peace. By the end of the second century, when the island was relatively secured, the storm had seemingly passed; several decades of prosperity, civilized amenities, and shelter under Rome's powerful military allowed the Britons a respite from fear and deprivation. The possibility that such a powerful empire could crack was unthinkable; it was beyond reality. Yet the storm thundered again in all its fury when the Romans withdrew from Britain.

Arthur was enmeshed in such a situation. Had he been born in the eye of the storm a century and a half earlier, he undoubtedly would have been recorded in *Roman* history. But the vortex of the storm had passed, and Arthur was destined to be recorded in a history much more obscured for succeeding generations. He lived during a time of rapid and often violent change. With barbarism pressing in on all sides, his parents killed in the misfortunes of war, and his country on the brink of annihilation, this king, a lone beacon of hope, optimism, and confidence, deflected catastrophe for approximately half a century. He seemingly lost in the end anyway, but the succeeding generations who can judge him deny that. Arthur has managed to survive into the twenty-first century, and he has done it because of all those persevering qualities which are honorable, truthful and just.

Appendix A: A Century and a Half of Dark-Age History

Date	Event	Comments
	The three-generational ancestral line immediately preceding Cunedda—Tacitus, Paternus, and Æternus—bore Roman names.	Of the three, Paternus acquired the title "Of the Red Robes," a mark of some kind of Romanized authority or office, meaning it would be logical to link his migration to the vacuum of authority left by Magnus Maximus's campaign in Gaul. (*History of Wales*, p. 51, J. Davies.)
	If Paternus is equated with the epithet Magnus Maximus as the evidence suggests, then Æternus would be equated with Vortigern the Over-King, and his son, Brydw, known most commonly as Cunedda but recorded as Vortimer the Over-Prince in the *Historia Brittonum*, would be Æternus's son as the Welsh genealogies proclaim.	Phrase 8 of the inscription on Eliseg's Pillar would therefore have to be interpreted that Paternus/Maximus had a son named Æternus/Vortigern and a daughter named Severa, accounting for the incestuous brother/sister relationship between Severa and Vortigern. (Phrase 8, "The Pillar of Eliseg," *Valle Crucis Abbey*, p. 48, J. Knight.)
		A variation is recorded in the *Historia Brittonum* as a father/daughter relationship between Vortigern and Severa. (*Nennii: Historia Britonum*, Chapter 39, Josephus Stevenson, p. 30.)
		Brydw/Cunedda/Vortimer was the offspring born of that relationship.

Date	Event	Comments
		(Phrase 8, "The Pillar of Eliseg," *Valle Crucis Abbey*, p. 48, J. Knight.)
383–388	Maelgwyn's ancestors—namely Tacitus and perhaps his son Paternus/Maximus—returned from the Manau Gododdin 146 years before Maelgywn reigned.	(*N:HB*, Chapter 62, p. 52, J. Stevenson.)
409–410	At this time, because the strength of the Romans was weakened in the five Britains, the Britons were ravaged by an incursion of *Saxones*. (The beginning of Roman abandonment.)	(*Chronica Gallica a CCCCLII.*) Year I of Theodosius II. *Hac tempestate prae valentudine Romanorum vires funditus attenuatae Britanniae Saxonum incursione devastatae.*
413–415	Birth of Hengist	Floruit: 428–458 Life span: 413–473
422	Birth of Ambrosius Aurelianus. His father, more commonly known as Utherpendragon, head of the Dragon clan, was Constantius III, who was appointed co-emperor of the West by Honorius. His mother was Ygerna, of Welsh royalty, who became Constantius's concubine when the co-emperor took command in Britain after he re-secured Gaul for Honorius. The logistics of this union explains information which was recorded in the Welsh chronicles at the turn of the millennium: Cador (father = Gorlois/mother = Ygerna) is listed as Ambrosius' half-brother (father = Constantius III/mother = Ygerna).	The discord between Ambrosius and Vitalinus, 437 minus 15, Arthur's age at coronation = 422. Throughout the centuries many names and epithets will come to be associated with Ambrosius, particularly "Riothamus" and "Arthur," suggesting an accurate title of Arthurex Ambrosius or Riardd Ambrosius. (*N: HB*, Chapter 66, p. 55, J. Stevenson.)
425	Because of Rome's inexorable withdrawal, two rival factions struggle for insular supremacy, causing internecine warfare which lasts not just four decades, but for a hundred years.	(*N: HB*, Chapter 31, pp. 23–24, J. Stevenson.) (*ASC*, Entry 423, pp. 10–11, G. N. Garmonsway.)
	One coalition embraced the legacy left by the Romans, and hence	(*DE*, Chapters 22, 23, p. 26, M. Winterbottom.)

Date	Event	Comments
425 (*cont.*)	acquired the appellation of *Romanitas*, whose leader, Ambrosius Aurelianus, survived the devastation and emerged as a successor by virtue of his heritage to rightfully claim the title of king.	
	The opposing confederation, led by Æternus who became known as Vortigern the Over-King, sought to build a new Britain independent of Roman influence.	
	Because of Ambrosius's youthfulness and the fear for his safety, he is taken to Brittany and Vortigern assumes the kingship.	(*N: HB*, Chapters 31, 36, pp. 23, 27, J. Stevenson.) (*N: HB*, Chapters 40, 41, 42, pp. 30–34, J. Stevenson.) (*HKB*, pp. 151, 155, 158, L. Thorpe.)
428	Saxon *Adventus* One. The emperor of the Western Roman Empire—not Æternus the Over-King as mistakenly interpreted—invokes a typical Roman policy and solicits Saxon help to defend the island from the Picts and the Irish.	(*DE*, Chapters 23.3–24, pp. 26–27, M. Winterbottom.) Valentinian III is the Roman Emperor of the West, but because he was a child, his mother (Galla Placidia) actually ruled.
434–435	Ambrosius, son of a Roman *consulibus*, has an encounter with Vortigern and his wizards. Vortigern gives the boy Emrys the kingdoms of western Britain and flees to the north of Wales.	(*N: HB*, Chapters 40–41, pp. 30–31, J. Stevenson.) The story of Emrys in the *HB* gives rise to Monmouth's coining the name of Ambrosius Merlinus, subsequently dropping the name of Ambrosius and creating the birth of a new character in Arthurian romances, thus adding another epithet to Riardd Ambrosius.
437	The quarrel between Vitalinus and Ambrosius. Although this passage is traditionally interpreted as warfare between Vitalinus as a representative of Vortigern and Ambrosius, both Vitalinus and Ambrosius as representatives of *Romanitas* and are opposed to Vortigern as a usurper.	(*N: HB*, Chapter 66, p. 55, J. Stevenson.)

Date	Event	Comments
437 (*cont.*)	Although Ambrosius is named king, instead of ascending to the throne in place of Æternus the Over-King, the young boy takes refuge in Brittany; Vitalinus (Guithelinus) as the guardian of Ambrosius convinces him to cross the Channel so that he will not be assassinated.	(*HKB*, Part Four, The House of Constantine, pp. 186–187, L. Thorpe.)
	Birth of Octha	Floruit: 452–482 Life span: 437–497
440–450	Brydw's/Cunedda's/Vortimer's ancestors, Paternus of the Red Robes and Æternus, who became the Over-King, migrated from the Manau Gododdin to what became Wales 146 years before the beginning of Maelgwyn's reign.	(*N: HB*, Chapters 14 and 62, pp. 11, 52, J. Stevenson.)
	But Brydw's/Cunedda's/Vortimer's involvement in warfare against the *Scotti* and the *Saxones* did not commence until the 440s to 450s.	(*AB*, p. 128, L. Alcock.) ("From Gododdin to Gwynedd: reflections on the story of Cunedda," *Studia Celtica*, XXIV/XXV, ftnts 6, 39, R. G. Gruffydd.) (*SSWM*, p. 7, M. L. Jones.)
442	The Saxon Revolt should more accurately be labeled as the Welsh Revolt against the encroaching Saxons.	(*Chronica Gallica a. CCCCLII.*) Year XVIIII of Theodosius after the death of Honorius: Death of Honorius Flavius, 423 + 19 = 442. *Brittanie usque ad hoc tempus variis cladibus eventibusque la[cera]tae in dicionem Saxonum rediguntur.)*
	Saxon *Adventus* Two: the second major coming of the Saxons is commanded by Hengist and Horsa.	(*Chronica Gallica a. DXI: XVI.*) *Britanniae a Romanis Amissae in dicionem Saxonum cedunt.* (*DE*, Chapters 23–24, pp. 26, 27, M. Winterbottom.)
446	The plea to Aëtius for help.	(*DE*: Chapter 20, ms V, Polydore Vergil.) (*ASC:* Entry 443, Parker/Laud Chronicle.)
		The plea for Roman intercession is based upon the conflicts between *Romanitas* and *Barbaria,* not between Ancient Britons and invading German Saxons. This

Date	Event	Comments
446 (*cont.*)		dispute links Arthur's name to Octha in the later decades.
447–457	Brydw/Cunedda as Vortimer begins intense warfare against the *Saxones*. For some unexplicable reason, Vortimer's reign splits that of Vortigern's, and Vortimer fights four pitched battles against the impious easterners.	(*N: HB*, Chapters 43, 44, pp. 34, 35, J. Stevenson.)
449	Saxon *Adventus* Three: Hengist and Horsa returned in force for Vortigern was their friend and because his wife Rowena was Hengist's daughter.	(*ASC*: Entry 449, pp. 12, 13, G. N. Garmonsway.) (*DE*: Chapter 23.5, pp. 26–27, M. Winterbottom.) (*N: HB*, Chapter 45, p. 36, J. Stevenson.)
450	The birth of Cerdic, fifth son of Cunedda, who plays a major role in this era, including being an interpreter for Vortigern and becoming a king of the West Saxons in his later life.	Floruit: 465–495 Life span: 450–510
	Octha, Cerdic, and Riardd Ambrosius become friends and later comrades with Briton salvation as a common cause. The relationship deteriorates into a powerful rivalry when Cerdic switches allegiance and sides with Octha, becoming a West Saxon leader. Their rivalry continues to the Battle of Badon when Octha is killed and culminates at the Battle of Camlann where Cerdic and Riardd both die.	(*The Mabinogion*, "How Culhwch Won Olwen," pp. 144–145, 174, J. Gantz.) (*The Mabinogion*, "The Dream of Rhonobwy," pp. 183, 190–191, J. Gantz.) (*HKB*, p. 261, L. Thorpe.)
451	Aëtius's last great Roman victory over Attila and the Huns near Chalons-sur-Marne.	
455	In this year Hengist and Horsa fought against Vortimer (mistakenly listed in the *Anglo-Saxon Chronicle* as Vortigern), and his brother Horsa was killed there. Brydw/Cunedda/Vortimer is the Welsh leader in this second battle,	(*ASC*, Entry 455, pp. 12, 13, G. N. Garmonsway.) (*N: HB*, Chapter 44, pp. 34–35, J. Stevenson.)

Date	Event	Comments
455 (*cont.*)	and in addition to Horsa, Catigern is also killed.	
	Octha comes down from the north.	(*N: HB*, Chapter 56, pp. 47–48, J. Stevenson.)
	Hengist and his son Octha succeeded to the kingdom and jointly rule until 473.	(*ASC:* Entry 455, p. 12, G. N. Garmonsway.)
456–458	In this interim, Brydw/Cunedda/Vortimer has two more intense conflicts with the *Saxones*, the third in the open country near the Inscribed Stone, and the fourth at a place called Tanet. This talented military tactician then disappears from insular history.	(*N: HB*, Chapter 44, pp. 34–36, J. Stevenson.)
457		Leo I becomes Emperor of the East.
458	Hengist massacres Vortigern's council. Essex, Sussex, Middlesex, and other districts are ceded to Hengist as part of Vortigern's ransom.	(*N: HB*, Chapter 46, pp. 37–38, J. Stevenson.)
459–460	The second migration to Brittany. Some survivors of the internal struggles made for lands beyond the sea; others held out, though not without fear, in their own land.	(*DE:* Chapter 25.1–2, pp. 27–28, M. Winterbottom.)
460–461	The victories of Ambrosius Aurelianus	(*DE:* Chapters 25.3, 26.1, p. 28, M. Winterbottom.) (*N: HB*, Chapter 48, pp. 30–31, J. Stevenson.)
	In the eleventh year of Cerdic, Arthur (i.e., Ambrosius Aurelianus) began to rule over the Britons.	(*CsAGE,* Ch. XXXII, p. 73, J. Carley.)
467	Anthemius appointed Emperor of the West by Leo I.	(Jordanes, *Gothic History.*)
469–470	Riothamus and the Battle of Angers: Odovacer and the Saxons	(Gregory of Tours, *Historia Francorum.*)

Date	Event	Comments
469–470 (*cont.*)	came to Angers, and when Odovacer reached the city, Childeric, King of the Franks, arrived the next day and took the city. The *Saxones* and Romans then fought each other. The *Saxones* turned tail and many of them fell to the Roman pursuit.	
	Sidonius's letter to Riothamus, Riardd Ambrosius.	(*Sidonius: Poems and Letters.*)
	Euric the Visigoth after a long fight routed Riotimus, king of the Britons, before the Romans could join him. The Britons were expelled from Bourg-de-Déols, and when Riotimus had lost a great part of his army, he fled to the Burgundians, a neighboring tribe allied to the Romans. Riothamus's disappearance into friendly territory gives rise to the resurrection/regeneration motif. When he resurfaces again in Britain as Arthur, another epithet attaches itself to Ambrosius Aurelianus.	(Jordanes: *Gothic History.*) (Gregory of Tours: *Historia Francorum.*) During the period of time before Ægidius's death, he and his son Syagrius are strong in Gaul, while Euric is dealing with internal struggles, which means that the Visigoths were not threatening invasions until the later half of the decade. After Ægidius's death during the great plague, Syagrius assumed the kingship and continued, with Rhiardd as an ally, the battles against the *Saxones* and Visigoths.
473	In this year Hengist and Octha fought against the Welsh	(*ASC*, Entry 473, pp. 14, 15, G. N. Garmonsway.)
	In this year Hengist died.	Last mention of Hengist: *ASC* Entry 473.
	In this year Octha became sole successor to the kingdom and reigned for twenty-four years.	Emendation of 488 to 473 in *ASC:* Æsc entry in the middle of South Saxon kingships.
475	The year traditionally set for Arthur's rise to the throne, ostensibly because this year occurs fifteen years after Ambrosius's victory, and legends tell of Arthur's being coronated at fifteen.	Ambrosius Aurelianus's victory and last mention in history: 460 + Arthur's age of 15 at succession = 475.
		This is the year when the epithet "Arthur" is coined, referring to the regeneration of Riothamus on the island after his defeat on the continent: Ambrosius Aurelianus becomes first Riothamus and then Arthur.

Date	Event	Comments
477	This is the year in which Ælle, the first Bretwalda, is invited into Britain from Germany by Octha and Cerdic to fight against the Welsh.	(*N: HB*, end of C. 56, p. 49, J. Stevenson.) (*ASC*, Entry 477, pp. 14, 15, G. N. Garmonsway.)
494–495	In this year Cerdic and his son [Creoda] landed at Cerdicesora with five ships and fought against the Welsh.	(Genealogical Preface of *ASC:* separate document in ms Ā: A.D. 494.) (*ASC*, Entry 495, pp. 14, 15, G. N. Garmonsway.)
	Cerdic, who has treacherously sided with the English *Saxones* and challenged Arthurex Ambrosius/Riardd Ambrosius, is the son of Welsh-born Brydw/Cunedda/Vortimer .	
497	Battle of Badon: Viroconium: Riardd Ambrosius fought against Octha and Cerdic at the Wrekin and Octha is killed there. Cerdic is granted amnesty and given the territory of West Saxon.	(*Annales Cambriae* in *British History*. Entry 516 minus nineteen years lunar adjustment = 497, p. 45, J. Morris.) (*De Excidio:* penning the ms., 541 minus 44 = 497.) (*ASC*: equated with entry 495, Cerdic's battle against the Welsh.)
	Birth of Gildas.	(*De Excidio:* penning the ms., 541 minus 44 = 497.)
	Death of Octha, reign of twenty-four years. Octha's twenty-four reign: 473 plus 24 = 497.	(*ASC:* Parker Chronicle, 473 = last entry for Hengist, implying his death, Octha's second succession.) ("HCWO" in *The Mabinogion*, Osla Big Knife is Arthur's comrade.) ("DOR" in *The Mabinogion*, Osla Big Knife fights against Arthur at Badon.) (*N: HB,* Octha involved in all twelve of Arthur's campaigns.) (*HOKB*, Octa and Chedric are companions in Britain.)
500	Six years after Cerdic and his son Creoda landed, they acquired the land of Wessex (Hampshire and Somerset) which become part of Cerdic's West Saxon kingdom in Wales and the midlands.	(Genealogical Preface: separate document ms Ā: 500.) (Ætherweard: CÆ: Entry 500.) (*CsAGE,* Ch. XXXIII, p. 73, J. Carley.)

Date	Event	Comments
508+	In this year Cerdic and his son Creoda kill a Welsh king and five thousand men with him.	(*ASC*, Entry 508, pp. 14, 15, G. N. Garmonsway.) (*N: HB*, Chapter 56, p. 48, J. Stevenson.)
	Cerdic evidently breaks his fealty with Riardd Ambrosius, and when routed a second time, the *Saxones*, with reinforcements from the continent, began a new series of incursions in the typical pattern.	
516–519	The Battle of Camlann: Charford?/Caman Llan?	(*AC:* Entry 537 minus 19 years lunar adjustment = 518.)
	Death of Riardd Ambrosius [Arthur].	(*AC:* Entry 537 minus 19 years lunar adjustment = 518.)
	Death of Cerdic.	Genealogical Preface: Entry 500 + Cerdic's reign of 16 years = 516. (*ASC:* Entry 534 minus Creoda's reign of 18 years = 516.)
	Cerdic and Creoda obtained the kingdom and from that day on the West Saxons have reigned.	(*ASC:* Entry 519.)
534	In this year [Creoda], son of Cerdic, died.	(*ASC:* emendation of Entry 534 and insertion of lost generation; Creoda inherits kingdom in 516 + reign of 18 years = 534.)
	Cynric succeeded to the kingdom and ruled for twenty-six years.	(*ASC:* Entry 534, Parker and Laud chronicles.)
541	Gildas writes the *DE*.	
560–61	In this year Cynric died and Ceawlin, the second Bretwalda, succeeded to the kingdom in Wessex.	(Genealogical Preface.) (*ASC:* Entry 560.)

Appendix B: Two Tales of *The Mabinogion*

Very close chronologically to Monmouth's work are the pre-romance bardic tales of *The Mabinogion*. These stories, like the Monmouth manuscript, are balanced between history and fiction. *The Mabinogion* has two tales directly related to the historic Arthur. From them an incredible framework can be constructed giving bits and pieces about Arthur's ancestry, comrades, and enemies; about the chronology of events in post–Roman Britain and the circumstances leading up to civil war and continental encroachment; about geographic probabilities which belie an explanation by pointing to a fanciful imagination; about other authentic figures in Arthur's milieu; and finally about the evolutionary process of molding history into legends and romances of the later centuries. Monmouth, too, surprisingly expands Arthurian data provided by the *Historia Brittonum* from a mere reference to Arthur in Book 56 to a full-fledged chapter titled "Arthur of Britain." In preceding chapters he additionally provides the intervening reigns of three kings—Vortigern; Arthur's uncle Aurelius Ambrosius (who is historically based as Ambrosius Aurelianus in both Gildas's and Nennius's works); and Arthur's father, Utherpendragon. Monmouth's work is between polarities; at times what he tries to pawn off as history is laughably absurd, and at other times he has a confounding uncanniness of tying diverse, unimpeachable historical sources into a tidy package, accurate far beyond the possibility of coincidence.

One segment of *The Mabinogion* is "How Culhwch Won Olwen," a tale featuring Arthur's first cousin. Although Arthur is an active rather than a passive participant in the story, he plays an almost insignificant role. "The Dream of Rhonabwy," however, focuses upon the Battle of Badon in which Arthur is a central figure. These two tales in combination convey a significant amount of information about Arthur as enumerated in the following table.

"How Culhwch Won Olwen"	"The Dream of Rhonabwy"
Arthur's Relatives:	*Arthur's Relatives:*
Culhwch, first cousin	Caradawg Strong Arm, chief advisor and first cousin
Gormant, son of Rica, a brother on his mother's side	Llacheu, a son
Llygardrudd Emys, uncle	March, son of Meirchyawn, first cousin

"How Culhwch Won Olwen"

Gwrvoddw, uncle
Gwenhwyvar, wife
Gwydre, son

Personal Items and Weapons:

A four-cornered purple mantle with a red-gold apple worth a hundred cows in each corner.
Caledvwlch, his sword

Rhongomynyad, his spear
Wynebgwrthucher, his shield
Carnwennan, his knife
Prydwen, his ship

Arthur's Warriors:

Kei
Bedwyr
Caw of Scotland
Gildas Albanius, son of Caw
Hueil, son of Caw
Talyessin the poet
Osla Big Knife

Arthur's Enemies:

Twrch Trwyth

Battles:

at Camlann, Morvran, whom the enemy thought was a devil
at Camlann, Sanddev, whom the enemy thought was an angel
Saint Kynwyl, who lived through the Battle of Camlann
Gwynn Hyvar, one of nine who planned the Battle of Camlann

"The Dream of Rhonabwy"

Medraut, a nephew and foster son

Personal Items and Weapons:

Gwynn, his mantle, having red-gold apples in each corner and the magical property of rendering a person invisible.
His sword, with a design of two serpents embossed upon its golden hilt

Arthur's Warriors:

Kei, the handsomest man in the kingdom
Howel, son of the Emhyr of Brittany
Caw of Scotland
Gildas Albanius, son of Caw
Rhun son of Maelgwn of Gwynedd
Avaon, son of Talyessin
Gwalchmei, son of Gwyar
Peredur Long Spear
Cadwr, Earl of Cornwall

Arthur's Enemies:

Osla Big Knife, at the battle of Caer Vaddon, the Fortress of the Baths
Medrawd, at the Battle of Camlann
Owein, at the Battle of Caer Vaddon
Gwres, at the Battle of Caer Vaddon

Battles:

Iddawg, who wove the Battle of Camlann
The Battle of Badon at Caer Vaddon, the Fortress of the Baths
Caer Vaddon located at a ford on the River Severn
Arthur on the offensive at Caer Vaddon

Osla Big Knife, one of the defenders at Caer Vaddon.

"How Culhwch Won Olwen"

Arthur's Court:

Kelliwic, in Cornwall

"The Dream of Rhonabwy"

Arthur's Court:

unnamed, in Cornwall

Chapter Notes

Chapter 1: New Perspectives of Ancient Insular History

1. Leslie Alcock, *Arthur's Britain*, p. 4.
2. Alcock, p. 1.
3. See Eilert Ekwall, *The Concise Oxford Dictionary of English Place-names*, p. 139 under the entry of "Darent," and pp. 142–143 under the entry "Derwent."
4. Ekwall, p. 139 under the entry "Darwen."
5. John Morris, *The Age of Arthur*, pp. 91–92.
6. Norma Goodrich, *King Arthur*, p. 11.
7. Goodrich, p. 6.
8. Goodrich, p. 6.
9. Goodrich, p. 7.
10. Frank D. Reno, *The Historic King Arthur*, pp. 297–298 and p. 308.
11. Goodrich, p. 27.
12. W. F. Skene, *The Four Ancient Books of Wales*, p. 34.
13. Thomas O'Sullivan, *The De Excidio of Gildas: Its Authenticity and Date*, p. 22, footnote 90. In addition to the original source—C. E. Stevens, "Gildas Sapiens," *English Historical Review*, LVI (1941), p. 363—O'Sullivan adds that this great epidemic "ties in quite well with the chronology of the *De Excidio* narrative."
14. Alcock, *Arthur's Britain*, pp. 108–109.
15. O'Sullivan, *The De Excidio of Gildas*, pp. 91–92.
16. O'Sullivan, p. 117.
17. O'Sullivan, pp. 117–118.
18. Michael Winterbottom, *Gildas: The Ruin of Britain and other works*, p. 33.
19. John Morris, *British History*, entry 547, p. 85; Thomas O'Sullivan's discussion in *The De Excidio of Gildas*, p. 82.
20. Richard Barber's comments about Rhos and Walwen's grave in *The Figure of Arthur*, p. 115.
21. An "Ogham stone" is any monument or grave marker which is inscribed with slash-like ancient Irish script called Ogham. The word, not uncommonly, is eponymic in its origins. P. B. Ellis, in his book *The Druids*, indicates on p. 126 that the origin of the word is *Ogmios*, a Gallic root, from whence came the Irish word *Ogma* and the British word *Ogmia*, all which are references to the God of Eloquence and Literature.
22. Pamphlet, "The Church of St. Brynach, Nevern, Pembrokeshire," published by E. L. Jones & Son, Printers, Cardigan, Third Edition reprinted May 1994, p. 2.
23. Winterbottom, *Gildas: The Ruin of Britain and other works*, p. 31.
24. Alcock, *Arthur's Britain*, p. 122; O'Sullivan, *The De Excidio of Gildas*, p. 103.

25. Rachel Bromwich, *The Beginnings of Welsh Poetry,* p. 9.
26. O'Sullivan, p. 103.
27. O'Sullivan, p. 106.
28. Morris, *Age of Arthur,* p. 513.
29. Morris, p. 125.
30. Morris, pp. 127 and 207; Alcock, *Arthur's Britain,* p. 123.
31. Morris, p. 203.
32. For a detailed explanation, see Reno, *The Historic King Arthur,* pp. 26–37, plus all of Chapter 3, pp. 66–123.
33. Alcock, *Arthur's Britain,* pp. 32–33.
34. Alcock, pp. 82–83.
35. Josephus Stevenson, *Nennii: Historia Brittonum,* footnote 22, p. 50.
36. Alcock, *Arthur's Britain,* p. 241.
37. Alcock, p. 246.
38. Stevenson, footnote 25, p. 28.
39. Morris, *The Age of Arthur,* p. 292.
40. Eilert Ekwall, *The Concise Oxford Dictionary of English Place-names,* p. 86.
41. All of these sites border the northern Welsh territories; it doesn't seem logical, therefore, to base the assumption that Darenth or River Derwent in Kent are unquestionably the sites of the battle at Derguentid simply on the authority of interpolated headings by some scribe doctoring an early manuscript.
42. Morris, *British History,* p. 31 for English, p. 72 for Latin.
43. See Alcock, *Arthur's Britain,* pp. 104–105, and mid–p. 109.
44. Josephus Stevenson, *Nennii,* p. 29.
45. See Reno, *The Historic King Arthur,* Chapter 5, "The Geography of Badon."
46. Charles Plummer, *Two of the Saxon Chronicles Parallel,* p. 12.
47. J. A. Giles, *Six Old English Chronicles,* p. 399.
48. Morris, *British History,* p. 28.
49. Stevenson, *Nennii,* p. 47.
50. See Reno, *The Historic King Arthur,* Chapter 3, "Cardinal and Ordinal Years," Hengist's death-year and floruit, p. 113 and Table 12 on p. 114.
51. Plummer, *Two Saxon Chronicles Parallel,* p. 3.
52. See *The Arthur of the Welsh,* p. 24. Thomas Charles–Edwards defines Bretwalda, found in the Parker Chronicle, as "British ruler," and defines Brytenwalda (Breotenwalda), found in the other versions of the Chronicle, as "Ruler of Britain." However, he feels that there is no genuine difference of meaning between the two. Yet there is, in fact, a very important difference. "British ruler" indicates that ethnically the ruler is Briton, but "Ruler of Britain" suggests that a foreign king could be ruling in Britain. Although this is a crucial difference for defining the terms, the two phrases are commonly considered synonymous. Because of this accepted condition, the two terms are viewed as interchangeable in this text. Nevertheless, the conclusions reached by this author about the definition of Bretwalda would definitely lean toward "Brytenwalda," Ruler of Britain, since he would be a German–Saxon king.
53. Geoffrey Ashe, *The Discovery of King Arthur,* p. 133.
54. Alcock, *Arthur's Britain,* pp. 321–322.
55. Morris, *The Age of Arthur,* p. 329.
56. Morris, footnote 317.1, p. 587.
57. John Davies, *A History of Wales,* pp. 62–63.
58. Peter Blair, *Roman Britain and Early England,* p. 274.
59. The reconciliation of dates between *The Anglo-Saxon Chronicle* and its Genealogical Preface as proposed by Frank Reno, *The Historic King Arthur,* pp. 62-63.

60. Reno, *The Historic King Arthur,* pp. 181–182.
61. G. N. Garmonsway, *The Anglo-Saxon Chronicle,* pp. 14 or 15.
62. Bromwich, *The Beginnings of Welsh Poetry: Studies by Ifor Williams,* Chapter VI, "Wales and the North," p. 71 and footnote.
63. G. N. Garmonsway, Parker Chronicle, p. 14, or Laud Chronicle, p. 15.
64. Ekwall, *The Concise Oxford Dictionary of English Place-names,* p. 319.
65. Reno, *The Historic King Arthur,* p. 12.
66. Wade-Evans, *The Emergence of England and Wales,* pp. 3–4, footnote 3 on p. 6, and p. 15.
67. Winterbottom, *Gildas: The Ruin of Britain and other works,* p. 28.
68. Blair, *Roman Britain and Early England,* p. 242.
69. Blair, p. 177.
70. Garmonsway, *The Anglo-Saxon Chronicle,* p. 16.

Chapter 2: Other Early Manuscripts

1. For an explanation of these calibrations, see Leslie Alcock, *Arthur's Britain,* pp. xvii, 6, 18, and 104; for specific application to Arthur's age, see Frank Reno, *The Historic King Arthur,* Chapter 3.
2. James Carley, ed./trans., *The Chronicle of Glastonbury Abbey,* pp. 73–75.
3. A. W. Wade-Evans, *The Emergence of England and Wales,* pp. 11 and 22, note 1.
4. Norris Lacy, *The Arthurian Encyclopedia,* p. 235.
5. Josephus Stevenson's Preface, *Gildas: De Excidio,* pp. vi through xiv, including all of the footnotes which he provides on those pages.
6. Carley, p. 75.
7. Carley, p. 283, footnote 115.
8. A. Campbell, *The Chronicle of Æthelweard,* p. 11.
9. Alcock, *Arthur's Britain,* p. 294.
10. Alcock, p. 77.
11. Charles Mierow, *Jordanes: The Origin and Deeds of the Goths,* p. 74.
12. Geoffrey Ashe, *The Discovery of King Arthur,* p. 103.
13. Acton Griscom, *The Historia Regum Britanniae of Geoffrey of Monmouth,* p. 19.
14. Griscom, p. 22.
15. Griscom, p. 102.
16. For a convincing point of view, read specifically Chapters III (pp. 19–25), VII (pp. 99–113), and VIII (pp. 114–147). In the first segment of Chapter VII, Griscom lays down a base that no qualified Welsh or Breton authority who is well-versed in those two languages has ever translated the Welsh/Breton chronicles so that they could be objectively and impartially compared to Monmouth's work to accurately determine what material of Geoffrey's was invention, and what was copied from these manuscripts as an earlier source. In the second section of that same chapter, Griscom writes of the unfounded attacks upon Monmouth's character, and of the unscholarly, unjustified judgments which have been made by "expert Latinists, recognized historians, and special students" who have absolutely no expertise—and in some instances have not even read the manuscripts—in Welsh or Breton—and yet those same individuals presume to talk with authority about them. Griscom ends this particular chapter by writing that "I have recently called attention to the fact which seems to have escaped the notice of scholars, that the Dingestow Court MS. in its turn is indisputably a copy of something earlier (p. 112)."

In Chapter VIII he elaborates upon his theory that the Welsh/Breton chronicles *precede* Monmouth's works, giving supportive evidence of why he believes such, including the highly complex discussion of what experts have said and what they have not said, of how material was misleading, and of how some points were misinterpreted. The misinformation which has sprung from all this, has left, according to Griscom, not only Monmouth with a besmirched reputation but true British history neglected and hence still undiscovered.

17. Griscom, pp. 22–23.
18. Griscom, p. 24, plus footnote 2 on that page.
19. Griscom, p. 25.
20. Michael Curley, *Geoffrey of Monmouth,* p. 11.
21. Curley, p. 11.
22. Curley, pp. 11–12.
23. Curley, p. 12.
24. Curley, p. 13.
25. Griscom, p. 104.
26. Griscom, p. 101.
27. Griscom, p. 99.
28. Griscom, p. 106.
29. Griscom, p. 114.
30. Griscom, p. 133.
31. R. H. Fletcher, *The Arthurian Material in the Chronicles,* pp. 117–118.
32. Fletcher, p. 251.
33. John Morris, *British History,* p. 26.
34. Michael Winterbottom, *Gildas: the Ruin of Britain and Other Works,* p. 28.
35. Winterbottom, pp. 29–30.
36. D. P. Simpson, *Cassell's Latin Dictionary,* p. 421.
37. Simpson, *Cassell's Latin Dictionary,* pp. xii, xiii.
38. Lewis Thorpe, *Geoffrey of Monmouth: The History of the Kings of Britain,* p. 214.
39. John Morris, *British History,* p. 80 for the Latin, p. 40 for the translation.
40. Thorpe, p. 215.
41. Thorpe, pp. 215–216.

Chapter 3: Riardd Ambrosius

1. Kenneth Jackson, "Arthur in Early Welsh Verse," *Arthurian Literature in the Middle Ages,* ed. R. S. Loomis, p. 2.
2. Rachel Bromwich, "Celtic Elements in Arthurian Romance: A General Survey," *The Legend of Arthur in the Middle Ages,* ed. P. B. Grout et. al., p. 42.
3. Bromwich, p. 42.
4. Richard Barber, *The Figure of Arthur,* pp. 37–38.
5. Graham Phillips and Martin Keatman, *King Arthur: The True Story,* p. 128.
6. Eilert Ekwall, *The Concise Oxford Dictionary of English Place-names,* First Edition, 1936, p. 12.
7. Alan Orr Anderson and Marjorie Ogilvie Anderson, *Adomnan's Life of Saint Columba,* pp. 132–133.
8. Rachel Bromwich, *The Beginnings of Welsh Poetry,* p. 10.
9. Bromwich, p. 10.
10. J. S. P. Tatlock, *The Legendary History of Britain,* Chapter VI, "Arthur," p. 216.

11. Tatlock, p. 217.
12. Tatlock, p. 218.
13. Tatlock, p. 219.
14. Tatlock, p. 221–222.
15. E. K. Chambers, *Arthur of Britain,* p. 169.
16. Geoffrey Ashe, *The Discovery of King Arthur,* p. 112.
17. Ashe, p. 113.
18. Ashe, p. 113.
19. John Morris, *British History,* p. 33.
20. Ashe, p. 113.
21. Norris Lacy, *The Arthurian Encyclopedia,* p. 454.
22. Charles Mierow, *Jordanes: The Origin and Deeds of the Goths,* p. 74.
23. W. B. Anderson, ed. and trans., *Sidonius: Poems and Letters, Volume I,* p. 35.
24. Michael Winterbottom, *Gildas: The Ruin of Britain and Other Works,* p. 28.
25. John Morris, *The Age of Arthur,* p. 48.

Chapter 4: Who's Who: Ambrosius's Father, the *Superbus Tyrannus* Vortigern

1. Josephus Stevenson, *Nennii,* p. 21.
2. John Morris, *British History,* p. 25.
3. Stevenson, p. 21, footnote 14.
4. Michael Winterbottom, *Gildas: The Ruin of Britain and other works.* p. 28.
5. Stevenson, *Nennii,* p. 34.
6. Winterbottom, p. 151.
7. D. P. Simpson, *Cassell's Latin Dictionary,* p. 489.
8. Lewis Thorpe, *Geoffrey of Monmouth: The History of the Kings of Britain,* p. 258.
9. Robert Huntington Fletcher, *The Arthurian Material in the Chronicles,* pp. 117, 118.
10. Fletcher, p. 140.
11. Richard Brengle, *Arthur King of Britain,* p. 115.
12. Fletcher, p. 225.
13. Stevenson, *Nennii,* pp. xxiii and xxiv of his Preface, and footnotes 13 and 14, p. 21. Manuscripts D, E, G, K, P, and R are the later versions containing the variants.
14. Alcock, *Arthur's Britain,* p. 104.
15. Alcock, p. 104–105.
16. Bede, *A History of the English Church and People,* p. 55.
17. Alcock, *Arthur's Britain,* p. 320.
18. Alcock, p. 320; Norris Lacy, *The Arthurian Encyclopedia,* p. 608.
19. Alcock, p. 320.
20. Michael Wood, *In Search of the Dark Ages,* p. 43.
21. A. W. Wade-Evans, *The Emergence of England and Wales,* p. 133, note 3.
22. R. H. Fletcher, *The Arthurian Material in the Chronicles,* p. 5.
23. Michael Winterbottom, *Gildas: The Ruin of Britain and other works,* p. 26; J. A. Giles, *Six Old English Chronicles,* p. 310; Richard Barber, *The Figure of Arthur,* p. 44; Graham Phillips/Martin Keatman, *King Arthur: The True Story,* p. 64.
24. Lacy, p. 606.
25. Alcock, *Arthur's Britain,* p. 320; Ashe, *The Quest for Arthur's Britain,* p. 4.
26. Ashe, "The Arthurian Fact," *The Quest for Arthur's Britain,* p. 46.

27. Lacy, p. 608.
28. Winterbottom, p. 26.
29. Alcock, *Arthur's Britain,* p. 357.
30. Alcock, p. 357.
31. Alcock, p. 92.
32. Alcock, p. 99.
33. Collingwood, *Roman Britain and the English Settlements,* p. 206.
34. Collingwood, p. 313.
35. Collingwood, p. 318.
36. Alcock, *Arthur's Britain,* p. 106.
37. Alcock, p. 106.
38. Alcock, p. 92.
39. Alcock, p. 103.
40. Wade-Evans, *The Emergence of England and Wales,* p. 67.
41. Wade-Evans, p. 67.
42. Rachel Bromwich, *The Beginnings of Welsh Poetry,* p. 44.
43. Alcock, *Arthur's Britain,* p. 39.
44. Alcock, p. 359.
45. Myres, *Roman Britain and the English Settlements,* pp. 358–359.
46. Myres, p. 378–379.
47. Myres, p. 358.
48. Charles Plummer, *Two of the Saxon Chronicles Parallel,* entry A.D. 449, p. 443.
49. John Morris, *British History,* p. 32.
50. Morris, p. 31.
51. G. N. Garmonsway, *The Anglo-Saxon Chronicle,* p. 12.
52. Josephus Stevenson, *Nennii,* Section 44, pp. 34–35, footnote 1.
53. R. H. Fletcher, *The Arthurian Material in the Chronicle,* p. 18.
54. Stevenson, p. 35, footnote 1.
55. Stevenson, p. 36.
56. Morris, p. 32.
57. Rachel Bromwich, "The Welsh Triads," *Arthurian Literature in the Middle Ages: A Collaborative History,* supplies this information on pp. 45–46 although I've recorded it here in a different format. Additionally, Bromwich, in her translation of the second Unfortunate Disclosure writes that Arthur, in addition to Vortigern, disclosed the dragons, but that appears to be different from the original Welsh she provides directly above the translation. Because the Welsh Triads are so difficult to obtain, I have not yet been able to resolve the discrepancy.
58. Morris, p. 32.
59. Stevenson, p. 39.
60. For part of this complicated entwining of languages, see the section labeled the "Five languages in Britain" in Plummer, *Two of the Saxon Chronicle, Parallel,* p. 6.
61. Jeremy K. Knight, "The Pillar of Eliseg," *Valle Crucis Abbey,* pp. 46–48.
62. Hammer's entire article "Neglected British History", pp. 251–278 in the Proceedings of The British Academy 1917–1918. The four chronologies at the end are particularly helpful.
63. Alcock, *Arthur's Britain,* p. 34.

Chapter 5: Vortimer and Vitalinus: Arthurian Enigmas

1. Lewis Thorpe, *Geoffrey of Monmouth: The History of the Kings of Britain,* p. 161.
2. R. H. Fletcher, *Arthurian Material in the Chronicles,* p. 18.

3. Fletcher, p. 19.
4. Geoffrey Ashe, *The Discovery of King Arthur,* p. 203.
5. John Morris, *British History,* Chapter 43, p. 31.
6. For the full account, see Stevenson, *Nennii,* p. 35, footnote 1.
7. Morris, p. 32.
8. Fletcher, p. 23.
9. Leslie Alcock, *Arthur's Britain,* p. 359.
10. Alcock, p. 359.
11. Geoffrey Ashe, *King Arthur's Avalon,* p. 74
12. Geoffrey Ashe, *The Discovery of King Arthur,* pp. 97–98.
13. Stevenson, *Nennii,* pp. 34–35. See also footnote 20, p. 34.
14. Michael Winterbottom, *Gildas, The Ruin of Britain and other works,* p. 28.
15. Winterbottom, p. 26.
16. John Morris, p. 26.
17. Morris, p. 28.
18. Morris, p. 28.
19. Morris, p. 29.
20. Winterbottom, p. 28.
21. On p. xvii of his Preface, Stevenson writes "The history of the reign of Vortigern is interrupted to introduce a long account of the miracles of Germanus, which, upon a comparison of the passages by which it is immediately preceded and followed, seems to have formed no part of the original work." This is a reference to what is labeled as Germanus-Part I, but what Stevenson indicates on p. xviii of Preface, lines 3–6 is equally applicable to Germanus-Part 2 and Germanus-Part 3. Stevenson then additionally adds, "The Legend of Patrick then follows, although entirely unconnected with the context," and in a footnote suggests that it was an supplemental addendum to the work, "although it found its way into the text in all other copies."
22. Stevenson, p. 34, lines 19–22 and footnote 20.
23. This name appears as Brittu in John Morris's *The Age of Arthur,* p. 63, and as Brydw in the booklet *Valle Crucis Abbey,* p. 48.
24. Phillips and Keatman, *King Arthur: The True Story,* p. 92.
25. See Phillips and Keatman, p. 96, for the specific postulations, plus other premises continued on pp. 97–98.
26. Phillips and Keatman, pp. 92–97.
27. Norris Lacy, *The Arthurian Encyclopedia,* p. 607.
28. Michael Winterbottom, p. 26.
29. Rachel Bromwich, "The Welsh Triads," *Arthurian Literature in the Middle Ages,* p. 45.
30. Lewis Thorpe, *Geoffrey of Monmouth: The History of the Kings of Britain,* p. 162.
31. John Morris, *British History,* p. 33.
32. Lewis Thorpe, pp. 160–202.
33. Charles Plummer, *Two of the Saxon Chronicles Parallel,* p. 13.
34. Plummer, p. cxii, plus footnote 2.
35. See Plummer, p. cxii, footnote 3, and for discussion of Stuf and Wihtgar check entry 514, p. 13 and entry 544 on p. 14. Additionally, see Æthelweard's chronicle in Giles's book, for entry 514, p. 7, and entry 534 on p. 8; Æthelweard does not include an entry for 544, nor does he record Wihtgar's death.
36. J. A. Giles, *Six Old English Chronicles* p. 404.
37. Josephus Stevenson, *Nennii,* pp. 34–35.
38. Stevenson, p. 35, footnote 1.

39. Stevenson, p. 35, footnote 2.
40. Stevenson, p. 24.
41. Ekwall, *The Concise Oxford Dictionary of English Place-names,* p. 459.
42. Morris, *The Age of Arthur,* p. 64.
43. Ekwall, p. 398.
44. Ekwall, p. 388.
45. Ekwall, p. 385.
46. Ekwall, p. 386.
47. Morris, p. 214.
48. Clayton, Peter, *Guide to the Archaeological Sites of Britain,* pp. 139–140.
49. Ashe, *Discovery of King Arthur,* p. 197.
50. Morris, p. 294.
51. See Morris, *Age of Arthur,* footnote 294.1, p. 581 and footnote 324.2, p. 588.
52. Morris, *Age of Arthur,* p. 319.
53. Stevenson, p. 40, and footnote 1, p. 41.
54. Stevenson, p. 55.
55. Thorpe, p. 121.
56. Peter Hunter Blair, *Roman Britain and Early England: 55 B.C.–A.D. 871,* p. 58.
57. Michael Curley, *Geoffrey of Monmouth,* p. 31.
58. Curley, p. 138.
59. Eilert Ekwall, *The Concise Oxford Dictionary of English Place-names,* Fourth Edition, p. 199.
60. Thomas O'Sullivan, *The De Excidio of Gildas,* p. 103.
61. As an example, see O'Sullivan, pp. 102 to 106, including the footnotes on those pp.; Wade-Evans addresses the issue throughout his book, fairly heavily on pp. 101–109; Alcock cites material on Magnus Maximus in an attempt to calibrate the Dési migration from Ireland to Dyfed, p. 123.
62. O'Sullivan, p. 105.
63. In Wade-Evans, *The Emergence of England and Wales,* p. 25, note 2, he appears as Aircol; in Collingwood and Myres, *Roman Britain and the English Settlement,* Second Edition, p. 150, he appears as Calpurnius as an abbreviation of Sextus Calpurnius Agricola; in Webster, *The Cornovii,* p. 163, he is indexed as Gnaeus Julius Agricola; Alcock, *Arthur's Britain,* also provides a background, pp. 123–124.
64. Webster, *The Cornovii,* p. 43.
65. Webster, p. 44.
66. Webster, p. 45.
67. Peter Clayton, p. 174.
68. For a translation of the inscription on Eliseg's Pillar, see Jeremy K. Knight, "The Pillar of Eliseg," in the booklet *Valle Crucis Abbey,* by D. H. Evans, pp. 47–48; for the Germanus material, see Stevenson, *Nennii,* pp. xvii–xviii of the Preface.
69. O'Sullivan, *The De Excidio of Gildas,* p. 103, and Wade-Evans, *The Emergence of England and Wales,* p. 25.
70. Alcock, *Arthur's Britain,* p. 122.
71. O'Sullivan, p. 103. The primary source is "The Expulsion of the Dési," p. 113, which was edited and translated by Kuno Meyer in *Y Cymmrodor,* XIV, 1901.
72. Alcock, p. 123.
73. William Skene, *The Four Ancient Books of Wales,* p. 43.
74. Leslie Alcock, p. 103.
75. Translated from Stevenson, *Nennii,* Book 49, pp. 40–41. A minor but noteworthy point for those who trace the name: In John Morris, *British History,* the name

of Vitalinus's father is given as "Gloiu" in both Section 49 and in the index, an unfortunate transposition.

76. During a discussion about Gloucester in a segment of "Caratacus and Boudicca" in *Roman Britain and the English Settlements,* R. G. Collingwood writes in a footnote on p. 95 that there's no proof that the Romans ever had a fortress at Gloucester, but in his writings Tacitus records a legionary fortress was built in the country of the Silures (or at least on its borders). However, this reference cannot be to Caerleon-on-Usk, and "not only is Gloucester the natural place for it, but the shape and size of the Roman town there are exactly those of a legionary fortress ... ."

77. Collingwood, p. 94.

78. For a brief but comprehensive history of Gloucester, including several excellent maps, see John Wacher, *The Towns of Roman Britain,* pp. 137–155.

79. Translated from Stevenson, *Nennii,* p. 55.

80. John Morris, *Age of Arthur,* p. 73, identifies the battle as Guoloph or Wallop in Hampshire, and likewise suggests that Vitalinus is the proper name for the epithet Vortigern on pp. 56 and 74. Alcock, *Arthur's Britain,* p. 105, also relates that the battle is a reference to Wallop in Hampshire, but Wade-Evans, *The Emergence of England and Wales,* p. 69, footnote 4, sets it near Grampound, the Roman *Voluba,* in Cornwall, and Phillips/Keatman, *King Arthur: The True Story,* p. 95, identify it as the River Wallop in Shropshire.

81. Lewis Thorpe, *Geoffrey of Monmouth: The History of the Kings of Britain,* p. 262.

82. Thorpe, p. 149.

83. Thorpe, p. 151.

84. See each of the following sources. Leslie Alcock, *Arthur's Britain,* p. 107: "Aëtius [was] a previous commander in Gaul, whose third consulship began in 446." Graham Phillips and Martin Keatman, *King Arthur: The True Story,* p. 66: "As [Aëtius's] third term began in 446 and the fourth in 453, the plea for help must have occurred at some point between these two years." Geoffrey Ashe, *The Discovery of King Arthur,* p. 42: "In 446 we have an authentic document [the letter to Aëtius], or at least, extracts from it." John Morris, *The Age of Arthur,* pp. 39, 40, 77, and 513 are all entries assigning the date of 446 to the Aëtius letter. R. G. Collingwood, Book IV, "The End of Roman Rule," *Roman Britain and the English Settlements,* p. 301 writes that Britain's hope of Roman help was abandoned in 446 after the appeal to Aëtius was ignored.

85. Collingwood, p. 301.

86. Thorpe, p. 152.

87. This author's translation from Stevenson, *Nennii,* p. 55.

88. Thorpe, p. 169.

89. Thorpe, p. 221.

90. Michael Winterbottom, *Gildas: The Ruin of Britain and Other Works,* p. 28.

91. John Morris, *British History,* p. 26.

92. Thorpe, p. 155.

93. Thorpe, p. 155.

94. Leslie Alcock, *Arthur's Britain,* p. 109.

95. Alcock, p. 105.

96. Pamphlet, *The Church of St. Brynach, Nevern, Pembrokeshire,* pp. 5–6.

97. John Morris, *The Age of Arthur,* p. 71.

Chapter 6: The Breach of Colors: Cunedda's Role in Civil War

1. Wade-Evans, *The Emergence of England and Wales,* p. 104.
2. Leslie Alcock, *Arthur's Britain,* p. 38.

3. Josephus Stevenson, *Nennii,* Chapter 14, pp. 11–12.
4. Stevenson, Chapter 62, p. 52.
5. Alcock, p. 128.
6. John Morris, *British History,* p. 37.
7. J. A. Giles, *Six Old English Chronicles,* p. 414.
8. Alcock, pp. 126–127.
9. Alcock, p. 126.
10. Wade-Evans, pp. 6–7.
11. Wade-Evans, p. 68, footnote 1.
12. Wade-Evans, p. 7, footnote 1.
13. *The Four Ancient Books of Wales*, Volume I, facing p. of Chapter 1, p. 1.
14. Stevenson, pp. 52–53.
15. D. P. Simpson, *Cassell's Latin Dictionary,* p. 557.
16. Alcock, p. 95.
17. Alcock, p. 120.
18. Rachel Bromwich, *The Beginnings of Welsh Poetry,* p. 53.
19. See Bromwich, pp. 75, 77, and 124, including footnote 7.
20. Kenneth Jackson, *The Gododdin,* p. 72. For the entire explanation, read pp. 69–75.
21. Wade-Evans, pp. 104–105.
22. J. G. Evans, *The Book of Taliesin,* pp. 69–70.
23. John Morris, *Y Cymmrodor,* the magazine of the Honourable Society of Cymmrodorion, xxviii, p. 209.
24. Alcock, p. 98.
25. Alcock, p. 128.
26. Wade-Evans, pp. 6–7 and 104.
27. Alcock, p. 106.
28. Wade-Evans, p. 7.
29. Stevenson, p. 12.
30. Alcock, p. 254.
31. I. A. Richmond, *Roman Britain,* p. 54.
32. Richmond, p. 54.
33. Bromwich, in *The Beginnings of Welsh Poetry,* on p. 10 writes that "Another common element in personal names was *cu* "dog," Irish *cu,* Welsh *ci,* for "warrior, hero," by the Irish and the Welsh. The genetive was *cunos.* In compounds the stem was lengthened to *cuno-* (on the analogy of second declension formations), when it formed the first element, as in *Cunorix, Cunovalos, Cunotegirnos."* She gives further details about the formation of the name Maglocunus, thus linking Cunedda and Maelgwn genealogically. O'Sullivan, on p. 27 of his text, is specifically analyzing the name "Cuneglasus," but defines several other terms which appear as an appositive for this name.
34. Josephus Stevenson, *Gildas: De Excidio Britanniæ,* p. 37.
35. Michael Winterbottom, *Gildas: The Ruin of Britain and Other Works,* p. 29.
36. Stevenson, p. 39.
37. Stevenson, p. 40.
38. Stevenson, p. 41.
39. O'Sullivan, *The De Excidio of Gildas,* p. 27.
40. Stevenson, p. 42.
41. Bromwich, "Celtic Element in Arthurian Romance," *The Legend of Arthur in the Middle Ages,* p. 55.
42. Alcock, *Arthur's Britain,* pp. 128–129.

43. Wade-Evans, *The Emergence of England and Wales,* p. 101, footnote 4.

44. Gildas uses the Latin term *vermes* which, not surprisingly, traces back to Greek. What is interesting, however, is that the Greek word *draconta* meant "monstrous worm" and was defined synonymously as "serpent." The Latin word *draco* derived from the Greek *draconta,* but its meaning became "dragon," connoting something different from "worm" or "serpent."

45. Skene, *The Four Ancient Books of Wales,* pp. 257, 258.

46. Winterbottom, p. 28.

Chapter 7: The Breach of Colors: *Romanitas* Versus Cunedda's Progeny and the Saxons

1. Leslie Alcock, *Arthur's Britain,* Chapter Twelve, from pp. 358 to the end of the text, p. 364.

2. Lewis Thorpe, *Geoffrey of Monmouth: The History of the Kings of Britain,* p. 169.

3. Alcock, *Arthur's Britain,* p. 34.

4. Alcock, p. 179.

5. Alcock, pp. 214–215.

6. Alcock, *The Quest for Arthur's Britain,* "Wales in the Arthurian Age," pp. 90–91.

7. Alcock, pp. 80–81.

8. Thorpe, p. 195.

9. Jeffrey Grantz, *The Mabinogion,* "How Culhwch Won Olwen," p. 140.

10. Gantz, p. 137.

11. Gantz, "The Dream of Rhonobwy," *The Mabinogion,* p. 185.

12. Gantz, p. 185, footnote 8.

13. Gantz, pp. 23–24.

14. For these names, see *The Mabinogion,* p. 148.

15. Gantz, "The Dream of Rhonabwy," *The Mabinogion,* p. 185.

16. Stevenson, *Nennii,* Chapter 37, p. 28. Manuscripts D, E, and P use the name of Cerdic.

17. J. A. Giles, *Six Old English Chronicles,* Chapter 37, p. 399.

18. Richard Barber, *The Figure of Arthur,* p. 86.

19. G. N. Garmonsway, *The Anglo-Saxon Chronicle,* the Parker Chronicle, p. 14, and the Laud Chronicle, p. 15.

20. Charles Plummer, *Two of the Saxon Chronicles Parallel,* p. 12. See also Geoffrey Ashe, *The Quest for Arthur's Britain,* "Extending the Map," p. 158, and also Geoffrey Ashe, *The Discovery of King Arthur,* p. 198.

21. Geoffrey Garmonsway, The Parker Chronicle, p. 16.

22. Geoffrey Ashe, *The Quest for Arthur's Britain,* "Extending the Map," pp. 158–159.

23. Ashe, p. 159.

24. John Morris, *The Age of Arthur,* p. 588, footnote 324.2.

25. Peter Clayton, *Guide to the Archaeological Sites of Britain,* p. 174.

26. Kathryn Grabowski and David Dumville, *Chronicles and Annals of Mediaeval Ireland and Wales,* p. 225.

27. James Carley, *The Chronicle of Glastonbury Abbey,* p. 73.

28. Carley, p. 75.

29. Carley, p. 81.

30. In conjunction with his adjustments of the dates, see Leslie Alcock, *Arthur's Britain,* pp. 45–55, *Arthur's Britain,* p. xvii of the Preface, and *Was This Camelot?,* pp. 215–216.

31. Ashe, *The Quest for Arthur's Britain,* p. 159; Ashe, *The Discovery of King Arthur,* p. 197; John Morris, *The Age of Arthur,* pp. 41, 67–70, 204.

32. Geoffrey Ashe's use of this term in *The Discovery of King Arthur.*

33. John Morris, *British History,* p. 29.

34. J. A. Giles, *Six Old English Chronicles,* p. 400.

35. Josephus Stevenson, *Nennii,* p. 29, plus footnote 14.

36. D. P. Simpson, *Cassell's Latin Dictionary,* p. 255.

37. The term for a Welsh story teller is *cyfarwydd* (coo-far'-oo-with); its plural is *cyfarwyddiaid* (coo-far-oo-with'-ee-ad).

38. Arthur Wade-Evans, *The Emergence of England and Wales,* pp. 66 through 69. As a support, see also footnote 1 on p. 67, where he cites an individual name Hodgkin.

39. Graham Webster, *The Cornovii,* p. 89.

40. Webster, *Wall: Roman Site: Staffordshire,* London: English Heritage, Second Edition, p. 7.

41. Webster, p. 3.

42. Webster, p. 4.

43. Webster, p. 4.

44. Webster, p. 6.

45. Webster, p. 3.

46. Webster, *The Cornovii,* p. 91.

47. Webster, Wall: *Roman Site,* p. 18.

48. Webster, p. 8.

49. Jeffrey Gantz, *The Mabinogion* pp. 144–145.

50. Gantz, p. 174.

51. Gantz, p. 183.

52. Gantz, p. 190–191.

53. See Alcock, *Arthur's Britain,* "Preface to the Pelican Edition," p. xvii, and Alcock, *Was This Camelot?,* "The Battle of Badon," pp. 215–216.

54. Lewis Thorpe, editor/translator, *Geoffrey of Monmouth: The History of the Kings of Britain,* p. 161.

Chapter 8: Arthur's Battles with the Saxons

1. Rachel Bromwich, *The Beginnings of Welsh Poetry: Studies by Sir Ifor Williams,* p. 132.

2. Bromwich, pp. 126–127.

3. John Morris, *The Age of Arthur,* p. 513.

4. Norris Lacy, *The Arthurian Encyclopedia,* p. 25.

5. Kenneth Jackson, *The Gododdin,* p. 112.

6. Patrick Sims-Williams, *The Arthur of the Welsh,* "The Early Welsh Arthurian Poems," p. 38.

7. See *The Arthur of the Welsh,* Introduction, pp. 8–9.

8. See *The Arthur of the Welsh,* Introduction, p. 9, and Jerry Gantz's introduction in *The Mabinogion,* p. 29.

9. *The Arthur of the Welsh,* Introduction, p. 10.

10. Brynley Roberts, *The Arthur of the Welsh,* "Culhwch ac Olwen, The Triads, Saints' Lives," pp. 73–74.
11. Roberts, p. 78.
12. Roberts, p. 89.
13. Stevenson, *Nennii,* footnote 4, p. 48.
14. Giles, *Six Old English Chronicles,* footnote 1, p. 408.
15. Leslie Alcock, *Arthur's Britain,* p. 63.
16. Eilert Ekwall, *The Concise Oxford Dictionary of English Place-names,* p. 199.
17. Stevenson, p. 48.
18. Stevenson, p. 48, footnote 5.
19. Ekwall, p. 138.
20. Giles, footnote 2, p. 408.
21. Alcock, pp. 65–66.
22. S. G. Wildman, *The Black Horsemen,* p. 43.
23. Ekwall, p. 388.
24. Ekwall, p. 358
25. Ekwall, p. 386.
26. Stevenson, p. 48, footnote 7.
27. See once again Leslie Alcock, *Arthur's Britain,* p. 67, where he claims that Bassas is one of three Arthurian battles that is impossible to locate in the sense that its name cannot be identified with any known place today.
28. Giles, *Six Old English Chronicles,* p. 408, double-daggered footnote.
29. Phillips and Keatman, *King Arthur: The True Story*, p. 172.
30. Rachel Bromwich, *The Beginnings of Welsh Poetry: Studies by Sir Ifor Williams,* Chapter VIII, p. 148.
31. Geoffrey Ashe, *Discovery of King Arthur,* p. 109.
32. Stevenson, *Nennii,* p. 48, and Morris, *British History,* p. 76.
33. Morris, *British History*, p. 35.
34. Morris, *The Age of Arthur,* p. 111.
35. Morris, pp. 218–219.
36. Giles, p. 408.
37. Alcock, *Arthur's Britain,* p. 61.
38. Alcock, p. 160.
39. Alcock, p. 359.
40. Alcock, p. 359.
41. Translated from Josephus Stevenson, *Nennii,* pp. 47–49.
42. R. G. Collingwood, *Roman Britain and the English Settlements,* pp. 114–116.
43. Alcock, *Arthur's Britain,* p. 61.
44. Morris, *The Age of Arthur,* p. 123.
45. Ekwall, p. 86, under the entry for Catterick.
46. E. K. Chambers, *Arthur of Britain,* p. 202.
47. Rachel Bromwich, *The Beginnings of Welsh Poetry,* p. 133.
48. Bromwich, p. 133.
49. Bromwich, p. 152.
50. Translated from Josephus Stevenson, *Nennii,* p. 48.
51. Robinson quotes this story in its entirety, *Two Glastonbury Legends,* p. 20, and indicates that John of Glastonbury has evidently omitted something, which suggests that John himself copied the story from somewhere.
52. Fletcher, *The Arthurian Material in the Chronicles,* p. 32.
53. Josephus Stevenson, *Nennii, Historia Britonum,* Chapter LVI, p. 49, footnote 4. Stevenson explains earlier, on p. xxv of his own Preface, that this Jerusalem story

is peculiar to MS "K," which was written in the thirteenth century, with many additions interpolated in the margins, which were then later introduced into the text of other copies.

54. Barber, *The Figure of Arthur,* p. 101.
55. For the entire passage, see Barber, pp. 102–103.
56. Chambers, p. 17.
57. Stevenson, p. 48, footnote 9.
58. Stevenson, also p. 48, footnote 9.
59. Alcock, p. 67.
60. Graham Webster, *The Cornovii,* pp. 18–19.
61. J. A. Giles, *Six Old English Chronicles,* p. 408, footnote.
62. Giles, p. 386.
63. Peter Clayton, *Guide to the Archaeological Sites of Britain,* pp. 129–132.
64. Graham Webster, *The Cornovii,* p. 4.
65. Stevenson, p. 48, footnote 16.
66. Webster and Barker, *Wroxeter: Roman City,* p. 15.
67. Webster and Barker, pp. 18–19.
68. Stevenson, p. 48, footnote 17.
69. John Morris, *British History,* p. 35.
70. See Patrick Sims-Williams, "The Early Welsh Arthurian Poems," in *The Arthur of the Welsh,* pp. 40 and 42.
71. Eilert Ekwall, *Dictionary of English Place-Names,* p. 458.
72. Patrick Sims-Williams, *The Arthur of the Welsh,* "The Early Welsh Arthurian Poems," p. 40.
73. Sims-Williams, p. 41.
74. Sims-Williams, p. 42.
75. Sims-Williams, pp. 42–43.
76. See Josephus Stevenson, *Nennii,* pp. xxi—xxxii for dating of various manuscripts, and footnote 1, p. 49, for variations in each manuscript.
77. Chambers, p. 202.
78. Geoffrey Ashe, *The Discovery of Arthur*, pp. 117–118.
79. Frank Reno, *The Historic King Arthur,* pp. 285–291.
80. The reader is directed to Reno, *The Historic King Arthur,* Chapter 5, "The Geography of Mount Badon," pp. 140–179.

Chapter 9: The Strife of Camlann

1. Frank Reno, *The Historic King Arthur,* Chapter 3, "The Cardinal and Ordinal Years for the Arthurian Chronology," pp. 115–116 for the chronological aspect, and Chapter 6, "The Geography of Camlann," pp. 179–195 for the geographic aspect.
2. Leslie Alcock, *Arthur's Britain,* p. 67.
3. Josephus Stevenson's original Latin versions, *Nennii,* pp. 47 and 48, particularly the footnotes in reference to Manuscript *a.*
4. Stevenson, *Nennii,* p. 47, footnote 13.
5. D. P. Simpson, *Cassell's Latin Dictionary,* p. 205.
6. Simpson, p. 394.
7. Michael Winterbottom, *Gildas: The Ruin of Britain and Other Works,* p. 28.
8. Stevenson, Chapter 42, lines 6 and 7, p. 34.
9. G. N. Garmonsway, *The Anglo-Saxon Chronicle,* "The Parker Chronicle," p. 16, and "The Laud Chronicle," p. 17.
10. James, Carley, ed., *The Chronicle of Glastonbury Abbey,* p. 75.

11. *The Church of St. Brynach, Nevern, Pembrokeshire,* p. 2.
12. *The Church of St. Brynach, Nevern, Pembrokeshire,* p. 5.
13. Reno, *The Historic King Arthur,* pp. 92–95.
14. *The Church of St. Brynach, Nevern, Pembrokeshire,* p. 5.
15. Stevenson, p. 55.
16. *The Church of St. Brynach, Nevern, Pembrokeshire,* p. 6.
17. Alcock, pp. 105, 110, 358, and 436.
18. Alcock, p. 105.
19. Lewis Thorpe, *The History of the Kings of Britain,* p. 262.
20. John Morris, *British History,* p. 33.
21. Michael Winterbottom, *Gildas: The Ruin of Britain and Other Works,* p. 28.
22. Winterbottom, p. 28.
23. John Morris, p. 45.
24. Leslie Alcock, p. 48.
25. Alcock, p. 50.
26. Rachel Bromwich, et. al., *The Arthur of the Welsh,* p. 3.
27. "How Culhwch Won Olwen," *The Mabinogion,* pp. 142, 143, 145.
28. *The Mabinogion,* pp. 180–181.
29. Lewis Thorpe, ed., *Geoffrey of Monmouth: The History of the Kings of Britain,* pp. 221, 237, 257–58 for details of Mordred, and pp. 259–261 for information on the battle of Camblam.
30. Thorpe, pp. 257–258.
31. For a detailed discussion, read Lewis Thorpe's "Introduction," pp. 9–37, and "Notes to the Introduction," pp. 38–45.
32. Phillips and Keatman, *King Arthur: The True Story,* p. 37.
33. Phillips and Keatman, pp. 152–153.
34. Phillips and Keatman, p. 159.
35. Thomas O'Sullivan, *The De Excidio of Gildas,* Chapter VI, "The Dates of the Five Gildasian Princes," pp. 108–133
36. For a full discussion see MacArthur, "The Identification of Some Pestilences Recorded in the Irish Annals," *Irish Historical Studies, VI,* 1948–49, pp. 169–188. (See O'Sullivan, p. 84, footnote 35.)
37. Nora Chadwick, "Early Culture and Learning in North Wales," *Studies in the Early British Church,* p. 35. (See O'Sullivan, pp. 90–91, and footnote 17.)
38. Blair, "The Origins of Northumbria," *Archaeologia Aeliana, 4th ser. xxv,* 1947, p. 24. (See O'Sullivan, p. 91, footnote 18.)
39. See Alcock, *Arthur's Britain,* p. 129, O'Sullivan, *The De Excidio of Gildas,* p. 91, and Frank Reno, Chapter 3, Cardinal Year #9 on Cunedda.
40. Thomas O'Sullivan, *The De Excidio of Gildas,* p. 91.
41. Winterbottom, *Gildas: The Ruin of Britain and other works,* Phillimore: London and Chichester, 1978. The p. and section number follow each specific listing.
42. Lewis Thorpe, *Geoffrey of Monmouth: The History of the Kings of Britain,* pp. 200–201.
43. D. P. Simpson, editor, *Cassell's Latin Dictionary,* p. 95.

Epilogue

1. Rachel Bromwich, *The Beginnings of Welsh Poetry: Studies of Sir Ifor Williams,* p. 70.
2. John Morris, *The Age of Arthur,* p. 17.
3. Morris, p. 66.

4. Morris, p. 17.
5. Morris, p. 18.
6. Morris, p. 66.
7. William Skene, *The Four Ancient Books of Wales,* pp. 42–45.
8. Michael Winterbottom, *Gildas: The Ruin of Britain and other works,* p. 28.
9. R. G. Collingwood, *Roman Britain and the English Settlements,* pp. 317–318.
10. Rachel Bromwich, et. al., *The Arthur of the Welsh,* p. 1 of the Introduction.
11. P. B. Ellis, *The Druids,* p. 205. In this same section Ellis also comments upon Monmouth's *Historia Regum Britanniae* and although he is aware of the shortcomings of Monmouth's work as being controversial, he also realizes its important historical influence. Some of his interesting commentary on pp. 205–206 attests to the reason why these works (The *De Excidio,* the *Historia Brittonum,* and Monmouth's work) cannot be summarily dismissed as non-history, because each contains bare facts which are historically verifiable.
12. T. Charles-Edwards, *The Arthur of the Welsh,* "The Arthur of History," p. 16.
13. John Davies, *A History of Wales,* p. 48.
14. T. Charles-Edwards, *The Arthur of the Welsh,* "The Arthur of History," p. 15.
15. Charles-Edwards, pp. 16–17.
16. David Dumville, *Arthurian Literature,* "The Historical Value of the *Historia Brittonum,* pp. 1–26.
17. Lapidge/Dumville, eds., *Gildas: New Approaches,* p. 54.
18. Geoffrey Ashe, *The Discovery of King Arthur,* p. 84.
19. Charles-Edwards, p. 19.
20. Charles-Edwards, p. 19.
21. Charles-Edwards, p. 21.
22. Rachel Bromwich, et. al., *The Arthur of the Welsh,* "Introduction," p. 3.
23. Charles-Edwards, p. 23.
24. See *Roman Britain and the English Settlements,* Second Edition, 1937, Book V, "The English Settlements," Section XX, "The Sources for the Period: Angles, Saxons, and Jutes on the Continent," pp. 325–350.
25. J. N. L. Myres, *Roman Britain and the English Settlements,* pp. 326–327.
26. Myres, p. 327.
27. Myres, p. 347.
28. Myres, p. 350.
29. Leo Sherley-Price, translator, *A History of the English Church and People,* p. 56.
30. Myres, p. 343.
31. Myres's footnote 1, p. 337; he views the material about the three specific tribes as an insertion by Bede.
32. G. N. Garmonsway, *The Anglo-Saxon Chronicle,* p. 12.
33. Garmonsway, p. 13.
34. John Morris, *British History,* p. 26.
35. Peter Beresford Ellis, *Caesar's Invasion of Britain,* pp. 20–21.
36. See specifically pp. 338 through 347 of *Roman Britain and the English Settlements,* Book V, "The English Settlements."
37. Winterbottom uses the term "Saxon" (Section 23, p. 26) but does exonerate himself on p. 150; he indicates that he means *Saxones,* the Roman term, and then clarifies even further that the British preferred the term *Engle.*
38. Morris, *British History,* p. 28.
39. Reno, *The Historic King Arthur,* "Ambrosius Aurelianus as Vortimer," pp. 267–274.

40. Charles-Edwards, *The Arthur of the Welsh*, p. 21.

41. Charles-Edwards, p. 19.

42. Stevenson, *Nennii*, p. xxx.

43. Alcock, p. 246. Refer to the entire discussion of the Ogham stones. Alcock writes not only that the Dési tribe would have had the chief responsibility for the introduction of Irish customs onto the island [p. 241], but adds that the heaviest concentration of Ogham and Latin inscriptions was in Dyfed, the area where the dynasty of the Dési ruled. The Dési would have encountered familiar characteristics on the island where they came across in the late fourth century [p. 268].

44. Stevenson, footnote 22, p. 50.

45. Alcock, *Arthur's Britain*, p. 102.

46. Blair, *Roman Britain and Early England*, p. 165.

47. Blair, p. 158.

48. G. N. Garmonsway, *The Anglo-Saxon Chronicle*, Parker Chronicle, Entry 443, p. 12; Laud Chronicle, Entry 443, p. 13.

49. Garmonswsay, pp. 12, 13.

50. Graham Webster and Philip Barker, "Wroxeter: Roman City," p. 28.

51. Webster and Barker, p. 28.

Glossary of Terms and Proper Names

This glossary has been formatted and cross-referenced for expediency. Some terms which might initially seem to be common knowledge are associated with narrower, connotative explanations because they stem from the research and findings of my earlier book, The Historic King Arthur, *and this text.*

***Adventi* of the Saxons**—According to Arthurian scholar Leslie Alcock, there were three distinctive "comings" of the Saxons: The first *Adventus* was in approximately 428, the second around 442, and the third in 449-450. In *The Historic King Arthur* Hengist and Horsa were identified as the leaders for the second and third *Adventi.*

adventus (pl. *adventi*)—Latin term literally meaning "arrival" or "coming," applied in context here to the migration or movement into Britain by the *Saxones,* a generic ethnic reference to English Saxons, German Saxons, Angles, Jutes, and Frisians.

Ælle—First Saxon to be designated as *Bretwalda,* a German Saxon who conquered territories in Britain. It has been erroneously interpreted that his territories are along the southern coast, and he is typically referred to as a South Saxon, but evidence shows that his locus is in the Midlands. *See* Bretwalda; Cymen.

Æsc—(Oesc)—Common name for Octha as it appears in *The Anglo-Saxon Chronicle. See also* Arthur: comrades; Arthur: enemies; Octa; Osla Big Knife.

Æternus (Edern in the *Book of Taliessin* XLVI)—Cunedda's father, of Roman lineage. *See also* Paternus; Tacitus; Vortigern.

Æthelbert—Third German Saxon to be designated as *Bretwalda.* His role, however, is minor as a king in Kent. *See* Bretwalda.

Aëtius—Roman general under Valentinian III, recipient of Britain's letter of appeal.

Agælesthrep—Site listed in *The Anglo-Saxon Chronicle* under entry 455 where Horsa was killed, most often translated as Episford on the sole premise that it is in Kent.

Agned—Arthur's eleventh battle on a mount called Agned. Variants: Agned Cathbregomion, Bregion, Cathbregyon, Agned Thabregomion, Agned Cathregonnon.

This text's ascription of probabilities: none, but Geoffrey Ashe's ascription has not yet been refuted. *See* Angers.

agnomen—Latin for a surname, often bestowed as a title of honor, or, fondly, as a nickname. See *cognomen; nomen; praenomen.*

alae—Roman term for cavalry.

Albion—Roman name for Britain derived from *albus,* meaning "White Island."

Aldborough—Tribal capital of the Brigantes territory, also known as Isurium Brigantum.

Allobroges—Literally, "men from another country," distinctive from *kombrogi,* fellow-countrymen, based upon *com-,* "together" or "unified." *See* Cymry; Welsh.

Ambris (Mount)—According to Geoffrey of Monmouth, the site where Hengist massacred Vortigern's Council of Elders. When Aurelius Ambrosius became king, he dedicated this site by having Merlin move Stonehenge here from Ireland. Unfortunately, Monmouth's manuscript is vague, indicating perhaps that he was referring to either the Amesbury or Avebury site of the macabre slaughter. *See* Killarus.

Ambrosius Aurelianus—One of the few proper names used by Gildas in the *De Excidio.* He is of royal Roman heritage, and in the *Historia Brittonum*, he is referred to as Emrys and Merlinus. In Geoffrey of Monmouth's *History of the Kings of Britain,* his name appears as Aurelius Ambrosius, Arthur's uncle and Utherpendragon's brother. Geoffrey of Monmouth also titles Aurelius Ambrosius as "Merlinus Ambrosius," later dropping part of the name and having Merlin emerge as a separate entity. *See* Fleuriot, Leon; Lucius Domitius Aurelianus; Merlin; Riardd Ambrosius.

Amlawdd the Great—Ygerna's father according to the Welsh chronicles. Although unnamed, Culhwch's mother was also Amlawdd's daughter, and hence Ygerna's sister.

"ancient book"—Term used by Geoffrey of Monmouth to refer to one of his ancient sources for the *History of the Kings of Britain. See* Geoffrey of Monmouth; *liber vetustissimus.*

Aneirin—Sixth-century bard, associated with the north, whose poem *The Gododdin,* has survived.

Angel—Term used to refer to a person from Angeln. It has become distinctive from the word "Angle," a person from Anglia. *See also* Angeln.

Angeln—Modern term for Bede's expression, Angulus, referring to the base of the Schleswig-Jutland peninsula, the original homeland of the Angles who settled in Britain. *See also* Angel; Angle.

Angers—Site which Geoffrey Ashe lists as a probability for Arthur's eleventh battle, equated with Agned.

Angle, Anglian—Term which must be distinctive from the word "Saxon," applicable to the inhabitants of the east midlands in Britain whose original homeland was Angeln.

Anglia—Territories east of the midlands in Britain, associated with original settlers from Anglen. The territories later became East Anglia, Middle Anglia, and Mercia.

Anglice—General term for Germanic settlers in Britain who were not Frisian.

Anglo-Saxon Chronicle—One of the four major ancient manuscripts used to delineate the Arthurian milieu. By reconciling it with its Genealogical Preface and using those emendations in conjunction with the *De Excidio,* the *Historia Brittonum,* and the *Annales Cambriae,* an accurate chronology can be devised for the Arthurian Age.

Angulus—Bede's term for Angeln.

Annales Cambriae—The Welsh chronicle which records Arthur's name twice. The year Nulla (0) is equated to the Christian reckoning of A.D. 444, ± two years. For Year 72, which converts to 516, Arthur's victorious battle at Mont Badonicus against the Saxons is recorded; his fateful battle at Camlann is listed in Year 93, A.D. 537. *The Historic King Arthur* emends those dates to A.D. 497 and A.D. 518 based upon a lunar adjustment of a nineteen-year cycle. See Dionysius Exiguus, Victorius of Aquitaine.

Aquae Sulis—Name derived from Sulis Minerva (the Celtic-Roman goddess), this Roman name was used until the A.D. 700s for modern-day Bath. Partially based upon this, the modern site of Bath was rejected as the possible site of Mount Badon in the book *The Historic King Arthur.*

Arddus (Arthus)—According to *The Historic King Arthur*, the epithet on which Arthur's name is built. *Ardd-* or *arth-* is an old Welsh affix meaning "high," leading to the term Arthurex, meaning "High King."

argoad—Term derived from two affixes, the first, *ar-* meaning "on" or "in," and the second meaning "wood" or "forest," associated with Arthur's seventh battle. See also *cellidon.*

Armorica—Another term for Brittany, literally meaning "on the sea." *See also* Letavia; Little Britain.

Arthur—*See* Ambrosius Aurelianus; Arthursus; Riardd Ambrosius; Riothamus.

Arthursus—A name referring to Arthur coined by Graham Phillips/Martin Keatman and derived from the Brythonic word "Arth" plus the Latin word for bear, "Ursus." They suggest that his original title may have been Arthursus, later being shortened to Arthur.

Artur, Artus—The variable proper names as proposed by J. S. P. Tatlock. These are, however, epithets which became the proper name for Arthur. Artus is derived from the Welsh *arddus,* with the double-d pronounced as an unvoiced "th-." "Arddus," meaning "high," was a genitive descriptor for Ambrosius Aurelianus which became an epithet, followed by the Latin *-us* suffix to give the Welsh word prestige, and what evolved was the term "Arddurex" (pronounced "Arthurex"), for the High King Ambrosius.

atavus—Latin term specifically meaning great-great-great grandfather, or generically, "an ancestor."

Avalon—An ancient term applied to Arthur's burial site at Glastonbury, but having strong otherworldly overtones.

Aurelius Ambrosius—Geoffrey of Monmouth's fictional counterpart of Ambrosius Aurelianus; Utherpendragon's brother, Arthur's uncle. As king, he is succeeded by his brother.

Badon, Mount Badon—Arthur's twelfth battle at Mount Badonicus. Variants:

none. This text's ascription of probabilities: Wroxeter and its neighboring hill of the Wrekin. See also *Annales Cambriae*.

barberia—Latin generic term for the barbarians, specifically the *Scotti*, Picts, and *Saxones*.

Bassas—Arthur's sixth battle on the shores of the River Bassas. Variants: Bass Rock, Basing, Bassa, Basse, Lusas. This text's ascription of probabilities: the shores of Basse Bretagne.

Basse Bretagne—Coastal area of Brittany, also called Lower Brittany. *See* Haute Bretagne.

bellum—Latin word for "war" or "battle." When used in conjunction with *dux* as a title for Arthur *(dux bellorum)*, it would suggest a title such as chief commander, or in modernistic terms, the commander-in-chief, the supreme leader or ruler of military forces. See *discordium; proelium*.

blazon—Insignia on knightly shields. One tradition recorded by John of Glastonbury relates that Arthur's original blazon was three red lions on a silver background. Thirteenth-century manuscripts depict Arthur's blazon as three gold crowns against a blue or a red background, which later changes to thirteen gold crowns on a blue or red background. Once Arthur is Christianized the blazon on his shield becomes a silver cross on a green background, with the Virgin and her Son on the dexter canton of the cross.

Book of Taliesin—Manuscripts and fragments by the poet Taliesin which have survived: one is Peniarth MS 16 of the thirteenth century, and the other is Peniarth MS 2 dating to the first quarter of the fourteenth century. Both collections record the name of Arthur.

Bretwalda (Breotenwalda, Brytenwalda)—Saxon term which has traditionally been translated and defined to mean "British ruler" or "Ruler of Britain." "British ruler" indicates that ethnically the ruler is Briton, but "Ruler of Britain" suggests that a foreign king could be ruling in Britain. Although this is a crucial difference for defining the terms, the two words are commonly considered as synonymous. This text uses all three forms synonymously, but concludes that the definition should more accurately be "a German Saxon who allied with his English Saxon compatriots and conquered kingdoms in Britain." The later Bretwaldas were Rædwald of East Anglia; Edwin, Oswald, and Oswy of Northumberland; and Egbert of the West Saxons. *See also* Ælle; Æthelbert; Ceawlin.

Britanni—Generic term used by the Romans referring to all peoples and all tribes who were settled on the island of Britain; the term included all the provincials of the Roman empire who settled as natives and therefore fell under the protectorate of the empire.

Brittany—A country on the northwestern shores of the mainland occupied by the Welsh and other Celts during several back-and-forth migrations, and hence having strong ties to Britain. Also called Armorica, Letavia, Little Britain.

Brydw—A name on Eliseg's Pillar which applies to Vortimer/Cunedda/Elesa. Although the names of Vortigern's other sons appear on the Pillar, Vortimer's name is missing. But because the *Historia Brittonum* praises Vortimer by relating that he is loved by the Britons and blessed by Germanus, and Brydw is praised in the same way on the Pillar, it is linked to Cunneda, whose name is also enigmatically absent from the pillar. *See also* Elesa; Vortimer.

Brythonic—A form of the Ogham language which spread to Britain and later replaced the earlier Goidelic style. *See* Ogham.

burgi—Old English term meaning "fort" or "fortified town."

Cador—According to the *Brut Tysilio* , Cador is the son of Gorlois, Duke of Cornwall, and Eigr (Igraine). Cador is also called Arthur's brother "on his mother's side." *See* Constantine III.

Caerwent—Tribal capital of the Silures territory, also known as Venta Silurum.

Caer Liwelydd, Caer Lliwelydd, Caer Ligualid—Terms used in the *Historia Brittonum* and the Book of Taliessin XLVI to refer to Carlisle, Cunedda's southern homeland.

Caer Luit Coyt—Another name for Wall-by-Lichfield, Octha's stronghold as proposed by this text and *The Historic King Arthur. See* Kaerluideoit; Wall.

Caer Vadon—Another term for Bath, derived from Baddon.

Cæint—Latin word used to identify territories given by Vortigern to the *Saxones,* specifically to Hengist and Horsa. Compare to Chent.

Caister-by-Norwich—Tribal capital of the Iceni territory, also known as Venta Icenorum.

calculi—Computation of genealogies used to introduce to the British Easter Tables.

Caledvwlch—Welsh name for Arthur's sword. *See* Excalibur.

Caman Llan—The most recent consideration as a possibility for the site of Camlann. *Caman* is a brook near Nevern in Wales, which acts as a boundary for a sacred enclosure called a *Llan,* commonly used to separate the secular land of the chieftain from the ecclesiastic land of the priest. *See* Camlann, Battle of.

Camblam—Geoffrey of Monmouth's term for Camlann, Arthur's last battle.

Camboglanna—A geographic region just to the northwest of Hadrian's Wall. The term literally means "crooked bank" and is often used in etymologically identifying Arthur's fatal battle. *See* Camlann, Battle of.

Camelodunum—*See* Colchester.

Camlann, Battle of—A reference to Arthur's last battle. See *Annales Cambriae;* Caman Llan ; Camblam; Charford.

Canterbury—Tribal capital of Kentish territory, also known as Durvonarum Cantiacorum.

cantref,* plural *cantrefi—An ancient Welsh land measurement made up of 100 trefydd (townships). *See also* cymwd; gwlad; trefydd.

Carlisle—Cunedda's settlement when he first came down from the north. *See* Caer Ligualid; Caer Liwelydd.

Carnwennan—Arthur's knife.

castello—A vaguely defined term meaning "fort," "fortification," or "castle," applied to Arthur's eighth battle.

castra—Latin word normally translated as "fortress," but more specifically used to mean a legionary base. One such base was located at Gloucester in the first century.

Cat Coit Celidon—Arthur's seventh battle at Cat Coit Celidon. Variants: Catoit Celidon, Cacoit Celidan, Caledonia. This text's ascription of probabilities: Clun Forest near Kerry, the Argoed of central Bretagne.

catulus—In Latin, a reference to any young animal, suggesting that kits (foxes), cubs (lions and bears), etc., would be included in this generic term. *See* whelp.

Cavall—Arthur's dog; the spelling is also Cabal, Caball.

Ceawlin—Son of Cynric, the second Saxon to be designated as *Bretwalda,* and the first from the West-Saxon house. As a German-Saxon king in Britain, he regained the kingdom of Wessex, which his great-grandfather Cerdic had originally obtained through a pact with Arthur. *See* Bretwalda; Cerdic; Cynric.

cellidon—Old Welsh prefix *celli-* meaning "forest" or "woods," combined with the root *-don* meaning "hill" or "mountain." See also *argoad.*

Celli wig—Arthur's enigmatic court as recorded in the Welsh chronicles. Its variant spellings are listed as Celli Wic, Celliwig, Celliwic, Kelliwic, Kelliwig, Kelli Wig, or Kelli Wic, and its most common locale is listed as somewhere in Cornwall. *The Historic King Arthur,* however, puts forth the theory that it refers to a forest grove near the present village of Kerry in the old Latin province of Cornovii, not Cornwall.

Cerdic—(Ceredig, Ceretic) Like Arthur, Cerdic's identity is triadic; there are three Cerdics during the Arthurian period, each which has traditionally been viewed as a separate individual, but viewed as a single entity in *The Historic King Arthur.* They are Cerdic, the young interpreter for Vortigern; Cerdic, the fifth son of Cunedda; and Cerdic, the later West Saxon king. The floruits and life spans overlap, and the aging process coincides. Based upon material in the Genealogical Preface of *The Anglo-Saxon Chronicle,* he died in 518, which would have been the time of Arthur's fatal battle at Camlann. See Cheldric; Chelric; Cherdic; Creoda.

Cerdicesford—A geographic locale incorrectly used interchangeably with Cerdicesora. *The Historic King Arthur* identifies this site as North Charford near the south-central coast. Compare with Cerdicesora.

Cerdicesora—Commonly confused with Cerdicesford, this site is localized in Ceredigion, Wales, according to *The Historic King Arthur.* Compare with Cerdicesford.

Chambers, E. K.—Writer of *Arthur of Britain* in 1964 who tied together the two name-forms of Ambrosius Aurelianus and Arthur but did not pursue the possibility. *See* Fleuriot, Leon; Uriscampum; William.

Charford—Southern site commonly associated with Cerdicesford in entry 519 of the *Anglo-Saxon Chronicle. See* Cerdicesford; Cerdicesora.

Cheldric—A Saxon who crosses the English Channel to fight in the Battle of Badon, and is killed by Cador on the Isle of Thanet, according to Monmouth. *See* Cerdic.

Chelric—In *History of the Kings of Britain,* replaces Cerdic as a Saxon leader in league with Mordred against Arthur at the Battle of Camlann. *See* Cerdic.

Chent—Latinized term for Kent in southeastern Britain, commonly misidentified as Hengist's, Horsa's, and Octha's kingdom, Compare to Cæint.

Cherdic—This individual appears as Octa's companion in Monmouth's *History of the Kings of Britain* when Hengist summons his son to come to Britain and settle in the north. *See* Cerdic.

chronology, calibration—*See* Dionysiac and/or Victorian chronological calibration; lunar cycle.

Chretien de Troyes—One of the most well-known Arthurian romance writers of the fifteenth century. He coined the term "Camelot" for Arthur's court, about nine centuries after Arthur's era.

Cirencester—Tribal center of the Dubonni, also called Corinium Dobunnorum, the second largest city of Roman Britain. *See* Londonium; St. Albans; Wroxeter.

civitate*, plural *civitates—An urban settlement granted its own senate and magistrates, although normally made up of local aristocracy; hence, a Latin term for civil and administrative centers in Roman Britain. See also *colonia; municipium; vicus.*

coal—Although this mineral was mined, wood remained the major source for baths and fuels in Roman Britain. Sometimes, however, it appears that coal was used for ritualistic purposes at places such as Aquae Sulis (Bath).

cognomen—Latin term for family or last name. See *agnomen; nomen; praenomen.*

cohort—One of ten divisions of an ancient Roman legion.

Colchester—Also known by its native name, Camelodunum, in addition to Colonia Victricensis, this city was the first of four *coloniae* in Britain, founded in A.D. 49. It was the most prominent city in southeast Britain before the Roman conquest. *See* Gloucester; Lincoln; York.

colonia*, plural *coloniae—Latin term referring to settlements for retired legionnaires. There were four coloniae in Britain: Colchester, Gloucester, Lincoln, and York. See also *municipium, civitate, vicus.*

Colonia Nervia—Another term for Glevum, the Roman name for Gloucester.

colors of rank—Colors play a vital role is signifying authority. The color purple expressed power and position in the Roman empire and filtered down to endowed jurisdiction among subjects and sub-kings. The color red also was significant in the early Briton territories. *See* dragon insignia; mantles.

"compacting"—The technique of early scribes listing both major and minor historical events in a very abbreviated series.

"conquered the kingdom"—One translation from Latin describing the acquisition of territory by a force of arms. *See also* "granted the kingdom;" "succeeded to the kingdom."

Constans—In Geoffrey of Monmouth's work, Constaus was the eldest son and brother of Ambrosius and Utherpendragon. He was treacherously manipulated and then murdered through Vortigern's devious plot.

Constantine—According to Monmouth's narrative, Aurelius Ambrosius is the direct descendant of Constantine. Unfortunately, there are so many Constantines and Constantiuses, plus usurpers, that it becomes virtually impossible to pinpoint Ambrosius's father. In the strictest sense of its meaning, this text hypothesizes (rather than theorizes) that Constantius III was Ambrosius's father.

Constantine III—A king whom Gildas Badonicus referred to as "*leænæ Damnoniæ tyrannicus catulus,*" "the tyrant cub of the filthy lioness of Dumnonia," Dumnonia being the earlier term for Cornwall. This same king appears in the Welsh *Bruts* as Cador's son, and in both the *Bruts* and Geoffrey of Monmouth's *History of the Kings of Britain* as the successor to Arthur. A more accurate identification would be Constantine the Briton.

Constantinus, Flavius Claudius—Known as Constantine according to the available histories, this usurper was a common soldier acclaimed emperor in Britain in 406 or 407. However, because he was executed in Ravenna in 411, his reign and death are outside the chronological feasibilities as Ambrosius's father.

Constantius III—Based upon the available histories, the most likely candidate for Ambrosius's father.

consul—Latin term applied to Ambrosius Aurelianus's father in the *Historia Brittonum.* The definition is akin to the one for "magistrate," but more specifically it means "a powerful, commissioned official representing the interests of the appointing country to manage the administrative and judicial functions of a subjugated foreign nation."

Corinium Dobunnorum—*See* Cirencester.

Cornwall—The modern name for the southwestern peninsula of the island. This Welsh term, meaning "the people from Cornovii" evolved in the 700s, a couple of centuries after Arthur's historical period. Prior to that the territory was known by the Latin term Dumnonii.

Creoda—Son of Cerdic, listed in the Genealogical Preface of the *Anglo-Saxon Chronicle,* but ignored in the *Chronicle* itself. *See* Cerdic; Cynric.

Culhwch—Arthur's first cousin; he, like Arthur, has a purple mantle with a red-gold apple in each corner.

Cunedag (Cunedda)—One of the most important figures in insular history. According to the *Historia Brittonum,* he migrates from the north to protect the new empire from the *Scotti,* but also becomes embroiled in civil war between the Britons and the Saxons. His progeny, particularly Cerdic, Enniaun Gert, Eugein Dantguin, and Maglocunus become prominent figures in Welsh/Saxon histories. See Brydw; Elesa; Vortimer.

cunos—Clan affix in Welsh meaning "lion," as in Cunorix, Cunedda, Maglocunus.

cyfarwydd (pl. = cyfarwyddiaid)—Welsh term for trained bards, masters of their trade in the transmission of oral tradition.

cyfarwyddyd—Traditional tales transmitted by the Welsh bards.

Cymen—One of Ælle's sons. His name is a cognate of Cymry and Cumru, a peculiarity since he is the son of a German Saxon.

Cymry, Cymru—Welsh and Wales, terms used by the Welsh to identify themselves, from *kombrogi,* meaning fellow countrymen. *See* its antonym, Allobroges; and its synonym, Welsh.

cymwd, **plural** *cymydau*—Ancient Welsh land measurement made up of fewer than a hundred townships, usually combined to form a cantref. *See also* cantref; gwlad; trefydd.

Cynric—Son of Creoda, incorrectly listed as the son of Cerdic in *The Anglo-Saxon Chronicle,* but properly listed in the Genealogical Preface. *See* Ceawlin; Cerdic; Creoda.

De Antiquitate Glastonie Ecclesie—Manuscript written by William of Malmsbury for Glastonbury Abbey. Fortunately for the all the succeeding generations,

Malmsbury himself included the first part of this manuscript in a subsequent edition of another of his works, titled *Gestis Regum Anglorum,* around 1140 because of the appalling number of interpolations added to the *De Antiquitate* without Malmsbury's knowledge.

(River) Dee—Northern river boundary given for Cunedda's territory in the ancient manuscripts. *See* Dubr Duiu, River Teifi.

De Excidio et Conquestu Britanniae—Commonly shortened to the *De Excidio,* Gildas Badonicus's manuscript.

De Instructione Principis—Written by Giraldus Cambrensis, its main contribution of Arthurian information is Arthur's exhumation at Glastonbury Abbey's cemetery in 1191.

Derguentid—Latin form of the word referring to Vortimer's second battle in the *Historia Brittonum. See* Derwent (River).

Derventio—A common root based upon *derva* and *entio* meaning "oak near a river" or "river where oaks were common." Variations of the word are Derwent, Darwent, Darwen, Darent, Darenth, and Dart, with spelling throughout the centuries compounding the problem: Deruuent, Deowentan, Derewent, Derventione, Diorente, Dærentan, Daerintan, Dærætan, Tarent. Later, new descriptors were added: Lower Darwen, Over Darwen, Netherderwent.

Derwent—*See* Derguentid, Derventio.

> **River**—Site of Vortimer's second battle as listed in the *Historia Brittonum,* identified as Darenth in some translations. There is a River Derwent in western Kent which flows northward to the Thames, another which flows north-south between the city of York and the North Sea, a third which originates about twenty miles east of Manchester and flows into the River Trent, and a fourth originating in the Cumbrian Mountains and flowing into the Solway Firth on the western coast of Wales at Workington.

> **village**—Derived from Derventio, the same root for river names. Several which must be considered as possible locations for Vortimer's battle are Darwen and a Lower Darwen near the mouth of the River Ribble in Lancashire, another in the central part of northern Wales six miles southwest of Ruthin, a Darenth in the southeast suburbs of London in Kent, and a Derwen in northern Wales about 18 miles from the coast. *See* Derventio.

Dionysiac calibration—Chronological reckoning devised by Dionysius Exiguus in A.D. 525 based upon the Incarnation (Birth) of Christ, different by twenty-eight years from the Victorian method of calibration. *See* lunar cycle; Victorian calibration.

Dionysius Exiguus—The individual who devised a chronological method of reckoning in A.D. 525 based upon the Incarnation (Birth) of Christ.

discordium—Latin word used in the *Historia Brittonum* to describe the dissension between Vitalinus and Ambrosius. *The Historic King Arthur* interprets that word as much more moderate than "battle" or "war," settling upon "discord" or "disagreement." See *bellum; proelium.*

draco—Latin term meaning "dragon." It was borrowed from the Greek word *drákön,* meaning "monstrous worm or serpent."

dragon insignia—The dragon as a heraldic symbol was a standard used by the Romans. On the island the Cymry, too, used it as such, and it became indelibly etched as King Arthur's blazon by Geoffrey of Monmouth, assigned first to Utherpendragon and carried on by Arthur. *See* colors of rank.

"Dream of Rhonabwy"—Oldest Welsh prose tale giving the most detail about Arthur's Battle of Badon.

Dubglas—Arthur's second, third, fourth, and fifth battles at the River Dubglas. Variants: Douglas, Dulas, Dulais, Dawlish, Dowlish, Divelish, Blackwater, Dunglas, Duglas. This text's ascription of probabilities: River Douglas.

Dubr Duiu (River)—Welsh term for the River Dee, a common Cymry northern boundary.

Dumnonii—Roman name for the southwestern peninsula of the island. *See* Cornwall.

dux—Roman term meaning, literally or figuratively, "guide, conductor, leader, ruler, or military commander." Its application as a title for Arthur in the *Historia Brittonum* would be either "ruler" or "military commander," probably more accurately as "commander-in-chief."

Eigr—Name for Ygerna (Igraine) as it appears in the *Brut Tysilio.* Eigr is listed as the daughter of Amlaudd the Great.

Elesa—Cerdic's father as listed in *The Anglo-Saxon Chronicle,* a doublet for Cunedda in the Welsh genealogies as proposed in this text. *See* Brydw; Vortimer.

Eliseg (Eliset) Pillar—An Ogham stone dating from the ninth century, erected near Llangollen in northeastern Wales, dedicated in honor of Eliseg, King of Powys. Among others, Vortigern's name is part of the inscription.

emperor—Term commonly used for Arthur in *The Mabinogion.* See *imperator.*

Emrys—Welsh term like Gwledic, Wledig, meaning the overlord of a country or territory.

English Saxons—Those Saxons who had migrated to Britain during Roman occupation, and had hence become known to the Romans by the generic term *Brittanni,* since they had been there for at least a couple of generations. Arthur's battles are mainly against the English Saxons, which is why Gildas Badonicus refers to these conflicts as "civil" or "internal" wars. See German Saxons; home, homeland.

englynion—Early Welsh term for a metrical, three-lined rhyming poem which was used to preface a prose tale. These verses emerged as the eleventh- and twelfth-century Triads, called in Welsh *Trioedd Ynys Prydein,* Triads of the Island of Britain.

Enniaun Girt—Seventh son of Cunedda, Cerdic's older brother, and Eugein Dantguin's father. *See* Cerdic; Cunedda; Owein.

epithet—A title so commonly used for an individual that it replaces his real name.

Esla—Anglo-Saxon name in the *Chronicle* for Vortigern, who has been identified by this book as Æternus.

Ethelwerd (Æthelweard) Chronicle—An excellent supplement to *The Anglo-Saxon Chronicle* which supplies some information not contained in the latter. The former relates that in 494 (a one-year differentiation from the *ASC)* Cerdic and Cynric (an error which must be corrected to Creoda) landed at Cerdicesora, and six years later (in A.D. 501) Wessex was annexed to the West Saxon kingdom, an entry which is not paralleled in the *ACS*. Both chronicles then complete the sequence at Year 519: Cerdic and [Creoda] inherit the *kingship* of West Saxon which includes Wessex, where they fight a battle at Cerdicesford, chronologically intersecting with Arthur's fateful battle at Camlann in 518.

Eubonia—Latin name for the Isle of Man, seen sometimes as Manay, Euboniamanay, and Mana, but not to be confused with Manau Gododdin.

Eugein—Etymological variant of the name Owein. *See* Owein.

Euric—Leader of the Visigoths who defeated Riothamus and his army at the Battle of Bourges in Gaul.

Excalibur—Arthur's sword. The name is derived from the Latin Caliburnus and the Welsh Caledvwlch, meaning "tempered steel."

Exeter—Tribal capital of the Dumnonii territory, also called Isca Dumnoniorum.

federates—Latin term for "confederates" or "allies," a word which was eventually adopted as a synonym for "West Saxons."

Fleuriot, Leon—Author of *Les Origins de la Bretagne* (published in 1980), which suggests that Arthur's name was somehow enigmatically connected to an epithet. Fleuriot writes of Riothamus as the great Briton leader whose Gallic campaigns contributed to the genesis of the Arthurian legends. More important, however, is his belief that Ambrosius Aurelianus's deeds were attributed to someone else named Arthur.

floruit—A general chronological measurement for a generation, usually thirty years. *See* life span; "reasonable age" concept.

fratrueli—Latin word in the *Historia Brittonum* describing the kinship between Octha and Ebissa. However, this word can mean a brother or—based upon citations from Cicero, Ovid, and Tacitus—sometimes a cousin or even a brother-in-law.

fulvus—Latin, meaning tawny, most commonly suggesting the color of a lion.

Gaelic Sea—The most logical interpretation of the site for one of Vortimer's battles, located along the western or northwestern coast of Wales. *See* Gallic Sea; *Gallici maris.*

Galla Placidia—Mother of Valentinian III and wife to Constantius III. According to postulations in this text, she is indirectly tied to Ambrosius Aurelianus through his father, Constantius III; also according to this text, Valentinian III has been identified as the *superbus tyrannus* in Gildas's *De excidio.*

Gallic Sea—Location most commonly given in translation for one of Vortimer's battles, most commonly identified as somewhere in Kent. *See* Gaelic Sea; *Gallici maris.*

Gallici maris—Original Latin term for the site of one of Vortimer's battles. *See* Gaelic Sea; Gallic Sea.

Geoffrey of Monmouth—First real narrator of the Arthurian saga, approximately six centuries after Arthur's death. See *The History of the Kings of Britain (Historia Regum Britanniae).*

German Saxons—Those relatives of English Saxons who lived on the continent. When civil war breaks out on the island, the English Saxons seek aid from their German counterparts. *See* English Saxons; home, homeland.

Gewissei—A later tribal territory overlapping the borderlands of the Silures, Dobunni, and Atrebates. Alternate names are Hwicci, Hrype, and Hræfn.

Gewisse—A slight variant of Gewissei, meaning "allies" or "compatriots." See also *federates.*

Gildas Albanius—One of the twenty-three sons of Caw King of Scotland. This particular Gildas is the subject of Caradoc's *Life of St. Gildas* and John of Glastonbury's *Cronica,* allegedly the saint who is buried at Glastonbury Abbey. This Gildas also appears in the tales of the *Mabinogion* as a character associated with Arthur.

Gildas Badonicus—A near-contemporary of Gildas Albanius, this Gildas was born in the same year that the Battle of Mount Badon was fought and wrote the *De Excidio* forty-four years later. The name of Arthur does not appear in the manuscript, but Gildas Badonicus does specifically mention Ambrosius Aurelianus just prior to his reference to the Badon battle.

Giraldus Cambrensis (Gerald of Wales)—See *De Instructione Principis.*

glano—See *glein-.*

Glastonbury (Abbey)—Arthur's alleged burial site. The Abbey and the Tor are often equated with the Isle of Avalon, not linked by Geoffrey of Monmouth, but commonly synonymous in the later romances.

Glastonbury Cross—The cross allegedly discovered during Arthur's exhumation at Glastonbury Abbey in 1191. Analysis has shown it to be of tenth-century origin, which has become the focus of controversy. The wording (translated) of the inscription varies from "Here lies buried the renown King Arthur with Guenevere his second wife in the Isle of Avalon," because he was supposedly entombed with his queen; to "Here lies buried the famous King Arthur in the Isle of Avalon," which makes no reference to Guinevere but does equate Glastonbury with the Isle of Avalon.

glein—An affix, based upon *glano-,* associated with the first of Arthur's battles, meaning "pure," "clean," or "holy."

Glein—Arthur's first battle at the River Glein. Variants: Gem, Glem, Glen, Cain, Glyme. This text's ascription of probabilities: Rivers Glyme, Cain.

Glevensium—Sometimes shortened to Glevum, this Roman legionary fort became Gloucester. *See also* Colonia Nervia.

Gloucester—Founded a couple of years after Lincoln, this was one of four *coloniae* in Britain, also known as Colonia Nervia Glevensium. It was abandoned as a legionary fortress when the legions moved westward to Caerleon to contain southern Wales. Geoffrey of Monmouth attributes the name of Gloucester to Gloui, father of Vitalinus. The name Vitalinus provides an important link as Arthur's (i.e., Ambrosius's) guardian. *See* Colchester; Lincoln; York.

Gododdin—Area just to the west of the Firth of Forth from whence Cunedda and his sons came.

Gododdin, The—Scottish poem written by Aneirin, which gives the earliest literary reference to Arthur.

Gogyrfan—Guinevere's father, most commonly known as Leodegrance. *See also* Old Oswestry.

Goidelic—Earliest form of the Ogham language. *See* Brythonic; Ogham.

"granted the kingdom"—One translation from Latin of how Cerdic acquired the West Saxon territory. According to John of Glastonbury, Arthur granted the kingdom to Cerdic because of Cerdic's pledge of fealty. *See* "conquered the kingdom;" "obtained the kingdom;" "succeeded to the kingdom."

"great death"—An expression for plague or pestilence. *See* Yellow Pestilence.

Gregory of Tours—In *The History of the Franks,* Gregory provides a detail of the Briton defeat at Bourges de Déols, though he makes no reference to Riothamus as the Briton leader.

Griscom, Acton—Scholar of the early 1900s who must rightfully be recognized for his expertise on Geoffrey of Monmouth. In addition to his knowledge of many of the 198 versions of Monmouth's *Historia Regum Britanniae,* he focuses upon the premise that the Welsh *Bruts,* including the *Tysilio,* could be Monmouth's *liber vetustissimus.* See *Brut Tysilio;* Welsh *Bruts.*

Guanhamara—Variation of Guinevere in Geoffrey of Monmouth's *The History of the Kings of Britain. See* Guinevere.

Guaul—The Latin term referring either to one of the Walls (Hadrian's or the Antonine), or a village by that name. *See* Wall.

Guenedota—Variant name for Gwynedd, Maelgwn's kingdom.

Guinevere—Arthur's queen. The Welsh Triads lists three Guyineveres: Gwynhwyfar, daughter of Cyrwryd Gwent; Gwenhwyfar, daughter of Gwythr ap Griedawl; and Gwenhwyfar, daughter of Gogfran the Giant. Another variation of her name is Guanhamara.

Guinnion (castello)—Arthur's eighth battle at the castello Guinnion. Variants: none. This text's ascription of probabilities: none.

Guithelinus—As Geoffrey of Monmouth's equivalent of Guitolin, Guithelinus is the Bishop of Gloucester promoted to Archbishop of London. He is instrumental in recruiting aid for Britain from Brittany, and he likewise becomes the guardian for both Ambrosius and Utherpendragon. *See* Vitalinus.

Guitolin—Original Latin term for Vitalinus. *See* Guithelinus; Vitalinus.

Gwenn—Arthur's mantle, purple with red-gold apples in each corner, which had the magical power of making a man invisible.

gwenn—Welsh affix commonly translated as "white." However, depending upon its context in various words and phrases, it could be interpreted as "pure," "chaste," "clean," "transparent," or "invisible." As a proper name, it refers to Arthur's mantle, but its name is interpreted as the magical quality of causing invisibility.

gwlad—Ancient Welsh political region subject to single rule and single dynasty, divided into various cantrefi, with each cantref divided into two or more cymydau. *See also* cantref; cymwd; trefydd.

Gwledic—Welsh variant for wledic, wledig, the ruler of a country.

Gwynedd—Maelgwn's kingdom.

Gwyr y Gogledd—Welsh expression meaning "Men of the North" and commonly used as a reference to Cunedda's clan.

hagiography—The biographies of saints or other religious venerated people.

Harleian 3895—Identification for a miscellany including the *Historia Brittonum* and the *Annales Cambriae.*

Haute Bretagne—Heavily wooded interior of Brittany, also called Upper Brittany. *See* Basse Bretagne.

heartland—Term used to refer to prime agricultural, political, and military centers in Britain. In the early manuscripts the reference is normally to the south-central part of the island, but it can also indicate the central midlands.

Hengist—English Saxon leader during the second and third *Adventi.* His brother Horsa and his son Octha (Æsc) were co-chieftains at various times.

heraldry—Use of shield insignia to identify knights. *See* blazon.

Heopwinesfleot—Site of Vortimer's third battle. This has traditionally been identified as Episford or Ebbsfleet in Kent, but Kent itself is an interpolated error.

Historia Brittonum—One of the earliest historical manuscripts which names Arthur, ascribed to a monk named Nennius. One section is devoted to Arthur and his twelve battles against the Saxons. Unfortunately, because it is laden with interpolations, misinterpretations, and incorrect headings, it must be read very analytically.

History of the Kings of Britain (Historia Regum Britanniae)—Printed during 1135, in this text, now commonly termed a "pseudohistory," Geoffrey of Monmouth detailed Arthur's origins, his ancestry, his allies and enemies, his activities both on the island and in Gaul, and his death. It is undoubtedly the most enigmatic book written about Arthur, a complex mixture of truth and fiction, based partly upon a source which Monmouth calls the *liber vetustissimus,* a "very ancient book." See *Brut Tysilio;* Welsh *Bruts.*

home, homeland—An expression used since the time of Gildas Badonicus in reference to the Saxons returning to their homeland or being forced to retreat to the homeland, which has traditionally been interpreted as a Saxon retreat to their homes across the sea. In point of fact, however, the *English* Saxons were settlers of the island and were retreating to their "eastern part of Britain." Only after their defeat at Mount Badon did they call for reinforcements from the *German* Saxon kings across the Channel. Therefore, a crucial distinction must be made between English and German Saxons. See *adventi* of the Saxons; English Saxons; German Saxons; *orientalis sacrilegorum.*

homolog—Two or more different names which knowingly or unknowingly apply to the same genetic individual.

Horsa—Hengist's brother and co-chieftain who was killed by Vortimer in a battle at Æglesthrepe.

Hrype—Tribal name eponymically responsible for geographic sites such as Repton in the Midlands. *See* Gewissei; Hwicci.

Hwicci—Tribal territory of the Gewissei, used by Bede.

imperator—Latin term for "emperor."

intera—Latin word crucial to the translation in the *Historia Brittonum,* meaning "meanwhile," "at length," "later," or "afterward." *The Historic King Arthur* interprets the word as "in the interim."

imperium—Latin term translated as "holding empire," occasionally used for the Roman emperors.

inscribed stones—General term used by Leslie Alcock to identify ancient monumental stones inscribed in Latin, in Ogham (Irish), or in both. The most relevant as they apply to Arthurian history are the Group I stones dating to the fifth, sixth, and seventh centuries. *See* Lapidem Tituli; Ogham.

Insula Oghgul—Original term used in the *Historia Brittonum* but incorrectly translated as "Angeln," leading to the false assumption that Hengist is consulting his own council rather than Vortigern's Council of Elders.

interpolation—Alteration or corruption of an ancient manuscript by inserting new or different material in the margins.

Isca Dumnoniorum—*See* Exeter.

Isle of Avalon—A site of many names: Witrin, Ynis Witrin, the Isle of Glass, the Isle of Apples, Fortunate Isles. In the later romances, it is identified as Arthur's burial site. *See* Glastonbury Abbey.

Isle of Man—*See* Eubonia.

Isurium Brigantum—*See* Aldborough.

Jordanes—In *The Origin and Deeds of the Goths,* he records the battle between Eurich King of the Visigoths, and Riothamus King of the Britons.

Kaerluideoit—Geoffrey of Monmouth's version of Caer Luit Coyt.

Kairliun—An older term, translated either as Caerleon-on-Usk or Chester-upon-Dee.

Kerriwic—Postulated as Arthur's court, interpolated as Kelliwic and Celliwic in the Welsh chronicles.

Killarus (Mount)—According to Geoffrey of Monmouth, the original site in Ireland where Stonehenge was located. Merlin, under the orders of Aurelius Ambrosius and the direction of Utherpendragon, uses his magic to move it to England.

lanio—Latin term used by Gildas Badonicus in the *De Excidio.* In its noun form it is defined as "butcher" or "executioner," but connotatively it can describe a slashing, lacerating predator.

Lapidem Tituli—Literally the "Titled" or "Inscribed" Stone, identifying one of Vortimer's battles against the Saxons near the shores of the Gallici Sea, erroneously interpreted as the *Gallic* rather than *Gaelic* Sea, since Group I Ogham stones are found in Wales and not along the southern coast of England. *See* Ogham stones.

lead—Roman Britain's most important mined metal. The three major-producing mines were in Derbyshire, Flintshire, and the Mendip Hills, which would, of course make these areas coveted for their resources.

Legend of St. Goeznovius—*See* William.

Leicester—Also known as Ratae Coritanorum, this was the tribal capital of the early Coritani territory.

Leodegrance—Name of Guinevere's father. He is also known as Gogyrfan or Gogfran. *See also* Old Oswestry.

Letavia—Another term for Brittany.

Letocetum—*See* Wall.

liber vetustissimus—What Geoffrey of Monmouth claims as the source for some his material, the "very ancient book." It is interpreted by Acton Griscom, among others, as a reference to the Welsh chronicles which Monmouth translated and incorporated into parts of his *History of the Kings of Britain.*

life span—In conjunction with a floruit, a general chronological measurement determined by adding fifteen years to either end of a floruit, giving a span of sixty years. *See* floruit; "reasonable age" concept.

Lincoln—Also called Lindum Colonia, was one of four *coloniae* in Britain, the site of a legionary fort prior to its switch farther north to York. Built in the 90s, it followed a traditional semi-military pattern similar to Colchester's layout. *See* Colchester; Gloucester; York.

Lindum Colonia—*See* Lincoln.

Little Britain—Geoffrey of Monmouth's term for Brittany. *See* Armorica, Letavia.

Llamrei—Arthur's horse, mentioned several times in "Culhwch and Olwen."

Llyfr Bwyn Rhydderch—Welsh term for *The White Book of Rhydderch.*

Llyfr Coch Hergest—Welsh term for *The Red Book of Hergest.*

Londinium—Largest city of Roman Britain, attacked and ravaged in its infancy by Boudicca. *See* Cirencester; St. Albans; Wroxeter.

Lucius Castus Artorius—A second-century Roman soldier, allegedly Arthur's namesake.

Lucius Domitius Aurelianus—Full name of Ambrosius's ancestor, Aurelian, a Roman emperor who ruled from A.D. 270-275. He was also called by an epithet of "Restitutor Orbis" (Restorer of the City) because of credit given him for building the Aurelian Wall around Rome. Many of Aurelian's campaigns were in Gaul, and from there he rescued Britain from pretenders during A.D. 271, 272, and 273. He was murdered by conspirators in 275. Geoffrey of Monmouth was undoubtedly aware of this when he named his "fictional" character Aurelius Ambrosius.

lunar cycle—An adaptation to chronological calibration based upon nineteen-year cycles. This meant, for example, that Arthur's Battle of Badon might have been fought in A.D. 490 according to the Dionysiac chronology, A.D. 499 according to the lunar adaptation, or A.D. 518 according to the Victorian table. *See* Dionysiac calibration; Victorian calibration.

Maelgwn—Variant name for Mailcun, Maglocunus.

maes-—Old English affix derived from *mære-*, used for several geographic sites, which means "boundary."

Maglocunus map Catgolaun Lauhir (Mailcun, Maelgwn)—One of the kings castigated by Gildas Badonicus in the *De Excidio.* In conjunction with this material, his death in 547, recorded in the *Annales Cambriae,* plays a crucial role in being able to establish a reliable chronology during the Arthurian age. He is likewise a key figure in determining Cunedda's migration from the north, as recorded in the *Historia Brittonum.* Maglocunus is the only tyrant who is described differently by Gildas; he is referred to as "insularis draco," the dragon of the island. Maglocunus, Cuneglasus, and Cunedag all have the same affix base, "-cunos-," meaning lion.

Maglocunus map Clutor—Ancestor of Maglocunus ap Lauhir dating to the fifth century, memorialized by a gravestone in St. Brynach's church in Nevern, Wales.

Mailcun—Variant name for Maglocunus, Maelgwn.

Manau Gododdin—Cunedda's northern homeland prior to his migration.

Manau Gustodin (Manau Gododdin, Manaw Gododdin)—Province from which Cunedda and his eight sons came, located at the western tip of the Firth of Forth, not to be confused with the earlier territory of Votadini or the later one of Gododdin.

mansio—Roman term for a hostel or a way station inn, usually used by imperial or official dignitaries. One of their special amenities was ordinarily a lavish bath annex.

mantle—A cloak; an important article of clothing which by its color signified the rank and authority of its wearer. For a Roman, the most prestigious flash of authority was purple; however, red, as exemplified by Patern Pesrut, or Paternus of the Red Robe, Cunedda's grandfather, also signified authority and rank. In two of the *Mabinogion* tales, Culhwch's and Arthur's mantles are purple brocade with red-gold apples in each corner.

maqi (mab, map, ap)—Goidelic terms meaning "son of."

Maximus, Magnus Clemens Maximus, Maxim Wletic—Usurper who in A.D. 383 proclaimed himself emperor while commanding troops in Britain, defeated Emperor Gratian in Gaul, and became recognized by Theodosius I, Emperor of the east. In an attempt to invade Italy he was defeated and beheaded by Theodosius in 388. However, he left an indelible mark in Britain, and many tribal leaders claimed ancestry from him.

mearc—Old English affix meaning "mark," "boundary mark," "boundary," "border," or "border district." It is a cognate of the Old English word *mierce,* which means Mercians, or literally translated, "borderers."

Mearcrædesburna—One of the sites where Ælle battles against the Welsh. In conjunction with the word "Welsh," its etymology is important in determining its locus, since it means "border" or "borderlands" and the kingdom of Mercia has the same cognate.

Medraut—Cognate of Mordred, which appears in the *Annales Cambriae.*

Medrod—Name appearing in the *Brut Tysilio* for Medraut in the *Annales Cambriae* and Mordred in Monmouth's *History of the Kings of Britain.*

Men of the North—*See* Gwyr y Gogledd; Manau Gustodin.

Merlin—Character invented by Geoffrey of Monmouth evolving from Aurelius Ambrosius and becoming a major figure in the later romances. *See* Ambrosius Aurelianus.

migration—Movement during the Arthurian period from Britain to the mainland or from the mainland to Britain. A term which applies also to Cunedda's movement from the Manau Gododdin territories to the south to subdue the *Scotti* infiltrating from Ireland.

Mirabilia—Latin term referring to the section of the *Historia Brittonum* known as "The Wonders of Britain."

Mordred—Name of Medraut as recorded in Geoffrey of Monmouth's *The History of the Kings of Britain.* Monmouth continuously confuses Mordred as either Arthur's bastard son or his nephew. *The Historic King Arthur* views Mordred as Arthur's nephew, and this text considers a link between Mordred and Maglocunus map Catgolaun Lauhir.

mortalitas magna—Latin for the "great death," usually in reference to a plague.

municipium*, plural *municipia—An existing urban settlement, granted special privileges by charter. See also *civitate; colonia; vicus.*

nobiliores—Latin term with several complex definitions. In its literal sense it can mean "celebrated," "renowned," or "well-known." In its *transferred* sense it means "noble," "of noble birth," and most important as it applies in this particular Arthurian context, "belonging to a family which had held the office of consul." See *consul.*

nomen—Latin term for middle name indicating a person's *gens* (clan). See *agnomen; cognomen; praenomen.*

"obtained the kingdom"—A crucial distinction in translation to separate it from other expressions such as "conquering the kingdom." In its Arthurian context, this refers to Cerdic's acquisition of Wessex; Arthur granted Cerdic these territories in return for Cerdic's pledge of fealty. *See* "conquered the kingdom;" "granted the kingdom."

Octha (Octa)—Common Briton name for one of Arthur's enemies according to the *Historia Brittonum.* In that work Arthur fights his twelve battles against Octha; the fight culminates in the Battle of Badon. Later, in *The History of the Kings of Britain* by Geoffrey of Monmouth, **Octa** is an enemy of Aurelius Ambrosius, Arthur's uncle, and Utherpendragon, Arthur's father. Upon Horsa's death he becomes co-chieftain with his father Hengist, and later allies himself with Cerdic. *See also* Æsc; Osla Big Knife.

Ogham—A form of the word Oghgul, meaning "Irish." Many stone memorials bearing the Ogham script exist throughout Wales and are peculiar to it. *See* Ogma.

Ogham stones—Gravestones or memorials derived from the word *Oghgul* meaning "Irish." The Ogham script is a unique alphabet composed of slash marks inscribed most commonly on the edges of markers. Of nearly two hundred stones classified as Group I, dating from the fifth, sixth and seventh centuries, approximately 140 of them are concentrated in the Gwynedd, Dyfed, and Brycheiniog territories of Wales; none, however, has ever been discovered in Kent. According to Peter Berresford Ellis, *Ogham* is an eponymic derivative from the name Ogma, who was the Irish God of Eloquence and Literature. *See* Ogham; Ogma.

Ogma—Irish God of Eloquence and Literature, derived from the Gallic god Ogmios, who also gave rise to the British god Ogmia. *See* Ogham; Ogham stone.

Old Oswestry—In literary tradition, the court of Gogyrfan, Guinevere's father. The site was previously known as Maes Cogwy.

orientali sacrilegorum—Term used by Gildas Badonicus in the *De Excidio* as a reference to the *Saxones* from the eastern part of the island, in Britannia Secunda. It literally translates to "sacrilegious easterners." Scholar Michael Winterbottom translates the term as "impious easterners." The term asserts a differentiation between these people (English Saxons) and German Saxons. See also *adventus.*

Osla Big Knife—Name for Octha as it appears in *The Mabinogion.* In "How Culhwch Won Olwen" Osla is one of Arthur's warriors (chasing Twrch Trwyth) and a comrade, but in "The Dream of Rhonabwy" he is his major enemy at the Battle of Badon. *See* Æsc; Octha.

Outigern (Dutigern)—A mysterious Briton king whose name appears only once in history. He fights against the English nation and might possibly figure into the calibration of Cunedda's migration from Manau Gododdin.

Owein—Although there are several figures named Owein in Arthuriana (such as Owein, son of Urien, and Owein, son of Maredudd), the one of prime importance is the Owein in "The Dream of Rhonabwy" of *The Mabinogion* and identified in *The Historic King Arthur* as the etymological variant of "Eugein Dantguin," son of Enniaun Girt and grandson of Cunedda who was Arthur's opponent in the symbolic gwddbwyll game, and hence an enemy of the king at the Battle of Badon. *See* Eugein.

Pa gur—Poem from *The Black Book of Carmarthen* in which Llachau and Kei are fighting "lions," a better interpretation for the affix "-cunos-." It also gives the name "Uthyr Pendragon," which Monmouth might have borrowed, and mentions Arthur's tenth battle several times .

Paternus (Patern Pesrut, Paternus of the Red Robe)—Cunedda's grandfather, obviously of Roman lineage, with the color red suggesting royalty, or at least special Roman recognition. *See also* Æternus; Tacitus.

pestifera lues—A plague identified shortly before the second Saxon *Adventus,* also labeled as the Plague of 442 by C. E. Stevens. *See* plague.

plague—See *mortalitas magna, pestifera lues,* Vad Velen; Yellow Pestilence.

praenomen—Latin term for first name. See *agnomen; cognomen; nomen.*

proelium—Latin word for "battle." See *bellum; discordium.*

Prydwen—Arthur's ship.

Pytheas—Greek navigator who recorded his travels about three centuries before the Romans invaded Britain. Although none of his work now exists, references in other sources give perceptive insights about Britain's agriculture, trade, and economy.

Rædwald—Fourth German Saxon to be designated as *Bretwalda.*

Ratae Coritanorum—*See* Leicester.

"reasonable age" concept—A life span judgment of approximately sixty years, so that extreme age in the ancient manuscripts will be viewed with suspicion as dual or missing generations. *See* floruit; life span.

Red Book of Hergest—Called the *Llyfr Coch Hergest* in Welsh, this is the most complete collection of Welsh manuscripts and fragments, compiled around 1400 and now preserved in the Bodleian Library at Oxford (Jesus Coll. MS 111). The *Red Book* lists thirty-two cities of Britain.

Renwein—Hengist's daughter and Vortigern's concubine, unnamed in the *Historia Brittonum,* but identified in Monmouth's *The History of the Kings of Britain.* She is sometimes called Rowena.

Rhiadaf—Welsh name for Riothamus.

Rhongomynyad—Arthur's spear or lance. It was commonly referred to by a shortened version "Rhon" or "Ron."

Rhos

cantref

In **Gwynedd** along the northern shoreline, part of Maglocunus's kingdom. According to the *Annales Cambriae,* this is where Maglocunus was infected with the Yellow Pestilence and perished.

in **Dyfed**, part of the southwestern peninsula.

township

In **Dyfed**, near the River Teifi bordering the old territory of Ceredigion.

In **Glamorganshire**, southern Wales.

Riardd Ambrosius—The name coined in *The Historic King Arthur* to refer to the triad Ambrosius Aurelianus, Riothamus, and Arthur, as being the same individual. Ambrosius is the only proper name (the factual historical figure of Roman royalty); *(Ri(a)-* means "King," and *(a)rdd-* (pronounced as an unvoiced "th-") means "high."

Riatham—Breton name for Riothamus.

Ribroit—Variant of Tribruit, Arthur's tenth battle. Ribroit is an interesting alternative because its root is based upon geographic names identifying boundaries of the Hrype tribe.

Rigotamos—Briton name for Riothamus.

Riothamus—Briton king of the 470s who crossed Ocean to join the Romans and Gauls in their fight against the barbarians. The term is literally an epithet, suggesting "Supreme King." See Arthur: epithets; Rhiadaf; Riatham; Rigotamos.

Rowena—*See* Renwein.

Romanitas—Term coined to refer to post-Roman tribes and leaders who remained loyal to Roman dominion even after abandonment from Britain and who actively sought their return.

Saesons—A synonymous term for the English, or the English Saxons, applicable by the Romans to all Frisian-speaking people settled in Britain. The Saesons mainly occupied what the Romans labeled as Britannia Secunda.

St. Albans—Also known as Verulanium, this was the third largest city in Roman Britain. *See also* Cirencester; Londinium; Wroxeter.

St. Brynach's Church at Nevern—Site of two bilingual fifth-century stones, the Great Celtic Cross, and Caman Llan. *See* Caman Llan; Maglocunus map Clutor; Vitalinus.

Saxon *Adventi*—See *Adventi* of the Saxons.

Saxones—Third-century Latin word for foreigners from the continent; it was a generic term for the Germanic tribes, including the Saxons, Angles, and Frisians.

Saxoniaid—Welsh term synonymously referring to the German (continental) Anglo-Saxons.

Saxons—Word borrowed from the Latin *Saxones* by the Welsh and Britons as *Saesons,* which over the centuries has blended in references to English Saxons, German Saxons, Angles, and Frisians. *See* English Saxons; German Saxons.

Scotti—Early term for the Irish migrants infiltrating the western and northwestern coast during the time of Gildas; not a reference to Scots.

scribal error—An inadvertent miscopy of a scribe in ancient manuscripts.

scuid—Old Welsh word meaning "shoulder." See *yagwydd.*

scuit—Old Welsh term meaning "shield." See *yaswyd.*

Searoburh—Saxon word for Old Sarum, just north of Salisbury. It is the heartland of southern Britain and the site of Saxon/Briton conflict.

seax—Saxon meaning "broad sword." In both "How Culhwch Won Olwen" and "The Dream of Rhonabwy" it is translated into "Big Knife" in reference to Osla.

shield—*See* blazon; heraldry; *scuit.*

Sidonius—Validates by name that Riothamus was in Gaul in A.D. 469 through a letter addressed to the Briton king.

Silchester—Atrebates tribal center, also referred to as Calleva Atrebatum.

silva—Latin term for "forest," used, for instance to describe Arthur's seventh battle, in "silva Celidonis."

"succeeded to the kingdom"—One translation from Latin suggesting the acquisition of a territory through inheritance. *See also* "conquered the kingdom;" "granted the kingdom."

superbus tyrannus—Gildas's term for the individual who invited the *Saxones* into Britain; later scribes assigned the epithet "Vortigern" to this term, but it more realistically applies generically to a Roman emperor, the supreme overlord.

Tacitus—Cunedda's great-grandfather, of Roman lineage. *See also* Æternus; Paternus.

Taliessen—A bard of the sixth century, whose poetry survived in bits and pieces. He also appears in some Welsh tales as a character.

tawny—A coloring or shading. See *fulvus.*

(River) Tebi, Teifi—River in central Wales which drains into Cardigan Bay at Cardigan; the Southern boundary of Cunedda's territory.

toises—Term for a Roman mile.

tor—British term for a craggy hill, commonly a site for a hill fort.

translocation—The displacement of an ancient geographic site, either because of faulty translations, inaccurate headings or subheadings, or the confusion of two or more sites with the same name.

transpicuousness—In Arthurian terms, the capability of clearly seeing and understanding the milieu of Arthur's time, including chronology, geography, events, and historical figures.

transvaluation—The re-evaluation of not only Arthurian history but also of satellite modifications which repudiate accepted standards not satisfactorily reconciled over the last fifteen centuries.

trefydd—Ancient Welsh term for a township, used in land measurements. *See* cantref; cymwd; gwlad.

Tribruit—Arthur's tenth battle at the River Tribruit. Variants: Ribroit, Trathtriuroit, Robroit. This text's ascription of probabilities: none.

tyranni—Gildas's term in Section C, chapters 27 through 36 of the *De Excidio* for the five contemporary kings whom he castigates.

Brut Tysilio—The *Brut* which melds almost perfectly with the *De Excidio,* the *Historia Brittonum,* the *History of the Kings of Britain,* and the *Mabinogion* genealogically, and with the *De Excidio,* the *Historia Brittonum,* the *Anglo-Saxon Chronicle,* and the *Annales Cambriae* chronologically. *See* Welsh *Bruts.*

Urbe Legionis—Arthur's ninth battle at the "city of legions." Variants: Kairliun.

The "city of legions" could be Caerleon, Chester, Colchester, Exeter, Gloucester, Lincoln, Usk, Wroxeter, or York. This text's ascription of probabilities: Wroxeter, based upon its locale and its association with the Battle of Badon. However, other hot spots of Welsh/Saxon conflicts could well have been at the ex-legionary fortresses of Caerleon, Usk, or Chester, since they are in Welsh territories.

Uriscampum—Chronicler of the 1170s who usually interpolated manuscripts of the 1130s and 1140s, including ones by Sigebert Gembloux, Beauvais, and Geoffrey of Monmouth, suggested as early as 1175 that Riothimir (Riothamus) should be identified with Arthur. *See* Chambers, E. K.; Fleuriot, Leon; William.

Utherpendragon—A "fictional" character invented by Geoffrey of Monmouth, the brother of Aurelius Ambrosius, the father of Arthur, and the paramour/husband of Ygerna. Historically, an epithet for Constantius III, Ambrosius Aurelianus's father.

Vad Velen—Term for the Yellow Pestilence which killed Maglocunus. According to tradition, Taliessin cursed Maglocunus, who sought refuge from the plague; he saw Vad Velen through the church keyhole in Rhos and perished as a consequence.

vallum—Term for a Roman rampart.

Venta Belgarum—*See* Winchester.

Venta Icenorum—*See* Caister-by-Norwich.

Venta Silurum—*See* Caerwent.

Verulamium—*See* St. Albans.

Victorian calibration—Chronological reckoning devised by Victorius of Aquitaine in A.D. 457 based upon the Passion (Death) of Christ, different from the Dionysiac method of calibration by twenty-eight years. *See* Dionysiac calibration; lunar cycle.

Victorius of Aquitaine—Individual who devised a chronological method of reckoning in A.D. 457 based upon the Passion (Death) of Christ, discovering in the process what is termed the Great Cycle of 532 years.

vicus*, plural *vicani—A settlement which grew outside the walls of military sites. See also *civitate; colonia; municipium.*

Viroconium Cornoviorum—Sometimes shortened to Viroconium, the Roman name for the capital of the Cornovii territory; also known as Wroxeter. *The Historic King Arthur* theorizes that Arthur's twelfth battle was fought just outside this city on a hill fort called the Wrekin.

Vitalinus—Son of Gloui, one of the most enigmatic figures of Welsh histories and genealogies. He has been traditionally identified as Vortigern's ally and Ambrosius's enemy, but *The Historic King Arthur* and this text identify him as an ally and guardian of Ambrosius and therefore Vortigern's enemy. His Latin name is actually Guitolin. *See* Gloucester; Guithelinus; Guitolin.

Vitalianus Stone—Located at St. Brynach's Churchyard in Nevern, this bilingual stone dates from the fifth century. Its Latin inscription reads *Vitaliani Emereto,* and its Ogham inscription translates to *Vitaliani. See* Guotolin.

Vortigern—The *superbus tyrannus* of Gildas, named in the *Historia Brittonum,* who assumed kingship in A.D. 425 immediately after the Roman abandonment. Tentatively suggested in this text as Æternus, Cunedda's father according to the Welsh genealogies, and Esla, Cerdic's grandfather, in *The Anglo-Saxon Chronicle.*

Vortimer—Son of Vortigern who appears only in the *Historia Brittonum,* but even there he is omitted from the genealogies. Viewed by some scholars as the Briton counterpart of the Roman Ambrosius Aurelianus, he splits Vortigern's reign and fights four battles against the Saxons. The word "Vortimer" is an epithet meaning "Over-King" and this text postulates that Cunedda is the name behind the epithet. *See* Brydw; Elesa.

Votadini—Early Latin name for the Gododdin territory.

Wall—Upon Octha's invitation into Britain, Hengist sends him to a locale by the name of Guaul in Latin, which enigmatically translates to Wall. *The Historic King Arthur* identifies this site as the Roman Letocetum, also known as Wall-by-Lichfield and Caer Luit Coyt, an important way station during the Arthurian age.

Wall-by-Lichfield—*See* Wall.

"wearing the purple"—Roman term used to signify someone of royal rank or authority.

Welsh—From *Wylisc,* Old English Anglican, Cæntish, meaning foreigner, the term used by the English Saxons for the Cymry.

Welsh *Bruts*—Welsh oral tradition which finally found its way into print around the 1100s. There are two controversies which spill over to the present day. The first is the disregard of competent Welsh scholars, which has prevented the Welsh *Bruts* from claiming their astonishing impact and appropriate niche in British history, a shortcoming which has still not been rectified since Acton Griscom's time. The second is the uncertainty of the *Bruts'* existence prior to or after the appearance of Monmouth's *Historia,* important because it could resolve the issue of whether or not the *Bruts* could be Monmouth's *liber vetustissimus. See* Geoffrey of Monmouth; Griscom, A.; *History of the Kings of Britain; Brut Tysilio.*

Wessex—Part of Cerdic's West Saxon kingdom, commonly identified as Hampshire and Somerset in southern England. *See* West Saxon.

West Saxon—Term for Cerdic's genealogical house. After Arthur grants Cerdic parts of Hampshire and Somerset, Cerdic's kingdom ranges from Wessex in southern England to Ceredigion on the western coast of Wales. "West Saxon," therefore, is a general term, and Ceredigion and Wessex are part of that kingdom.

whelp—Reference to a young animal, sometimes in a specific sense and at other times generically. "Whelp" specifically has come to mean a young dog or wolf, but generally, as in the *De Excidio,* it can refer to a lioness's young. See *catulus.*

White Book of Rhydderch—Early Welsh prose manuscript, *Llyfr Bwyn Rhydderch,* written around 1325 and preserved in two volumes, Peniarth 4 and 5, reposited in the National Library of Wales. Arthur's name appears in these preservations. The *White Book* refers to the list of the cities but does not identify them.

William—Scribe of the *Legend of St. Goeznovius* around 1019 whose work echoes Arthur's Gallic campaigns, thus suggesting a homolog with Riothamus. *See* Chambers, E. K.; Fleuriot, Leon; Uriscampum.

William of Malmsbury—See *De Antiquitate; Glastonie Ecclesie.*

Winchester—Tribal center of the Belgae, also called Venta Belgarum.

Wledic, Wledig—Welsh term for the ruler of a country; the overking of a territory. *See* Emrys; Gwledic.

(the) Wrekin—The hill fort just outside Viroconium (Wroxeter). *The Historic King Arthur* identifies this site as Arthur's twelfth battle, the Battle of Mons Badonicus.

Wroxeter—Tribal capital of the Cornovii territory, also called Viroconium Cornoviorum, the fourth largest city of Roman Britain. *See also* Cirencester; Londinium; St. Albans.

Wynebgwrthucher—Arthur's shield. Monmouth refers to Arthur's shield as Prydwn, but this seems to be a confusion.

yagwydd—Welsh word meaning "shoulder." See *scuid.*

yaswyd—Welsh word meaning "shield." See blazon; heraldry; *scuit.*.

Yellow Pestilence—The disease which killed Maglocunus in A.D. 547. *See* Vad Velen.

Ygerna (Igraine)—In the Romances, Arthur's mother.

York—One of four *coloniae* in Britain constructed in the 230s, the new legionary base as the Roman troops continued their thrust to the north. *See also* Colchester; Gloucester; Lincoln.

Bibliography

Alcock, Leslie. *Arthur's Britain.* New York: Viking Penguin, Inc., 1987.

_____. *"By South Cadbury is that Camelot ...": The Excavation of Cadbury Castle 1966–1970.* Hazell Watson and Viney Ltd., Aylesbury, Great Britain: Thames and Hudson, 1972.

_____. *Was This Camelot? Excavations at Cadbury Castle, 1966–1970.* New York: Stein and Day Publishers, 1972. (This text and the one immediately preceding are identical, including the same plates and drawings, except that one was printed in the United States and the other in Great Britain.)

Anderson, Alan Orr, and Marjorie Ogilvie Anderson. *Adomnan's Life of Columba.* Toronto and New York: Thomas Nelson and Sons Ltd., 1961.

Anderson, W. B., ed. and trans. *Sidonius: Poems and Letters, Volume 1.* Cambridge: Harvard University Press, reprinted 1956, 1963.

_____, ed. and trans. *Sidonius: Poems and Letters, Volume 2.* Cambridge: Harvard University Press, reprinted 1956, 1963.

Ashe, Geoffrey. "'A Certain Very Ancient Book': Traces of an Arthurian Source in Geoffrey of Monmouth's History," *Speculum* 56, 1981, 301–323.

_____, ed. *The Discovery of King Arthur.* New York: Henry Holt and Company, 1987.

_____. *King Arthur's Avalon: The Story of Glastonbury.* Glasgow: William Collins Sons and Co. Ltd, copyrighted 1957, tenth impression, 1987.

Ashe, Geoffrey. "The Origins of the Arthurian Legend," *Arthuriana,* Volume 5, Number 3, Fall 1995. Southern Methodist University: Dallas, Texas. 1–24.

_____. *The Quest for Arthur's Britain.* New York, Washington, London: Frederick A. Praeger Publishers, 1968.

_____, ed. *The Quest for Arthur's Britain.* Chicago: Academy Chicago Publisher, 1987.

Baines, Keith. "A Rendition in Modern Idiom," Sir Thomas Malory's *Le Morte D'Arthur.* New York: Bramhall House, 1957.

Barber, Richard, ed. *The Arthurian Legends: An Illustrated Anthology.* Yugoslavia: Dorset Press, a division of Marboro Books Corporation, by arrangement with Boydell & Brewer Ltd., 1985.

_____. *Arthur of Albion.* London: Barrie and Rockliff with Pall Mall Press, 1961.

_____. *The Figure of Arthur.* London: Longman Group Ltd., 1972.

_____. *The Knight and Chivalry.* New York: Harper & Row, Publishers, A Harper Colophon Book, 1970, 1974.

Baring-Gould, Sabine, and John Fisher. *The Lives of the British Saints.* 4 volumes, for the honourable Society of Cymmrodorion, London, 1907–1913.

Bede. *A History of the English Church and People.* New York: Dorset Press, 1985.

Blair, Peter Hunter. *Roman Britain and Early England, 55 B.C.–A.D. 871.* New York/London: W. W. Norton & Company by arrangement with Thomas Nelson and Sons Ltd., 1966.

Brengle, Richard L., ed. *Arthur, King of Britain: History, Romance, Chronicle, & Criticism.* New York: Meredith Publishing Company, 1964.

Bromwich, Rachel. "Celtic Elements in Arthurian Romance: A General Survey." *The Legend of Arthur in the Middle Ages,* edited by P. B. Grout, et. al. Cambridge: D. S. Brewer, an imprint of Boydell and Brewer Ltd., 1983.

_____, ed. *The Beginnings of Welsh Poetry: Studies by Sir Ifor Williams.* Cardiff: reprinted by permission of University of Wales Press, 1972.

_____, A.O.H. Jarman, and Brynley F. Roberts, eds. *The Arthur of the Welsh: The Arthurian Legend in Medieval Welsh Literature.* Cardiff: University of Wales Press, 1991.

Bullfinch, Thomas. *Bullfinch's Mythology,* particularly "King Arthur and His Knights," 367–525, and "The Mabinogion," 527–633. New York: Avenel Books, Crown Publishers, 1989.

Butler, H. E., ed. and trans. *The Autobiography of Giraldus Cambrensis.* London: Johnathan Cape, 1937.

Caldwell, Robert A. "*The Use of Sources in the* Variant *and Vulgate Versions of the* Historia Regum Britanniæ *and the Question of the Order of the Versions," Bulletin Bibliographique de la Société Internationale Arthurienne (Bibliographical Bulletin of the International Arthurian Society), Number 9, 1957,* 123–124.

Campbell, A., ed. *The Chronicle of Æthelweard.* Edinburgh: Thomas Nelson and Sons Ltd., 1962.

Carley, James P. *The Chronicle of Glastonbury Abbey: An Edition, Translation and Study of John of Glastonbury's Cronica Sive Antiquitates Glastoniensis Ecclesie.* trans. by David Townsend, Woodbridge, Suffolk: The Boydell Press, 1985.

_____. *Glastonbury Abbey: The Holy House at the Head of the Moors Adventurous* . New York: St. Martin's Press, 1988.

Chambers, E. K. *Arthur of Britain.* Cambridge: Speculum Historiale, 1964.

"The Church of St. Brynach, Nevern Pembrokeshire." Distributed pamphlet under the guidance of the Vicar, Churchwardens & Parishioners. Wales: Cardigan, H. L. Jones & Son, 3rd Edition, May 1994.

Clayton, Peter. *Guide to the Archaeological Sites of Britain.* London: B. T. Batsford Ltd., 1985.

Coles, J. M., and B. J. Orme. *Prehistory of the Somerset Levels.* Hertford: Stephen Austin and Sons Limited, 1982.

Colgrave, Betram, and R. A. B. Mynors, eds. *Bede's Ecclesiastical History of the English People.* Oxford: Clarendon Press, 1969.

Collingwood, R. G. and J. N. L. Myres. *Roman Britain and the English Settlements.* Oxford: The Clarendon Press, Second Edition, 1937.

Cowan, Janet, ed. *Sir Thomas Malory's Le Morte D'Arthur, Volume I.* Middlesex: Penguin Books, 1969.

_____. *Sir Thomas Malory's Le Morte D'Arthur, Volume II.* Middlesex: Penguin Books, 1969.

Cunliffe, Barry. *The Celtic World: An Illustrated History of the Celtic Race.* New York: published by Greenwich House, distributed by Crown Publishers, Inc., by arrangement with McGraw Hill Book Company, 1986.

_____. *The City of Bath.* New Haven: Yale University Press, 1986.

_____, selector and introducer. *Heywood Sumner's Wessex.* Wimbourne, Dorset: Rox Gasson Associates, 1985.

_____. *Iron Age Communities in Britain.* London: Routledge and Kegan Paul Ltd., 1974.

Curley, Michael J. *Geoffrey of Monmouth.* New York: Twayne Publishers, 1994.

Davies, John. *A History of Wales.* New York: Penguin Books, 1993.

Dowden, W. A. "Little Solsbury Camp," *Proceedings of the Bristol University Spelaeological Society,* #8 (1957), 18–29, and #9 (1962), 177–182.
Ekwall, Eilert. *The Concise Oxford Dictionary of English Place-names.* Oxford: by permission of Oxford University, Clarendon Press, 1936.
_____. *The Concise Oxford Dictionary of English Place-names,* fourth edition. Oxford: Clarendon Press, reprinted 1991.
Ellis, Peter Berresford. *Caesar's Invasion of Britain.* London: Book Club Associates, by arrangement with Orbis Publishing Limited, 1978.
_____. *The Druids.* Grand Rapids, Michigan: William B. Eerdmans Publishing Company, 1994.
Evans, D. H. "Valle Crucis Abbey," *Valle Crucis Abbey.* Cadw: Welsh Historic Monuments, 1987, 2–46.
Evans, D. Simon, ed. *Lives of the Welsh Saints,* by G. H. Doble. Cardiff: University of Wales Press, 1971.
Evans, J. Gwenogvryn, with the co-operation of John Rhys. *The Text of the Book of Llan Dav, Reproduced from the Gwnsaney Manuscript.* Oxford, 1893.
Evans, Sebastain, trans. *Geoffrey of Monmoth's History of the Kings of Britain.* New York: E. P. Dutton and Company, 1958.
Fairbairn, Neil, and Michael Cyprien. *A Traveller's Guide to the Kingdoms of Arthur.* United States and Canada: Historical Times, Incorporated, by special arrangement with Bell and Hyman Publishers Denmark House, London, 1983.
Fletcher, Robert Huntington. *The Arthurian Material in the Chronicles.* New York: Burt Franklin, 1966.
Ford, Patrick K., trans. *The Mabinogi and other Medieval Welsh Tales.* Berkeley and Los Angeles: University of California Press, 1977.
Forester, Thomas, ed. and trans. *The Chronicle of Henry of Huntingdon, Comprising the History of England, from the Invasion of Julius Caesar to the Accession of Henry II.* London: Henry G. Bohn, York Street, Covent Garden, 1853.
Gantz, Jeffrey, trans. *The Mabinogion.* New York: Viking Penguin Books, 1987.
Garmonsway, G. N., trans. and ed. *The Anglo-Saxon Chronicle.* London: J. M. Dent and Son Ltd., 1990.
Gibson, Edmond, trans. *Camden's Britannia, Newly translated into English with Large Additions and Improvements.* Printed by F. Collins, for A. Swale, at the Unicorn at the West-end of St. Paul's Church-yard, and A. & J. Churchil, at the Black Swan in Pater-noster-Row, 1695.
Giles, J. A., ed. *Six Old English Chronicles.* London: George Bell and Sons, 1885.
Godwin, Parke, *Firelord.* New York: Avon Books, a division of The Hearst Corporation, 1980.
Goodrich, Norma Lorre. *King Arthur.* New York, Toronto: Franklin Watts, 1986.
_____. *Merlin.* New York: Franklin Watts, 1987.
Grabowski, Kathryn, and David Dumville. *Chronicles and Annals of Mediaeval Ireland and Wales.* Woodbridge, Suffolk: The Boydell Press, 1984.
Gregory of Tours. *History of the Franks,* trans. by Ernest Brehaut. New York: Columbia University Press, 1916.
Griscom, Acton, and Robert Ellis Jones, trans. *The Historia Regum Britanniæ of Geoffrey of Monmouth.* London: Longmans, Green and Co., 1929.
Grout, P. B. et al., eds. *The Legend of Arthur in the Middle Ages.* Cambridge: D. S. Brewer, an imprint of Boydell & Brewer Ltd., 1983.
Hammer, Jacob. *Geoffrey of Monmouth Historia Regum Britanniæ: A Variant Version Edited from Manuscripts.* Cambridge, Massachusetts: The Mediaeval Academy of America, Publication No. 57, 1951.

_____. "Some Additional Manuscripts of Geoffrey of Monmouth's *Historia Regum Britanniae,*" *Modern Language Quarterly,* Volume Three, Number 2, June 1942.
Henken, Elissa R. *Traditions of the Welsh Saints.* Cambridge: D. S. Brewer, an imprint of Boydell & Brewer Ltd., 1987.
Hinde, Thomas, ed. *The Domesday Book: England's Heritage, Then and Now.* Avenel, New Jersey: Crescent Books, distributed by Random House Value Publishing, Inc., 1995.
Hopkins, Andrea. *The Book of Guinevere: Legendary Queen of Camelot.* New York, Avenel: Crescent Books, 1996.
Ingram, Reverend J., trans. *The Saxon Chronicle A.D 1 to A.D. 1154.* London: Studio Editions Ltd., 1993.
Jackson, Kenneth. "The Arthur of History," *Arthurian Literature in the Middle Ages,* ed. by R. S. Loomis. Oxford Clarendon Press, 1959, 1–11.
_____. "Arthur in Early Welsh Verse." *Arthurian Literature in the Middle Ages,* ed. by R. S. Loomis. Oxford: Clarendon Press, 1959.
_____, ed. and trans. *A Celtic Miscellany.* London: Routledge & Paul, 1951.
_____. *The Gododdin: The Oldest Scottish Poem.* Edinburgh: The University Press, 1969.
Jenkins, Elizabeth. *The Mystery of King Arthur.* London England: Michael O'Mara Books Limited, by arrangement with Rainbird Publishing Group Limited, 1990.
Knight, Jeremy. "The Pillar of Eliseg," *Valle Crucis Abbey.* Cadw: Welsh Historic Monuments, 1987.
Lacy, Norris J., ed. *The Arthurian Encyclopedia.* New York: Peter Bedrick Books, 1986.
Lapidge, Michael, and David Dumville, eds. *Gildas: New Approaches.* Dover New Hampshire: The Boydell Press, 1984.
Loomis, Roger Sherman, ed. *Arthurian Literature in the Middle Ages: A Collaborative History.* Oxford: The Clarendon Press, 1959.
Markdale, Jean, trans. by Christine Hauch. *King of the Celts: Arthurian Legends and Celtic Tradition.* Rochester, Vermont: Inner Traditions, first U.S. edition, 1994.
Matthews, Caitlin and John. *Ladies of the Lake.* London and San Francisco, California: The Aquarian Press, an Imprint of HarperCollins Publishers, 1992.
Matthews, John. *The Arthurian Tradition.* Rockport Maine: Element, Inc., 1994.
Mierow, Charles C. *Jordanes: The Origin and Deeds of the Goths.* Presented to the Faculty of Princeton University for the degree of Doctor of Philosophy. Princeton, New Jersey: Princeton University Press, 1908.
Mommsen, Theodor, ed. *Chronica Minora saec. IV. V. VI. VII.* Volume I, Berlin, 1892–1898.
Morris, John. *The Age of Arthur: A History of the British Isles from 350 to 650.* London: Weidenfeld and Nicolson, 1989.
_____, ed., trans. *Nennius: British History and the Welsh Annals.* London and Chichester: Phillimore and Co. Ltd., 1980.
O'Sullivan, Thomas. *The De Excidio of Gildas: Its Authenticity and Date.* Reprinted with permission of The Trustees of Columbia University Press, 1978.
Petrie, Sir W. M. Flinders, "Neglected British History," *The Proceedings of the British Academy, 1917–1918.* London: Published for the British Academy by Humphrey Milford, Oxford University Press, 251–275; 276–278.
Phillips, Graham, and Martin Keatman. *King Arthur: The True Story.* London: Century Random House, 1992.
Plummer, Charles, and John Earle, eds. *Two of the Saxon Chronicles Parallel with Supplementary Extracts from the Others.* Oxford: Clarendon Press, 1899.
Radford, C. A. Ralegh. "Glastonbury Abbey." *The Quest for Arthur's Britain.* Ed. Geoffrey Ashe. Chicago: Academy Chicago Publishers, 1987. 111–122.
Rahtz, Philip. "Excavations on Glastonbury Tor, Somerset, 1964–6," *The Archaeolog-*

ical Journal, Volume CXXVII, for the year 1970, 1–81. Leeds, England: W. S. Maney and Son Ltd., published by the Royal Archaelogical Institute, London, 1971.

_____. "Glastonbury Tor." *The Quest for Arthur's Britain.* Ed. Geoffrey Ashe. Chicago: Academy Chicago Publishers, 1987. 111–122.

_____. *Book of Glastonbury.* London: B. T. Batsford, Ltd./English Heritage, 1993.

Reno, Frank D. *The Historic King Arthur: Authenticating the Celtic Hero of Post-Roman Britain.* Jefferson, North Carolina, and London: McFarland & Company, Inc., 1996.

Rhys, John. *Studies in the Arthurian Legend.* Oxford: Clarendon Press, 1890.

Rhys, John. *Celtic Folklore: Welsh and Manx,* Volume 2. Oxford: The Clarendon Press, MDCCCCI [1951].

Richards, Reverend G. C., trans. *Imperial Rome.* London: G. Bell and Sons, Ltd., 1926.

Richmond, I. A. *Roman Britain*. New York: Barnes & Noble, Inc., 1963.

Robinson, J. Armitage. *Two Glastonbury Legends: King Arthur and St. Joseph of Arimathea.* Cambridge: The University Press, 1926.

Rutherford, Ward. *The Druids: Magicians of the West.* Wellingborough, Northamptonshire: The Aquarian Press, 1984.

Sherley-Price, Leo, trans. *Bede: A History of the English Church and People.* New York: Dorset Press, 1955.

Simpson, D. P. *Cassell's Latin Dictionary.* New York: Macmillan Publishing Company, 1968.

Skene, William F. *The Four Ancient Books of Wales Containing the Cymric Poems attributed to the Bards of the Sixty Century,* Volume I. Edinburgh: Edmonston and Douglas, 1868.

Spence, Lewis. *The Mysteries of Britain: Secret Rites and Traditions of Ancient Britain.* London: Studio Edition Ltd., 1994.

Stevenson, Josephus. *Gildas: De Excidio Britanniæ.* Vaduz: Kraus Reprint Ltd., Reprinted from a copy in the collections of the New York Public Library, 1964.

_____. *Nennii: Historia Brittonum.* Londini: Kraus Reprint Ltd., 1964.

Tatlock, J. S. P. *The Legendary History of Britain: Geoffrey of Monmouth's Historia Regum Britanniae and its Early Vernacular Versions.* Berkeley and Los Angeles: University of California Press, 1950.

Thorpe, Lewis, trans. *Geoffrey of Monmouth: The History of the Kings of Britain.* Middlesex, England: Penguin Books, 1966.

_____. *Gerald of Wales: The Journey through Wales/The Description of Wales.* New York: Penguin Books USA Inc., 1978.

Tolstoy, Nikolai. *The Coming of the King: The First Book of Merlin.* New York: Bantam Books, 1989.

Wacher, John. *The Towns of Roman Britain.* Berkeley and Los Angeles: University of California Press, 1974.

Wade-Evans, Arthur W. *The Emergence of England and Wales.* Cambridge: W. Heffer & Sons Ltd., 1959.

Webster, Graham. *The Cornovii.* Stroud, Glouchester: Alan Sutton Publishing Ltd., 1991.

_____. "Wall Roman Site," London: English Heritage, 1994.

_____, and Philip Barker. "Wroxeter: Roman City." London: English Heritage, 1993.

Webster, Kenneth G. T. *Guinevere: A Study of Her Abductions.* Milton Massachusetts: The Turtle Press, 1951.

Wildman, S. G. *The Black Horsemen: English Inns and King Arthur.* London: John Barker Publishers Ltd., 1971.

Williams, Ifor. *Lectures on Early Welsh Poetry.* Dublin: Dublin Institute for Advanced Studies, 1944.

Winterbottom, Michael, ed. and trans. *Gildas: The Ruin of Britain and Other Works.* Chichester, England: Phillimore and Co., Ltd., 1978 and Totowa, New Jersey: Rowman and Littlefield, 1978.

Wood, Michael. *In Search of the Dark Ages.* New York: Facts on File Publications, 1987.

Index